Fosdyke Saga Five

D1827593

£1.25

Fosdyke Saga Five

Further chronicles from the famous DAILY MIRROR strip

by BILL TIDY

WOLFE PUBLISHING LIMITED
10 EARLHAM STREET • LONDON WC2H 9LP

© Daily Mirror Newspapers Limited 1976
ISBN 0 7234 0697 9

Printed by C. Nicholls & Company Ltd
The Philips Park Press
Manchester
M11 4AU

Fosdyke Saga Five

The indomitable Fosdykes, tripe suppliers to the world, surge on from one mighty exploit to another. In Manchester, surrounded by a blaze of publicity, Sir Jos Fosdyke and his youngest son Tim are hard at work preparing Victoria's lily-livered swain for his next heavyweight boxing contest.

GOSH, DAD, IT'S ALMOST IMPOSSIBLE FOR BERT TO TRAIN WITH ALL OF THESE PRESSMEN BADGERING HIM...
...CAN'T WE MAKE A BREAK FOR IT ALONG THE CANAL?
J133
NO, TIM, IT'S NICE HERE IN THE PARK!

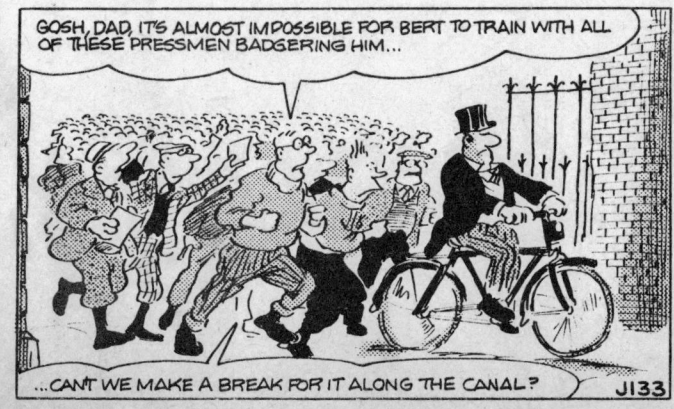

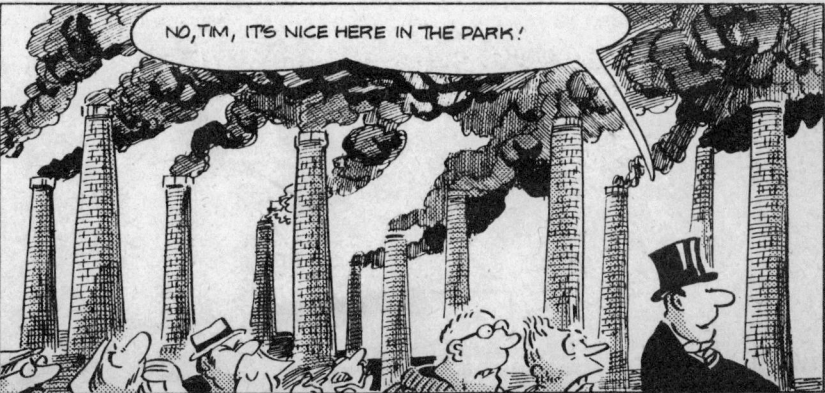

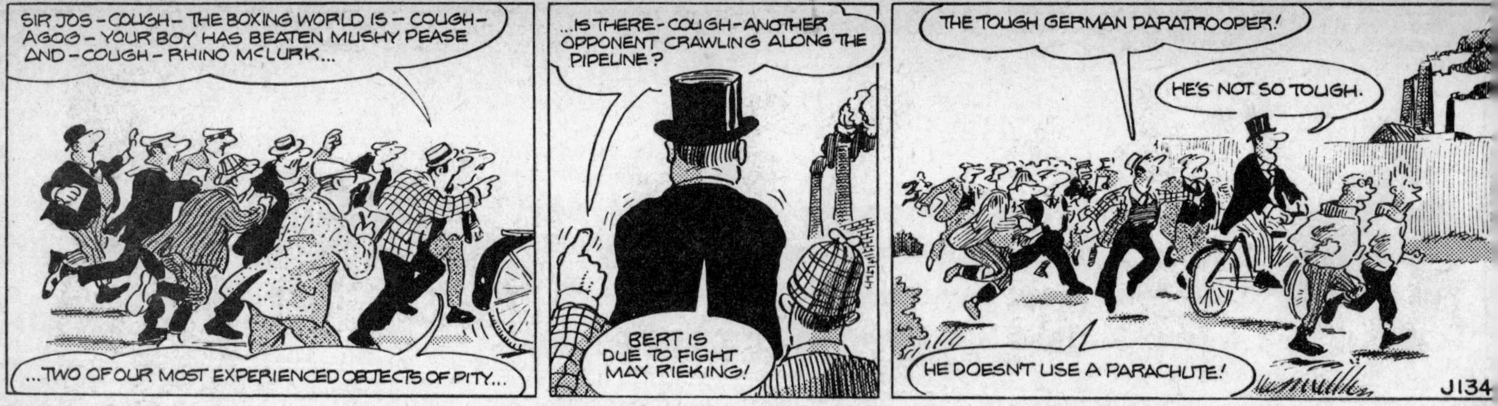
SIR JOS - COUGH - THE BOXING WORLD IS - COUGH - AGOG - YOUR BOY HAS BEATEN MUSHY PEASE AND - COUGH - RHINO McLURK...
...TWO OF OUR MOST EXPERIENCED OBJECTS OF PITY...
...IS THERE - COUGH - ANOTHER OPPONENT CRAWLING ALONG THE PIPELINE?
BERT IS DUE TO FIGHT MAX RIEKING!
THE TOUGH GERMAN PARATROOPER!
HE'S NOT SO TOUGH.
HE DOESN'T USE A PARACHUTE!
J134

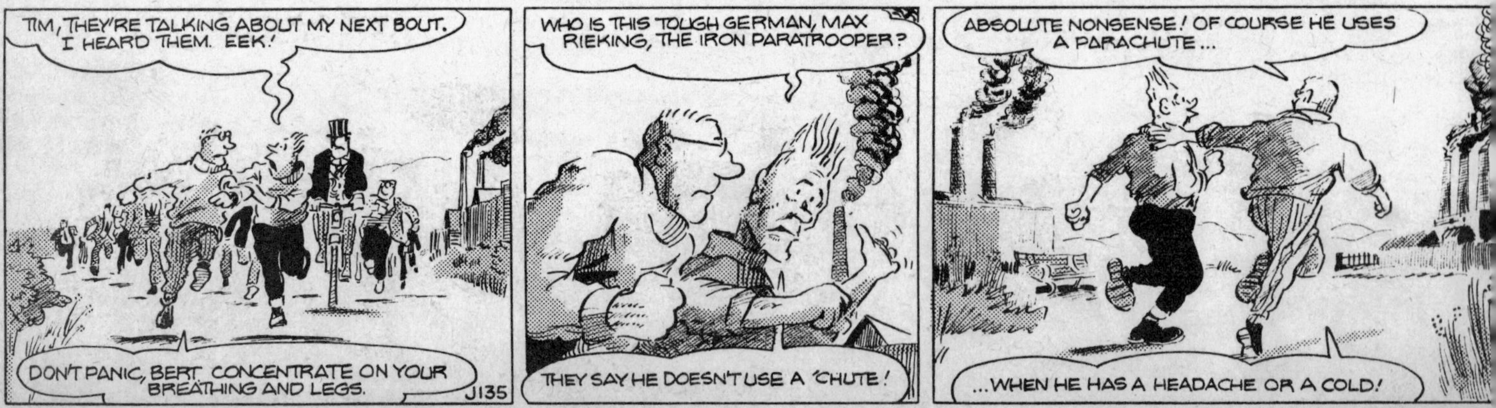
TIM, THEY'RE TALKING ABOUT MY NEXT BOUT. I HEARD THEM. EEK!
DON'T PANIC, BERT. CONCENTRATE ON YOUR BREATHING AND LEGS.
J135
WHO IS THIS TOUGH GERMAN, MAX RIEKING, THE IRON PARATROOPER?
THEY SAY HE DOESN'T USE A 'CHUTE!
ABSOLUTE NONSENSE! OF COURSE HE USES A PARACHUTE...
...WHEN HE HAS A HEADACHE OR A COLD!

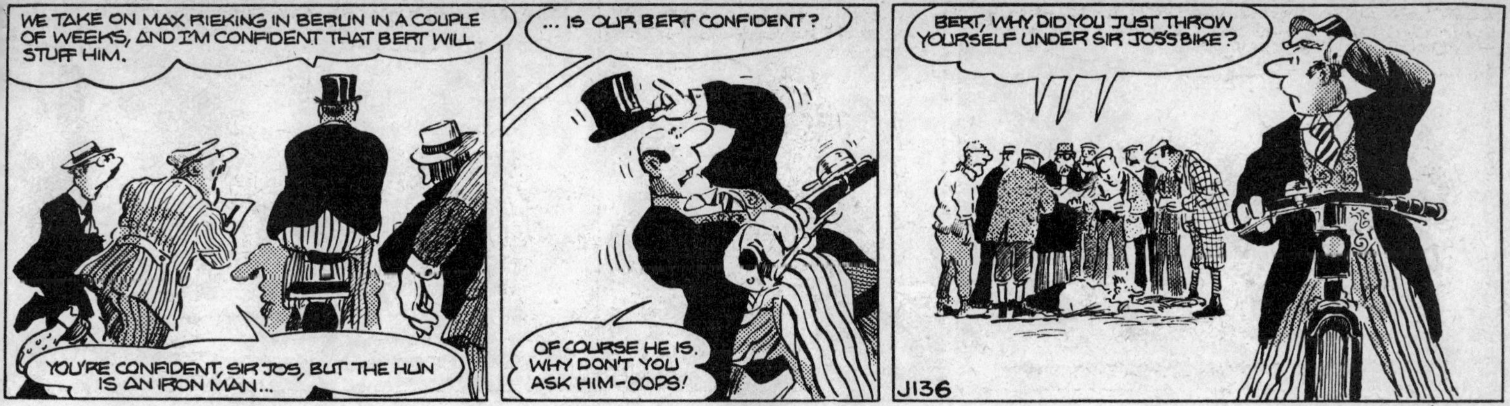
WE TAKE ON MAX RIEKING IN BERLIN IN A COUPLE OF WEEKS, AND I'M CONFIDENT THAT BERT WILL STUFF HIM.
YOU'RE CONFIDENT, SIR JOS, BUT THE HUN IS AN IRON MAN...
... IS OUR BERT CONFIDENT?
OF COURSE HE IS. WHY DON'T YOU ASK HIM-OOPS!
BERT, WHY DID YOU JUST THROW YOURSELF UNDER SIR JOS'S BIKE?
J136

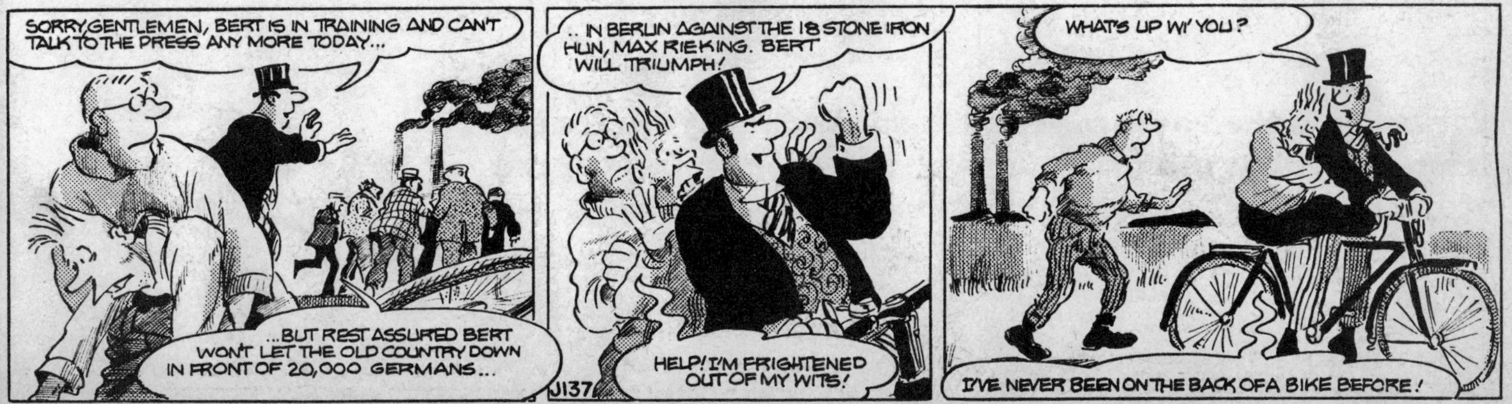
SORRY, GENTLEMEN, BERT IS IN TRAINING AND CAN'T TALK TO THE PRESS ANY MORE TODAY...
...BUT REST ASSURED BERT WON'T LET THE OLD COUNTRY DOWN IN FRONT OF 20,000 GERMANS...
.. IN BERLIN AGAINST THE 18 STONE IRON HUN, MAX RIEKING. BERT WILL TRIUMPH!
HELP! I'M FRIGHTENED OUT OF MY WITS!
J137
WHAT'S UP WI' YOU?
I'VE NEVER BEEN ON THE BACK OF A BIKE BEFORE!

At home that night...

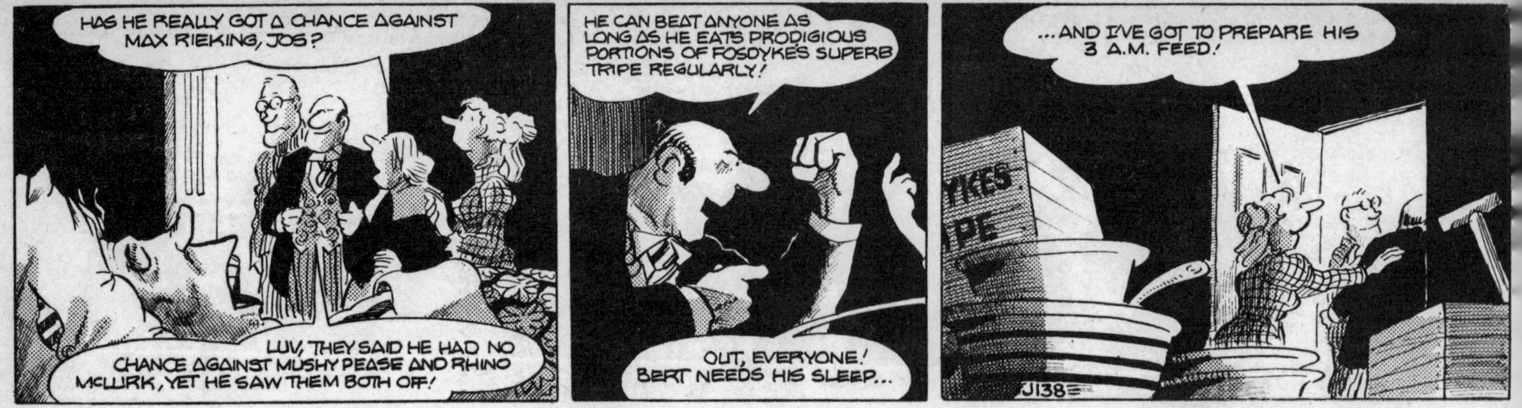
HAS HE REALLY GOT A CHANCE AGAINST MAX RIEKING, JOS?
LUV, THEY SAID HE HAD NO CHANCE AGAINST MUSHY PEASE AND RHINO McLURK, YET HE SAW THEM BOTH OFF!
HE CAN BEAT ANYONE AS LONG AS HE EATS PRODIGIOUS PORTIONS OF FOSDYKE'S SUPERB TRIPE REGULARLY!
OUT, EVERYONE! BERT NEEDS HIS SLEEP...
...AND I'VE GOT TO PREPARE HIS 3 A.M. FEED!
YKES
PE
J138

Far away in the Pacific, Albert Fosdyke, newly surfaced from a perilous bid to lay tripe on the deepest part of the ocean bed, climbs aboard his support ship, triumphant but grief-stricken...

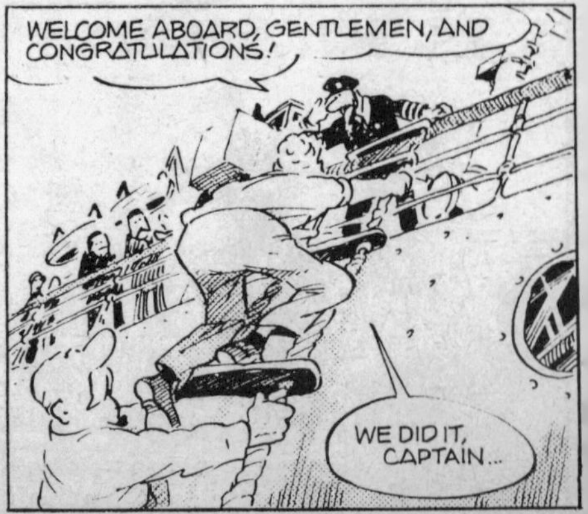
WELCOME ABOARD, GENTLEMEN, AND CONGRATULATIONS!
WE DID IT, CAPTAIN...

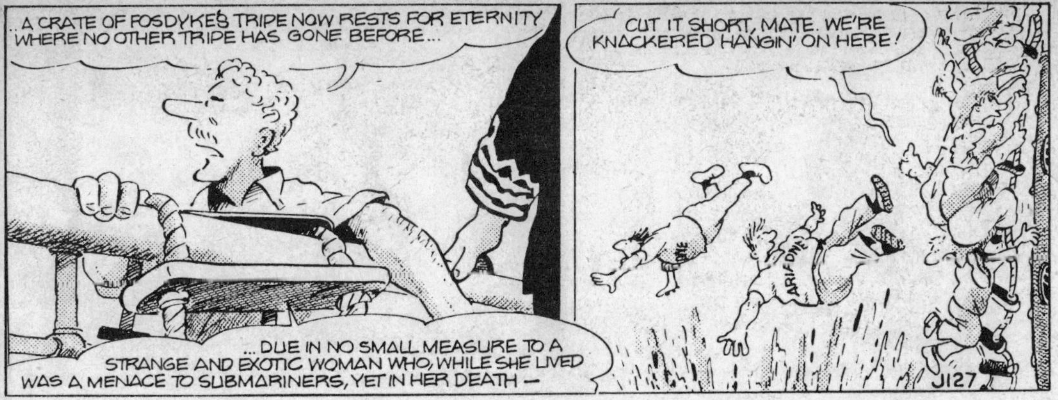
..A CRATE OF FOSDYKE'S TRIPE NOW RESTS FOR ETERNITY WHERE NO OTHER TRIPE HAS GONE BEFORE...
... DUE IN NO SMALL MEASURE TO A STRANGE AND EXOTIC WOMAN WHO, WHILE SHE LIVED WAS A MENACE TO SUBMARINERS, YET IN HER DEATH —
CUT IT SHORT, MATE. WE'RE KNACKERED HANGIN' ON HERE!
J127

Shortly afterwards...

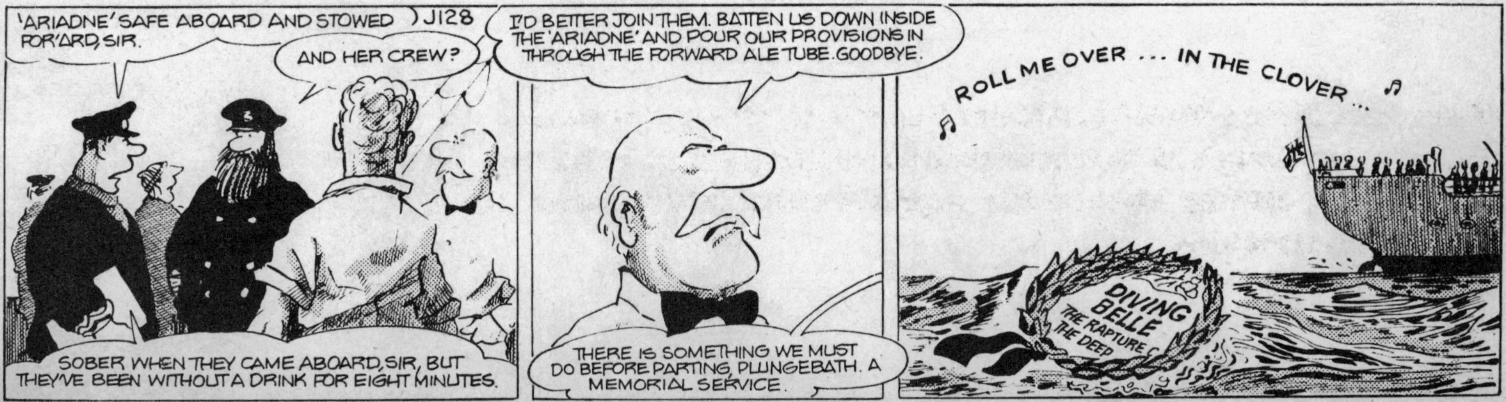
J128
'ARIADNE' SAFE ABOARD AND STOWED FOR'ARD, SIR.
AND HER CREW?
SOBER WHEN THEY CAME ABOARD, SIR, BUT THEY'VE BEEN WITHOUT A DRINK FOR EIGHT MINUTES.
I'D BETTER JOIN THEM. BATTEN US DOWN INSIDE THE 'ARIADNE' AND POUR OUR PROVISIONS IN THROUGH THE FORWARD ALE TUBE. GOODBYE.
THERE IS SOMETHING WE MUST DO BEFORE PARTING, PLUNGEBATH. A MEMORIAL SERVICE.
ROLL ME OVER ... IN THE CLOVER ...
DIVING BELLE
THE RAPTURE
THE DEEP

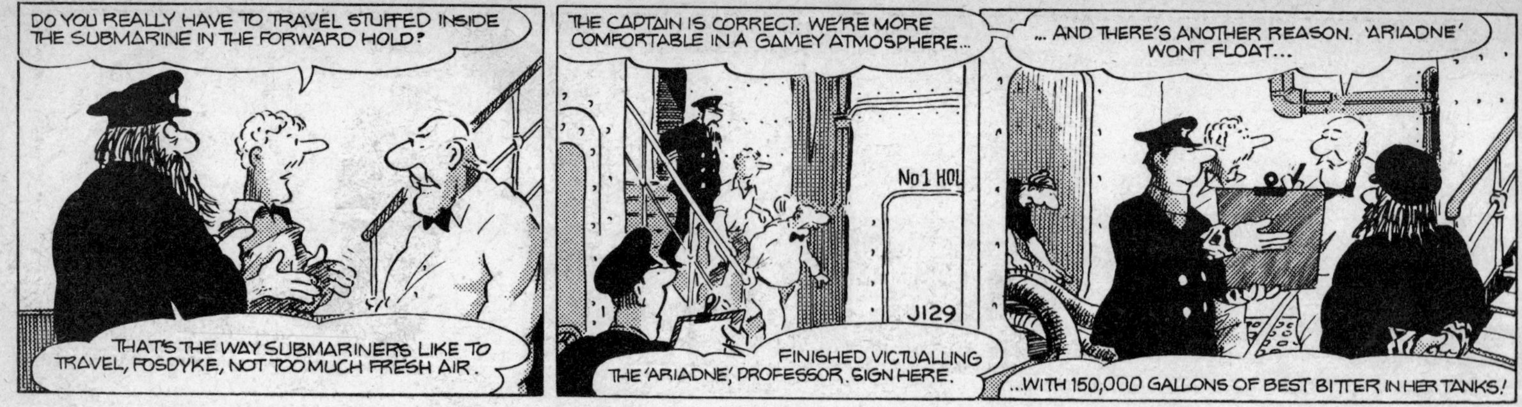
DO YOU REALLY HAVE TO TRAVEL STUFFED INSIDE THE SUBMARINE IN THE FORWARD HOLD?
THAT'S THE WAY SUBMARINERS LIKE TO TRAVEL, FOSDYKE, NOT TOO MUCH FRESH AIR.
THE CAPTAIN IS CORRECT. WE'RE MORE COMFORTABLE IN A GAMEY ATMOSPHERE...
No 1 HOL
J129
FINISHED VICTUALLING THE 'ARIADNE', PROFESSOR. SIGN HERE.
... AND THERE'S ANOTHER REASON. 'ARIADNE' WONT FLOAT...
...WITH 150,000 GALLONS OF BEST BITTER IN HER TANKS!

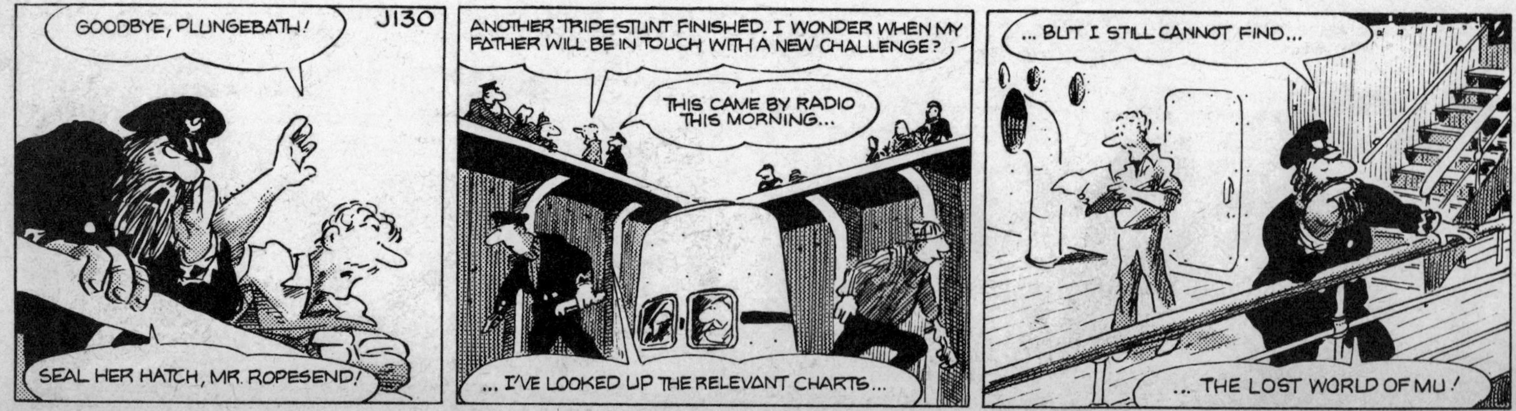
GOODBYE, PLUNGEBATH!
J130
SEAL HER HATCH, MR. ROPESEND!
ANOTHER TRIPE STUNT FINISHED. I WONDER WHEN MY FATHER WILL BE IN TOUCH WITH A NEW CHALLENGE?
THIS CAME BY RADIO THIS MORNING...
... I'VE LOOKED UP THE RELEVANT CHARTS...
... BUT I STILL CANNOT FIND...
... THE LOST WORLD OF MU!

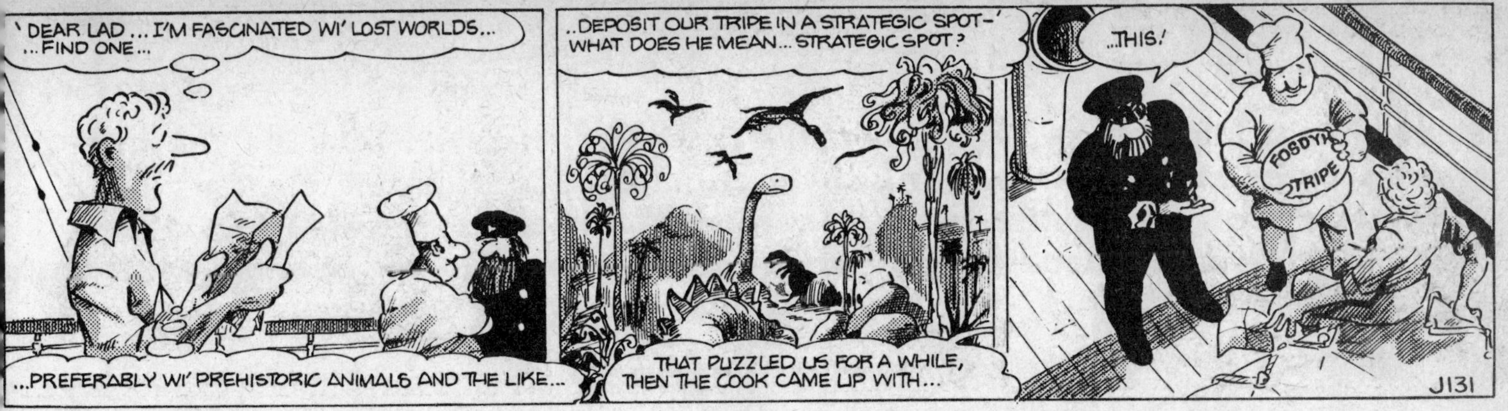
'DEAR LAD ... I'M FASCINATED WI' LOST WORLDS...
...FIND ONE...
...PREFERABLY WI' PREHISTORIC ANIMALS AND THE LIKE...
..DEPOSIT OUR TRIPE IN A STRATEGIC SPOT-' WHAT DOES HE MEAN... STRATEGIC SPOT?
THAT PUZZLED US FOR A WHILE, THEN THE COOK CAME UP WITH...
...THIS!
FOSDYK
TRIPE
J131

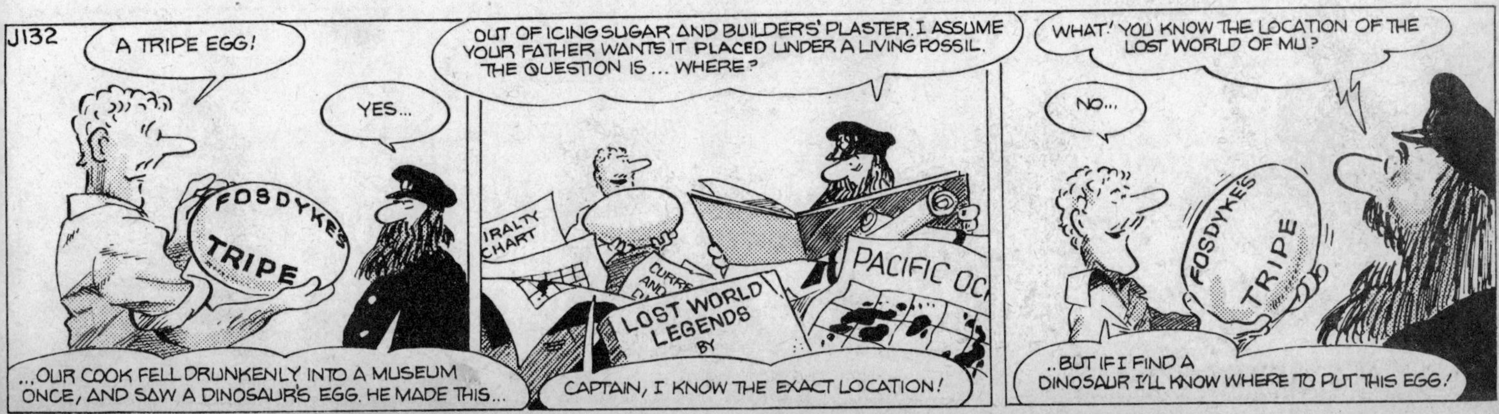
J132
A TRIPE EGG!
YES...
FOSDYKE'S
TRIPE
...OUR COOK FELL DRUNKENLY INTO A MUSEUM ONCE, AND SAW A DINOSAUR'S EGG. HE MADE THIS...
OUT OF ICING SUGAR AND BUILDERS' PLASTER. I ASSUME YOUR FATHER WANTS IT PLACED UNDER A LIVING FOSSIL. THE QUESTION IS ... WHERE?
IRALTY CHART
CURR AND
LOST WORLD LEGENDS BY
PACIFIC OC
CAPTAIN, I KNOW THE EXACT LOCATION!
WHAT! YOU KNOW THE LOCATION OF THE LOST WORLD OF MU?
NO...
FOSDYKE'S
TRIPE
..BUT IF I FIND A DINOSAUR I'LL KNOW WHERE TO PUT THIS EGG!

Meanwhile in Manchester, unknown to the Fosdykes, their life-long foe, the hate-crazed Roger Ditchley, has fallen into the clutches of the fanatical Dr. Thrumper, thwarted revenge specialist. In the washroom of St. Septyck's Nose Hospital Dr. Thrumper has used Ditchley as a decoy for the object of his own revenge, Sir Hugo Faynte-Pulse.

I'LL TELL YOU WHO I AM, YOU NOSE CRAZED MONSTER, FAYNTE-PULSE...
..I AM THRUMPER, THE MAN WHOSE WORK YOU LAUGHED TO SCORN YEARS AGO!
THRUMPER.. RAMPANT REVENGE.. I DIMLY RECALL CERTAIN THEORIES....
YES, YES?
..ILL CONCEIVED, CRACKPOT, OBSESSIVE AND QUITE STUPID.
HE REMEMBERS ME!
J121

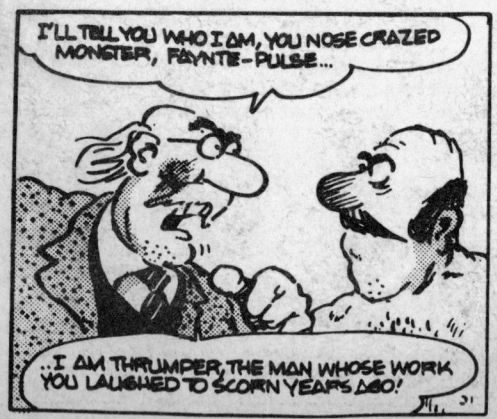

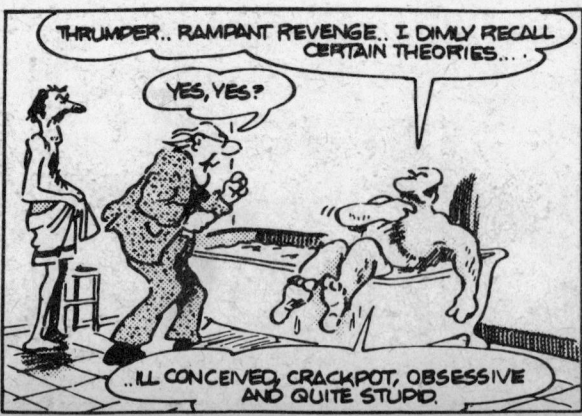

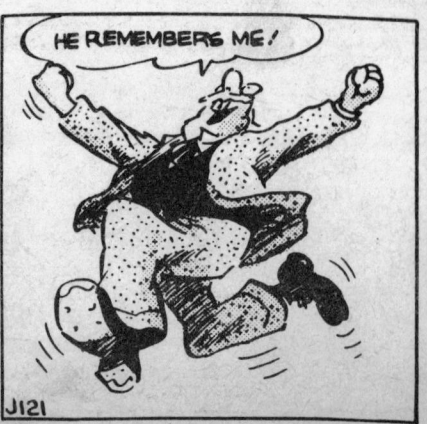

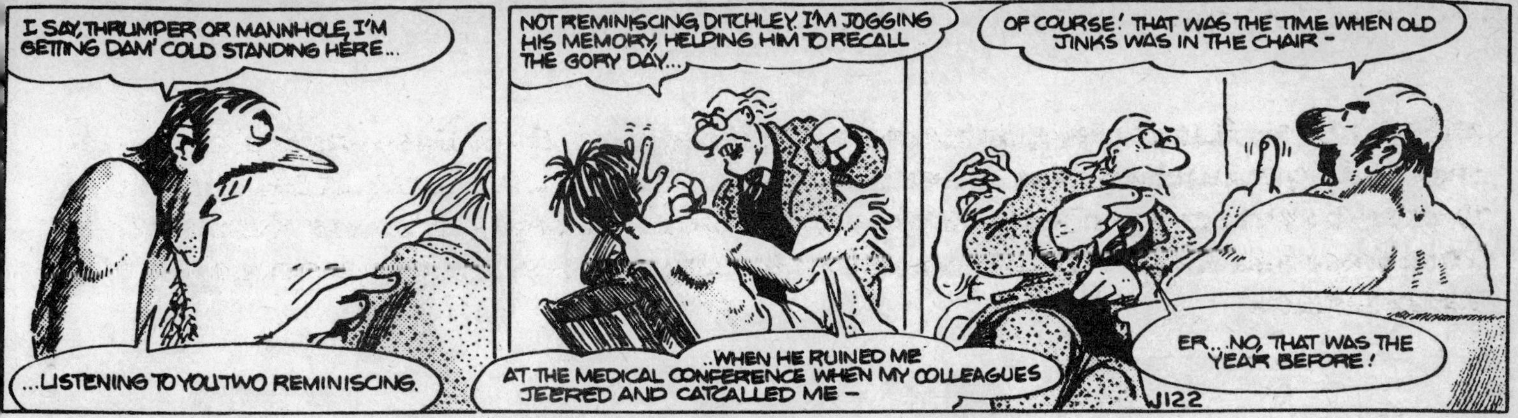
I SAY, THRUMPER OR MANNHOLE, I'M GETTING DAM' COLD STANDING HERE...
...LISTENING TO YOU TWO REMINISCING.
NOT REMINISCING, DITCHLEY. I'M JOGGING HIS MEMORY, HELPING HIM TO RECALL THE GORY DAY...
..WHEN HE RUINED ME AT THE MEDICAL CONFERENCE WHEN MY COLLEAGUES JEERED AND CATCALLED ME –
OF COURSE! THAT WAS THE TIME WHEN OLD JINKS WAS IN THE CHAIR –
ER...NO, THAT WAS THE YEAR BEFORE!
J122

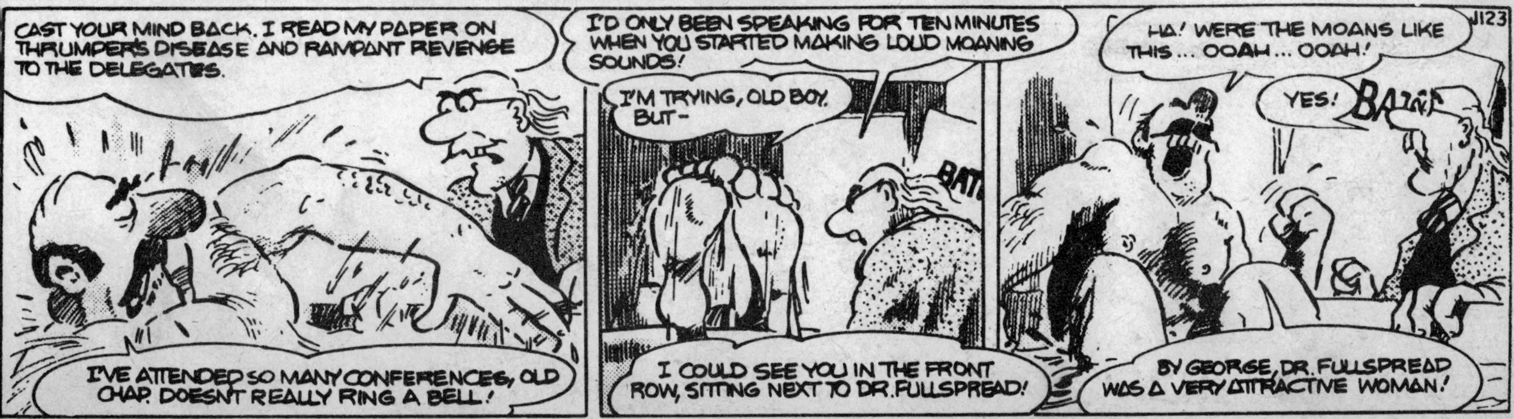
CAST YOUR MIND BACK. I READ MY PAPER ON THRUMPER'S DISEASE AND RAMPANT REVENGE TO THE DELEGATES.
I'VE ATTENDED SO MANY CONFERENCES, OLD CHAP. DOESN'T REALLY RING A BELL!
I'D ONLY BEEN SPEAKING FOR TEN MINUTES WHEN YOU STARTED MAKING LOUD MOANING SOUNDS!
I'M TRYING, OLD BOY. BUT –
I COULD SEE YOU IN THE FRONT ROW, SITTING NEXT TO DR. FULLSPREAD!
J123
HA! WERE THE MOANS LIKE THIS ... OOAH ... OOAH!
YES!
BY GEORGE, DR. FULLSPREAD WAS A VERY ATTRACTIVE WOMAN!

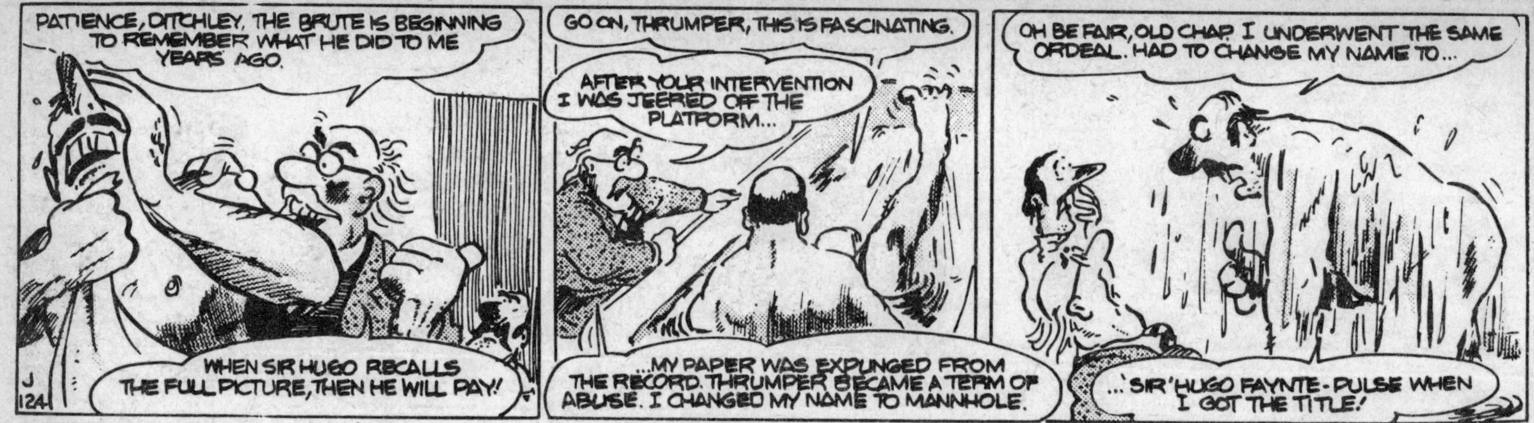
PATIENCE, DITCHLEY, THE BRUTE IS BEGINNING TO REMEMBER WHAT HE DID TO ME YEARS AGO.
WHEN SIR HUGO RECALLS THE FULL PICTURE, THEN HE WILL PAY!
GO ON, THRUMPER, THIS IS FASCINATING.
AFTER YOUR INTERVENTION I WAS JEERED OFF THE PLATFORM...
...MY PAPER WAS EXPUNGED FROM THE RECORD. THRUMPER BECAME A TERM OF ABUSE. I CHANGED MY NAME TO MANNHOLE.
OH BE FAIR, OLD CHAP. I UNDERWENT THE SAME ORDEAL.. HAD TO CHANGE MY NAME TO...
...'SIR' HUGO FAYNTE-PULSE WHEN I GOT THE TITLE!

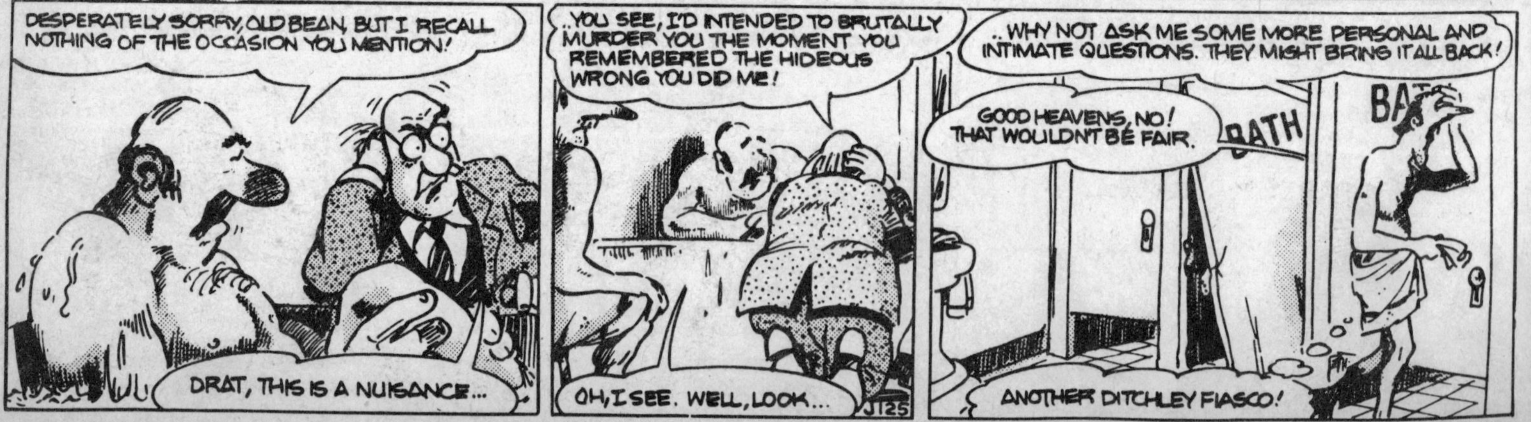
DESPERATELY SORRY, OLD BEAN, BUT I RECALL NOTHING OF THE OCCASION YOU MENTION!
DRAT, THIS IS A NUISANCE...
..YOU SEE, I'D INTENDED TO BRUTALLY MURDER YOU THE MOMENT YOU REMEMBERED THE HIDEOUS WRONG YOU DID ME!
OH, I SEE. WELL, LOOK...
..WHY NOT ASK ME SOME MORE PERSONAL AND INTIMATE QUESTIONS. THEY MIGHT BRING IT ALL BACK!
GOOD HEAVENS, NO! THAT WOULDN'T BE FAIR.
BATH
ANOTHER DITCHLEY FIASCO!

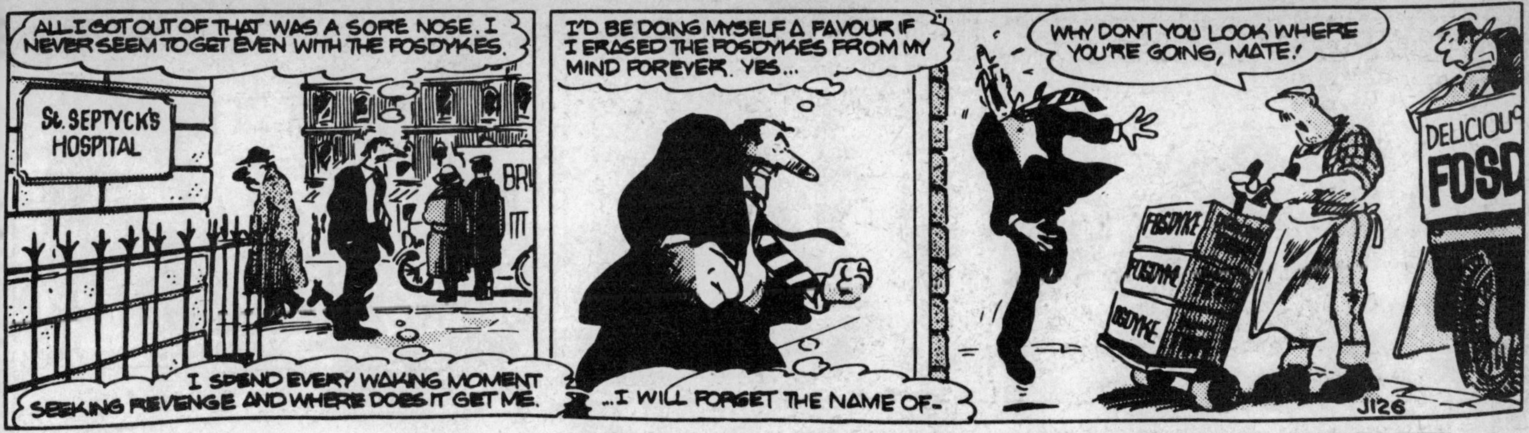
ALL I GOT OUT OF THAT WAS A SORE NOSE. I NEVER SEEM TO GET EVEN WITH THE FOSDYKES.
St. SEPTYCK'S HOSPITAL
I SPEND EVERY WAKING MOMENT SEEKING REVENGE AND WHERE DOES IT GET ME.
I'D BE DOING MYSELF A FAVOUR IF I ERASED THE FOSDYKES FROM MY MIND FOREVER. YES...
...I WILL FORGET THE NAME OF–
WHY DON'T YOU LOOK WHERE YOU'RE GOING, MATE!
FOSDYKE
DELICIOU
FOSD
J126

Some time later...

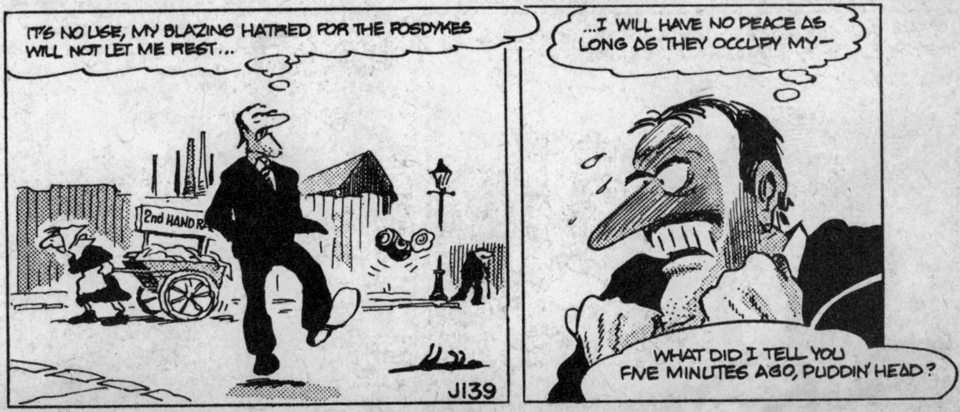
IT'S NO USE, MY BLAZING HATRED FOR THE FOSDYKES WILL NOT LET ME REST...
...I WILL HAVE NO PEACE AS LONG AS THEY OCCUPY MY–
WHAT DID I TELL YOU FIVE MINUTES AGO, PUDDIN' HEAD?
J139

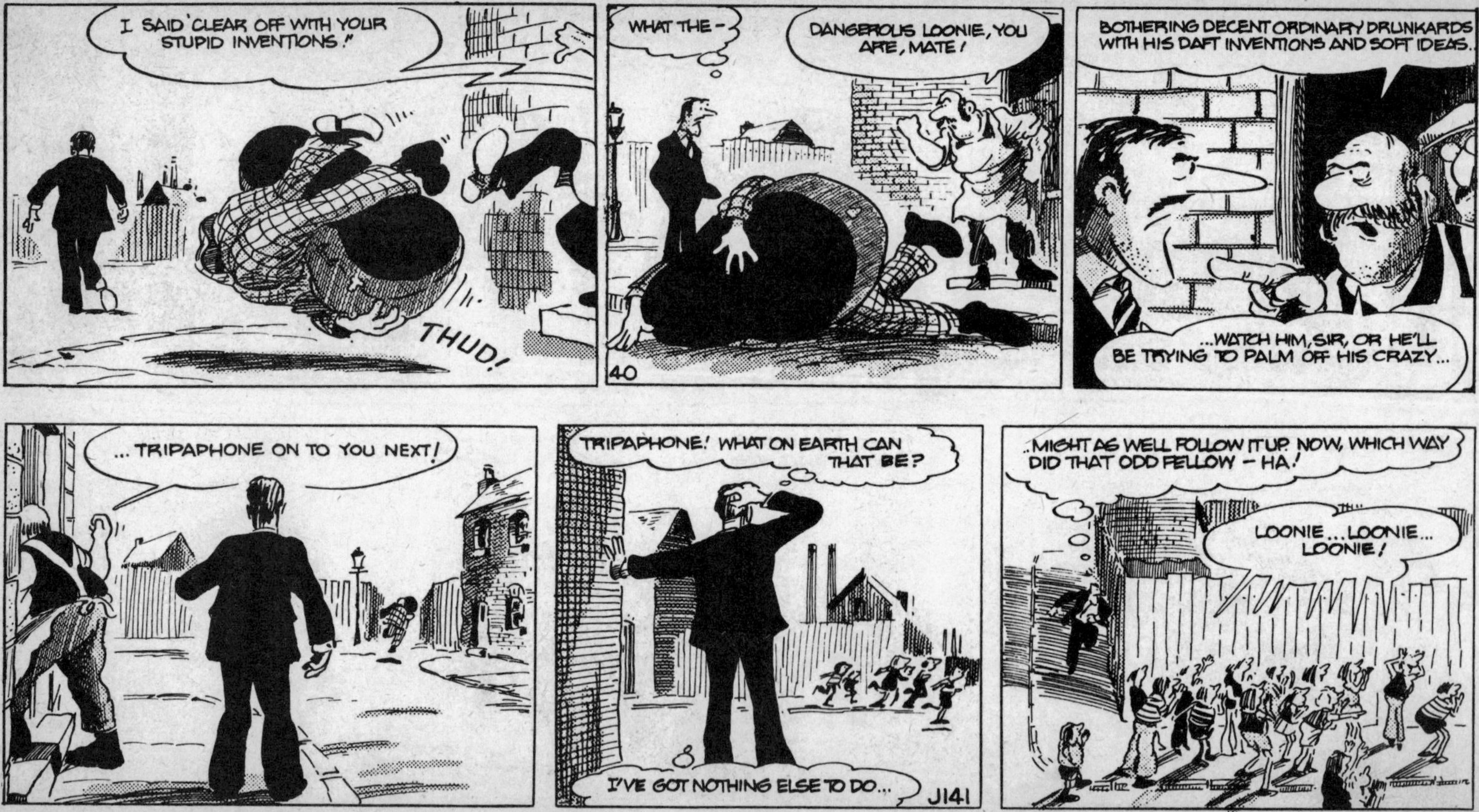
I SAID 'CLEAR OFF WITH YOUR STUPID INVENTIONS.'
THUD!
WHAT THE –
DANGEROUS LOONIE, YOU ARE, MATE!
40
BOTHERING DECENT ORDINARY DRUNKARDS WITH HIS DAFT INVENTIONS AND SOFT IDEAS..
...WATCH HIM, SIR, OR HE'LL BE TRYING TO PALM OFF HIS CRAZY...
... TRIPAPHONE ON TO YOU NEXT!
TRIPAPHONE! WHAT ON EARTH CAN THAT BE?
I'VE GOT NOTHING ELSE TO DO...
J141
..MIGHT AS WELL FOLLOW IT UP. NOW, WHICH WAY DID THAT ODD FELLOW – HA!
LOONIE... LOONIE... LOONIE!

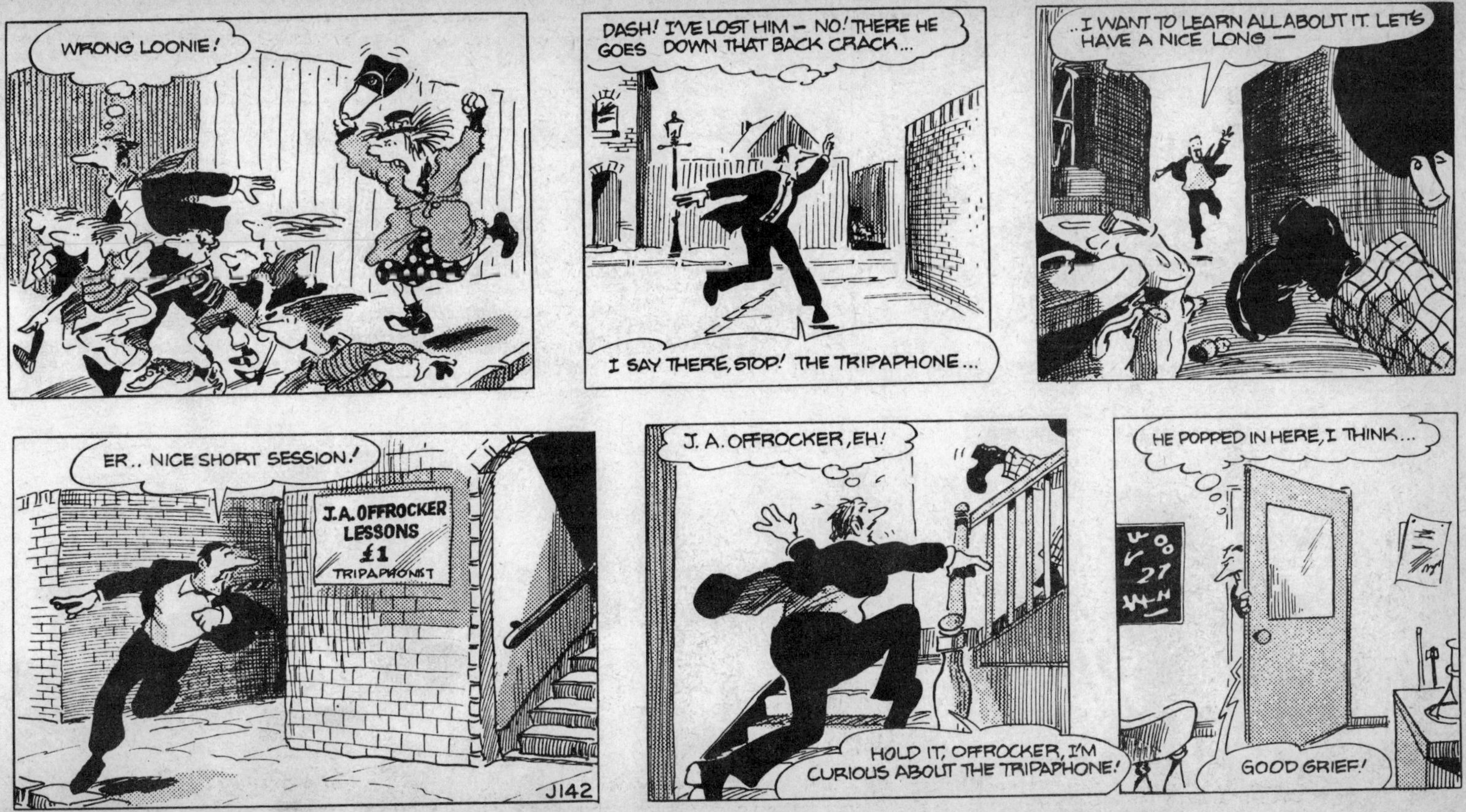
WRONG LOONIE!
DASH! I'VE LOST HIM – NO! THERE HE GOES DOWN THAT BACK CRACK...
I SAY THERE, STOP! THE TRIPAPHONE...
..I WANT TO LEARN ALL ABOUT IT. LET'S HAVE A NICE LONG –
ER.. NICE SHORT SESSION!
J.A. OFFROCKER LESSONS £1 TRIPAPHONIST
J142
J. A. OFFROCKER, EH!
HOLD IT, OFFROCKER, I'M CURIOUS ABOUT THE TRIPAPHONE!
HE POPPED IN HERE, I THINK...
GOOD GRIEF!

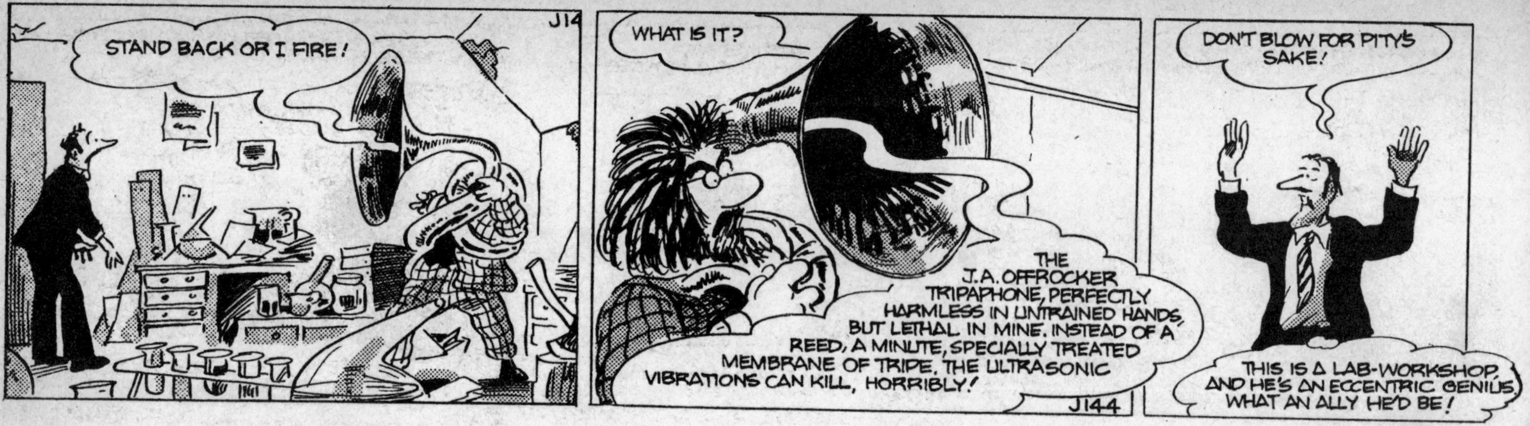
STAND BACK OR I FIRE!
WHAT IS IT?
THE J.A. OFFROCKER TRIPAPHONE, PERFECTLY HARMLESS IN UNTRAINED HANDS, BUT LETHAL IN MINE. INSTEAD OF A REED, A MINUTE, SPECIALLY TREATED MEMBRANE OF TRIPE. THE ULTRASONIC VIBRATIONS CAN KILL, HORRIBLY!
J144
DON'T BLOW FOR PITY'S SAKE!
THIS IS A LAB-WORKSHOP, AND HE'S AN ECCENTRIC GENIUS. WHAT AN ALLY HE'D BE!

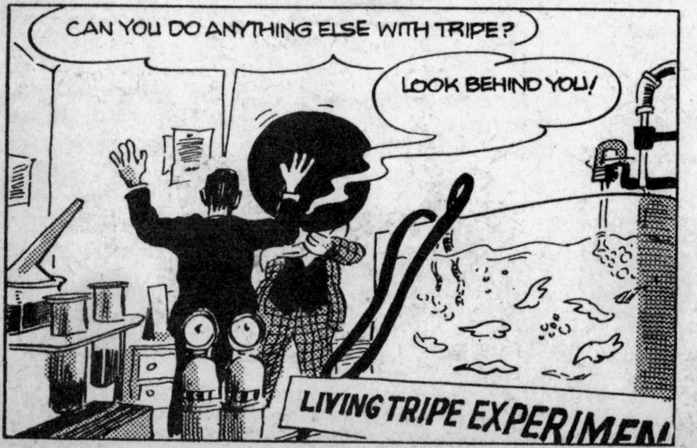
CAN YOU DO ANYTHING ELSE WITH TRIPE?
LOOK BEHIND YOU!
LIVING TRIPE EXPERIMEN

And on Albert's support ship...

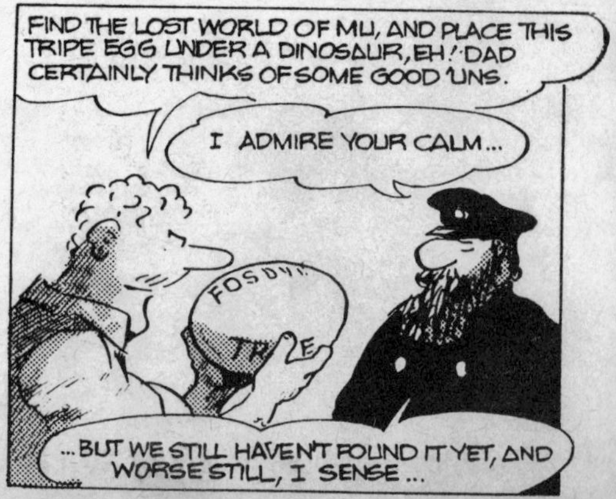
FIND THE LOST WORLD OF MU, AND PLACE THIS TRIPE EGG UNDER A DINOSAUR, EH! DAD CERTAINLY THINKS OF SOME GOOD 'UNS.
I ADMIRE YOUR CALM...
...BUT WE STILL HAVEN'T FOUND IT YET, AND WORSE STILL, I SENSE...

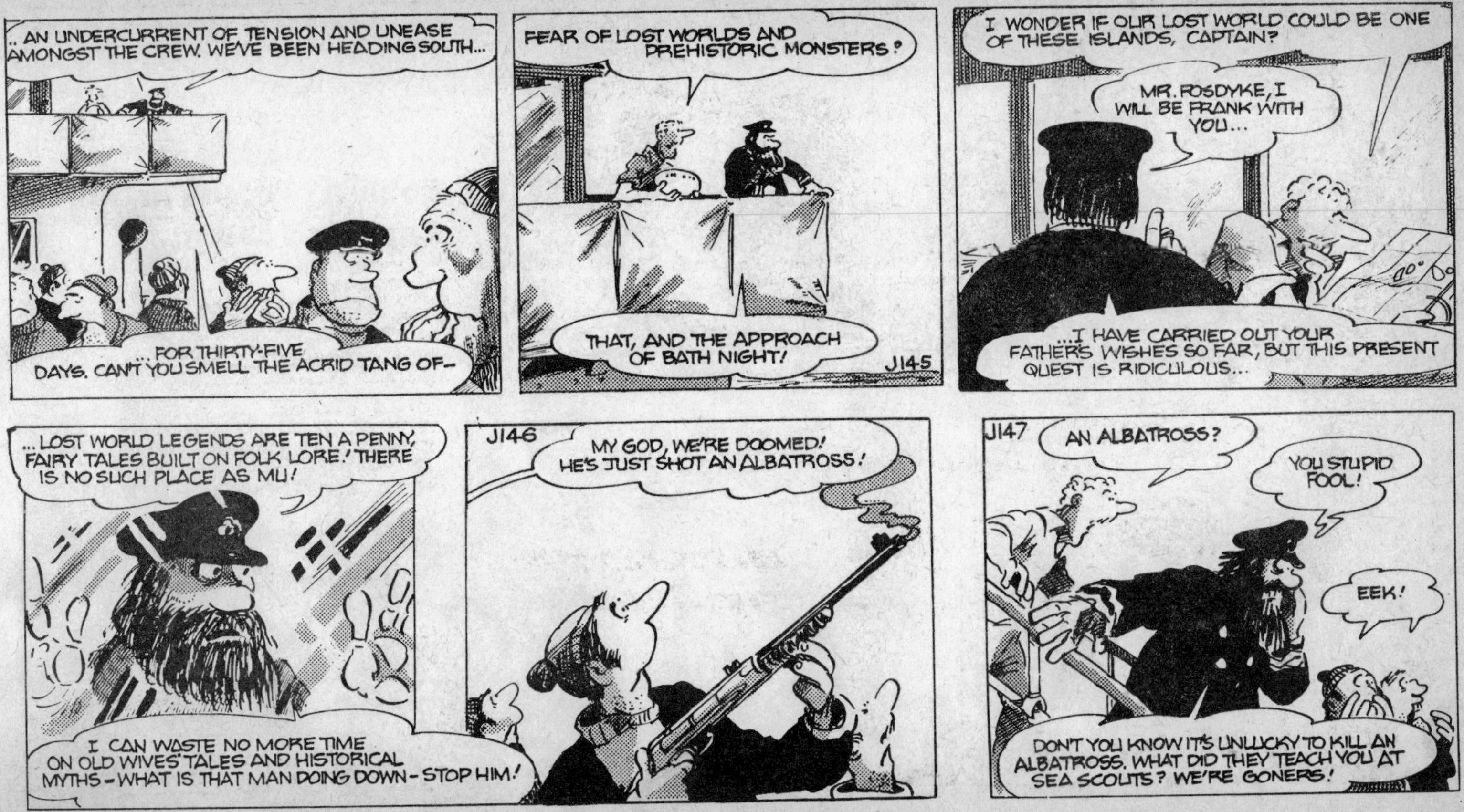
... AN UNDERCURRENT OF TENSION AND UNEASE AMONGST THE CREW. WE'VE BEEN HEADING SOUTH...
...FOR THIRTY-FIVE DAYS. CAN'T YOU SMELL THE ACRID TANG OF-
FEAR OF LOST WORLDS AND PREHISTORIC MONSTERS?
THAT, AND THE APPROACH OF BATH NIGHT!
J145
I WONDER IF OUR LOST WORLD COULD BE ONE OF THESE ISLANDS, CAPTAIN?
MR. FOSDYKE, I WILL BE FRANK WITH YOU...
...I HAVE CARRIED OUT YOUR FATHER'S WISHES SO FAR, BUT THIS PRESENT QUEST IS RIDICULOUS...
... LOST WORLD LEGENDS ARE TEN A PENNY, FAIRY TALES BUILT ON FOLK LORE! THERE IS NO SUCH PLACE AS MU!
I CAN WASTE NO MORE TIME ON OLD WIVES' TALES AND HISTORICAL MYTHS - WHAT IS THAT MAN DOING DOWN - STOP HIM!
J146
MY GOD, WE'RE DOOMED! HE'S JUST SHOT AN ALBATROSS!
J147
AN ALBATROSS?
YOU STUPID FOOL!
EEK!
DON'T YOU KNOW IT'S UNLUCKY TO KILL AN ALBATROSS. WHAT DID THEY TEACH YOU AT SEA SCOUTS? WE'RE GONERS!

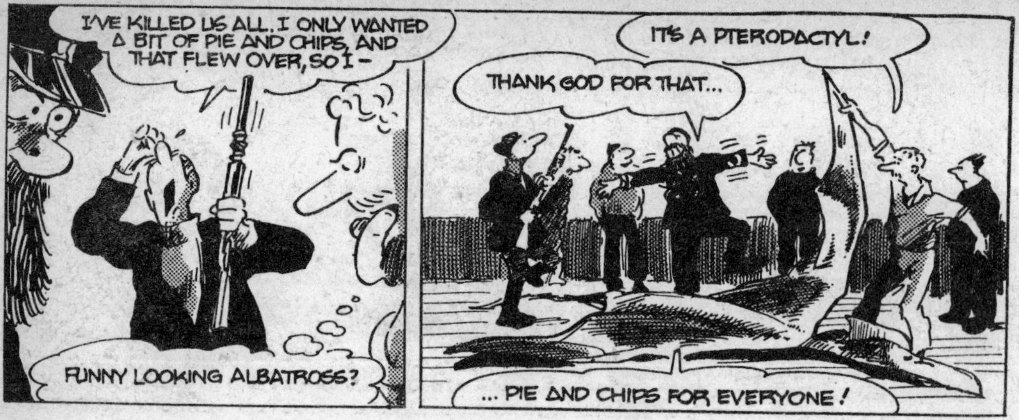
I'VE KILLED US ALL. I ONLY WANTED A BIT OF PIE AND CHIPS, AND THAT FLEW OVER, SO I –
FUNNY LOOKING ALBATROSS?
IT'S A PTERODACTYL!
THANK GOD FOR THAT...
... PIE AND CHIPS FOR EVERYONE!

So that evening in the Captain's cabin...

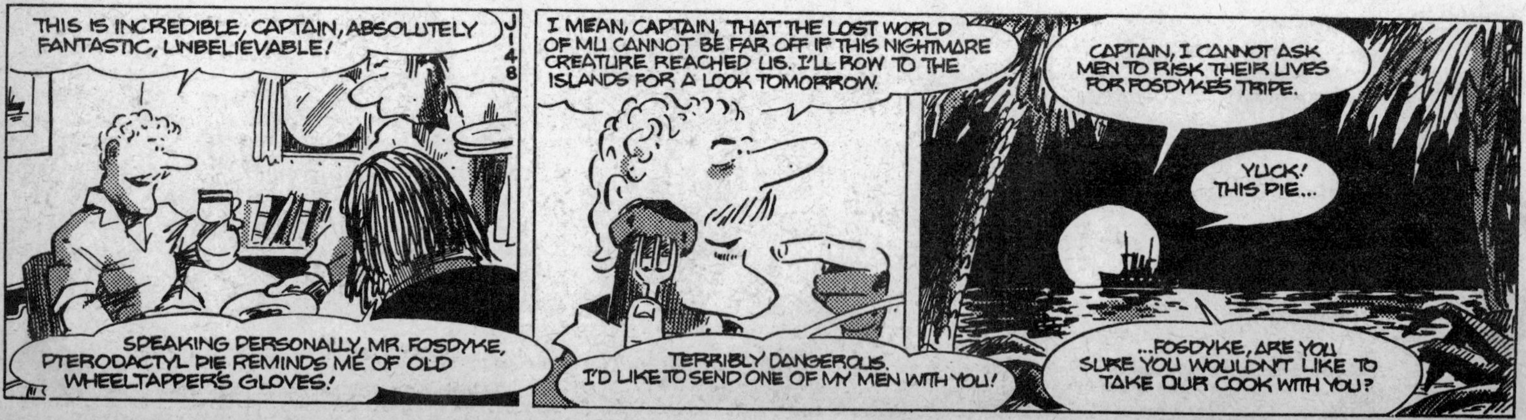
THIS IS INCREDIBLE, CAPTAIN, ABSOLUTELY FANTASTIC, UNBELIEVABLE!
SPEAKING PERSONALLY, MR. FOSDYKE, PTERODACTYL PIE REMINDS ME OF OLD WHEELTAPPER'S GLOVES!
J148
I MEAN, CAPTAIN, THAT THE LOST WORLD OF MU CANNOT BE FAR OFF IF THIS NIGHTMARE CREATURE REACHED US. I'LL ROW TO THE ISLANDS FOR A LOOK TOMORROW.
TERRIBLY DANGEROUS. I'D LIKE TO SEND ONE OF MY MEN WITH YOU!
CAPTAIN, I CANNOT ASK MEN TO RISK THEIR LIVES FOR FOSDYKE'S TRIPE.
YUCK! THIS PIE...
...FOSDYKE, ARE YOU SURE YOU WOULDN'T LIKE TO TAKE OUR COOK WITH YOU?

Next morning...

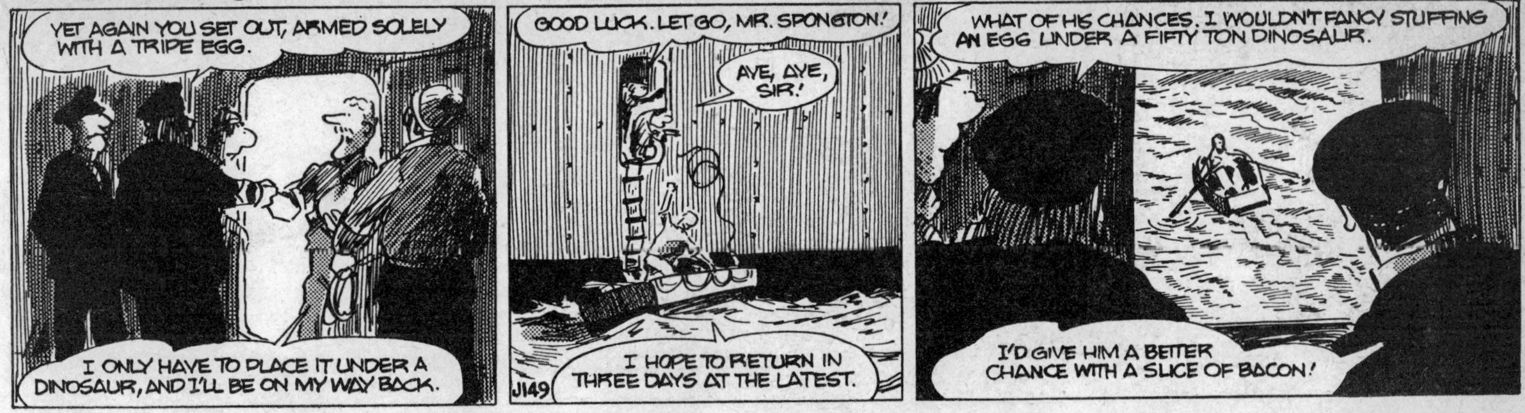
YET AGAIN YOU SET OUT, ARMED SOLELY WITH A TRIPE EGG.
I ONLY HAVE TO PLACE IT UNDER A DINOSAUR, AND I'LL BE ON MY WAY BACK.
GOOD LUCK. LET GO, MR. SPONGTON!
AYE, AYE, SIR!
I HOPE TO RETURN IN THREE DAYS AT THE LATEST.
J149
WHAT OF HIS CHANCES. I WOULDN'T FANCY STUFFING AN EGG UNDER A FIFTY TON DINOSAUR.
I'D GIVE HIM A BETTER CHANCE WITH A SLICE OF BACON!

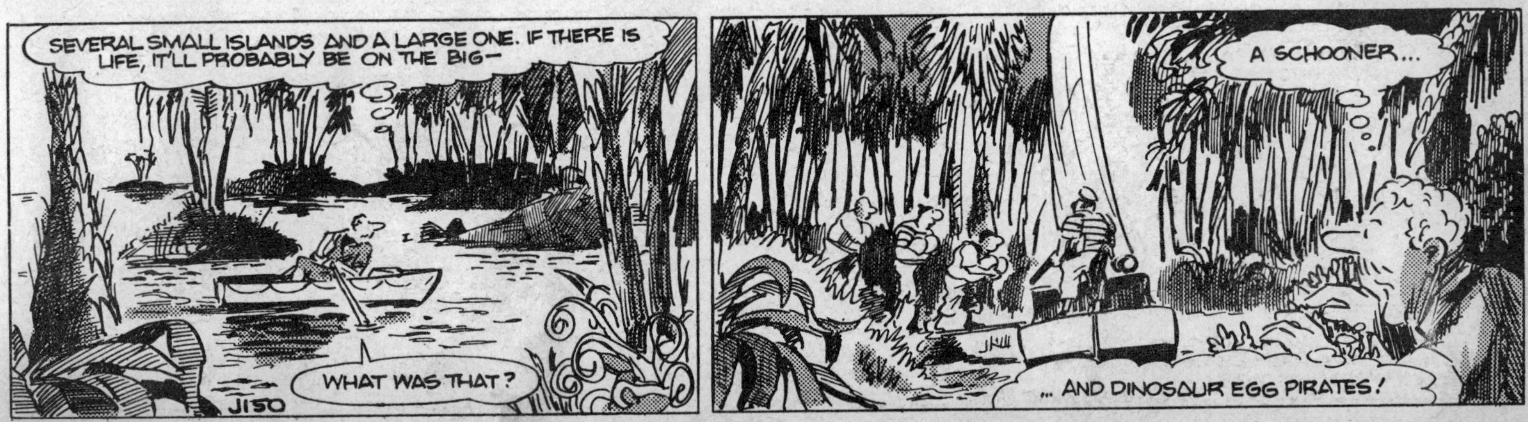
SEVERAL SMALL ISLANDS AND A LARGE ONE. IF THERE IS LIFE, IT'LL PROBABLY BE ON THE BIG—
WHAT WAS THAT?
J150
A SCHOONER...
... AND DINOSAUR EGG PIRATES!

At a Manchester gymnasium...

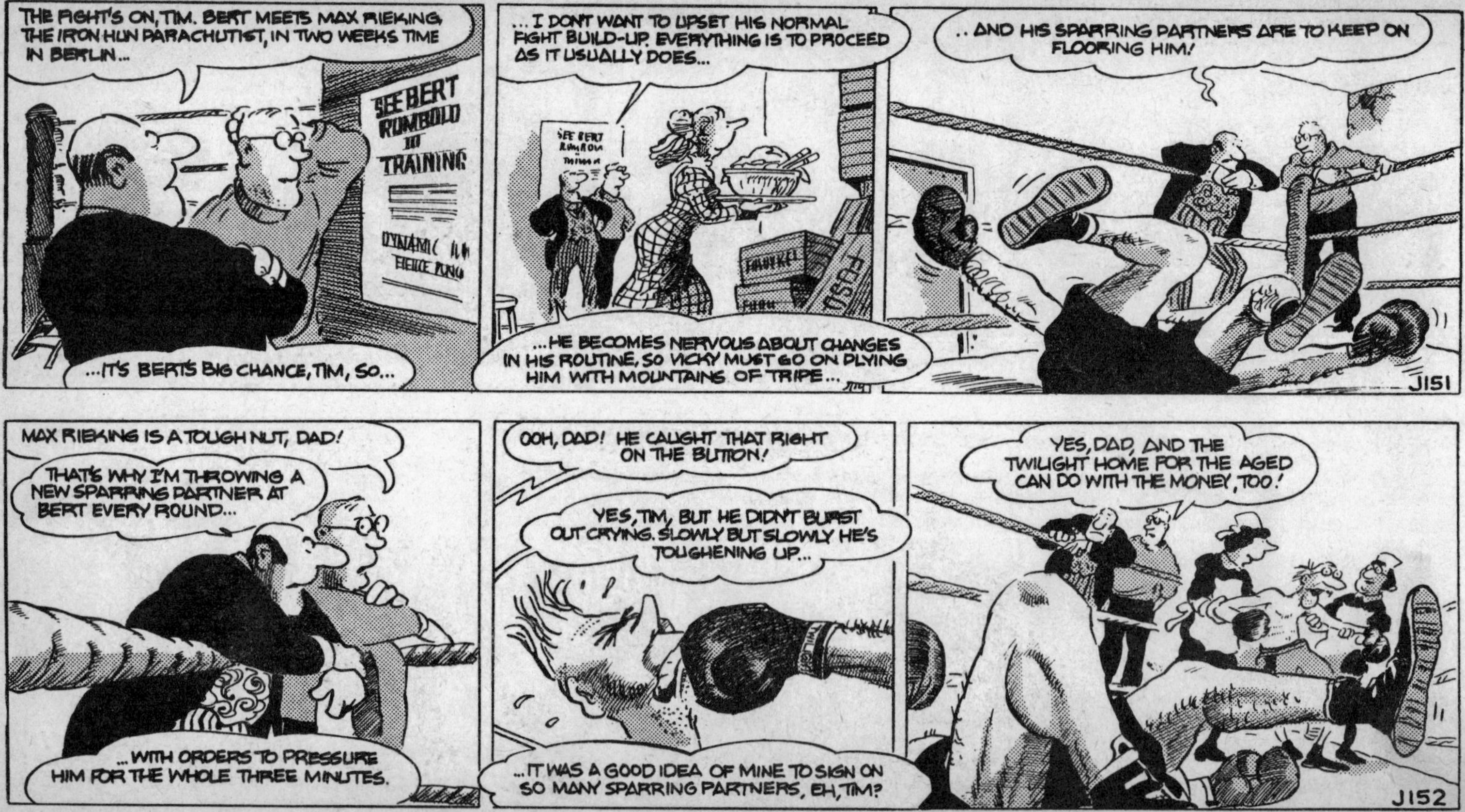

THE FIGHT'S ON, TIM. BERT MEETS MAX RIEKING, THE IRON HUN PARACHUTIST, IN TWO WEEKS TIME IN BERLIN...
SEE BERT RUMBOLD
TRAINING
...IT'S BERT'S BIG CHANCE, TIM, SO...
... I DON'T WANT TO UPSET HIS NORMAL FIGHT BUILD-UP. EVERYTHING IS TO PROCEED AS IT USUALLY DOES...
...HE BECOMES NERVOUS ABOUT CHANGES IN HIS ROUTINE, SO VICKY MUST GO ON PLYING HIM WITH MOUNTAINS OF TRIPE...
.. AND HIS SPARRING PARTNERS ARE TO KEEP ON FLOORING HIM!
J151
MAX RIEKING IS A TOUGH NUT, DAD!
THAT'S WHY I'M THROWING A NEW SPARRING PARTNER AT BERT EVERY ROUND...
... WITH ORDERS TO PRESSURE HIM FOR THE WHOLE THREE MINUTES.
OOH, DAD! HE CAUGHT THAT RIGHT ON THE BUTTON!
YES, TIM, BUT HE DIDN'T BURST OUT CRYING. SLOWLY BUT SLOWLY HE'S TOUGHENING UP...
...IT WAS A GOOD IDEA OF MINE TO SIGN ON SO MANY SPARRING PARTNERS, EH, TIM?
YES, DAD, AND THE TWILIGHT HOME FOR THE AGED CAN DO WITH THE MONEY, TOO!
J152

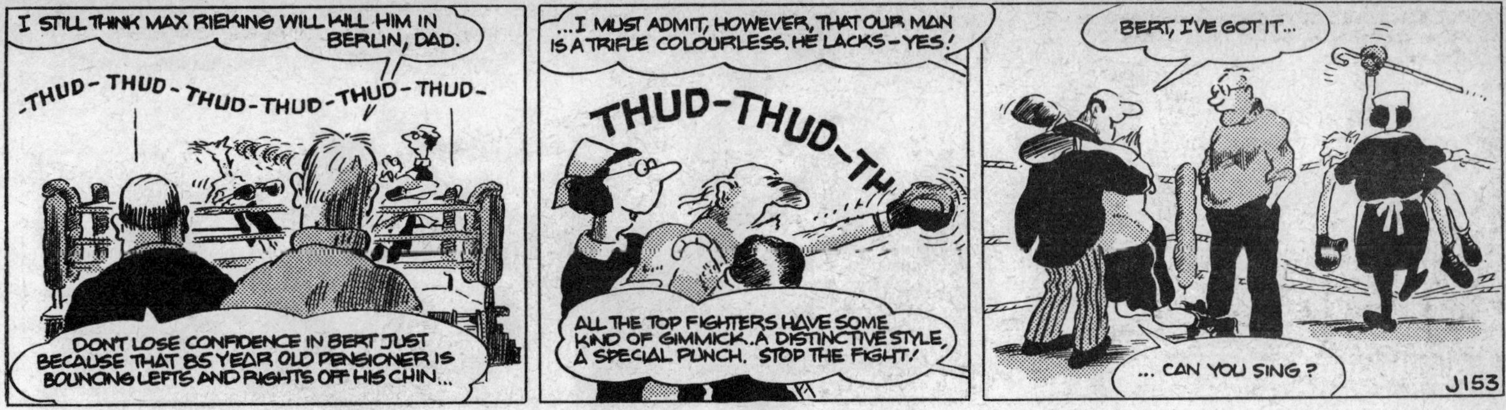
I STILL THINK MAX RIEKING WILL KILL HIM IN BERLIN, DAD.
-THUD - THUD - THUD-THUD-THUD - THUD-
DON'T LOSE CONFIDENCE IN BERT JUST BECAUSE THAT 85 YEAR OLD PENSIONER IS BOUNCING LEFTS AND RIGHTS OFF HIS CHIN...
...I MUST ADMIT, HOWEVER, THAT OUR MAN IS A TRIFLE COLOURLESS. HE LACKS - YES!
THUD-THUD-TH
ALL THE TOP FIGHTERS HAVE SOME KIND OF GIMMICK..A DISTINCTIVE STYLE, A SPECIAL PUNCH. STOP THE FIGHT!
BERT, I'VE GOT IT...
... CAN YOU SING ?
J153

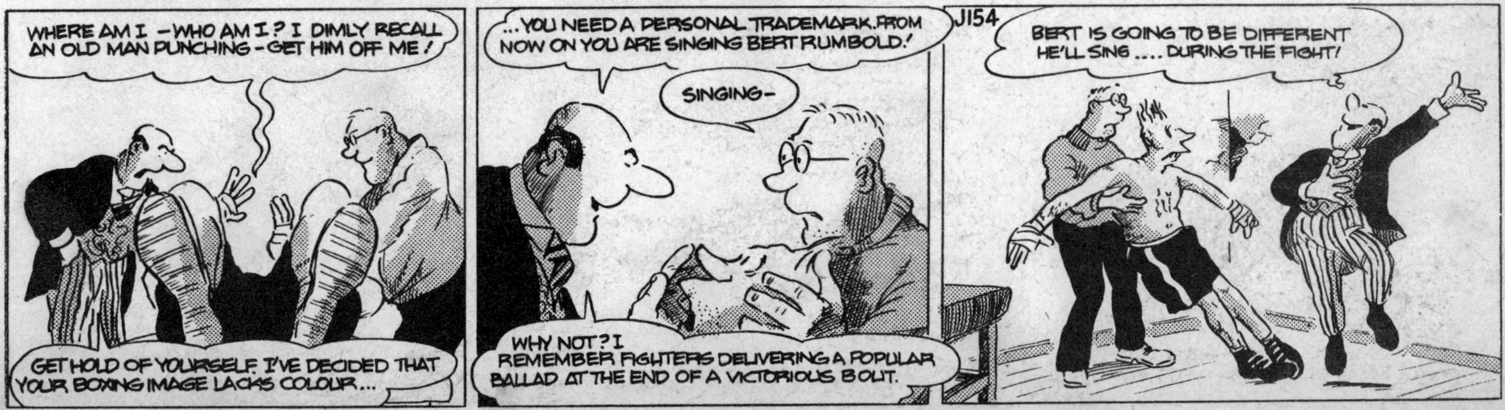
WHERE AM I -WHO AM I? I DIMLY RECALL AN OLD MAN PUNCHING - GET HIM OFF ME!
GET HOLD OF YOURSELF. I'VE DECIDED THAT YOUR BOXING IMAGE LACKS COLOUR...
...YOU NEED A PERSONAL TRADEMARK. FROM NOW ON YOU ARE SINGING BERT RUMBOLD!
SINGING-
WHY NOT? I REMEMBER FIGHTERS DELIVERING A POPULAR BALLAD AT THE END OF A VICTORIOUS BOUT.
J154
BERT IS GOING TO BE DIFFERENT HE'LL SING .... DURING THE FIGHT!

At the next training session...

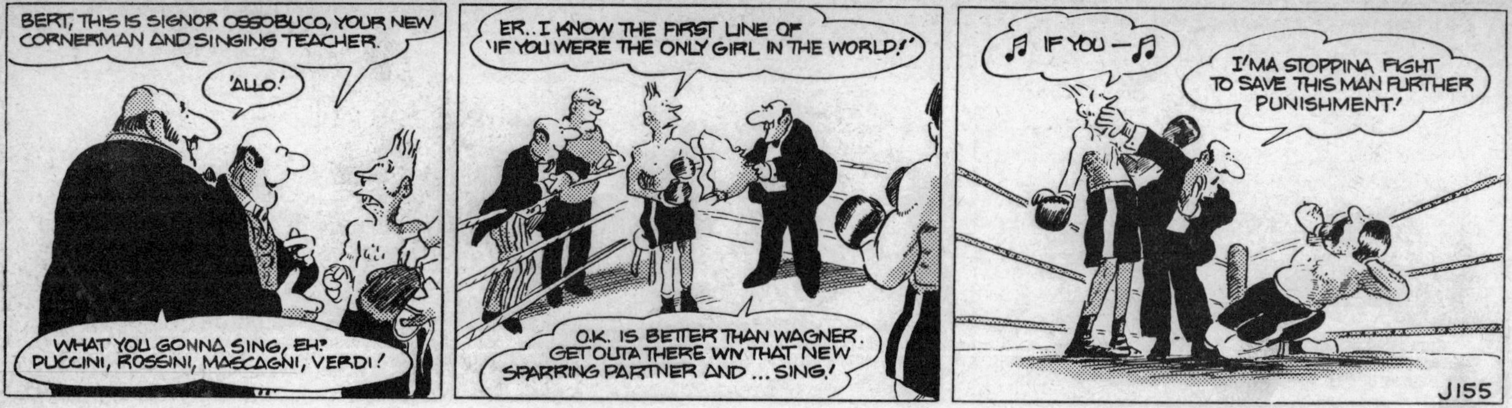
BERT, THIS IS SIGNOR OSSOBUCO, YOUR NEW CORNERMAN AND SINGING TEACHER.
'ALLO!
WHAT YOU GONNA SING, EH? PUCCINI, ROSSINI, MASCAGNI, VERDI!
ER.. I KNOW THE FIRST LINE OF 'IF YOU WERE THE ONLY GIRL IN THE WORLD!'
O.K. IS BETTER THAN WAGNER. GET OUTA THERE WIV THAT NEW SPARRING PARTNER AND ... SING!
♬ IF YOU — ♬
I'MA STOPPINA FIGHT TO SAVE THIS MAN FURTHER PUNISHMENT!
J155

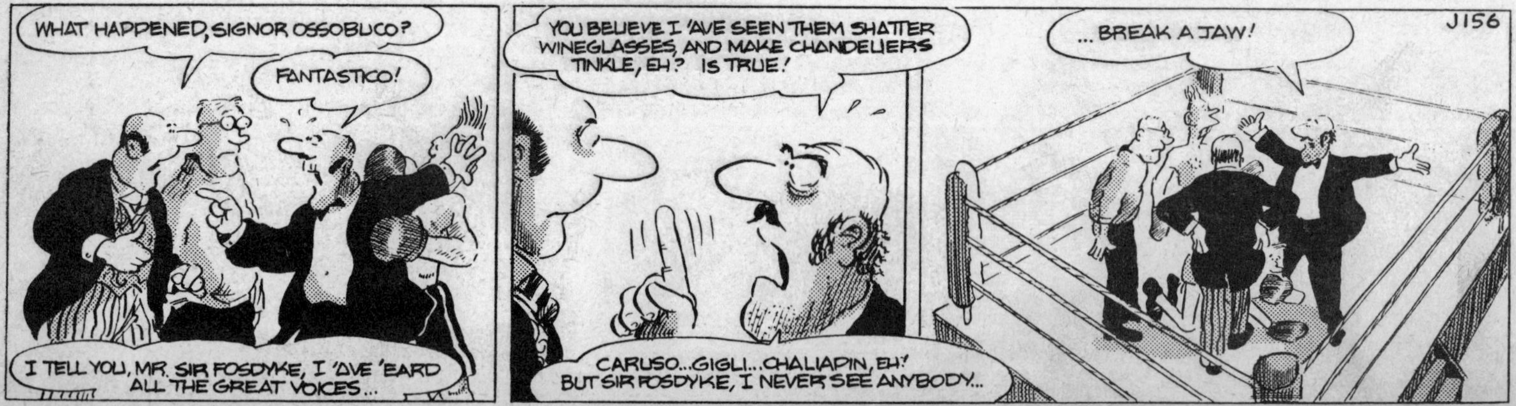
WHAT HAPPENED, SIGNOR OSSOBUCO?
FANTASTICO!
I TELL YOU, MR. SIR FOSDYKE, I 'AVE 'EARD ALL THE GREAT VOICES...
YOU BELIEVE I 'AVE SEEN THEM SHATTER WINEGLASSES, AND MAKE CHANDELIERS TINKLE, EH? IS TRUE!
CARUSO...GIGLI...CHALIAPIN, EH! BUT SIR FOSDYKE, I NEVER SEE ANYBODY...
... BREAK A JAW!
J156

Meanwhile, in J. A. Offrocker's laboratory...

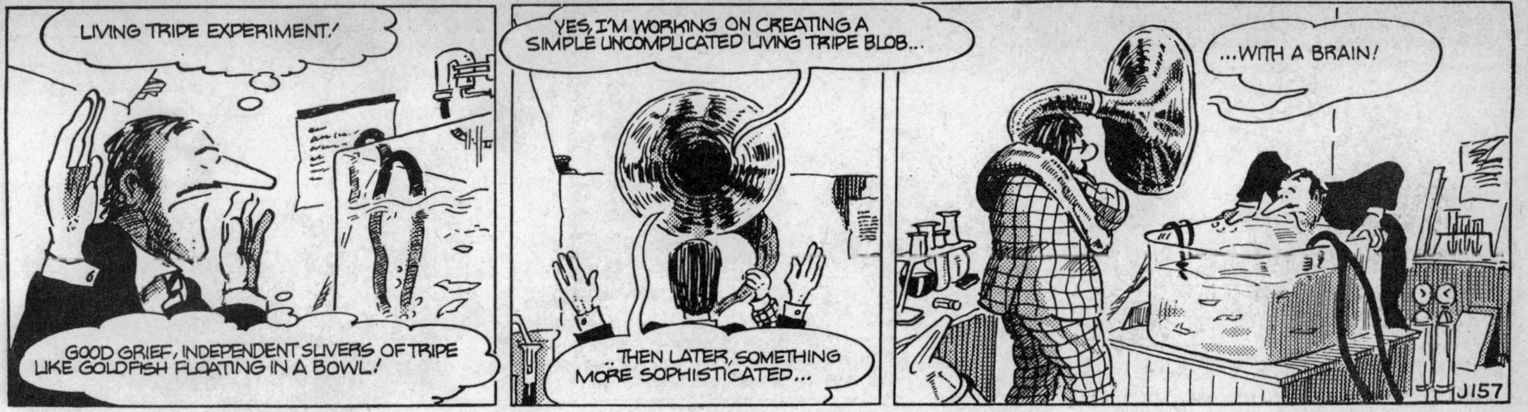

LIVING TRIPE EXPERIMENT!
GOOD GRIEF, INDEPENDENT SLIVERS OF TRIPE LIKE GOLDFISH FLOATING IN A BOWL!
YES, I'M WORKING ON CREATING A SIMPLE UNCOMPLICATED LIVING TRIPE BLOB...
..THEN LATER, SOMETHING MORE SOPHISTICATED...
...WITH A BRAIN!
J157

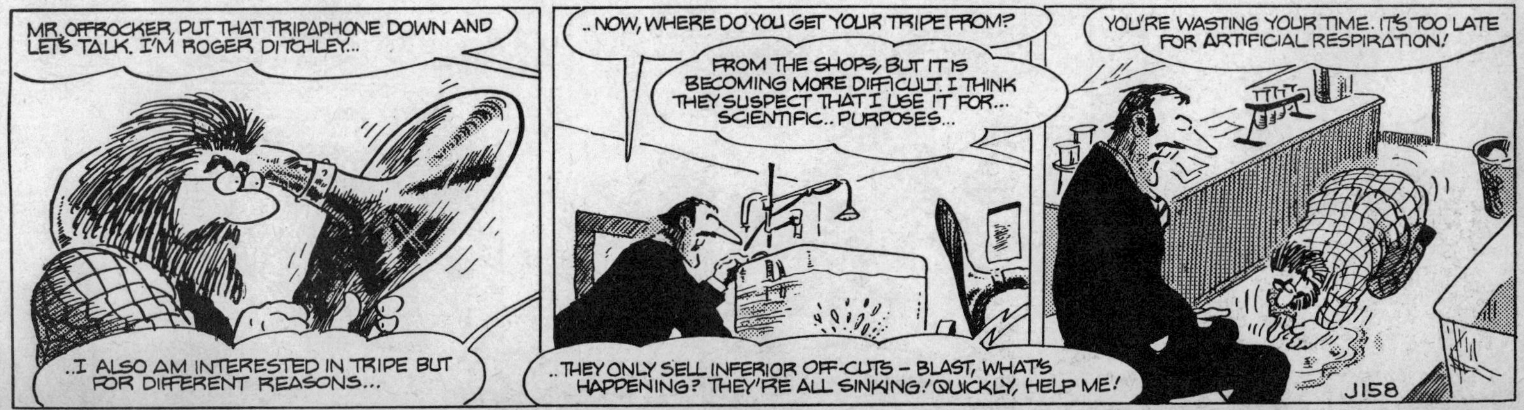

MR. OFFROCKER, PUT THAT TRIPAPHONE DOWN AND LET'S TALK. I'M ROGER DITCHLEY...
..I ALSO AM INTERESTED IN TRIPE BUT FOR DIFFERENT REASONS...
.. NOW, WHERE DO YOU GET YOUR TRIPE FROM?
FROM THE SHOPS, BUT IT IS BECOMING MORE DIFFICULT. I THINK THEY SUSPECT THAT I USE IT FOR... SCIENTIFIC.. PURPOSES...
..THEY ONLY SELL INFERIOR OFF-CUTS – BLAST, WHAT'S HAPPENING? THEY'RE ALL SINKING! QUICKLY, HELP ME!
YOU'RE WASTING YOUR TIME. IT'S TOO LATE FOR ARTIFICIAL RESPIRATION!
J158

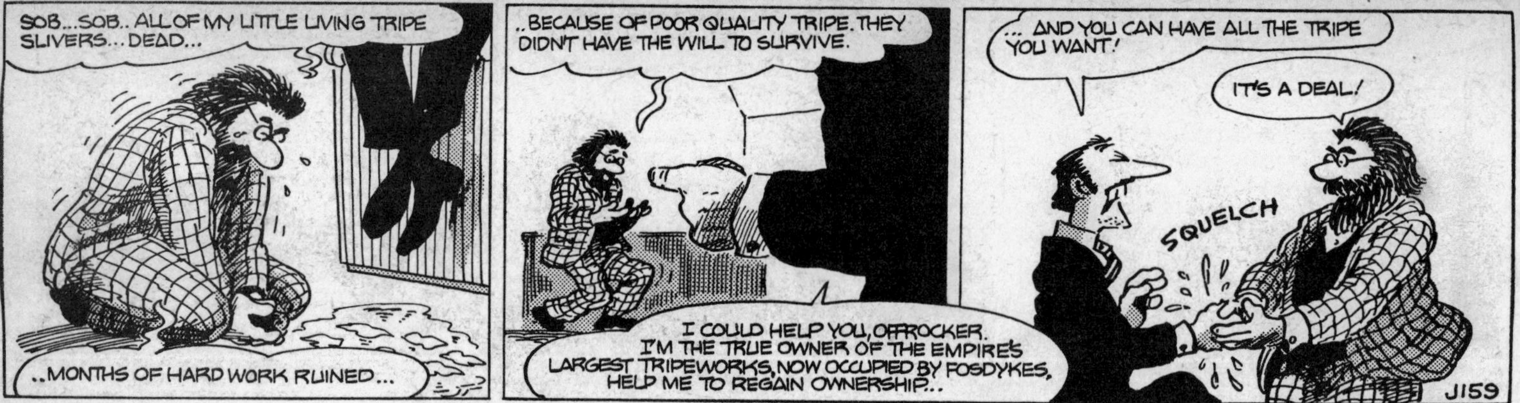
SOB...SOB.. ALL OF MY LITTLE LIVING TRIPE SLIVERS... DEAD...
..MONTHS OF HARD WORK RUINED...
..BECAUSE OF POOR QUALITY TRIPE. THEY DIDN'T HAVE THE WILL TO SURVIVE.
I COULD HELP YOU, OFFROCKER. I'M THE TRUE OWNER OF THE EMPIRE'S LARGEST TRIPEWORKS, NOW OCCUPIED BY FOSDYKES, HELP ME TO REGAIN OWNERSHIP...
... AND YOU CAN HAVE ALL THE TRIPE YOU WANT!
IT'S A DEAL!
SQUELCH
J159

And so the dastardly partnership goes into action...

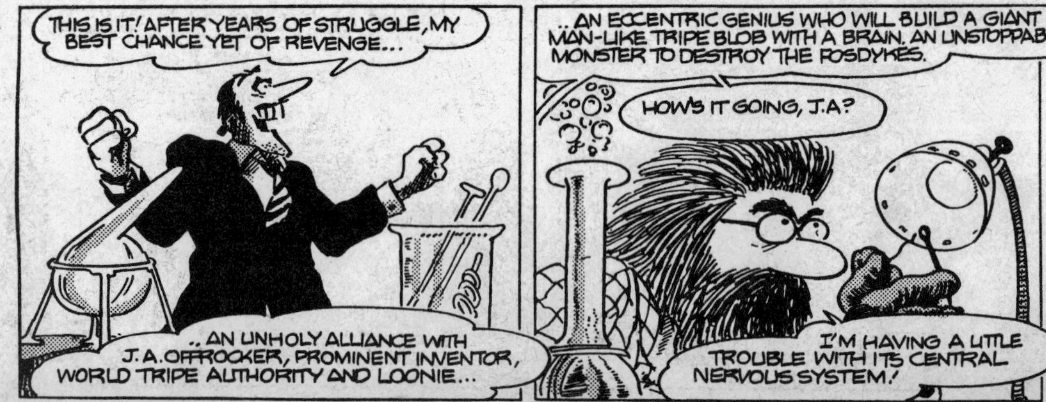
THIS IS IT! AFTER YEARS OF STRUGGLE, MY BEST CHANCE YET OF REVENGE...
.. AN UNHOLY ALLIANCE WITH J. A. OFFROCKER, PROMINENT INVENTOR, WORLD TRIPE AUTHORITY AND LOONIE...
.. AN ECCENTRIC GENIUS WHO WILL BUILD A GIANT MAN-LIKE TRIPE BLOB WITH A BRAIN. AN UNSTOPPABLE MONSTER TO DESTROY THE FOSDYKES.
HOW'S IT GOING, J.A?
I'M HAVING A LITTLE TROUBLE WITH ITS CENTRAL NERVOUS SYSTEM!

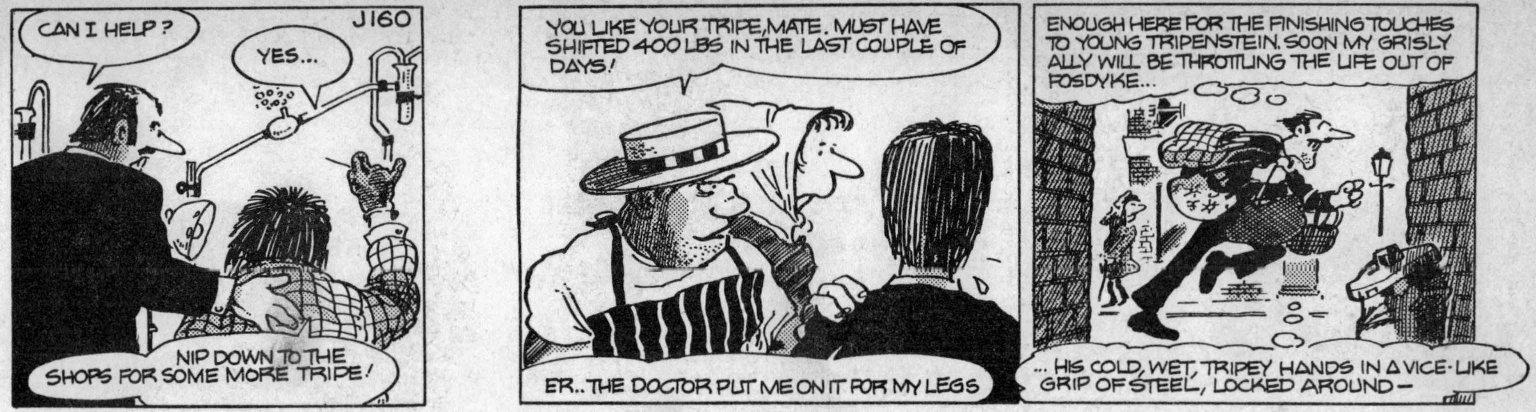
J160
CAN I HELP ?
YES...
NIP DOWN TO THE SHOPS FOR SOME MORE TRIPE!
YOU LIKE YOUR TRIPE, MATE. MUST HAVE SHIFTED 400 LBS IN THE LAST COUPLE OF DAYS!
ER.. THE DOCTOR PUT ME ON IT FOR MY LEGS
ENOUGH HERE FOR THE FINISHING TOUCHES TO YOUNG TRIPENSTEIN. SOON MY GRISLY ALLY WILL BE THROTTLING THE LIFE OUT OF FOSDYKE...
... HIS COLD, WET, TRIPEY HANDS IN A VICE-LIKE GRIP OF STEEL, LOCKED AROUND —

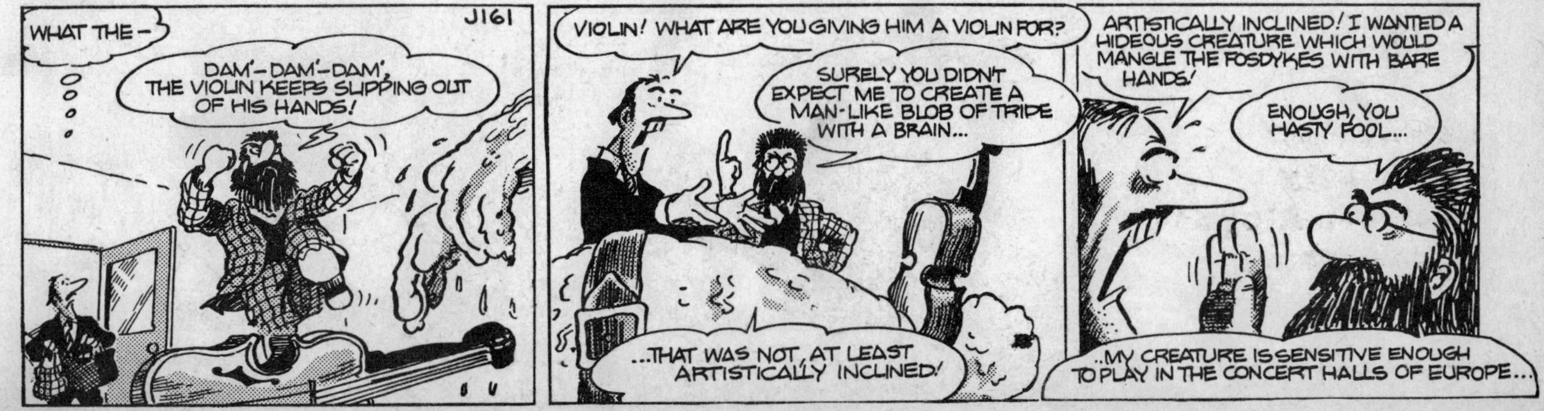
J161
WHAT THE —
DAM'— DAM'— DAM', THE VIOLIN KEEPS SLIPPING OUT OF HIS HANDS!
VIOLIN! WHAT ARE YOU GIVING HIM A VIOLIN FOR?
SURELY YOU DIDN'T EXPECT ME TO CREATE A MAN-LIKE BLOB OF TRIPE WITH A BRAIN...
...THAT WAS NOT, AT LEAST ARTISTICALLY INCLINED!
ARTISTICALLY INCLINED! I WANTED A HIDEOUS CREATURE WHICH WOULD MANGLE THE FOSDYKES WITH BARE HANDS!
ENOUGH, YOU HASTY FOOL...
...MY CREATURE IS SENSITIVE ENOUGH TO PLAY IN THE CONCERT HALLS OF EUROPE...

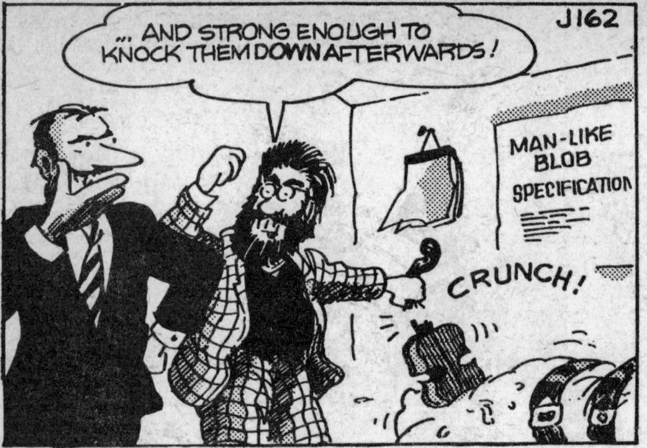
J162
... AND STRONG ENOUGH TO KNOCK THEM DOWN AFTERWARDS!
MAN-LIKE BLOB SPECIFICATION
CRUNCH!

Far away, in the lost world of Mu...

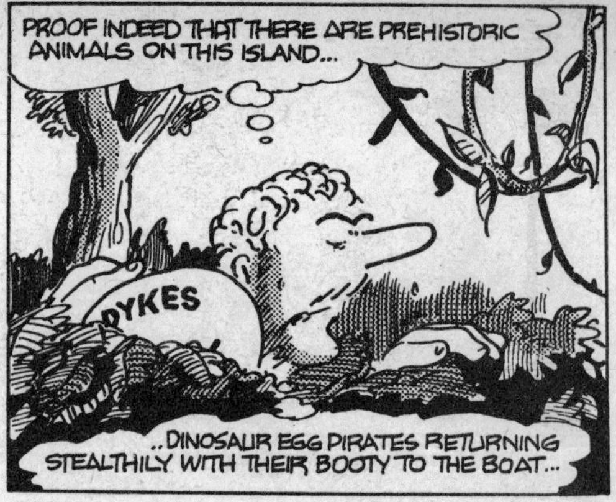
PROOF INDEED THAT THERE ARE PREHISTORIC ANIMALS ON THIS ISLAND...
DYKES
..DINOSAUR EGG PIRATES RETURNING STEALTHILY WITH THEIR BOOTY TO THE BOAT...

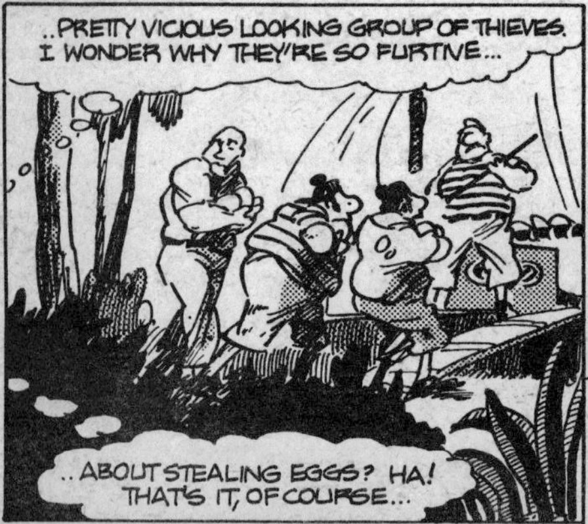
..PRETTY VICIOUS LOOKING GROUP OF THIEVES. I WONDER WHY THEY'RE SO FURTIVE...
.. ABOUT STEALING EGGS? HA! THAT'S IT, OF COURSE...

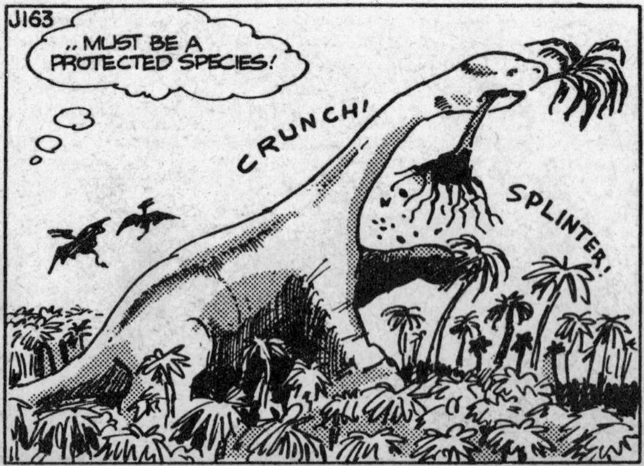
J163
.. MUST BE A PROTECTED SPECIES!
CRUNCH!
SPLINTER!

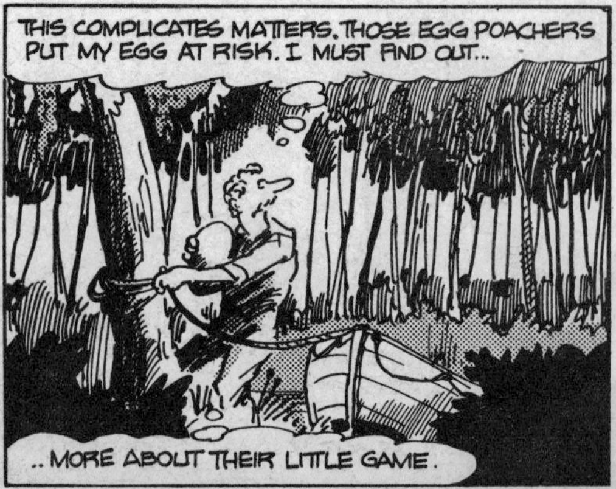
THIS COMPLICATES MATTERS. THOSE EGG POACHERS PUT MY EGG AT RISK. I MUST FIND OUT...
.. MORE ABOUT THEIR LITTLE GAME.

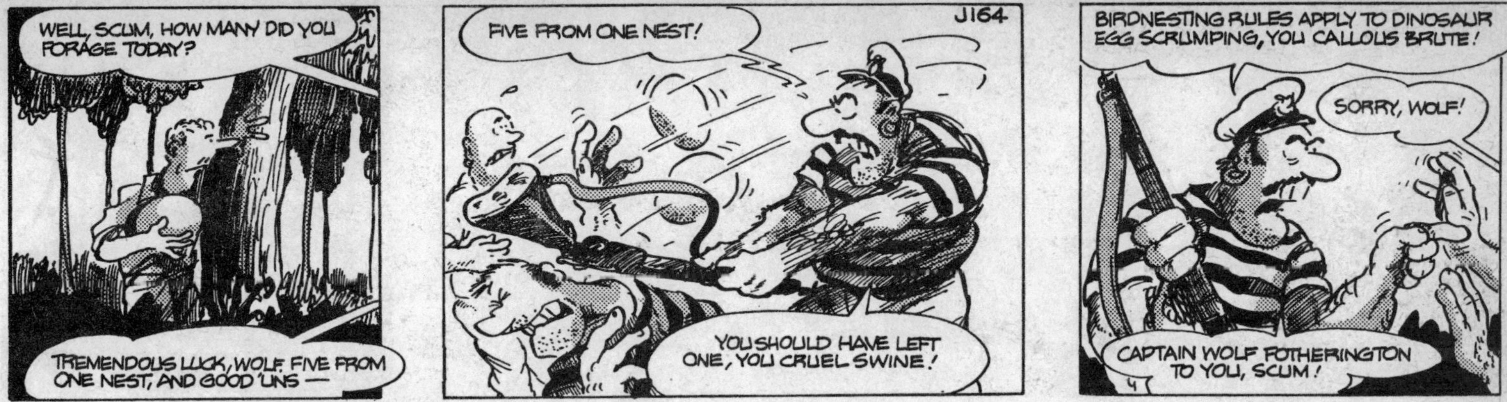
WELL, SCUM, HOW MANY DID YOU FORAGE TODAY?
TREMENDOUS LUCK, WOLF. FIVE FROM ONE NEST, AND GOOD 'UNS —
J164
FIVE FROM ONE NEST!
YOU SHOULD HAVE LEFT ONE, YOU CRUEL SWINE!
BIRDNESTING RULES APPLY TO DINOSAUR EGG SCRUMPING, YOU CALLOUS BRUTE!
SORRY, WOLF!
CAPTAIN WOLF FOTHERINGTON TO YOU, SCUM!

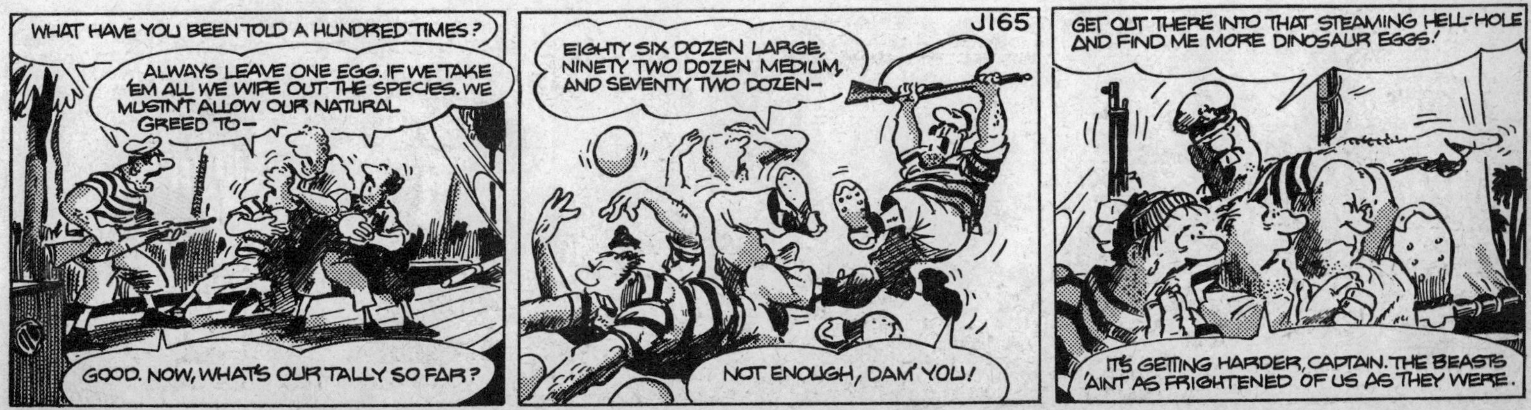
WHAT HAVE YOU BEEN TOLD A HUNDRED TIMES?
ALWAYS LEAVE ONE EGG. IF WE TAKE 'EM ALL WE WIPE OUT THE SPECIES. WE MUSTN'T ALLOW OUR NATURAL GREED TO–
GOOD. NOW, WHAT'S OUR TALLY SO FAR?
J165
EIGHTY SIX DOZEN LARGE, NINETY TWO DOZEN MEDIUM, AND SEVENTY TWO DOZEN–
NOT ENOUGH, DAM' YOU!
GET OUT THERE INTO THAT STEAMING HELL-HOLE AND FIND ME MORE DINOSAUR EGGS!
IT'S GETTING HARDER, CAPTAIN. THE BEASTS 'AINT AS FRIGHTENED OF US AS THEY WERE.

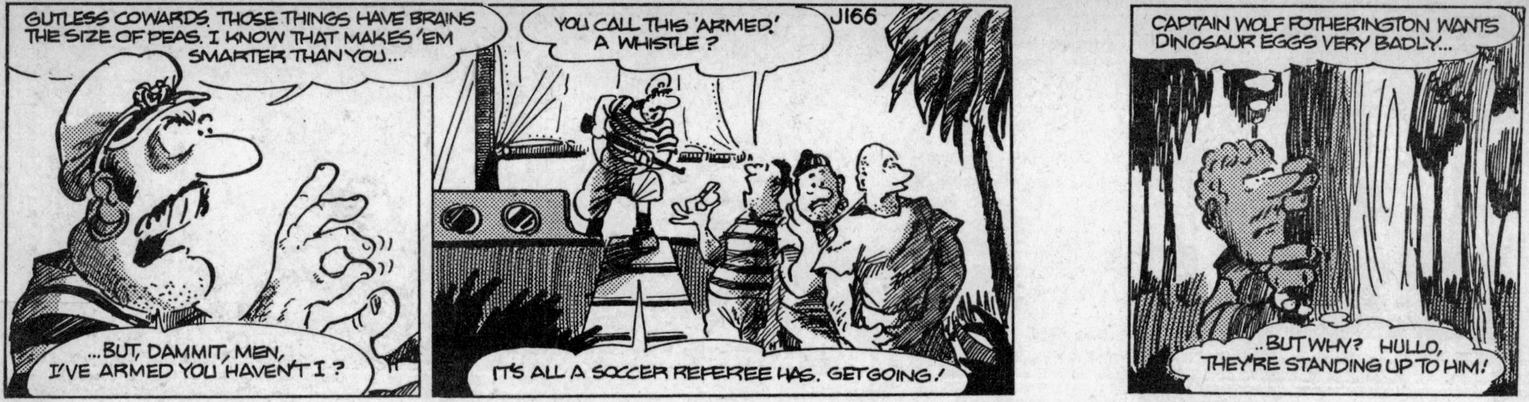
GUTLESS COWARDS. THOSE THINGS HAVE BRAINS THE SIZE OF PEAS. I KNOW THAT MAKES 'EM SMARTER THAN YOU...
...BUT, DAMMIT, MEN, I'VE ARMED YOU HAVEN'T I ?
J166
YOU CALL THIS 'ARMED.' A WHISTLE ?
IT'S ALL A SOCCER REFEREE HAS. GETGOING!
CAPTAIN WOLF FOTHERINGTON WANTS DINOSAUR EGGS VERY BADLY...
...BUT WHY? HULLO, THEY'RE STANDING UP TO HIM!

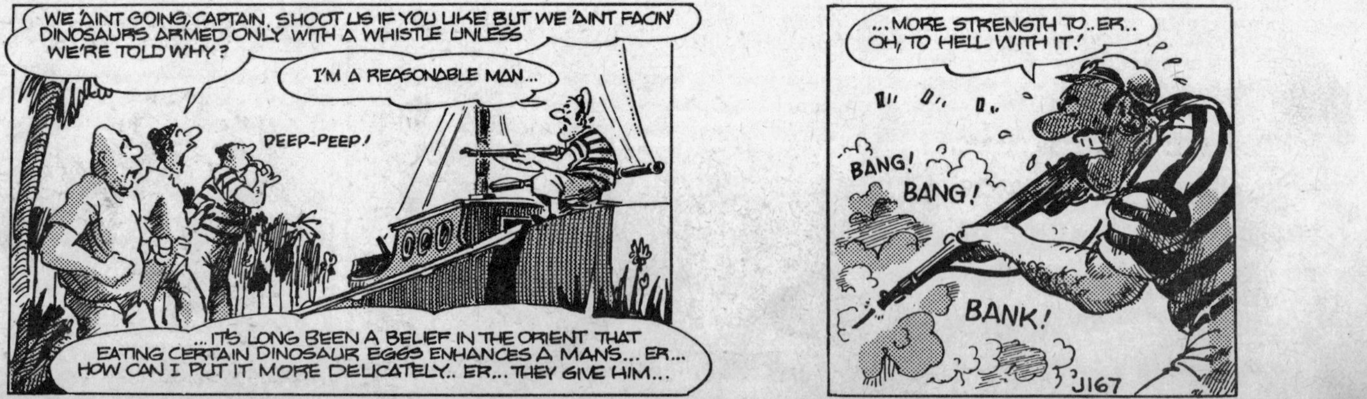
WE 'AINT GOING, CAPTAIN. SHOOT US IF YOU LIKE BUT WE 'AINT FACIN' DINOSAURS ARMED ONLY WITH A WHISTLE UNLESS WE'RE TOLD WHY ?
I'M A REASONABLE MAN...
PEEP-PEEP!
...IT'S LONG BEEN A BELIEF IN THE ORIENT THAT EATING CERTAIN DINOSAUR EGGS ENHANCES A MAN'S... ER... HOW CAN I PUT IT MORE DELICATELY.. ER... THEY GIVE HIM...
...MORE STRENGTH TO..ER.. OH, TO HELL WITH IT!
BANG!
BANG!
BANK!
J167

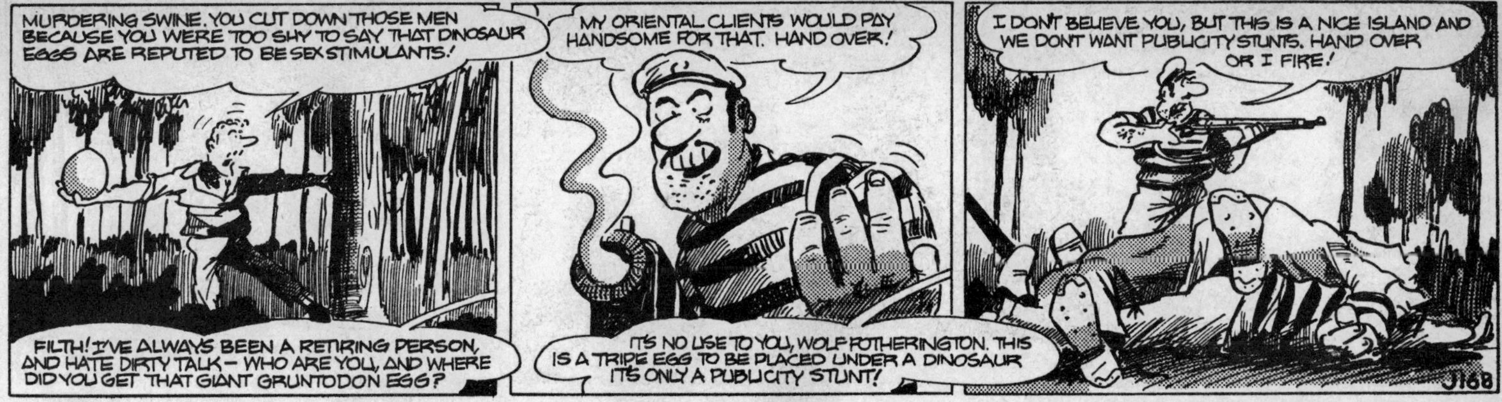
MURDERING SWINE. YOU CUT DOWN THOSE MEN BECAUSE YOU WERE TOO SHY TO SAY THAT DINOSAUR EGGS ARE REPUTED TO BE SEX STIMULANTS!
FILTH! I'VE ALWAYS BEEN A RETIRING PERSON, AND HATE DIRTY TALK – WHO ARE YOU, AND WHERE DID YOU GET THAT GIANT GRUNTODON EGG?
MY ORIENTAL CLIENTS WOULD PAY HANDSOME FOR THAT. HAND OVER!
IT'S NO USE TO YOU, WOLF FOTHERINGTON. THIS IS A TRIPE EGG TO BE PLACED UNDER A DINOSAUR IT'S ONLY A PUBLICITY STUNT!
I DON'T BELIEVE YOU, BUT THIS IS A NICE ISLAND AND WE DON'T WANT PUBLICITY STUNTS. HAND OVER OR I FIRE!
J168

In Manchester Bert's training programme reaches a crescendo...

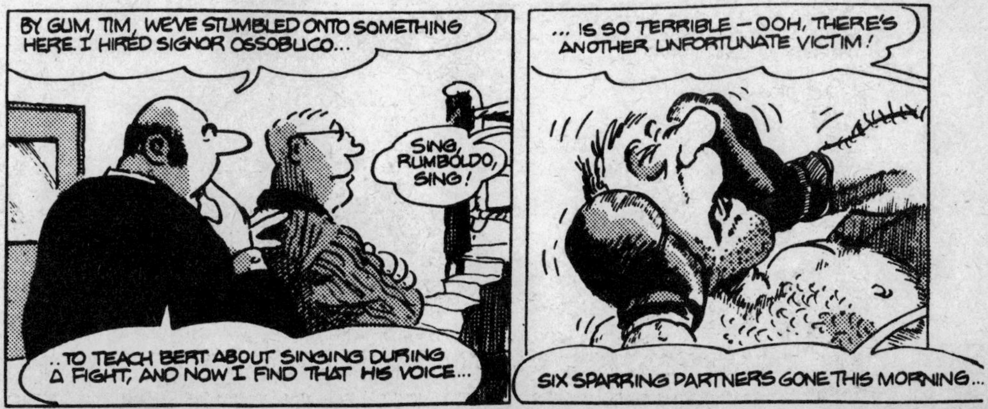
BY GUM, TIM, WE'VE STUMBLED ONTO SOMETHING HERE. I HIRED SIGNOR OSSOBUCO...
SING, RUMBOLDO, SING!
..TO TEACH BERT ABOUT SINGING DURING A FIGHT, AND NOW I FIND THAT HIS VOICE...
... IS SO TERRIBLE – OOH, THERE'S ANOTHER UNFORTUNATE VICTIM!
SIX SPARRING PARTNERS GONE THIS MORNING...

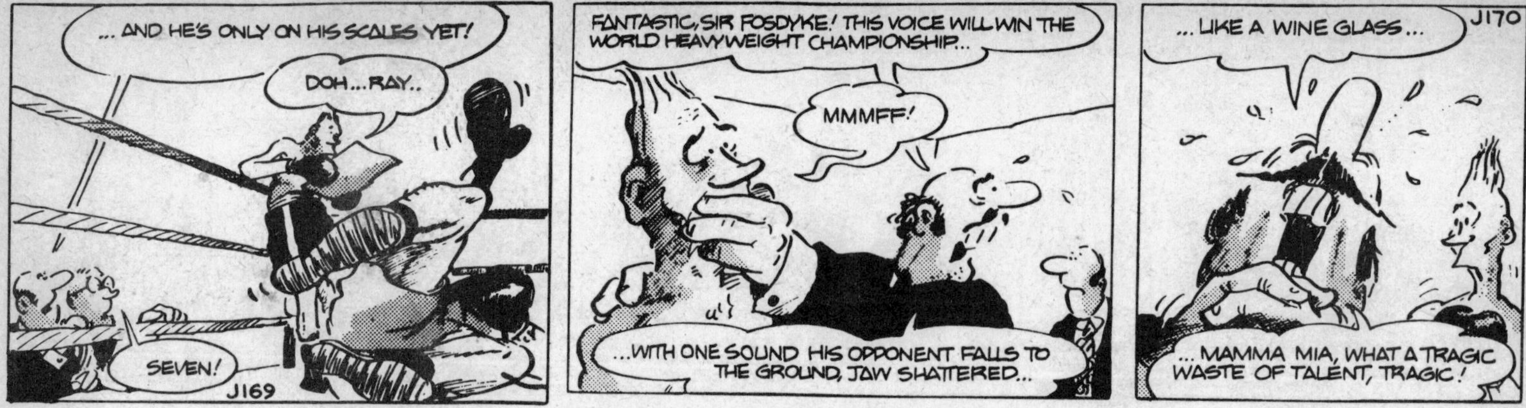
... AND HE'S ONLY ON HIS SCALES YET!
DOH... RAY..
SEVEN!
J169
FANTASTIC, SIR FOSDYKE! THIS VOICE WILL WIN THE WORLD HEAVYWEIGHT CHAMPIONSHIP...
MMMFF!
...WITH ONE SOUND HIS OPPONENT FALLS TO THE GROUND, JAW SHATTERED...
J170
... LIKE A WINE GLASS ...
... MAMMA MIA, WHAT A TRAGIC WASTE OF TALENT, TRAGIC!

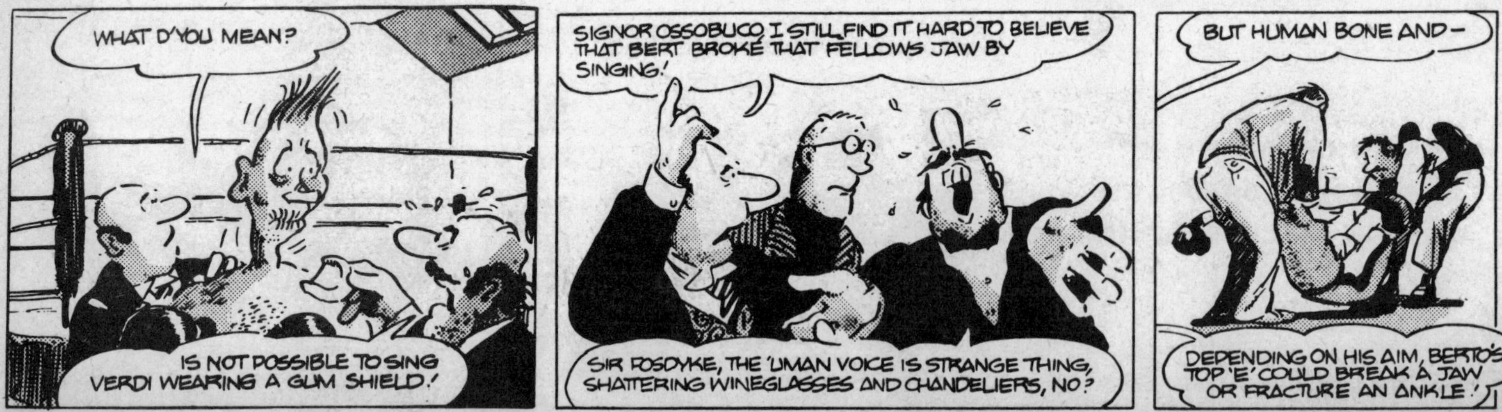
WHAT D'YOU MEAN?
IS NOT POSSIBLE TO SING VERDI WEARING A GUM SHIELD!
SIGNOR OSSOBUCO, I STILL FIND IT HARD TO BELIEVE THAT BERT BROKE THAT FELLOWS JAW BY SINGING!
SIR FOSDYKE, THE 'UMAN VOICE IS STRANGE THING, SHATTERING WINEGLASSES AND CHANDELIERS, NO?
BUT HUMAN BONE AND—
DEPENDING ON HIS AIM, BERTO'S TOP 'E' COULD BREAK A JAW OR FRACTURE AN ANKLE!

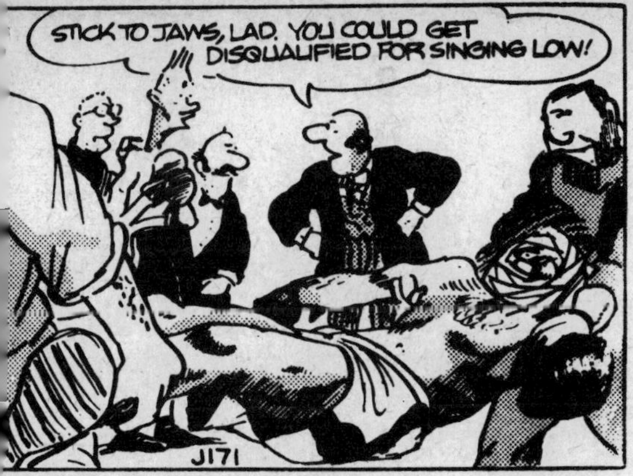
STICK TO JAWS, LAD. YOU COULD GET DISQUALIFIED FOR SINGING LOW!
J171

Outside the gymnasium the press hounds are still hot on the trail...

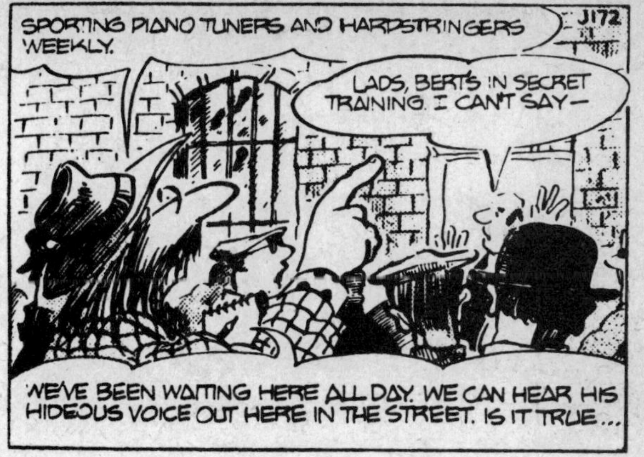
J172
SPORTING PIANO TUNERS AND HARDSTRINGERS WEEKLY.
LADS, BERT'S IN SECRET TRAINING. I CAN'T SAY—
WE'VE BEEN WAITING HERE ALL DAY. WE CAN HEAR HIS HIDEOUS VOICE OUT HERE IN THE STREET. IS IT TRUE...

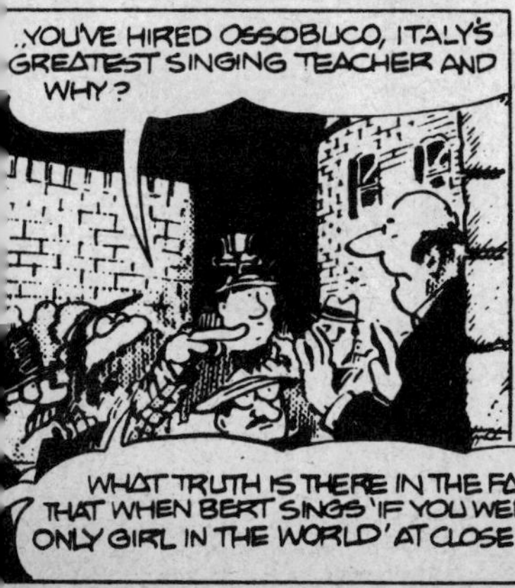
...YOU'VE HIRED OSSOBUCO, ITALY'S GREATEST SINGING TEACHER AND WHY?
WHAT TRUTH IS THERE IN THE FACT THAT WHEN BERT SINGS 'IF YOU WERE THE ONLY GIRL IN THE WORLD' AT CLOSE RANGE...

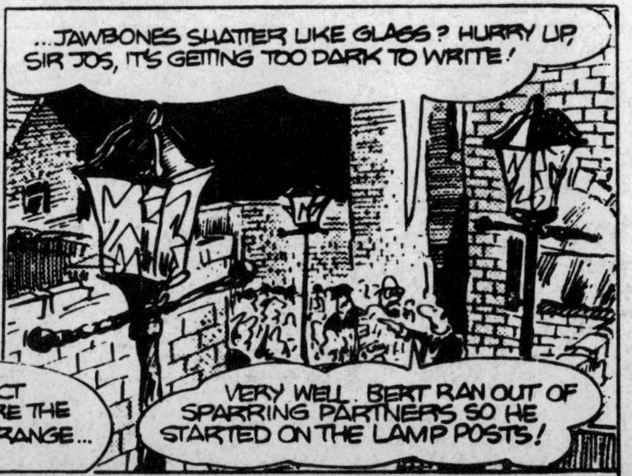
...JAWBONES SHATTER LIKE GLASS? HURRY UP, SIR JOS, IT'S GETTING TOO DARK TO WRITE!
VERY WELL. BERT RAN OUT OF SPARRING PARTNERS SO HE STARTED ON THE LAMP POSTS!

But inside the gymnasium...

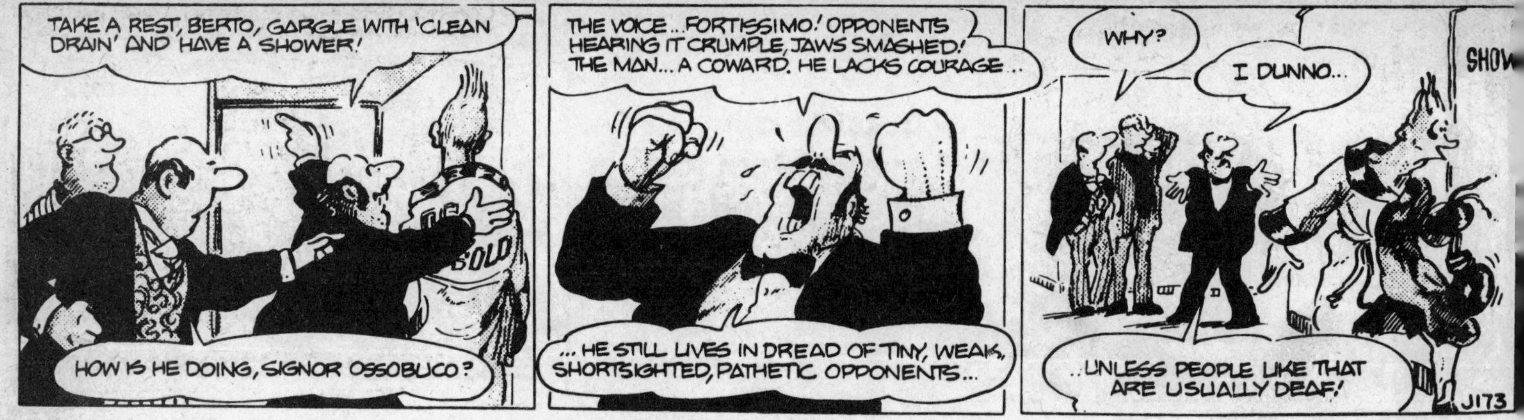
TAKE A REST, BERTO, GARGLE WITH 'CLEAN DRAIN' AND HAVE A SHOWER!
HOW IS HE DOING, SIGNOR OSSOBUCO?
THE VOICE... FORTISSIMO! OPPONENTS HEARING IT CRUMPLE, JAWS SMASHED! THE MAN... A COWARD. HE LACKS COURAGE...
... HE STILL LIVES IN DREAD OF TINY, WEAK, SHORTSIGHTED, PATHETIC OPPONENTS...
WHY?
I DUNNO...
..UNLESS PEOPLE LIKE THAT ARE USUALLY DEAF!
J173

And at last the goal is in sight...

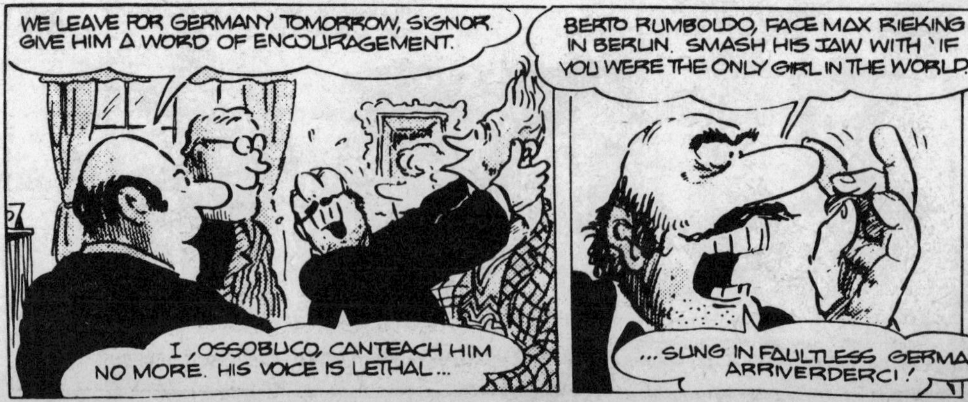
WE LEAVE FOR GERMANY TOMORROW, SIGNOR. GIVE HIM A WORD OF ENCOURAGEMENT.
I, OSSOBUCO, CAN TEACH HIM NO MORE. HIS VOICE IS LETHAL...
BERTO RUMBOLDO, FACE MAX RIEKING IN BERLIN. SMASH HIS JAW WITH 'IF YOU WERE THE ONLY GIRL IN THE WORLD'...
... SUNG IN FAULTLESS GERMAN. ARRIVERDERCI!

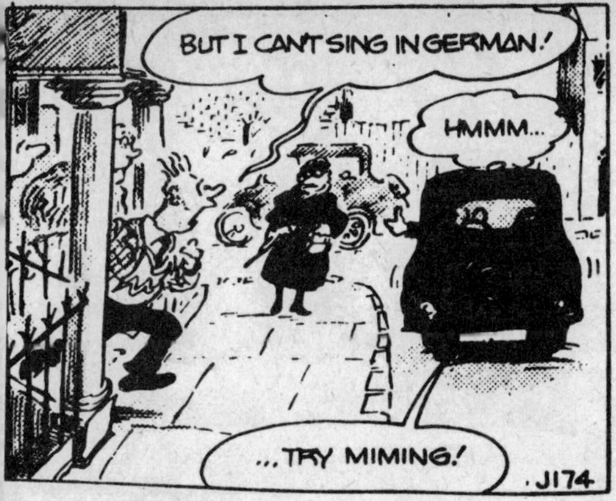
BUT I CAN'T SING IN GERMAN!
HMMM...
...TRY MIMING!
J174

Meanwhile, in the tripe laboratory...

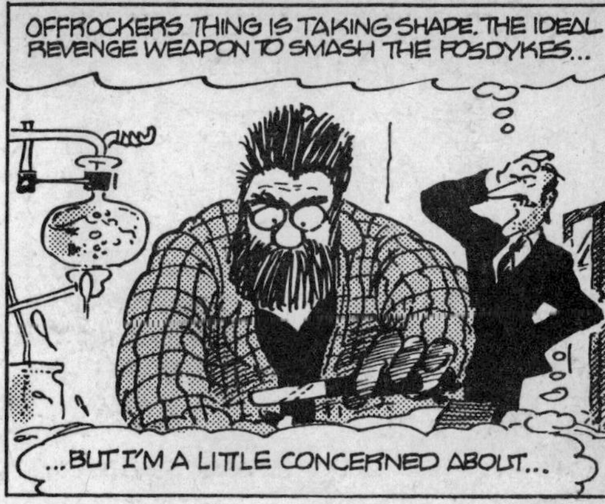
OFFROCKERS THING IS TAKING SHAPE. THE IDEAL REVENGE WEAPON TO SMASH THE FOSDYKES...
...BUT I'M A LITTLE CONCERNED ABOUT...

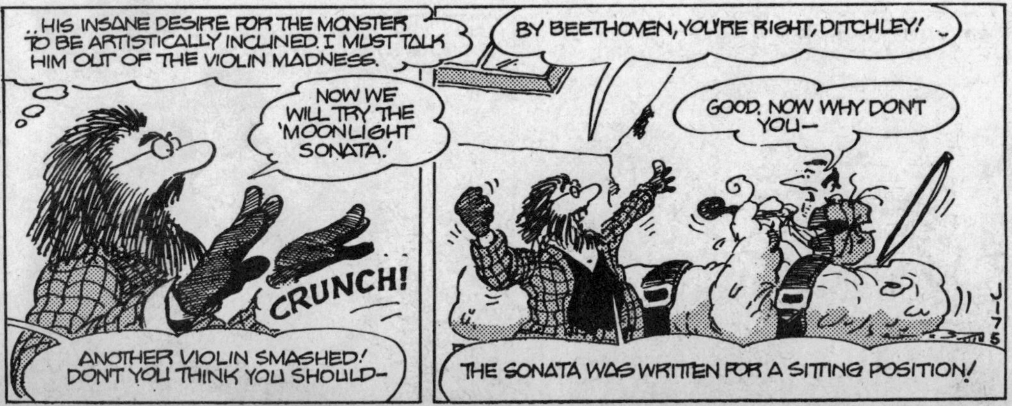
...HIS INSANE DESIRE FOR THE MONSTER TO BE ARTISTICALLY INCLINED. I MUST TALK HIM OUT OF THE VIOLIN MADNESS.
NOW WE WILL TRY THE 'MOONLIGHT SONATA.'
CRUNCH!
ANOTHER VIOLIN SMASHED! DON'T YOU THINK YOU SHOULD–
BY BEETHOVEN, YOU'RE RIGHT, DITCHLEY!
GOOD. NOW WHY DON'T YOU–
THE SONATA WAS WRITTEN FOR A SITTING POSITION!
J175

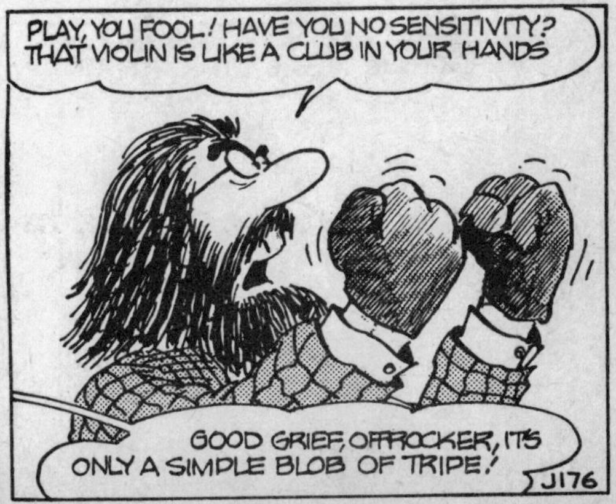
PLAY, YOU FOOL! HAVE YOU NO SENSITIVITY? THAT VIOLIN IS LIKE A CLUB IN YOUR HANDS
GOOD GRIEF, OFFROCKER, IT'S ONLY A SIMPLE BLOB OF TRIPE!
J176

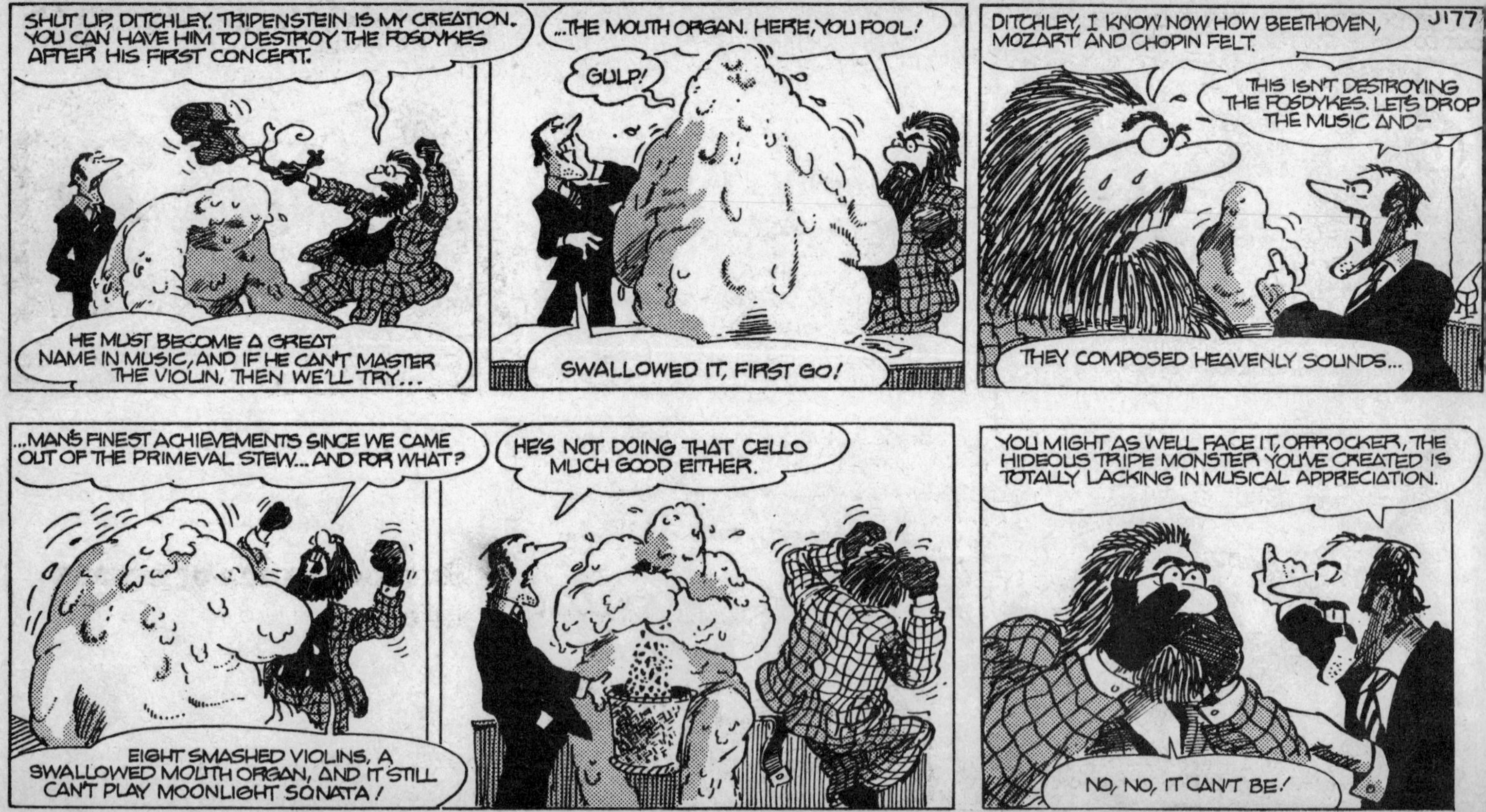
SHUT UP, DITCHLEY. TRIPENSTEIN IS MY CREATION. YOU CAN HAVE HIM TO DESTROY THE FOSDYKES AFTER HIS FIRST CONCERT.
HE MUST BECOME A GREAT NAME IN MUSIC, AND IF HE CAN'T MASTER THE VIOLIN, THEN WE'LL TRY...
...THE MOUTH ORGAN. HERE, YOU FOOL!
GULP!
SWALLOWED IT, FIRST GO!
J177
DITCHLEY, I KNOW NOW HOW BEETHOVEN, MOZART AND CHOPIN FELT.
THIS ISN'T DESTROYING THE FOSDYKES. LET'S DROP THE MUSIC AND—
THEY COMPOSED HEAVENLY SOUNDS...
...MAN'S FINEST ACHIEVEMENTS SINCE WE CAME OUT OF THE PRIMEVAL STEW... AND FOR WHAT?
EIGHT SMASHED VIOLINS, A SWALLOWED MOUTH ORGAN, AND IT STILL CAN'T PLAY MOONLIGHT SONATA!
HE'S NOT DOING THAT CELLO MUCH GOOD EITHER.
YOU MIGHT AS WELL FACE IT, OFFROCKER, THE HIDEOUS TRIPE MONSTER YOU'VE CREATED IS TOTALLY LACKING IN MUSICAL APPRECIATION.
NO, NO, IT CAN'T BE!

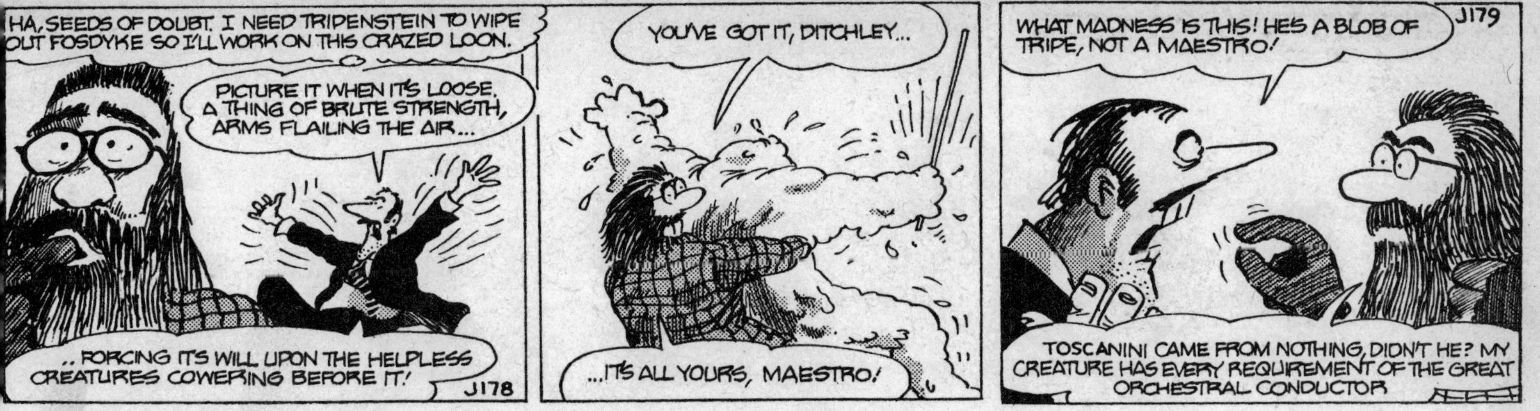
HA, SEEDS OF DOUBT. I NEED TRIPENSTEIN TO WIPE OUT FOSDYKE SO I'LL WORK ON THIS CRAZED LOON.
PICTURE IT WHEN IT'S LOOSE, A THING OF BRUTE STRENGTH, ARMS FLAILING THE AIR...
..FORCING IT'S WILL UPON THE HELPLESS CREATURES COWERING BEFORE IT!
J178
YOU'VE GOT IT, DITCHLEY...
...IT'S ALL YOURS, MAESTRO!
J179
WHAT MADNESS IS THIS! HE'S A BLOB OF TRIPE, NOT A MAESTRO!
TOSCANINI CAME FROM NOTHING, DIDN'T HE? MY CREATURE HAS EVERY REQUIREMENT OF THE GREAT ORCHESTRAL CONDUCTOR

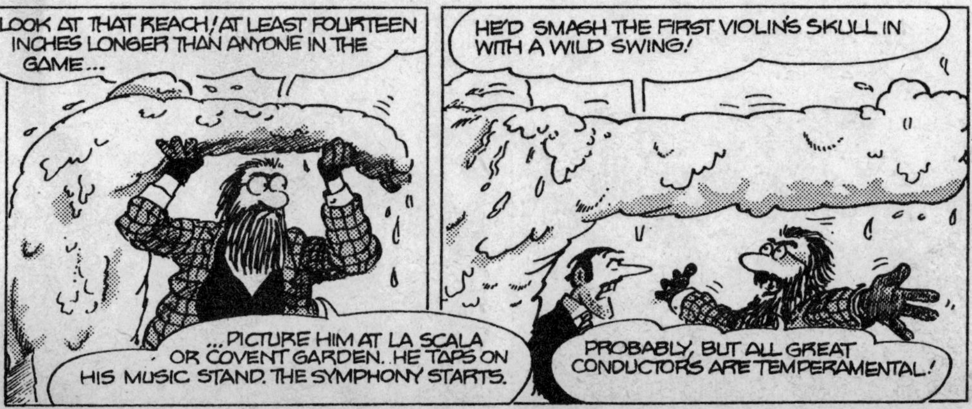
LOOK AT THAT REACH! AT LEAST FOURTEEN INCHES LONGER THAN ANYONE IN THE GAME...
...PICTURE HIM AT LA SCALA OR COVENT GARDEN. HE TAPS ON HIS MUSIC STAND. THE SYMPHONY STARTS.
HE'D SMASH THE FIRST VIOLIN'S SKULL IN WITH A WILD SWING!
PROBABLY, BUT ALL GREAT CONDUCTORS ARE TEMPERAMENTAL!

But thousands of batons later...

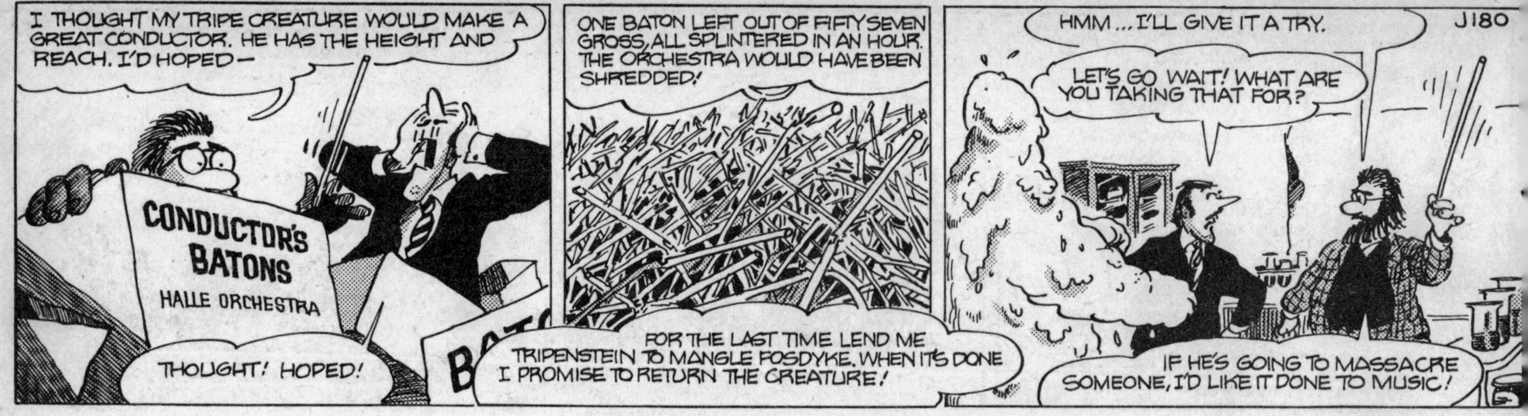
I THOUGHT MY TRIPE CREATURE WOULD MAKE A GREAT CONDUCTOR. HE HAS THE HEIGHT AND REACH. I'D HOPED—
CONDUCTOR'S BATONS
HALLE ORCHESTRA
THOUGHT! HOPED!
ONE BATON LEFT OUT OF FIFTY SEVEN GROSS, ALL SPLINTERED IN AN HOUR. THE ORCHESTRA WOULD HAVE BEEN SHREDDED!
FOR THE LAST TIME LEND ME TRIPENSTEIN TO MANGLE FOSDYKE. WHEN IT'S DONE I PROMISE TO RETURN THE CREATURE!
HMM ... I'LL GIVE IT A TRY.
J180
LET'S GO WAIT! WHAT ARE YOU TAKING THAT FOR?
IF HE'S GOING TO MASSACRE SOMEONE, I'D LIKE IT DONE TO MUSIC!

In the lost world of Mu, Albert finds himself in a desperate predicament.

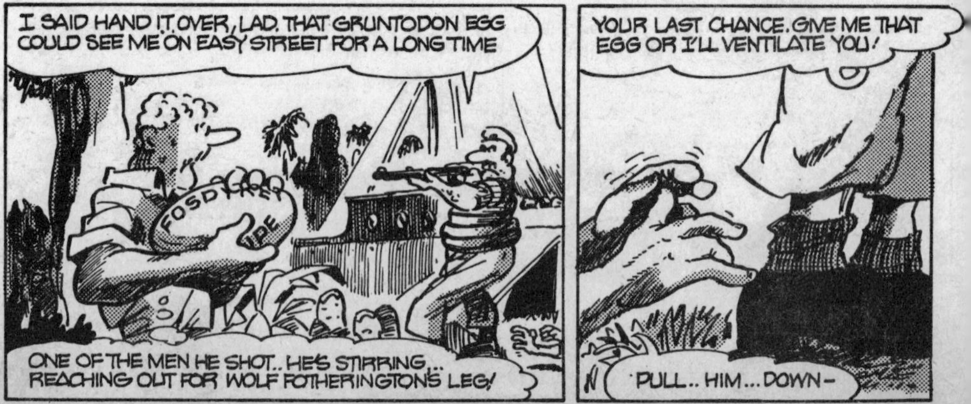
I SAID HAND IT OVER, LAD. THAT GRUNTODON EGG COULD SEE ME ON EASY STREET FOR A LONG TIME
FOSDYKE
ONE OF THE MEN HE SHOT.. HE'S STIRRING... REACHING OUT FOR WOLF FOTHERINGTON'S LEG!
YOUR LAST CHANCE. GIVE ME THAT EGG OR I'LL VENTILATE YOU!
PULL.. HIM... DOWN—

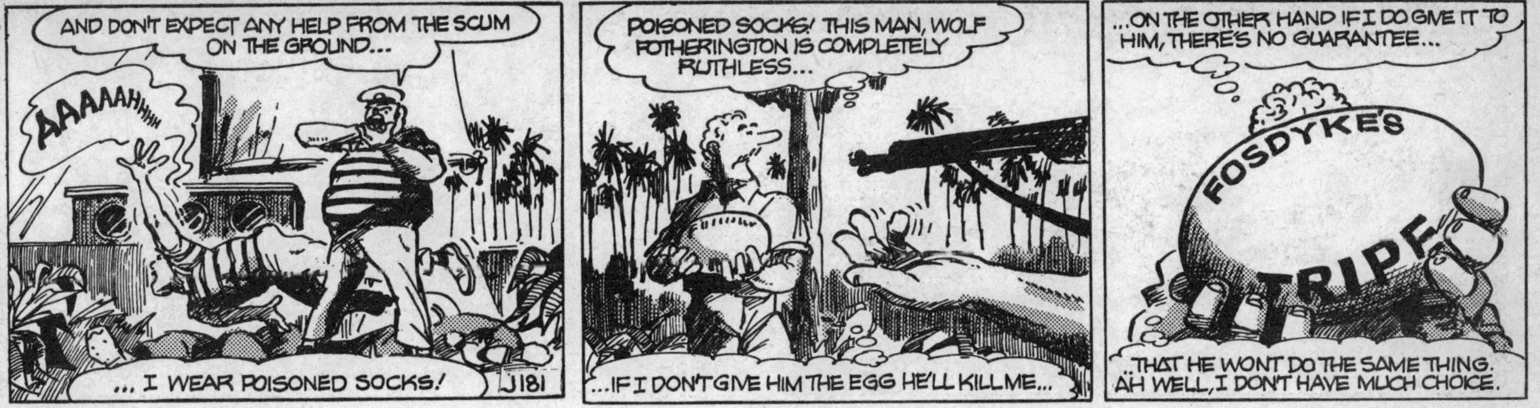
AND DON'T EXPECT ANY HELP FROM THE SCUM ON THE GROUND...
AAAAAHHhhh
... I WEAR POISONED SOCKS!
J181
POISONED SOCKS! THIS MAN, WOLF FOTHERINGTON IS COMPLETELY RUTHLESS...
...IF I DON'T GIVE HIM THE EGG HE'LL KILL ME...
...ON THE OTHER HAND IF I DO GIVE IT TO HIM, THERE'S NO GUARANTEE...
FOSDYKE'S
TRIPE
...THAT HE WONT DO THE SAME THING. AH WELL, I DON'T HAVE MUCH CHOICE.

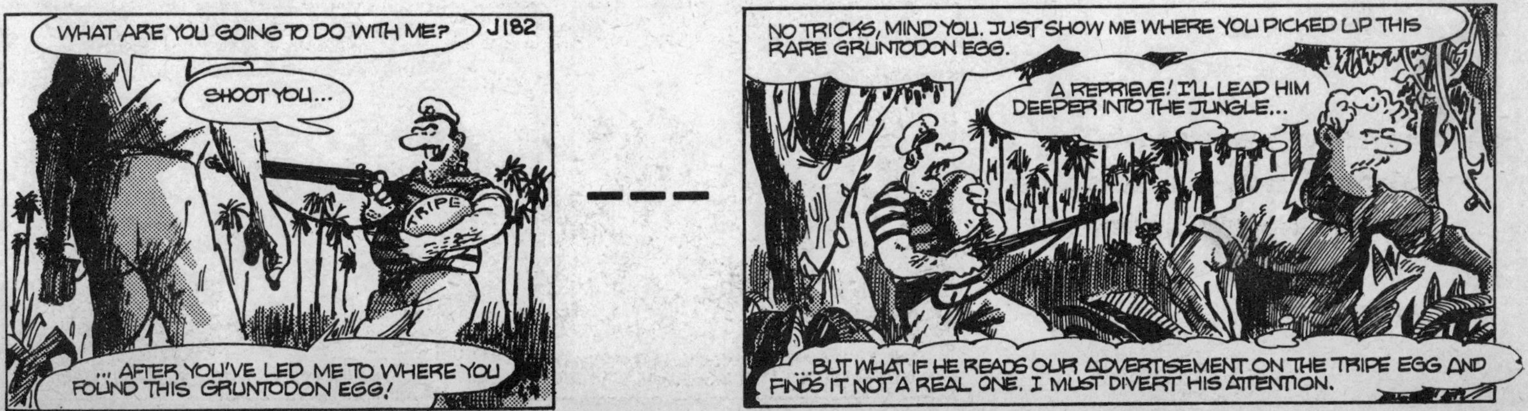
WHAT ARE YOU GOING TO DO WITH ME?
J182
SHOOT YOU...
TRIPE
... AFTER YOU'VE LED ME TO WHERE YOU FOUND THIS GRUNTODON EGG!
NO TRICKS, MIND YOU. JUST SHOW ME WHERE YOU PICKED UP THIS RARE GRUNTODON EGG.
A REPRIEVE! I'LL LEAD HIM DEEPER INTO THE JUNGLE...
...BUT WHAT IF HE READS OUR ADVERTISEMENT ON THE TRIPE EGG AND FINDS IT NOT A REAL ONE. I MUST DIVERT HIS ATTENTION.

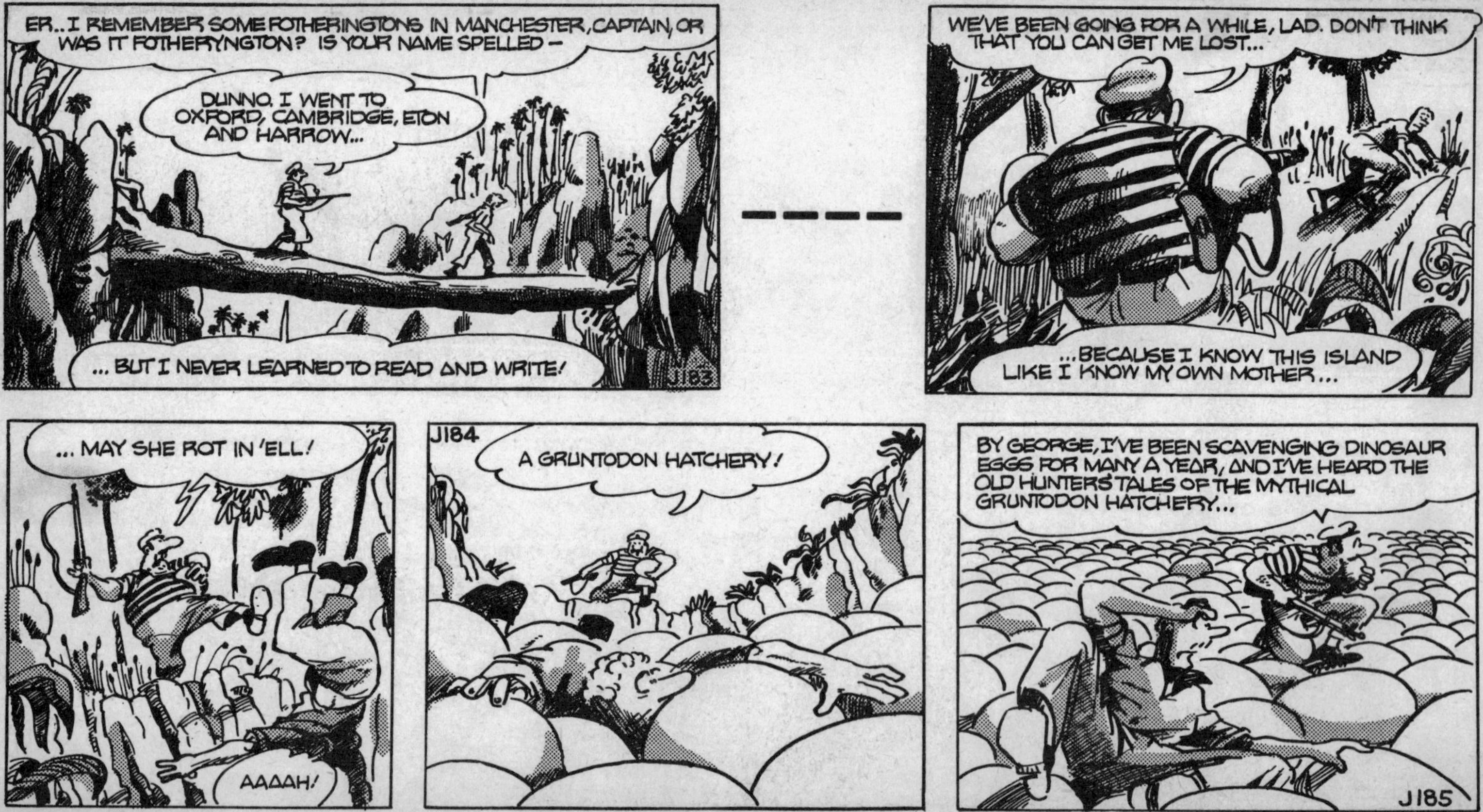
ER.. I REMEMBER SOME FOTHERINGTONS IN MANCHESTER, CAPTAIN, OR WAS IT FOTHERYNGTON? IS YOUR NAME SPELLED –
DUNNO. I WENT TO OXFORD, CAMBRIDGE, ETON AND HARROW...
... BUT I NEVER LEARNED TO READ AND WRITE!
J183
WE'VE BEEN GOING FOR A WHILE, LAD. DON'T THINK THAT YOU CAN GET ME LOST...
...BECAUSE I KNOW THIS ISLAND LIKE I KNOW MY OWN MOTHER...
... MAY SHE ROT IN 'ELL!
AAAAH!
J184
A GRUNTODON HATCHERY!
BY GEORGE, I'VE BEEN SCAVENGING DINOSAUR EGGS FOR MANY A YEAR, AND I'VE HEARD THE OLD HUNTERS' TALES OF THE MYTHICAL GRUNTODON HATCHERY...
J185

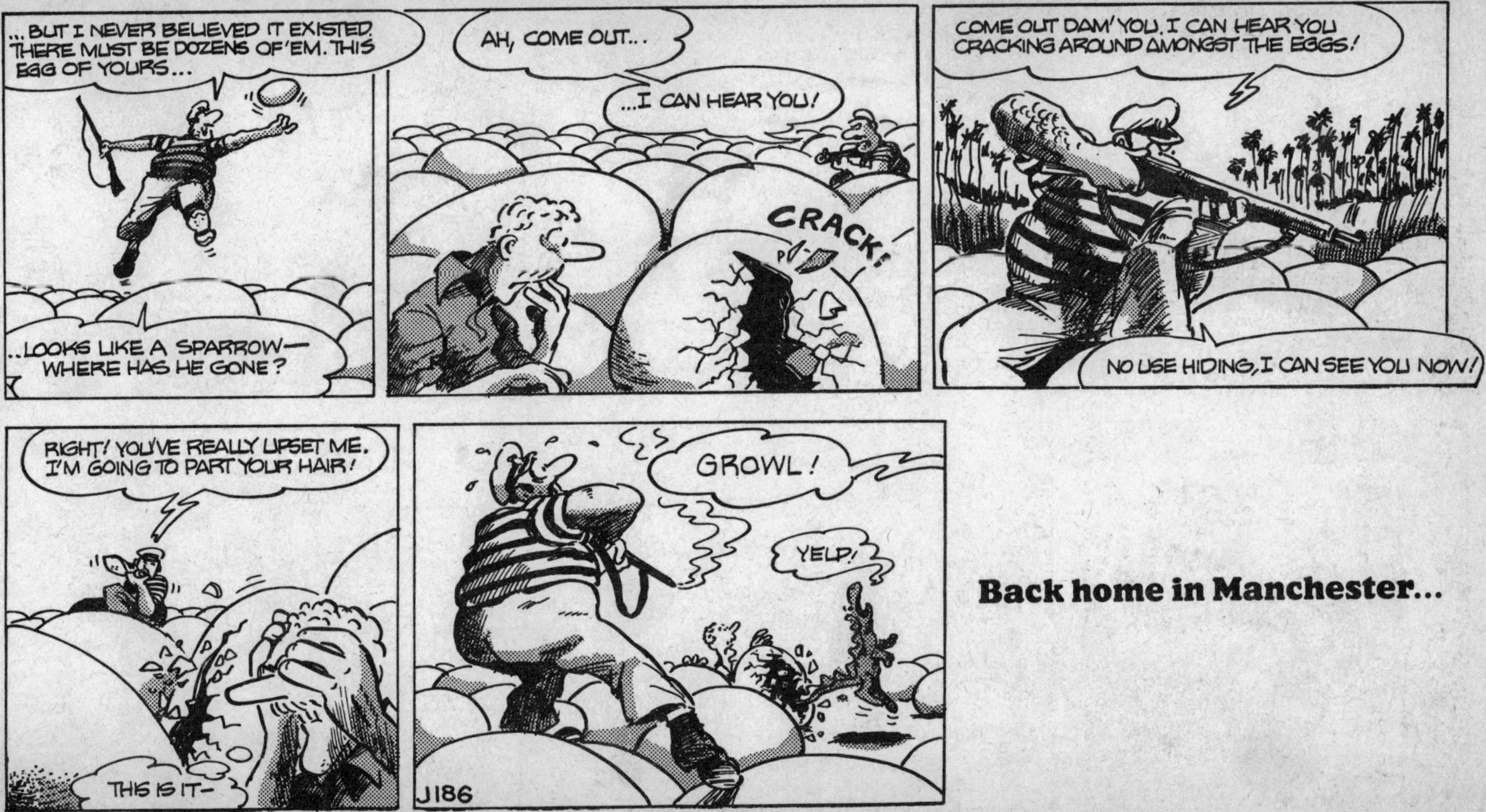
... BUT I NEVER BELIEVED IT EXISTED. THERE MUST BE DOZENS OF 'EM. THIS EGG OF YOURS ...
... LOOKS LIKE A SPARROW— WHERE HAS HE GONE?
AH, COME OUT...
...I CAN HEAR YOU!
CRACK!
COME OUT DAM' YOU. I CAN HEAR YOU CRACKING AROUND AMONGST THE EGGS!
NO USE HIDING, I CAN SEE YOU NOW!
RIGHT! YOU'VE REALLY UPSET ME. I'M GOING TO PART YOUR HAIR!
THIS IS IT—
GROWL!
YELP!
J186

Back home in Manchester...

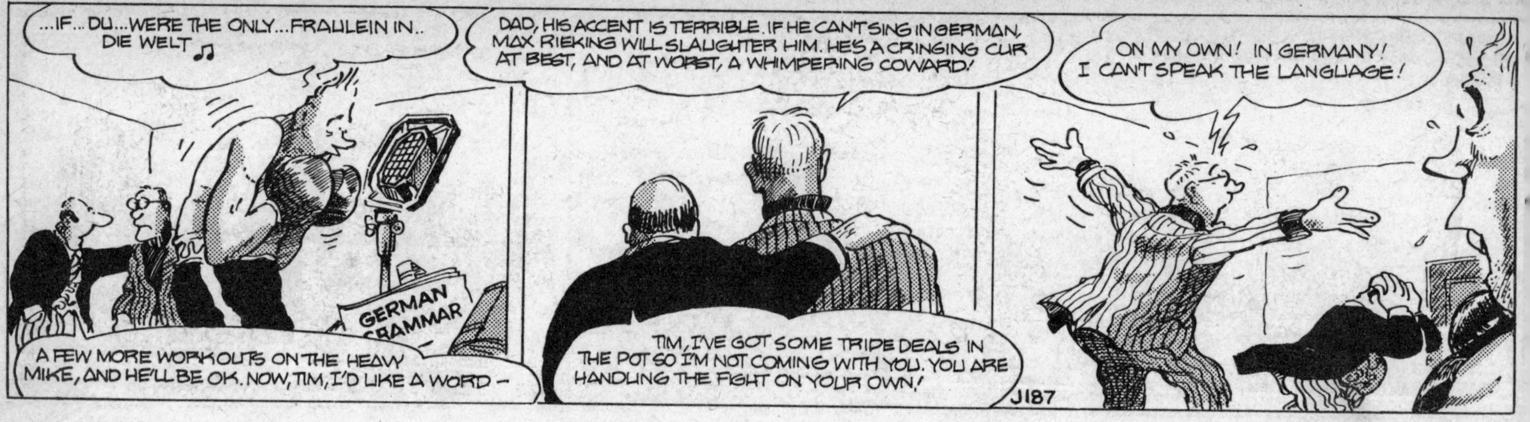
...IF...DU...WERE THE ONLY...FRAULEIN IN.. DIE WELT ♫
GERMAN GRAMMAR
A FEW MORE WORKOUTS ON THE HEAVY MIKE, AND HE'LL BE OK. NOW, TIM, I'D LIKE A WORD –
DAD, HIS ACCENT IS TERRIBLE. IF HE CAN'T SING IN GERMAN, MAX RIEKING WILL SLAUGHTER HIM. HE'S A CRINGING CUR AT BEST, AND AT WORST, A WHIMPERING COWARD!
TIM, I'VE GOT SOME TRIPE DEALS IN THE POT SO I'M NOT COMING WITH YOU. YOU ARE HANDLING THE FIGHT ON YOUR OWN!
J187
ON MY OWN! IN GERMANY! I CAN'T SPEAK THE LANGUAGE!

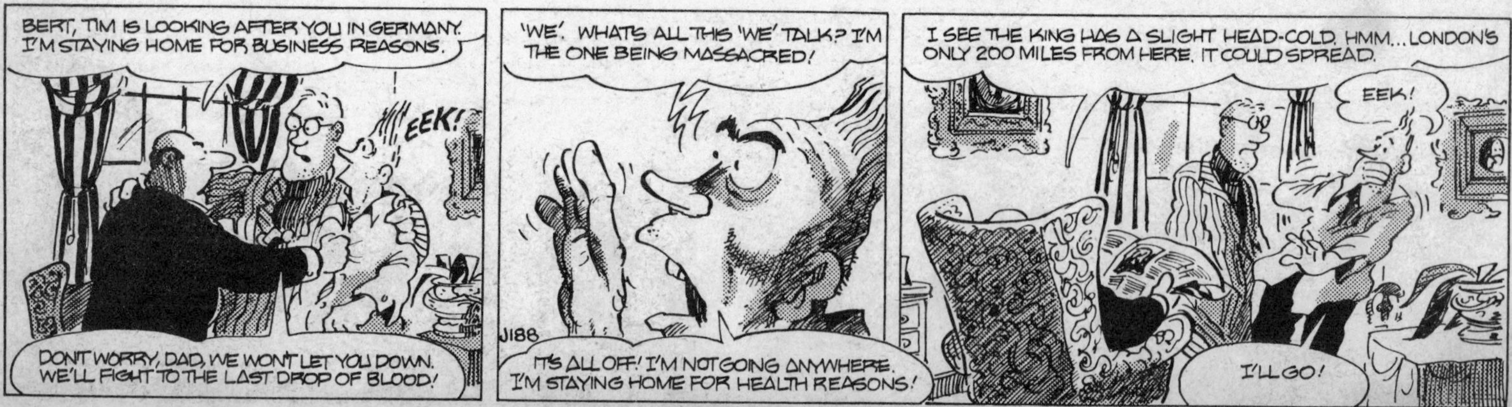
BERT, TIM IS LOOKING AFTER YOU IN GERMANY. I'M STAYING HOME FOR BUSINESS REASONS.
EEK!
DON'T WORRY, DAD, WE WON'T LET YOU DOWN. WE'LL FIGHT TO THE LAST DROP OF BLOOD!
'WE'. WHAT'S ALL THIS 'WE' TALK? I'M THE ONE BEING MASSACRED!
J188
IT'S ALL OFF! I'M NOT GOING ANYWHERE. I'M STAYING HOME FOR HEALTH REASONS!
I SEE THE KING HAS A SLIGHT HEAD-COLD. HMM... LONDON'S ONLY 200 MILES FROM HERE. IT COULD SPREAD.
EEK!
I'LL GO!

A few hours later...

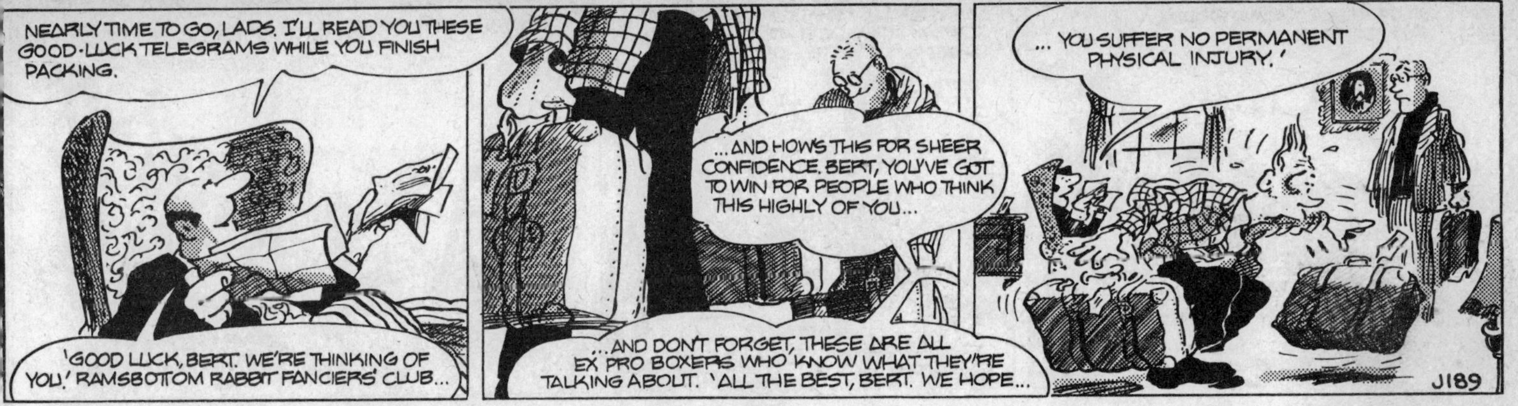
NEARLY TIME TO GO, LADS. I'LL READ YOU THESE GOOD-LUCK TELEGRAMS WHILE YOU FINISH PACKING.
'GOOD LUCK, BERT. WE'RE THINKING OF YOU.' RAMSBOTTOM RABBIT FANCIERS' CLUB...
...AND HOW'S THIS FOR SHEER CONFIDENCE. BERT, YOU'VE GOT TO WIN FOR PEOPLE WHO THINK THIS HIGHLY OF YOU...
...AND DON'T FORGET, THESE ARE ALL EX PRO BOXERS WHO KNOW WHAT THEY'RE TALKING ABOUT. 'ALL THE BEST, BERT. WE HOPE...
... YOU SUFFER NO PERMANENT PHYSICAL INJURY.'
J189

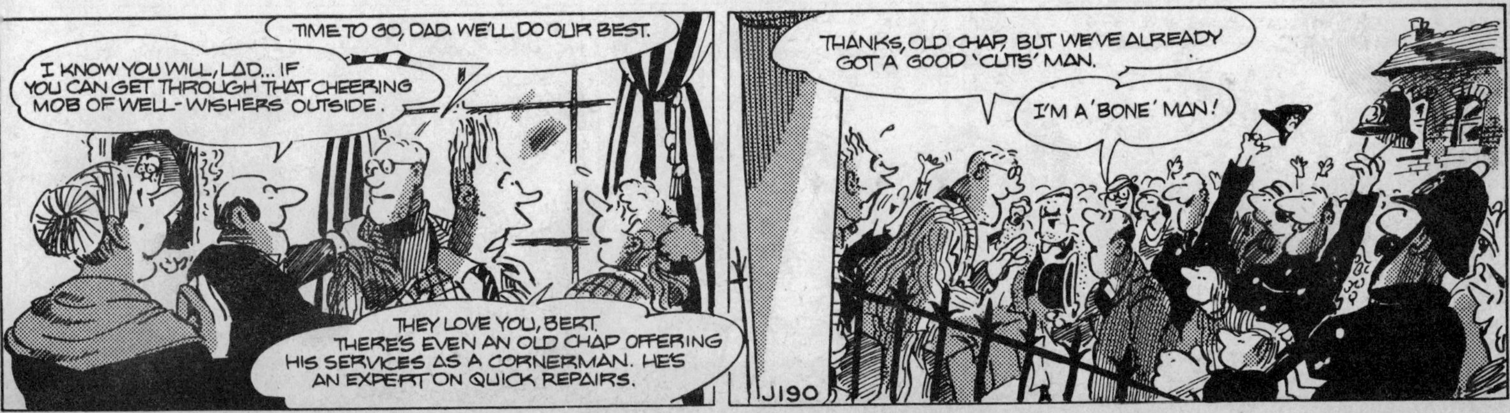
TIME TO GO, DAD. WE'LL DO OUR BEST.
I KNOW YOU WILL, LAD... IF YOU CAN GET THROUGH THAT CHEERING MOB OF WELL-WISHERS OUTSIDE.
THEY LOVE YOU, BERT. THERE'S EVEN AN OLD CHAP OFFERING HIS SERVICES AS A CORNERMAN. HE'S AN EXPERT ON QUICK REPAIRS.
THANKS, OLD CHAP, BUT WE'VE ALREADY GOT A 'GOOD 'CUTS' MAN.
I'M A 'BONE' MAN!
J190

At the airport…

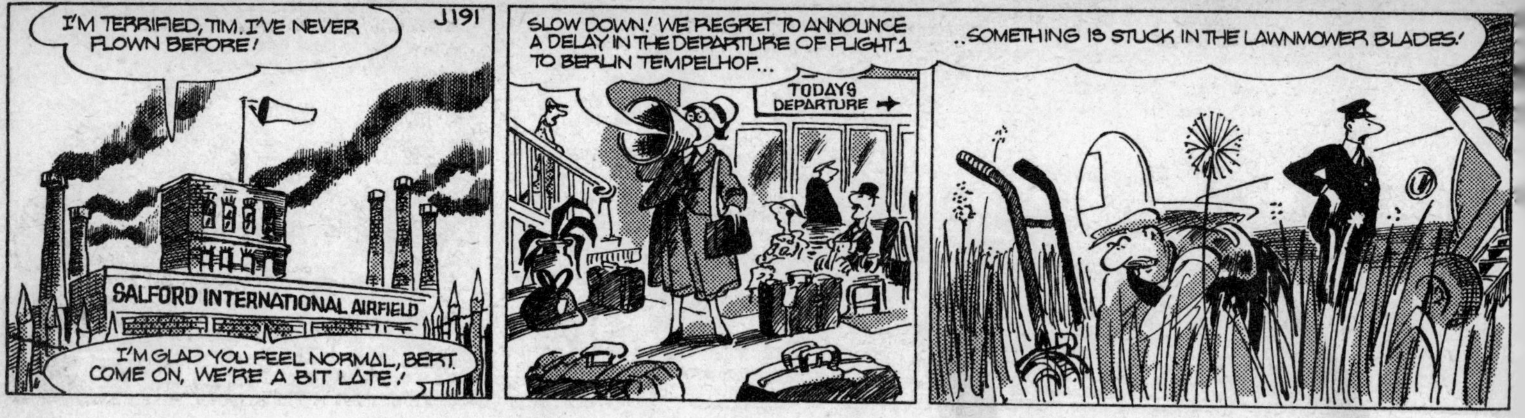

I'M TERRIFIED, TIM. I'VE NEVER FLOWN BEFORE!
J191
SALFORD INTERNATIONAL AIRFIELD
I'M GLAD YOU FEEL NORMAL, BERT. COME ON, WE'RE A BIT LATE!
SLOW DOWN! WE REGRET TO ANNOUNCE A DELAY IN THE DEPARTURE OF FLIGHT 1 TO BERLIN TEMPELHOF…
TODAYS DEPARTURE →
..SOMETHING IS STUCK IN THE LAWNMOWER BLADES!

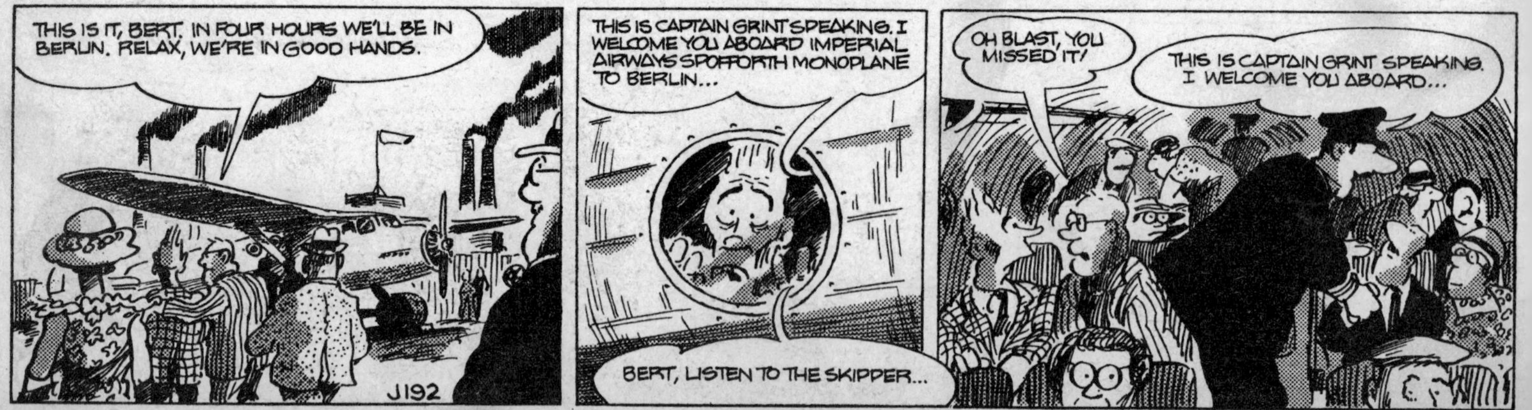

THIS IS IT, BERT. IN FOUR HOURS WE'LL BE IN BERLIN. RELAX, WE'RE IN GOOD HANDS.
J192
THIS IS CAPTAIN GRINT SPEAKING. I WELCOME YOU ABOARD IMPERIAL AIRWAYS SPOFFORTH MONOPLANE TO BERLIN…
BERT, LISTEN TO THE SKIPPER…
OH BLAST, YOU MISSED IT!
THIS IS CAPTAIN GRINT SPEAKING. I WELCOME YOU ABOARD…

And in J. A. Offrocker's laboratory...

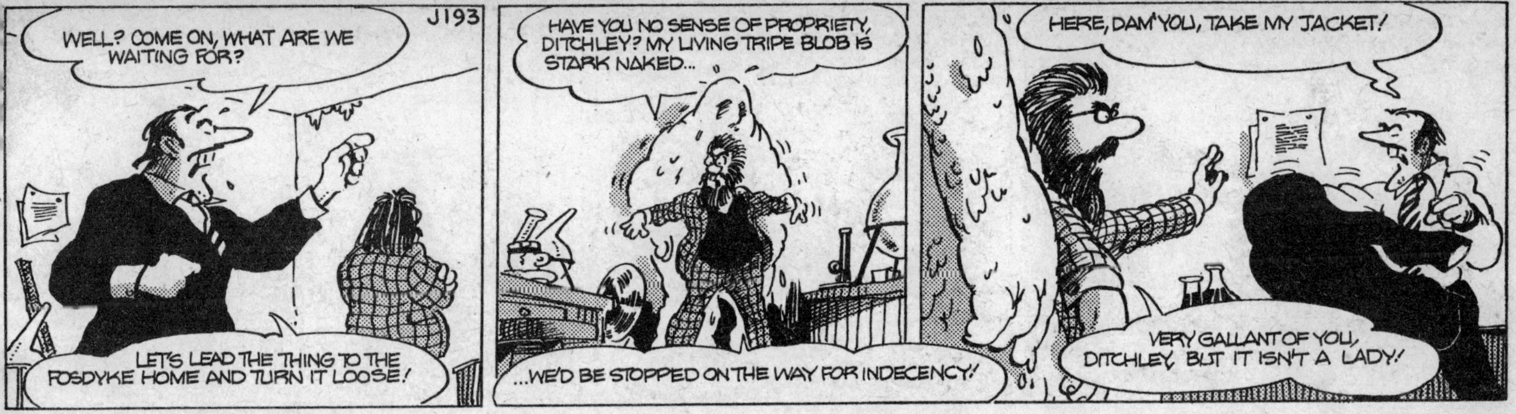
J193
WELL? COME ON, WHAT ARE WE WAITING FOR?
LET'S LEAD THE THING TO THE FOSDYKE HOME AND TURN IT LOOSE!
HAVE YOU NO SENSE OF PROPRIETY, DITCHLEY? MY LIVING TRIPE BLOB IS STARK NAKED...
...WE'D BE STOPPED ON THE WAY FOR INDECENCY!
HERE, DAM'YOU, TAKE MY JACKET!
VERY GALLANT OF YOU, DITCHLEY, BUT IT ISN'T A LADY!

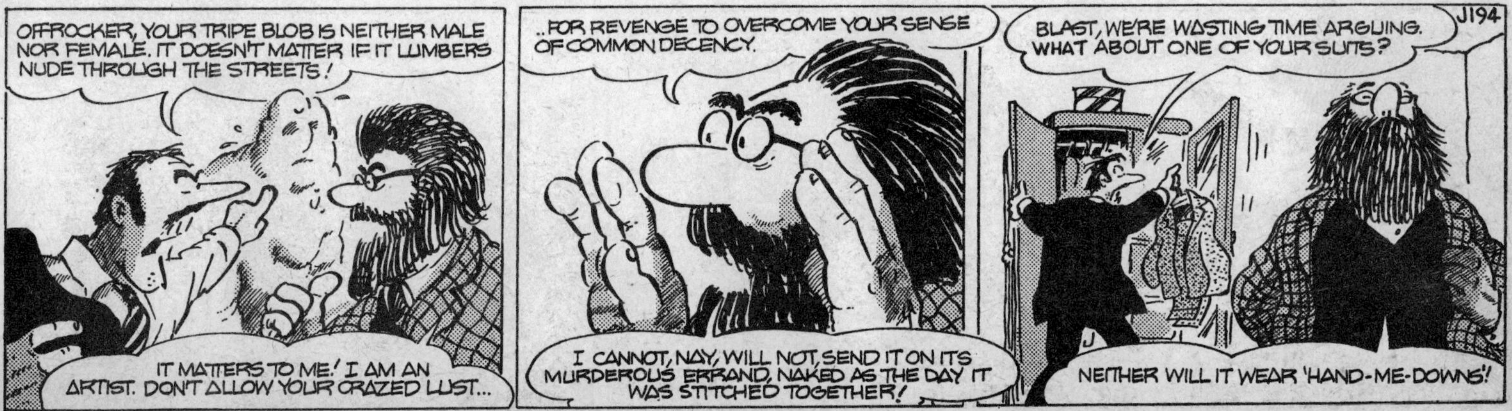
OFFROCKER, YOUR TRIPE BLOB IS NEITHER MALE NOR FEMALE. IT DOESN'T MATTER IF IT LUMBERS NUDE THROUGH THE STREETS!
IT MATTERS TO ME! I AM AN ARTIST. DON'T ALLOW YOUR CRAZED LUST...
..FOR REVENGE TO OVERCOME YOUR SENSE OF COMMON DECENCY.
I CANNOT, NAY, WILL NOT, SEND IT ON ITS MURDEROUS ERRAND, NAKED AS THE DAY IT WAS STITCHED TOGETHER!
J194
BLAST, WE'RE WASTING TIME ARGUING. WHAT ABOUT ONE OF YOUR SUITS?
NEITHER WILL IT WEAR 'HAND-ME-DOWNS'!

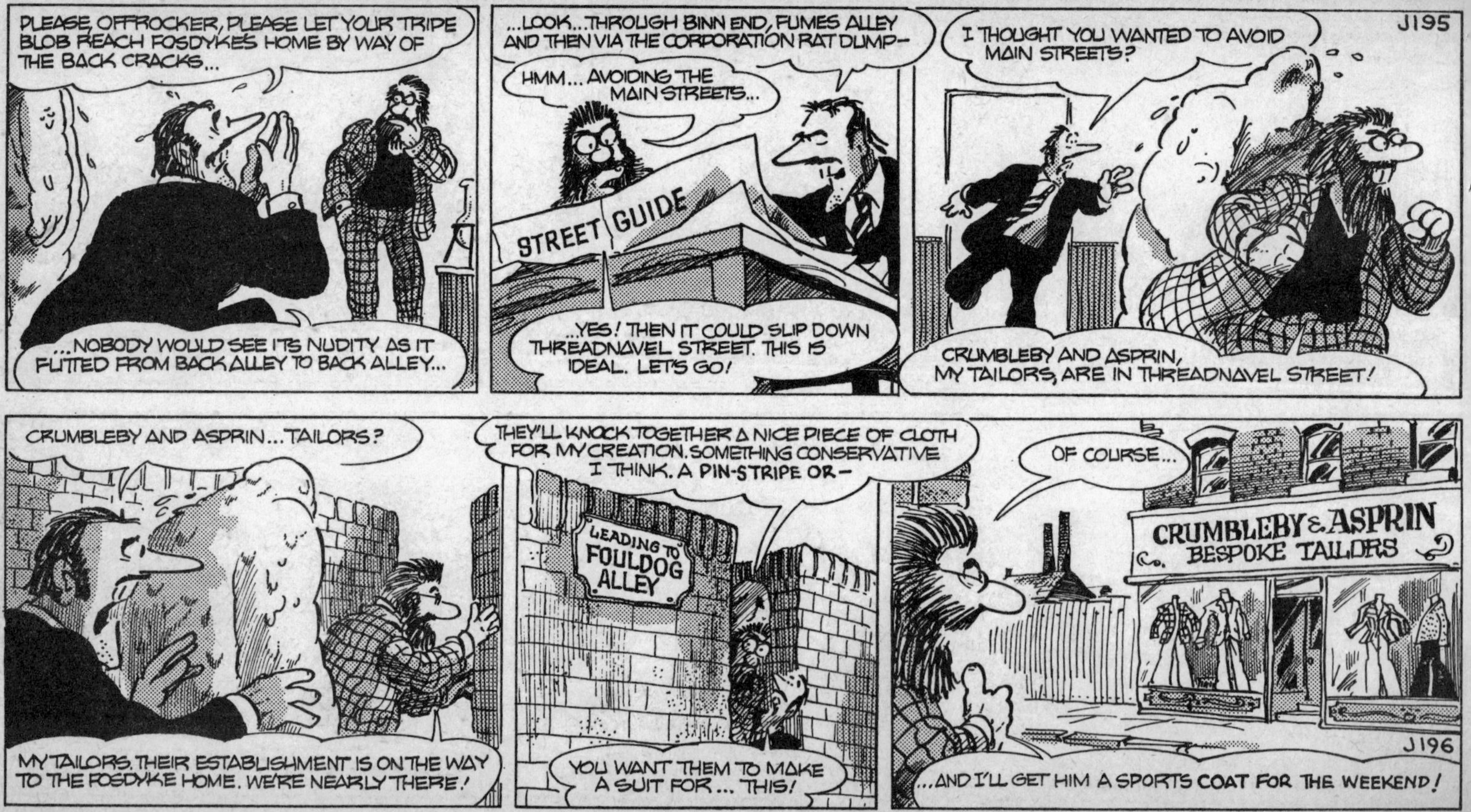
PLEASE, OFFROCKER, PLEASE LET YOUR TRIPE BLOB REACH FOSDYKE'S HOME BY WAY OF THE BACK CRACKS...
...NOBODY WOULD SEE ITS NUDITY AS IT FLITTED FROM BACK ALLEY TO BACK ALLEY...
...LOOK...THROUGH BINN END, FUMES ALLEY AND THEN VIA THE CORPORATION RAT DUMP–
HMM... AVOIDING THE MAIN STREETS...
STREET GUIDE
...YES! THEN IT COULD SLIP DOWN THREADNAVEL STREET. THIS IS IDEAL. LET'S GO!
J195
I THOUGHT YOU WANTED TO AVOID MAIN STREETS?
CRUMBLEBY AND ASPRIN, MY TAILORS, ARE IN THREADNAVEL STREET!
CRUMBLEBY AND ASPRIN... TAILORS?
MY TAILORS. THEIR ESTABLISHMENT IS ON THE WAY TO THE FOSDYKE HOME. WE'RE NEARLY THERE!
THEY'LL KNOCK TOGETHER A NICE PIECE OF CLOTH FOR MY CREATION. SOMETHING CONSERVATIVE I THINK. A PIN-STRIPE OR–
LEADING TO FOULDOG ALLEY
YOU WANT THEM TO MAKE A SUIT FOR ... THIS!
OF COURSE...
CRUMBLEBY & ASPRIN BESPOKE TAILORS
...AND I'LL GET HIM A SPORTS COAT FOR THE WEEKEND!
J196

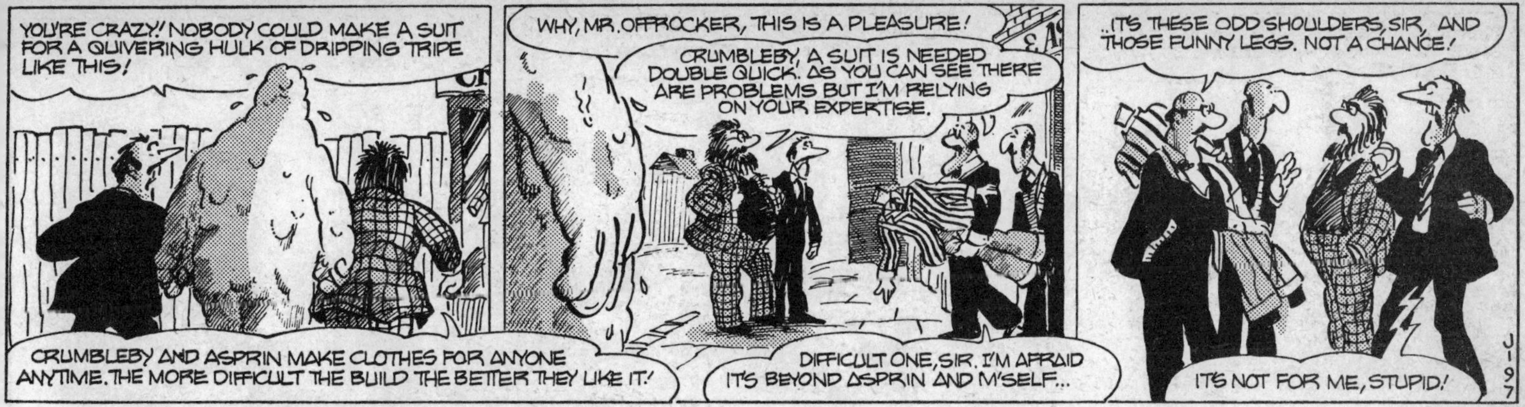
YOU'RE CRAZY! NOBODY COULD MAKE A SUIT FOR A QUIVERING HULK OF DRIPPING TRIPE LIKE THIS!
CRUMBLEBY AND ASPRIN MAKE CLOTHES FOR ANYONE ANYTIME. THE MORE DIFFICULT THE BUILD THE BETTER THEY LIKE IT!
WHY, MR. OFFROCKER, THIS IS A PLEASURE!
CRUMBLEBY, A SUIT IS NEEDED DOUBLE QUICK. AS YOU CAN SEE THERE ARE PROBLEMS BUT I'M RELYING ON YOUR EXPERTISE.
DIFFICULT ONE, SIR. I'M AFRAID IT'S BEYOND ASPRIN AND M'SELF...
..IT'S THESE ODD SHOULDERS, SIR, AND THOSE FUNNY LEGS. NOT A CHANCE!
IT'S NOT FOR ME, STUPID!
J197

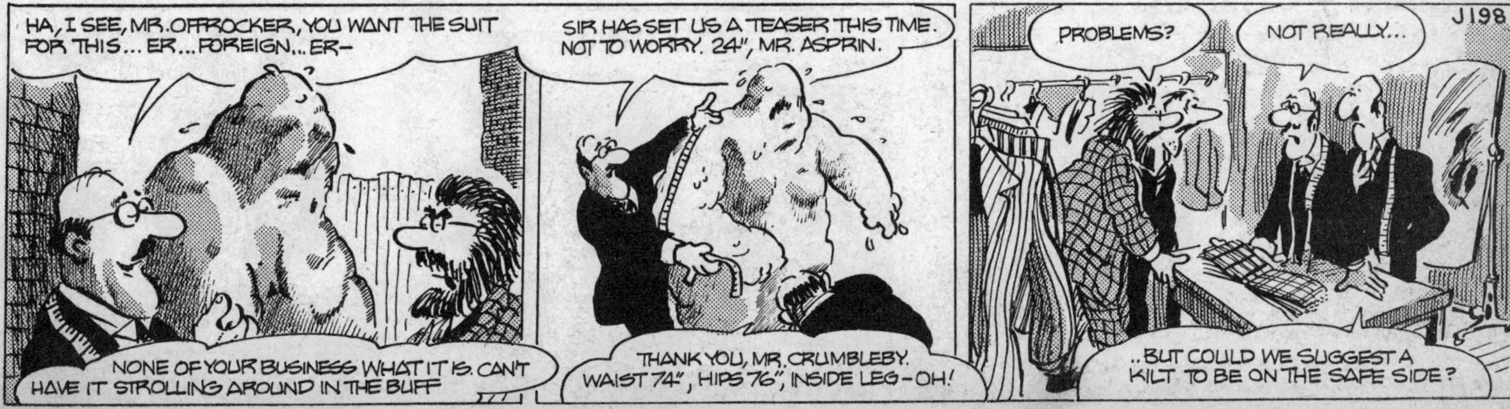
HA, I SEE, MR. OFFROCKER, YOU WANT THE SUIT FOR THIS... ER... FOREIGN... ER–
NONE OF YOUR BUSINESS WHAT IT IS. CAN'T HAVE IT STROLLING AROUND IN THE BUFF
SIR HAS SET US A TEASER THIS TIME. NOT TO WORRY. 24", MR. ASPRIN.
THANK YOU, MR. CRUMBLEBY. WAIST 74", HIPS 76", INSIDE LEG – OH!
J198
PROBLEMS?
NOT REALLY...
..BUT COULD WE SUGGEST A KILT TO BE ON THE SAFE SIDE?

Meanwhile, on the flight to Berlin...

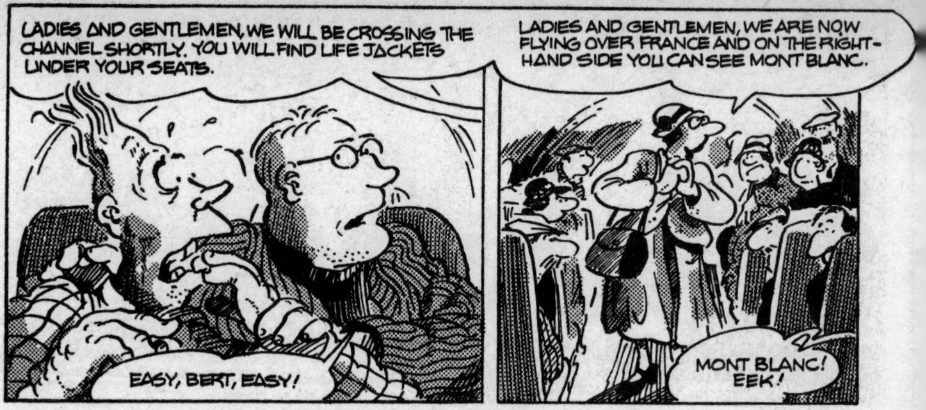
LADIES AND GENTLEMEN, WE WILL BE CROSSING THE CHANNEL SHORTLY. YOU WILL FIND LIFE JACKETS UNDER YOUR SEATS.
EASY, BERT, EASY!
LADIES AND GENTLEMEN, WE ARE NOW FLYING OVER FRANCE AND ON THE RIGHT-HAND SIDE YOU CAN SEE MONT BLANC.
MONT BLANC! EEK!

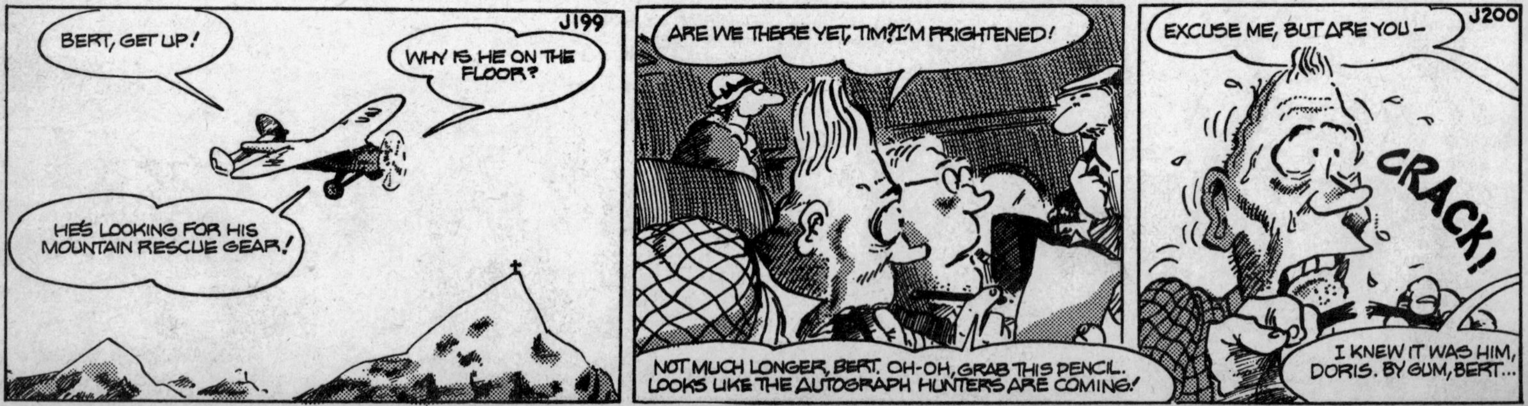
J199
BERT, GET UP!
WHY IS HE ON THE FLOOR?
HE'S LOOKING FOR HIS MOUNTAIN RESCUE GEAR!
ARE WE THERE YET, TIM? I'M FRIGHTENED!
NOT MUCH LONGER, BERT. OH-OH, GRAB THIS PENCIL. LOOKS LIKE THE AUTOGRAPH HUNTERS ARE COMING!
J200
EXCUSE ME, BUT ARE YOU –
CRACK!
I KNEW IT WAS HIM, DORIS. BY GUM, BERT...

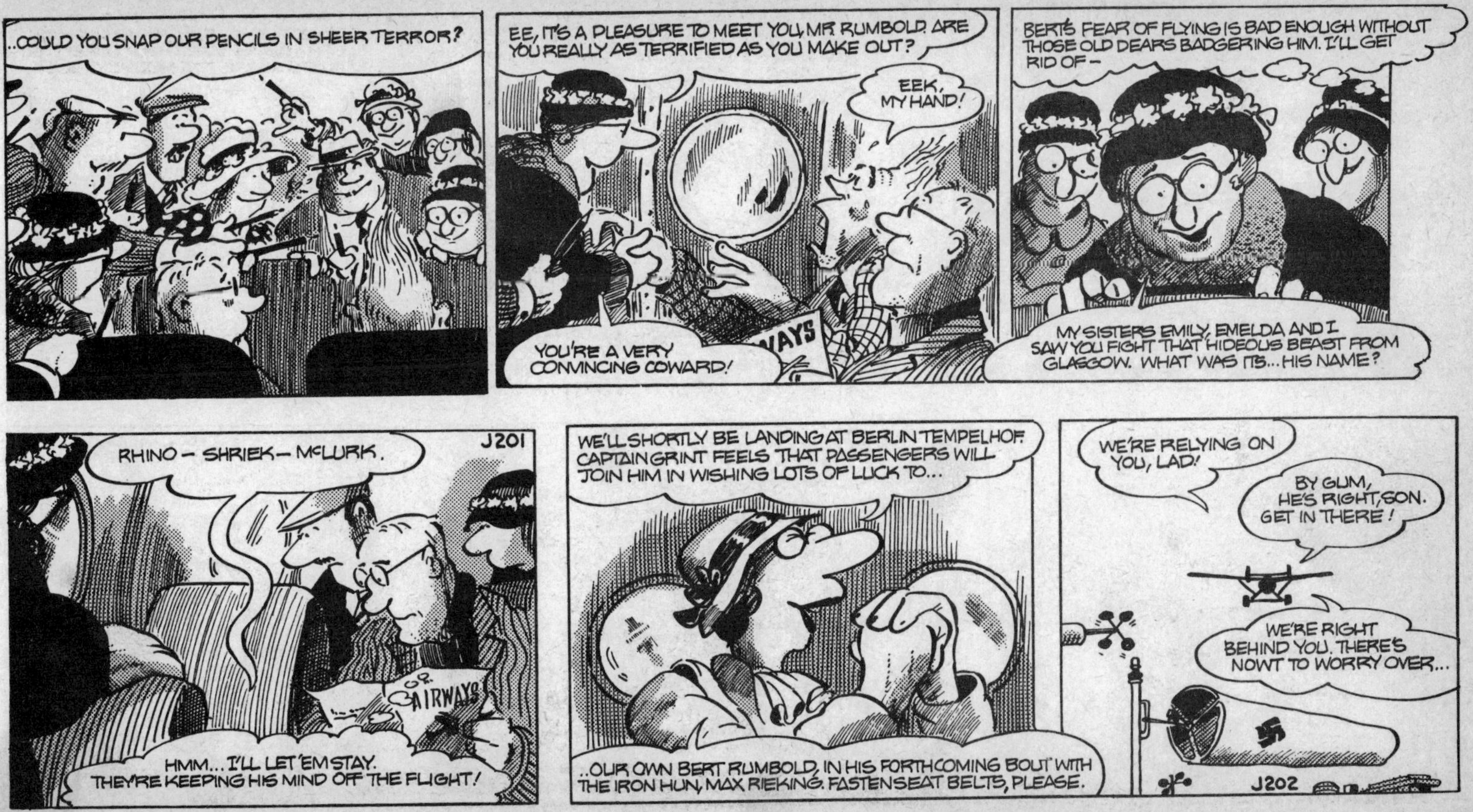
..COULD YOU SNAP OUR PENCILS IN SHEER TERROR?
EE, IT'S A PLEASURE TO MEET YOU, MR. RUMBOLD. ARE YOU REALLY AS TERRIFIED AS YOU MAKE OUT?
EEK, MY HAND!
YOU'RE A VERY CONVINCING COWARD!
WAYS
BERT'S FEAR OF FLYING IS BAD ENOUGH WITHOUT THOSE OLD DEARS BADGERING HIM. I'LL GET RID OF –
MY SISTERS EMILY, EMELDA AND I SAW YOU FIGHT THAT HIDEOUS BEAST FROM GLASGOW. WHAT WAS ITS... HIS NAME?
J201
RHINO – SHRIEK – McLURK.
HMM... I'LL LET 'EM STAY. THEY'RE KEEPING HIS MIND OFF THE FLIGHT!
AIRWAYS
WE'LL SHORTLY BE LANDING AT BERLIN TEMPELHOF. CAPTAIN GRINT FEELS THAT PASSENGERS WILL JOIN HIM IN WISHING LOTS OF LUCK TO...
..OUR OWN BERT RUMBOLD, IN HIS FORTHCOMING 'BOUT' WITH THE IRON HUN, MAX RIEKING. FASTEN SEAT BELTS, PLEASE.
WE'RE RELYING ON YOU, LAD!
BY GUM, HE'S RIGHT, SON. GET IN THERE!
WE'RE RIGHT BEHIND YOU. THERE'S NOWT TO WORRY OVER...
J202

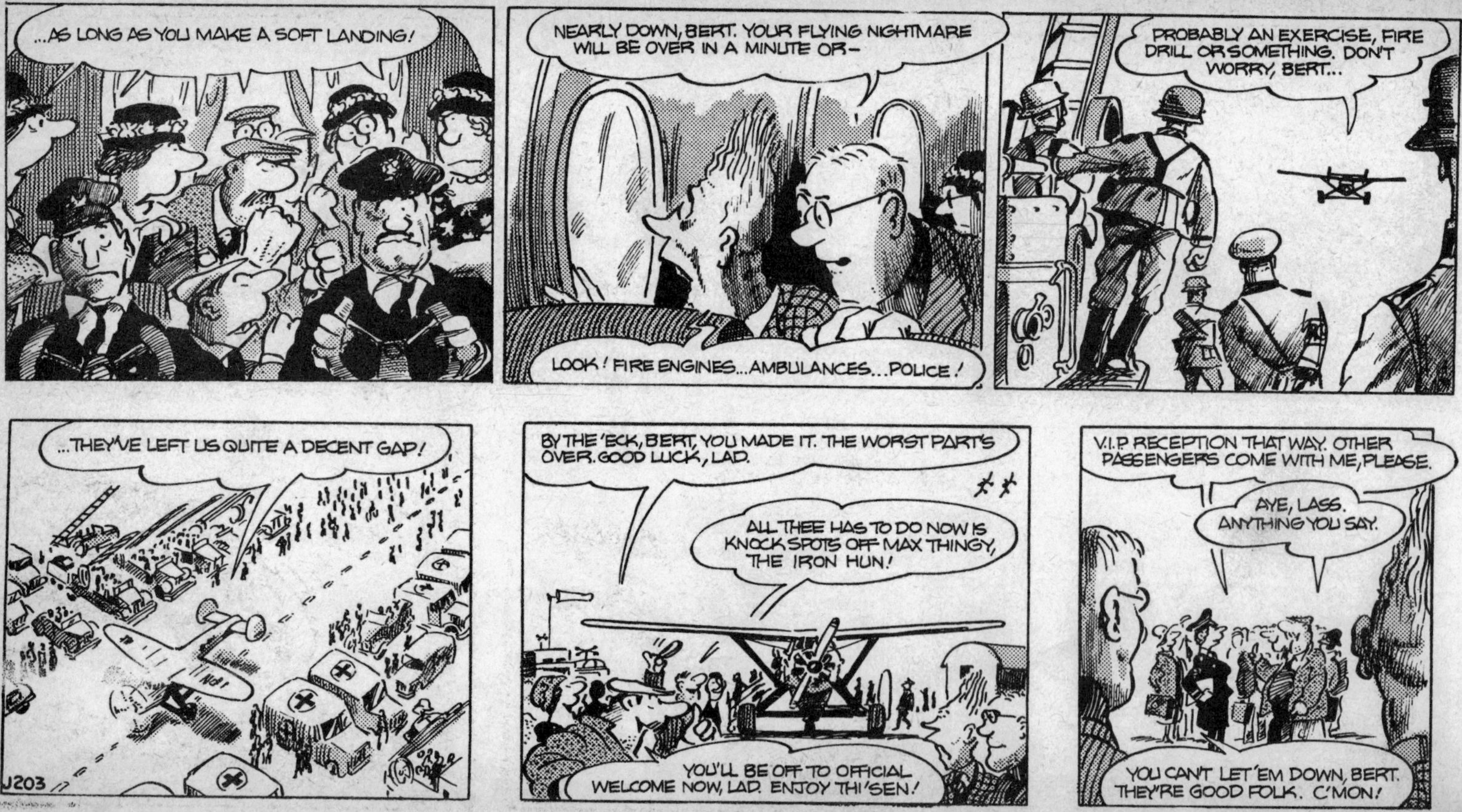
...AS LONG AS YOU MAKE A SOFT LANDING!
NEARLY DOWN, BERT. YOUR FLYING NIGHTMARE WILL BE OVER IN A MINUTE OR–
LOOK! FIRE ENGINES...AMBULANCES...POLICE!
PROBABLY AN EXERCISE, FIRE DRILL OR SOMETHING. DON'T WORRY, BERT...
...THEY'VE LEFT US QUITE A DECENT GAP!
J203
BY THE 'ECK, BERT, YOU MADE IT. THE WORST PART'S OVER. GOOD LUCK, LAD.
ALL THEE HAS TO DO NOW IS KNOCK SPOTS OFF MAX THINGY, THE IRON HUN!
YOU'LL BE OFF TO OFFICIAL WELCOME NOW, LAD. ENJOY THI'SEN!
V.I.P. RECEPTION THAT WAY. OTHER PASSENGERS COME WITH ME, PLEASE.
AYE, LASS. ANYTHING YOU SAY.
YOU CAN'T LET 'EM DOWN, BERT. THEY'RE GOOD FOLK. C'MON!

But in a nearby office...

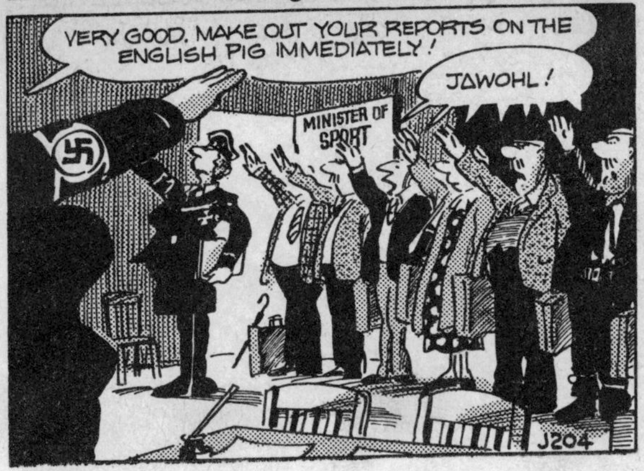
VERY GOOD. MAKE OUT YOUR REPORTS ON THE ENGLISH PIG IMMEDIATELY!
JAWOHL!
MINISTER OF SPORT

On the other side of the world danger looms over the gruntodon hatchery...

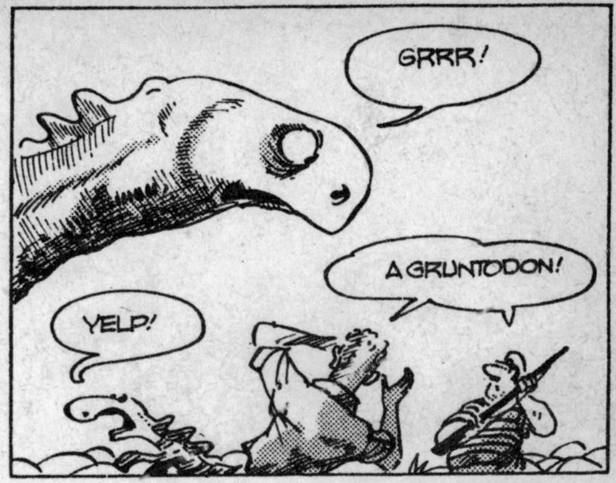
GRRR!
A GRUNTODON!
YELP!

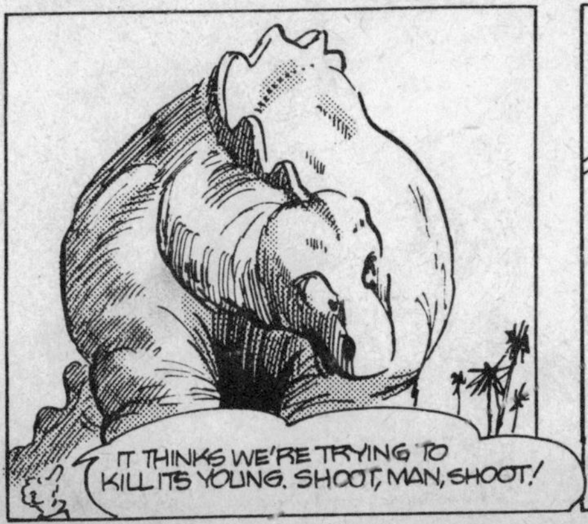
IT THINKS WE'RE TRYING TO KILL ITS YOUNG. SHOOT, MAN, SHOOT!

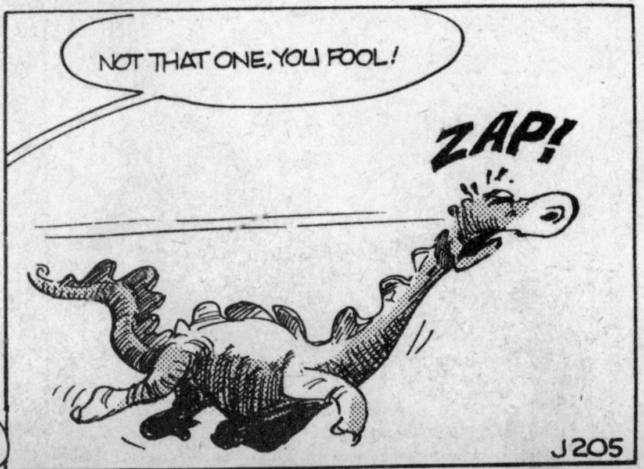
NOT THAT ONE, YOU FOOL!
ZAP!

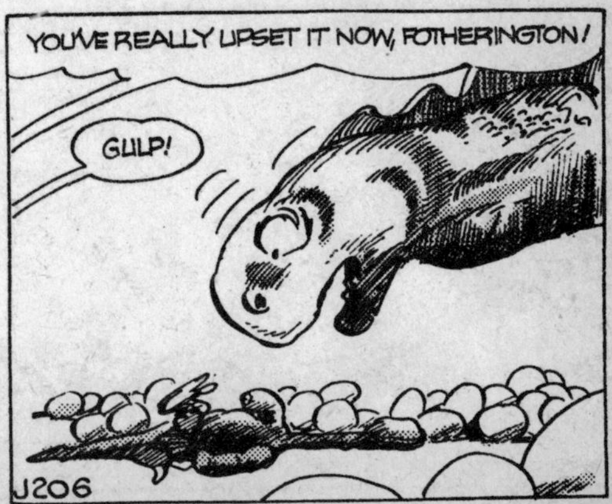
YOU'VE REALLY UPSET IT NOW, FOTHERINGTON!
GULP!

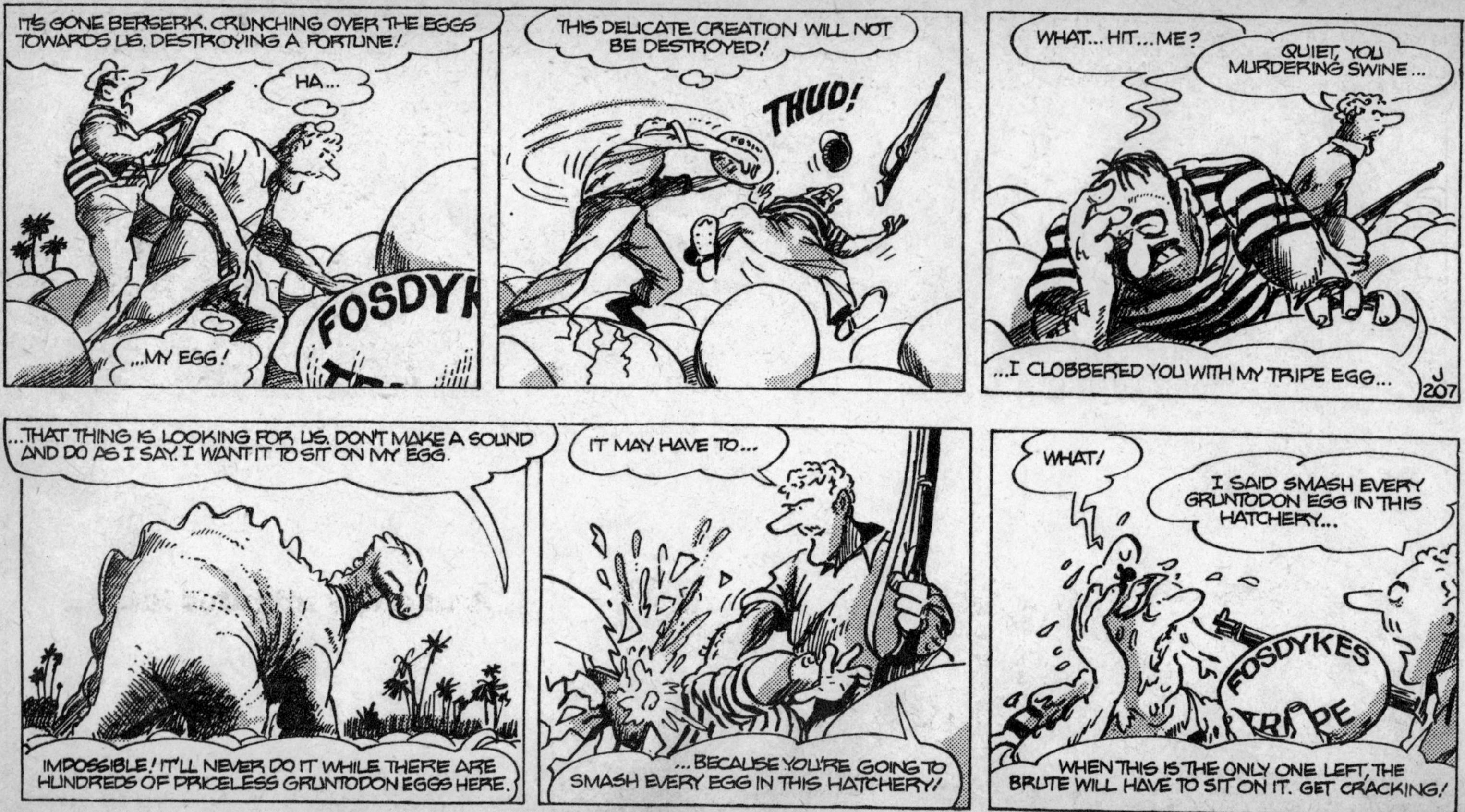
IT'S GONE BERSERK. CRUNCHING OVER THE EGGS TOWARDS US. DESTROYING A FORTUNE!
HA...
...MY EGG!
FOSDYK
THIS DELICATE CREATION WILL NOT BE DESTROYED!
THUD!
WHAT... HIT... ME?
QUIET, YOU MURDERING SWINE...
...I CLOBBERED YOU WITH MY TRIPE EGG...
J 207
...THAT THING IS LOOKING FOR US. DON'T MAKE A SOUND AND DO AS I SAY. I WANT IT TO SIT ON MY EGG.
IMPOSSIBLE! IT'LL NEVER DO IT WHILE THERE ARE HUNDREDS OF PRICELESS GRUNTODON EGGS HERE.
IT MAY HAVE TO...
...BECAUSE YOU'RE GOING TO SMASH EVERY EGG IN THIS HATCHERY!
WHAT!
I SAID SMASH EVERY GRUNTODON EGG IN THIS HATCHERY...
FOSDYKES TRIPE
WHEN THIS IS THE ONLY ONE LEFT, THE BRUTE WILL HAVE TO SIT ON IT. GET CRACKING!

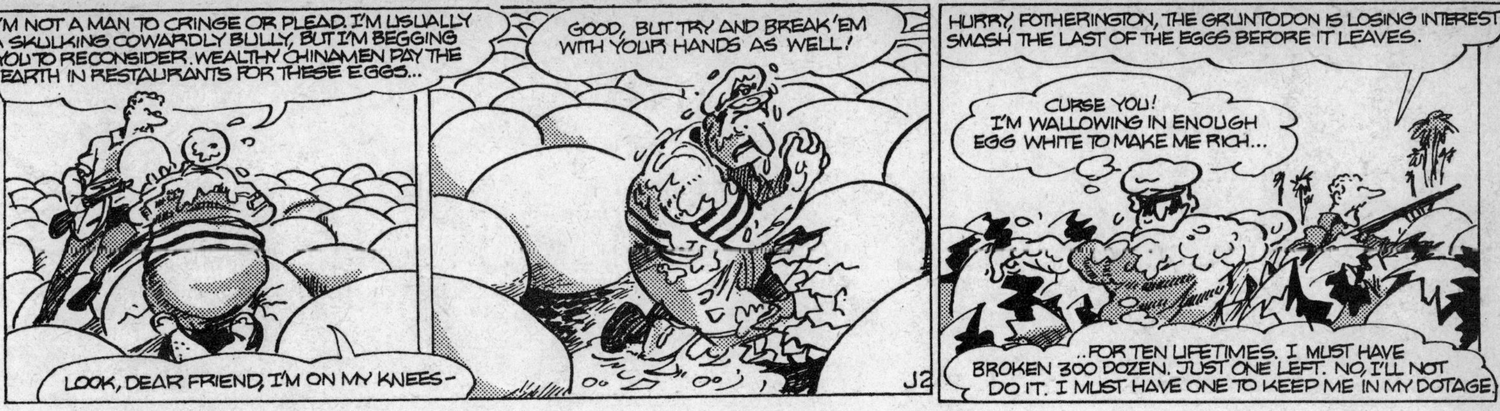
I'M NOT A MAN TO CRINGE OR PLEAD. I'M USUALLY A SKULKING COWARDLY BULLY, BUT I'M BEGGING YOU TO RECONSIDER. WEALTHY CHINAMEN PAY THE EARTH IN RESTAURANTS FOR THESE EGGS...
LOOK, DEAR FRIEND, I'M ON MY KNEES–
GOOD, BUT TRY AND BREAK 'EM WITH YOUR HANDS AS WELL!
J2
HURRY, FOTHERINGTON, THE GRUNTODON IS LOSING INTEREST. SMASH THE LAST OF THE EGGS BEFORE IT LEAVES.
CURSE YOU! I'M WALLOWING IN ENOUGH EGG WHITE TO MAKE ME RICH...
...FOR TEN LIFETIMES. I MUST HAVE BROKEN 300 DOZEN. JUST ONE LEFT. NO, I'LL NOT DO IT. I MUST HAVE ONE TO KEEP ME IN MY DOTAGE.

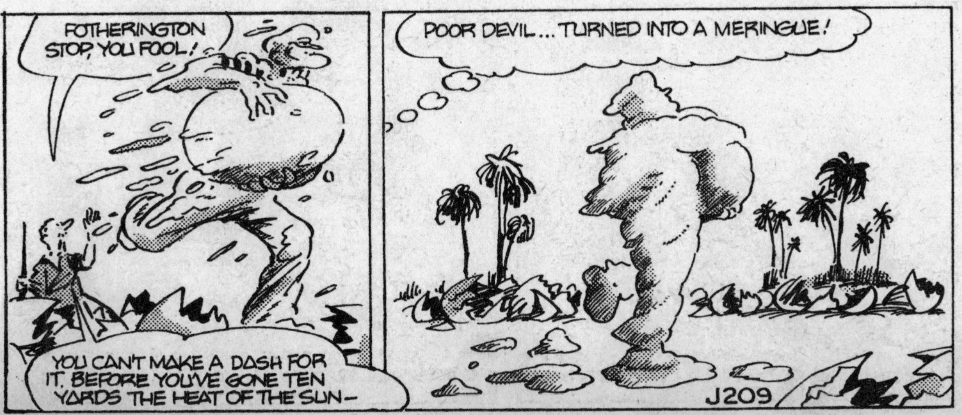
FOTHERINGTON STOP, YOU FOOL!
YOU CAN'T MAKE A DASH FOR IT. BEFORE YOU'VE GONE TEN YARDS THE HEAT OF THE SUN–
POOR DEVIL... TURNED INTO A MERINGUE!
J209

And a few minutes later...

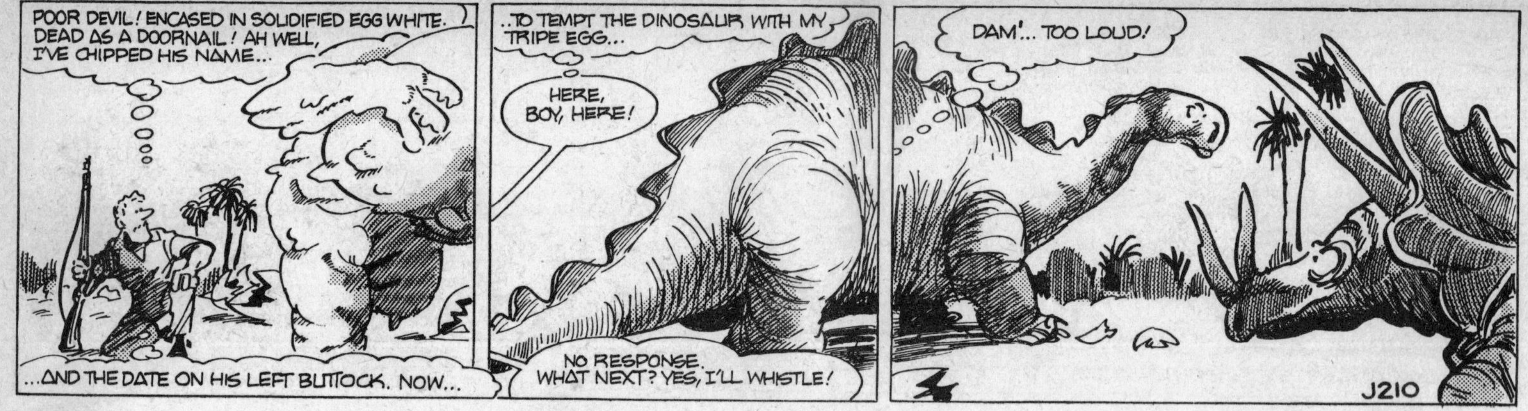
POOR DEVIL! ENCASED IN SOLIDIFIED EGG WHITE. DEAD AS A DOORNAIL! AH WELL, I'VE CHIPPED HIS NAME...
...AND THE DATE ON HIS LEFT BUTTOCK. NOW...
..TO TEMPT THE DINOSAUR WITH MY TRIPE EGG...
HERE, BOY, HERE!
NO RESPONSE. WHAT NEXT? YES, I'LL WHISTLE!
DAM'... TOO LOUD!
J210

Back in Manchester, in the establishment of Messrs. Crumbleby & Asprin, bespoke tailors...

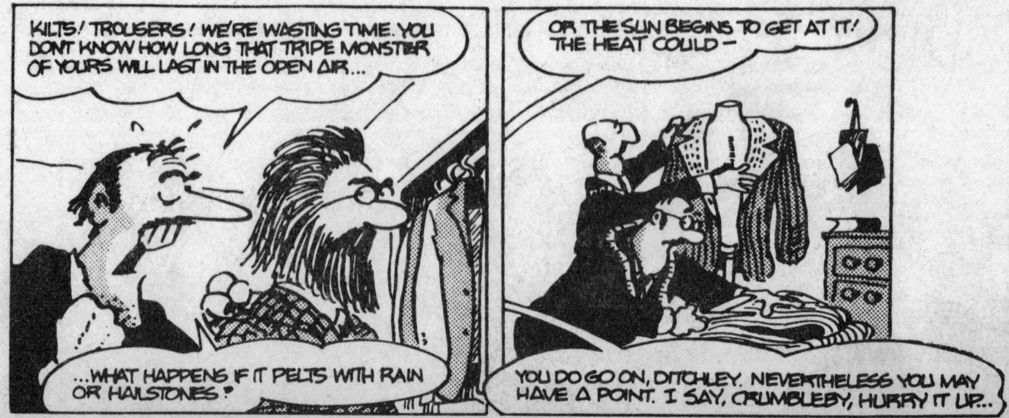
KILTS! TROUSERS! WE'RE WASTING TIME. YOU DONT KNOW HOW LONG THAT TRIPE MONSTER OF YOURS WILL LAST IN THE OPEN AIR...
...WHAT HAPPENS IF IT PELTS WITH RAIN OR HAILSTONES?
OR THE SUN BEGINS TO GET AT IT! THE HEAT COULD –
YOU DO GO ON, DITCHLEY. NEVERTHELESS YOU MAY HAVE A POINT. I SAY, CRUMBLEBY, HURRY IT UP...

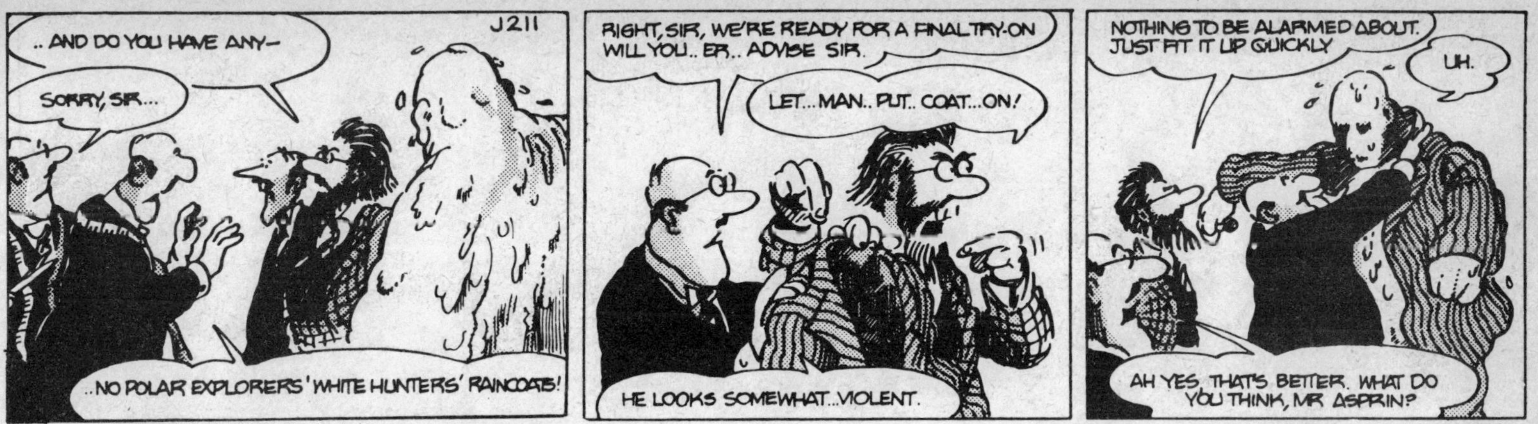
J211
.. AND DO YOU HAVE ANY—
SORRY, SIR...
..NO POLAR EXPLORERS' 'WHITE HUNTERS' RAINCOATS!
RIGHT, SIR, WE'RE READY FOR A FINAL TRY-ON WILL YOU.. ER.. ADVISE SIR.
LET...MAN.. PUT.. COAT...ON!
HE LOOKS SOMEWHAT...VIOLENT.
NOTHING TO BE ALARMED ABOUT. JUST FIT IT UP QUICKLY
UH.
AH YES, THAT'S BETTER. WHAT DO YOU THINK, MR ASPRIN?

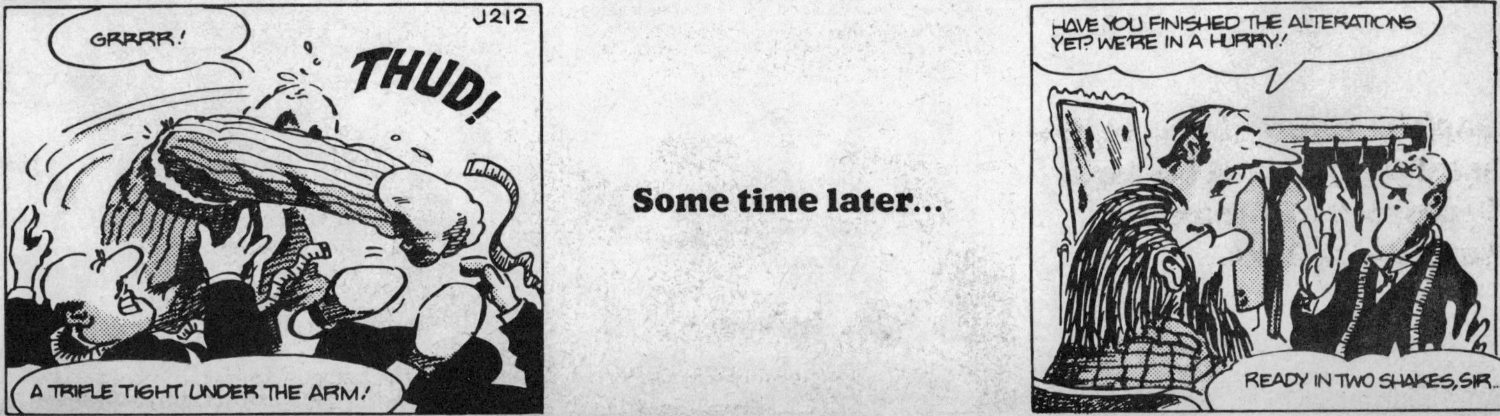
J212
GRRRR!
THUD!
A TRIFLE TIGHT UNDER THE ARM!
Some time later...
HAVE YOU FINISHED THE ALTERATIONS YET? WE'RE IN A HURRY!
READY IN TWO SHAKES, SIR...

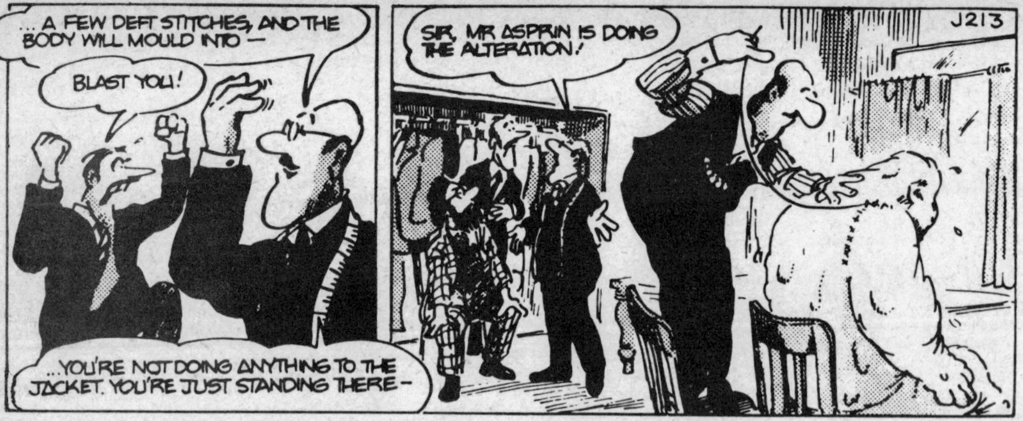
... A FEW DEFT STITCHES, AND THE BODY WILL MOULD INTO —
BLAST YOU!
...YOU'RE NOT DOING ANYTHING TO THE JACKET. YOU'RE JUST STANDING THERE —
SIR, MR ASPRIN IS DOING THE ALTERATION!
J213

And in a few minutes...

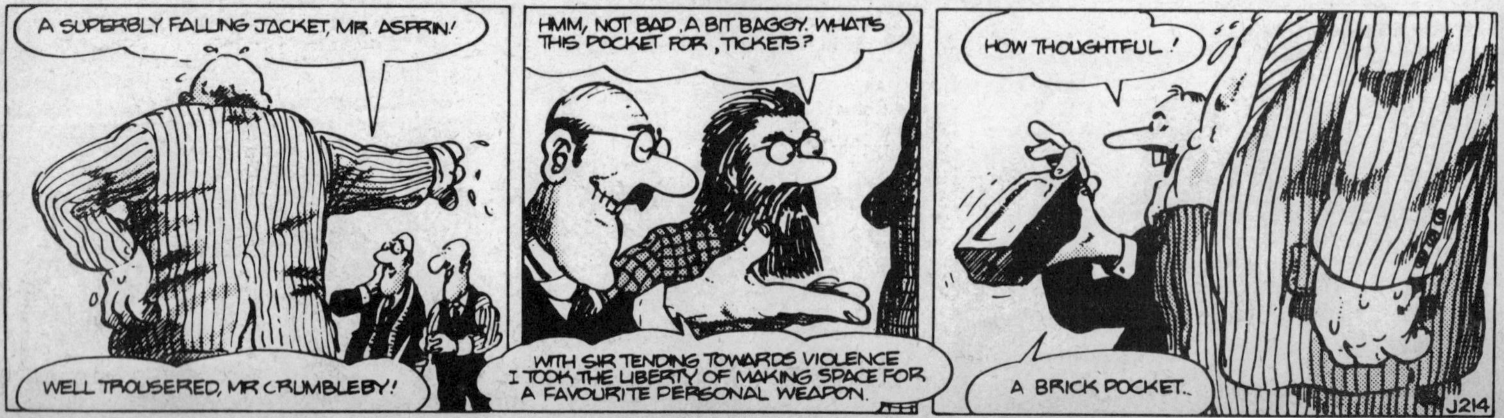
A SUPERBLY FALLING JACKET, MR. ASPRIN!
WELL TROUSERED, MR CRUMBLEBY!
HMM, NOT BAD. A BIT BAGGY. WHAT'S THIS POCKET FOR, TICKETS?
WITH SIR TENDING TOWARDS VIOLENCE I TOOK THE LIBERTY OF MAKING SPACE FOR A FAVOURITE PERSONAL WEAPON.
HOW THOUGHTFUL!
A BRICK POCKET..
J214

And as the avenging army moves off...

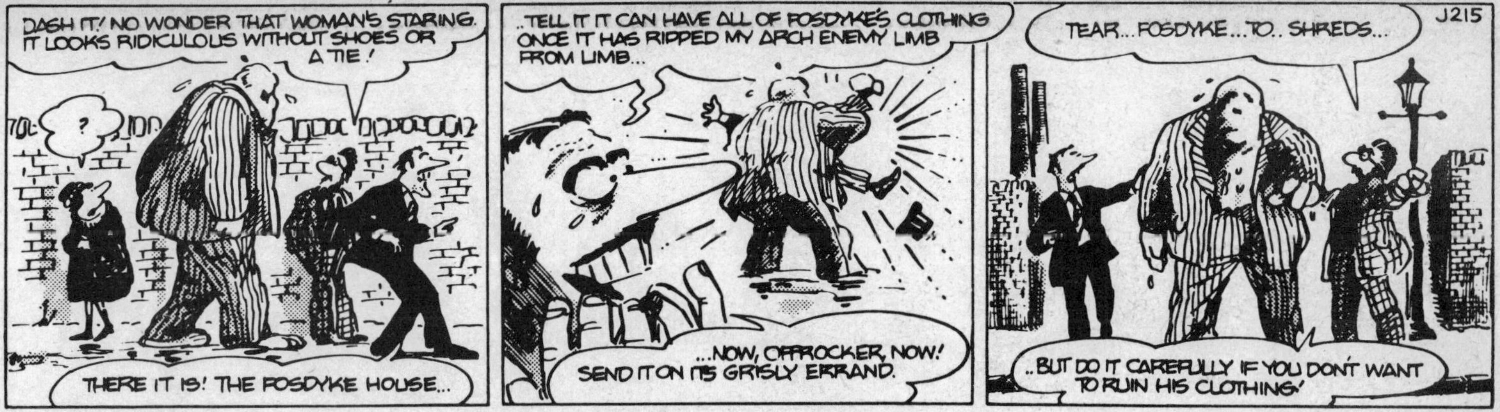
DASH IT! NO WONDER THAT WOMAN'S STARING. IT LOOKS RIDICULOUS WITHOUT SHOES OR A TIE!
?
THERE IT IS! THE FOSDYKE HOUSE...
..TELL IT IT CAN HAVE ALL OF FOSDYKE'S CLOTHING ONCE IT HAS RIPPED MY ARCH ENEMY LIMB FROM LIMB...
...NOW, OFFROCKER, NOW! SEND IT ON ITS GRISLY ERRAND.
J215
TEAR... FOSDYKE... TO.. SHREDS...
..BUT DO IT CAREFULLY IF YOU DON'T WANT TO RUIN HIS CLOTHING!

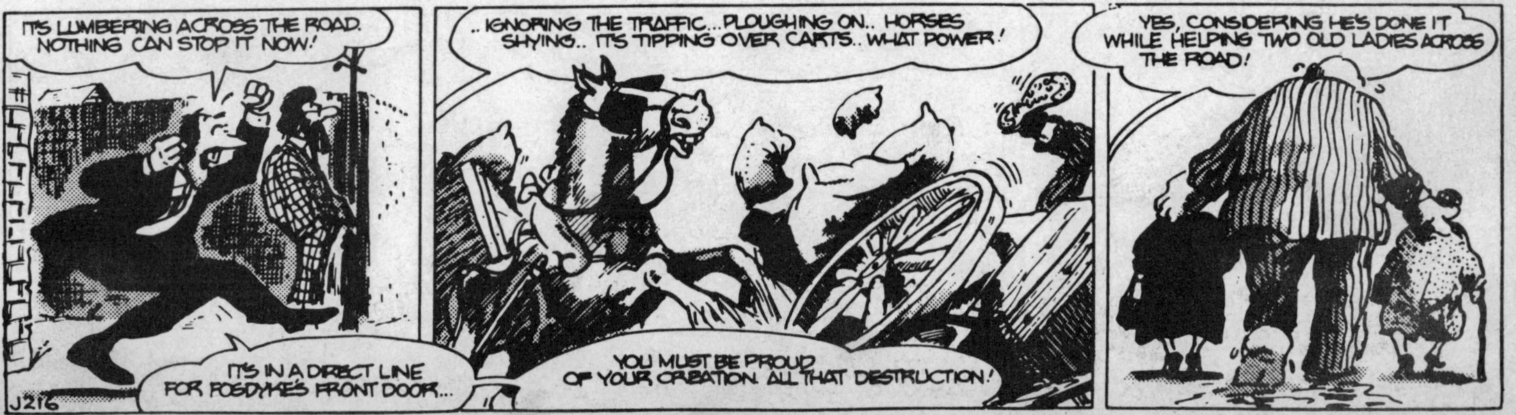
IT'S LUMBERING ACROSS THE ROAD. NOTHING CAN STOP IT NOW!
IT'S IN A DIRECT LINE FOR FOSDYKE'S FRONT DOOR...
J216
.. IGNORING THE TRAFFIC... PLOUGHING ON.. HORSES SHYING.. IT'S TIPPING OVER CARTS.. WHAT POWER!
YOU MUST BE PROUD OF YOUR CREATION. ALL THAT DESTRUCTION!
YES, CONSIDERING HE'S DONE IT WHILE HELPING TWO OLD LADIES ACROSS THE ROAD!

Meanwhile at the Berlin Ministry of Sport...

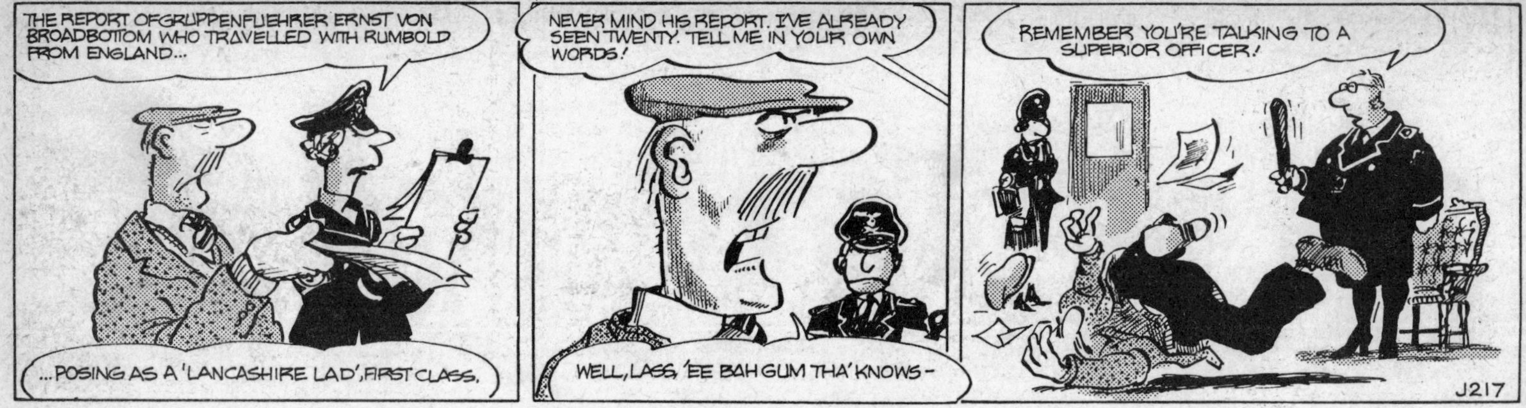
THE REPORT OFGRUPPENFUEHRER ERNST VON BROADBOTTOM WHO TRAVELLED WITH RUMBOLD FROM ENGLAND...
...POSING AS A 'LANCASHIRE LAD', FIRST CLASS.
NEVER MIND HIS REPORT. I'VE ALREADY SEEN TWENTY. TELL ME IN YOUR OWN WORDS!
WELL, LASS, 'EE BAH GUM THA' KNOWS –
REMEMBER YOU'RE TALKING TO A SUPERIOR OFFICER!
J217

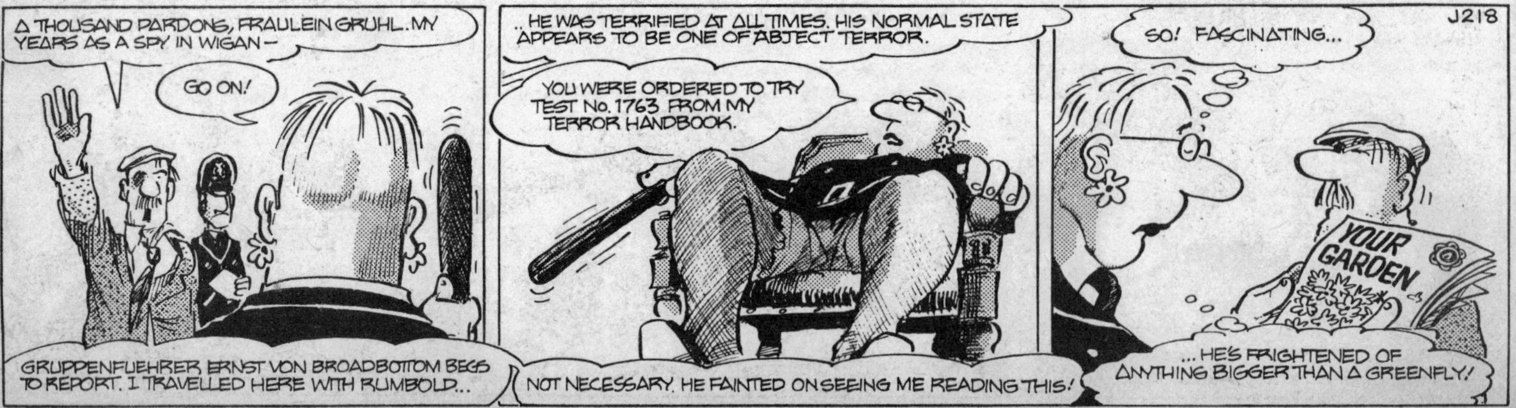
GRUPPENFUEHRER ERNST VON BROADBOTTOM BEGS TO REPORT. I TRAVELLED HERE WITH RUMBOLD...
A THOUSAND PARDONS, FRAULEIN GRUHL. MY YEARS AS A SPY IN WIGAN –
GO ON!
YOU WERE ORDERED TO TRY TEST No. 1763 FROM MY TERROR HANDBOOK.
NOT NECESSARY. HE FAINTED ON SEEING ME READING THIS!
..HE WAS TERRIFIED AT ALL TIMES. HIS NORMAL STATE APPEARS TO BE ONE OF ABJECT TERROR.
SO! FASCINATING...
YOUR GARDEN
...HE'S FRIGHTENED OF ANYTHING BIGGER THAN A GREENFLY!
J218

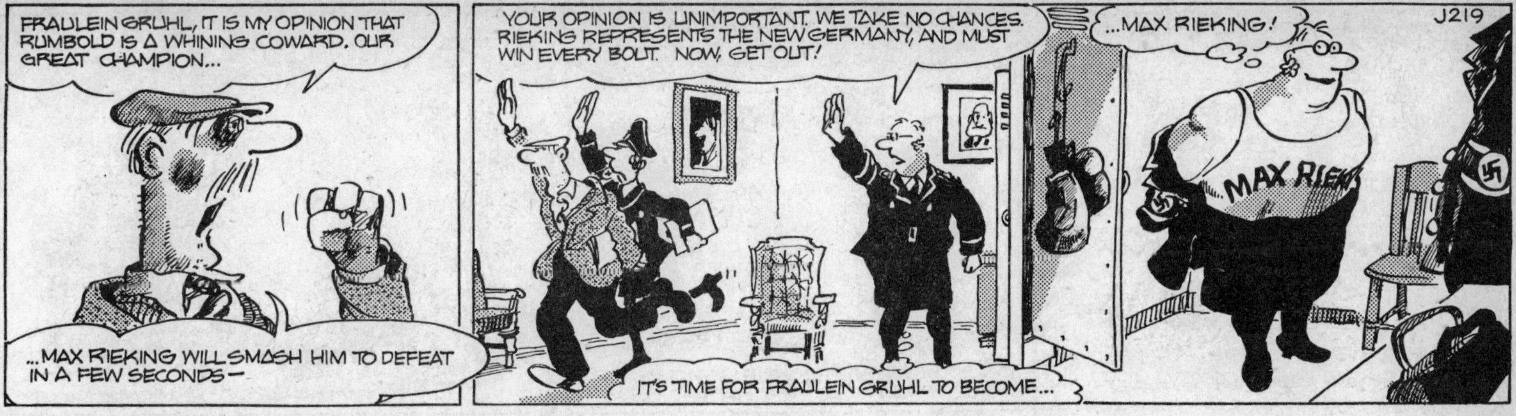
FRAULEIN GRUHL, IT IS MY OPINION THAT RUMBOLD IS A WHINING COWARD. OUR GREAT CHAMPION...
...MAX RIEKING WILL SMASH HIM TO DEFEAT IN A FEW SECONDS—
YOUR OPINION IS UNIMPORTANT. WE TAKE NO CHANCES. RIEKING REPRESENTS THE NEW GERMANY, AND MUST WIN EVERY BOUT. NOW, GET OUT!
IT'S TIME FOR FRAULEIN GRUHL TO BECOME...
...MAX RIEKING!
J219
MAX RIEK

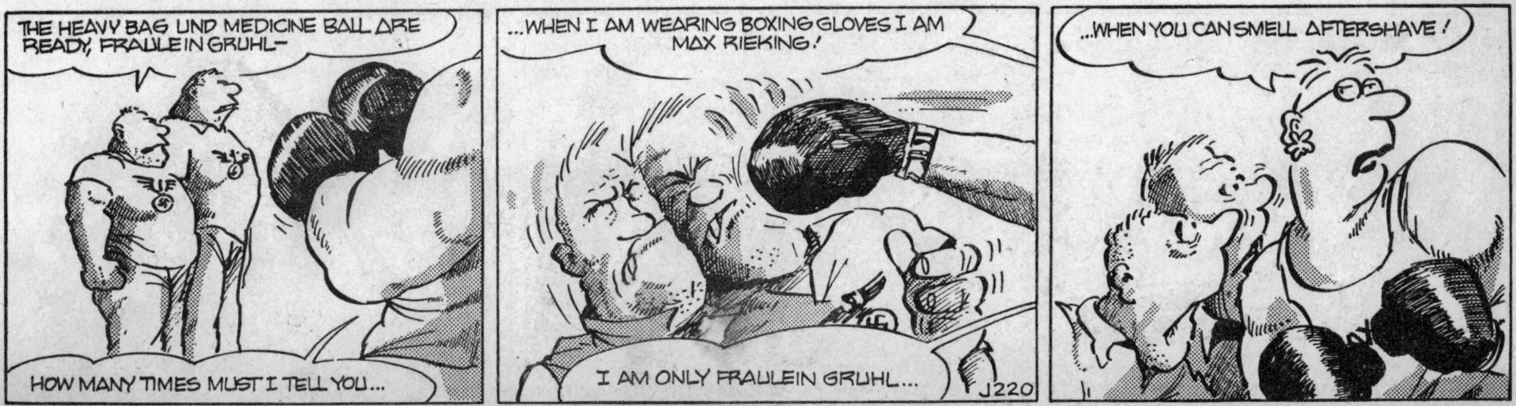
THE HEAVY BAG UND MEDICINE BALL ARE READY, FRAULEIN GRUHL—
HOW MANY TIMES MUST I TELL YOU...
...WHEN I AM WEARING BOXING GLOVES I AM MAX RIEKING!
I AM ONLY FRAULEIN GRUHL...
J220
...WHEN YOU CAN SMELL AFTERSHAVE!

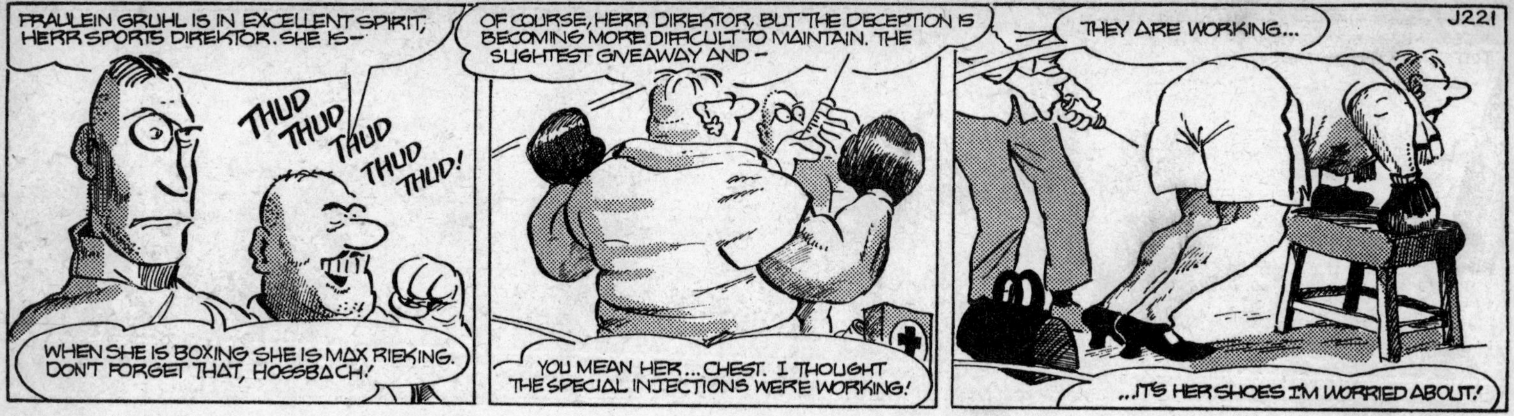
J221
FRAULEIN GRUHL IS IN EXCELLENT SPIRIT, HERR SPORTS DIREKTOR. SHE IS—
THUD THUD THUD THUD THUD!
WHEN SHE IS BOXING SHE IS MAX RIEKING. DON'T FORGET THAT, HOSSBACH!
OF COURSE, HERR DIREKTOR, BUT THE DECEPTION IS BECOMING MORE DIFFICULT TO MAINTAIN. THE SLIGHTEST GIVEAWAY AND—
YOU MEAN HER... CHEST. I THOUGHT THE SPECIAL INJECTIONS WERE WORKING!
THEY ARE WORKING...
...IT'S HER SHOES I'M WORRIED ABOUT!

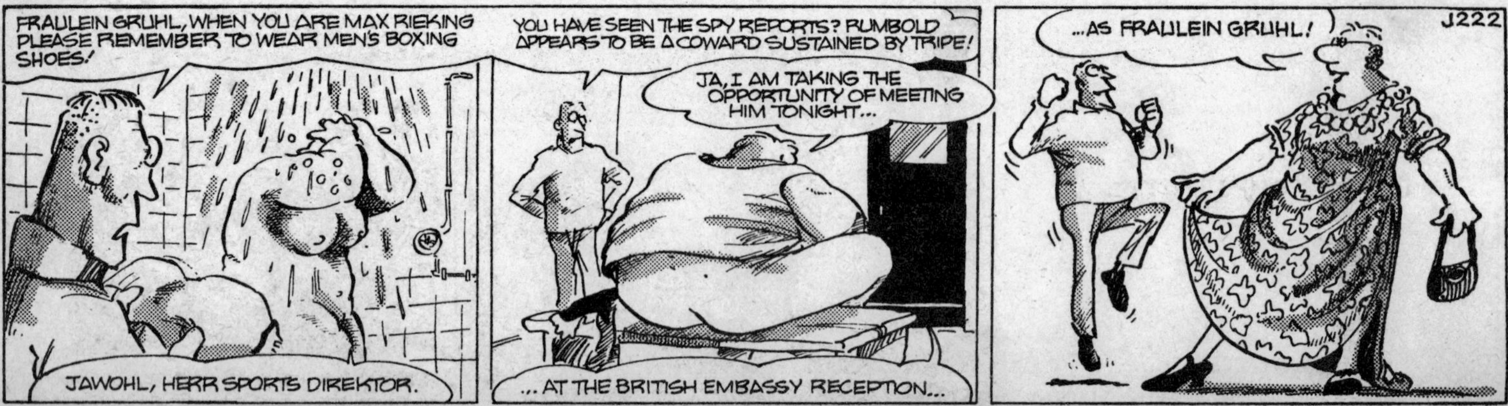
J222
FRAULEIN GRUHL, WHEN YOU ARE MAX RIEKING PLEASE REMEMBER TO WEAR MEN'S BOXING SHOES!
JAWOHL, HERR SPORTS DIREKTOR.
YOU HAVE SEEN THE SPY REPORTS? RUMBOLD APPEARS TO BE A COWARD SUSTAINED BY TRIPE!
JA, I AM TAKING THE OPPORTUNITY OF MEETING HIM TONIGHT...
... AT THE BRITISH EMBASSY RECEPTION...
...AS FRAULEIN GRUHL!

And on the island of Mu...

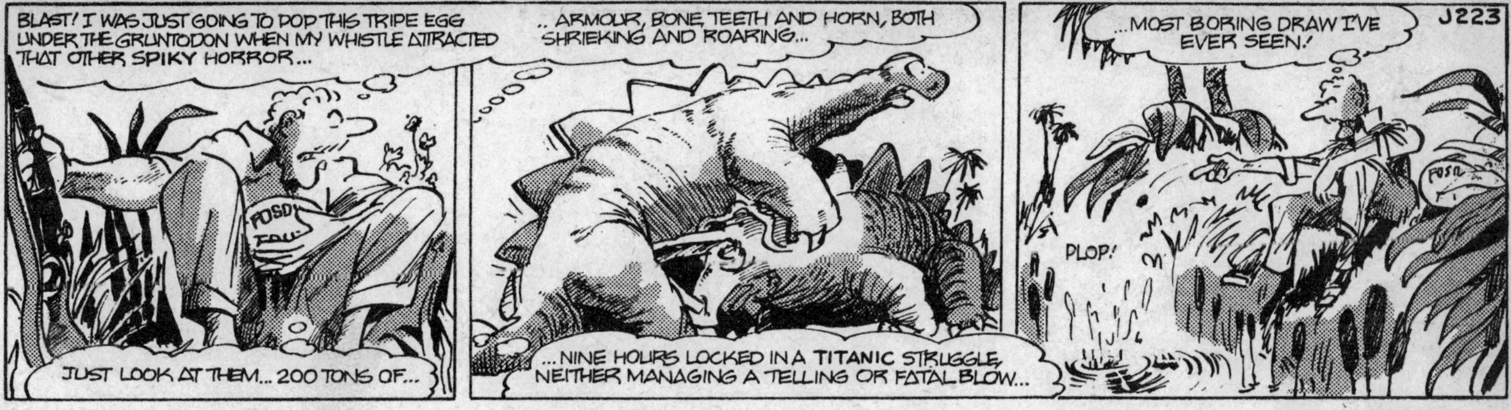
BLAST! I WAS JUST GOING TO POP THIS TRIPE EGG UNDER THE GRUNTODON WHEN MY WHISTLE ATTRACTED THAT OTHER SPIKY HORROR...
JUST LOOK AT THEM... 200 TONS OF...
.. ARMOUR, BONE, TEETH AND HORN, BOTH SHRIEKING AND ROARING...
...NINE HOURS LOCKED IN A TITANIC STRUGGLE, NEITHER MANAGING A TELLING OR FATAL BLOW...
J223
...MOST BORING DRAW I'VE EVER SEEN!
PLOP!

Some hours later...

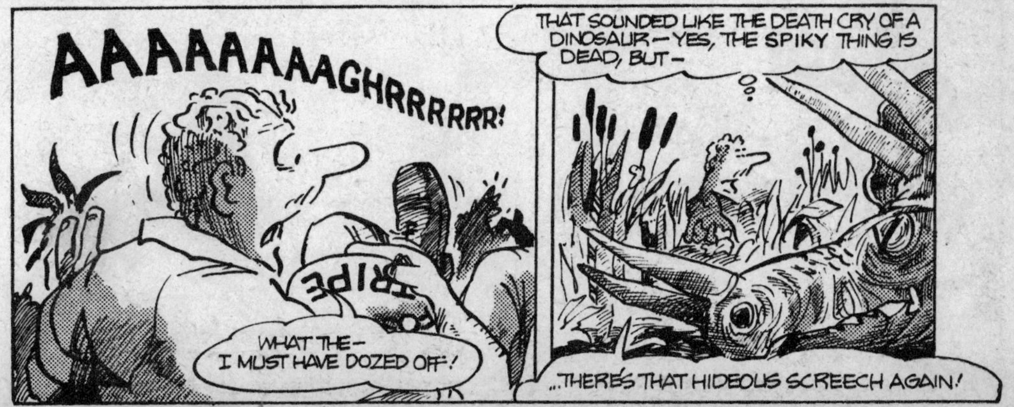
AAAAAAAAGHRRRRRRR!
WHAT THE— I MUST HAVE DOZED OFF!
THAT SOUNDED LIKE THE DEATH CRY OF A DINOSAUR—YES, THE SPIKY THING IS DEAD, BUT—
...THERE'S THAT HIDEOUS SCREECH AGAIN!

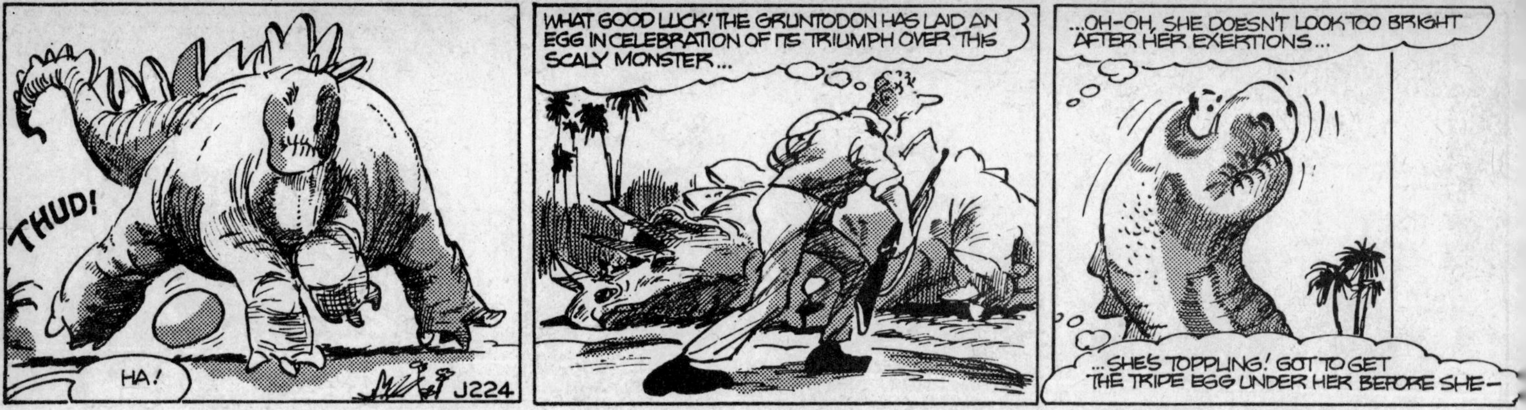
THUD!
HA!
J224
WHAT GOOD LUCK! THE GRUNTODON HAS LAID AN EGG IN CELEBRATION OF ITS TRIUMPH OVER THIS SCALY MONSTER...
...OH-OH, SHE DOESN'T LOOK TOO BRIGHT AFTER HER EXERTIONS...
...SHE'S TOPPLING! GOT TO GET THE TRIPE EGG UNDER HER BEFORE SHE—

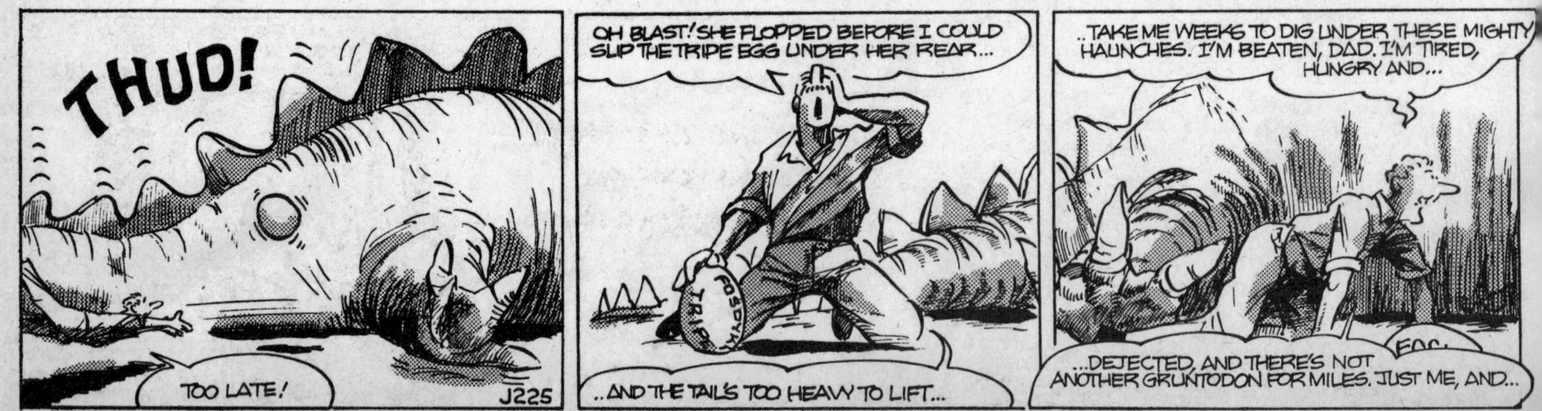
THUD!
TOO LATE!
J225
OH BLAST! SHE FLOPPED BEFORE I COULD SLIP THE TRIPE EGG UNDER HER REAR...
FOSDYKE TRIPE
..AND THE TAIL'S TOO HEAVY TO LIFT...
..TAKE ME WEEKS TO DIG UNDER THESE MIGHTY HAUNCHES. I'M BEATEN, DAD. I'M TIRED, HUNGRY AND...
...DEJECTED, AND THERE'S NOT ANOTHER GRUNTODON FOR MILES. JUST ME, AND...

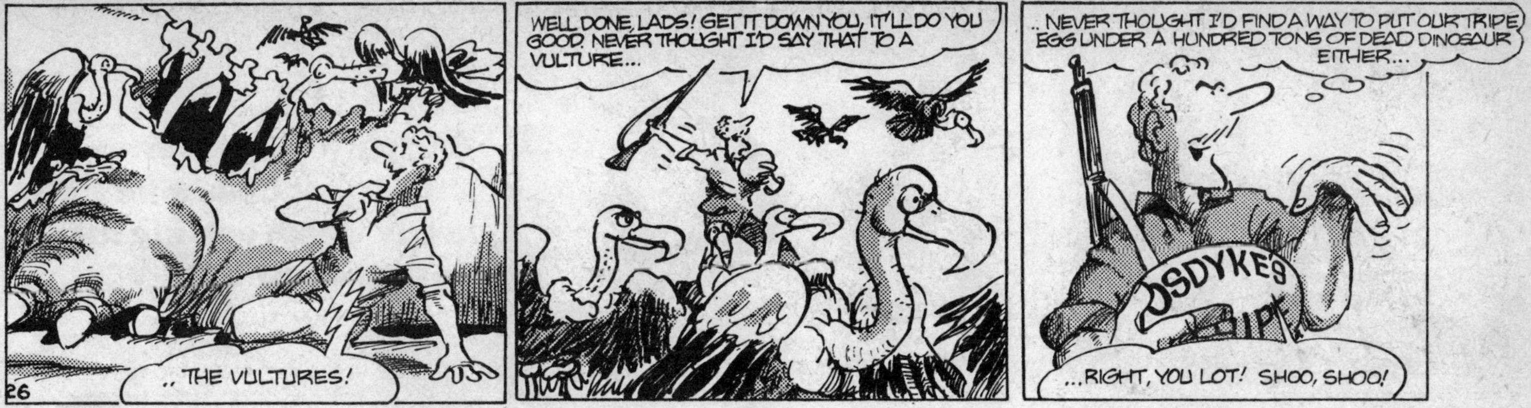
.. THE VULTURES!
26
WELL DONE, LADS! GET IT DOWN YOU, IT'LL DO YOU GOOD. NEVER THOUGHT I'D SAY THAT TO A VULTURE...
.. NEVER THOUGHT I'D FIND A WAY TO PUT OUR TRIPE EGG UNDER A HUNDRED TONS OF DEAD DINOSAUR EITHER...
OSDYKE'S
...RIGHT, YOU LOT! SHOO, SHOO!

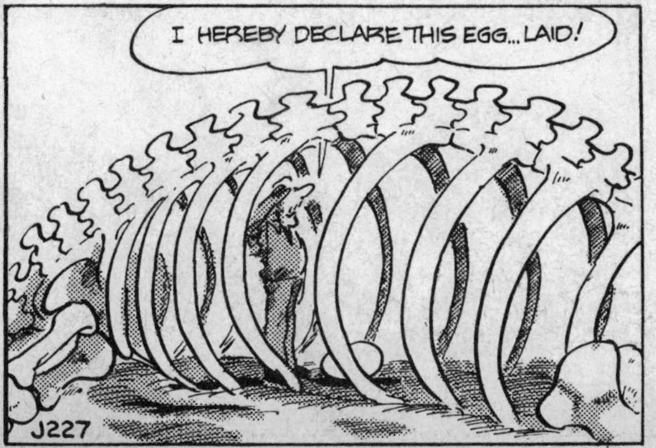
I HEREBY DECLARE THIS EGG... LAID!
J227

And so the victorious stunt man returns triumphantly to the shore.

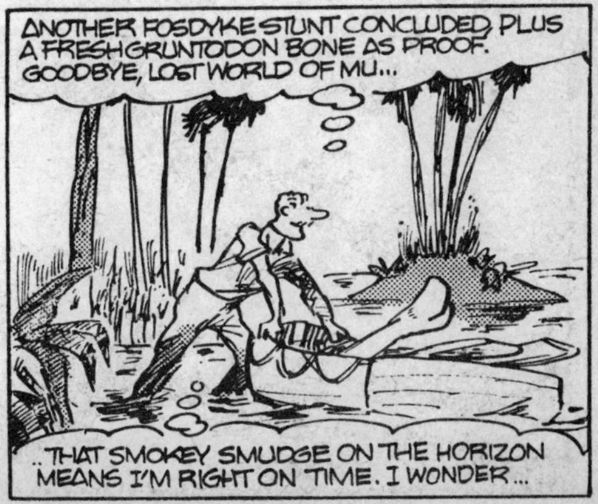
ANOTHER FOSDYKE STUNT CONCLUDED, PLUS A FRESH GRUNTODON BONE AS PROOF. GOODBYE, LOST WORLD OF MU...
..THAT SMOKEY SMUDGE ON THE HORIZON MEANS I'M RIGHT ON TIME. I WONDER...

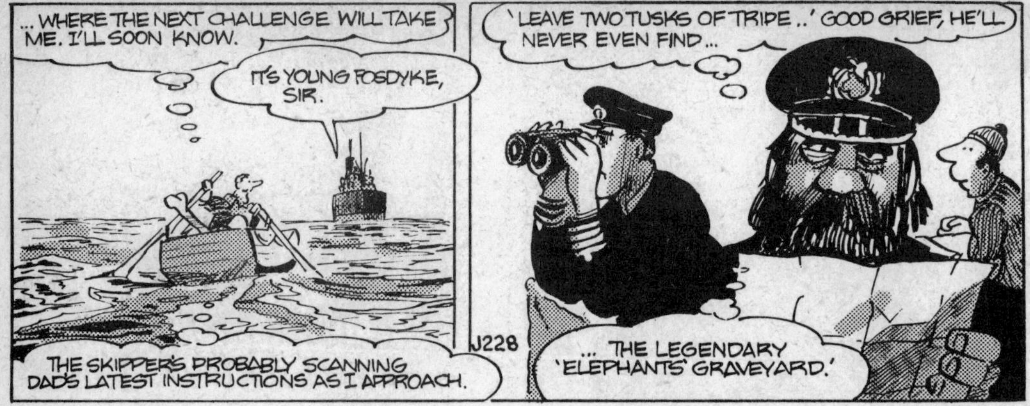
... WHERE THE NEXT CHALLENGE WILL TAKE ME. I'LL SOON KNOW.
IT'S YOUNG FOSDYKE, SIR.
THE SKIPPER'S PROBABLY SCANNING DAD'S LATEST INSTRUCTIONS AS I APPROACH.
'LEAVE TWO TUSKS OF TRIPE ..' GOOD GRIEF, HE'LL NEVER EVEN FIND ...
... THE LEGENDARY 'ELEPHANTS' GRAVEYARD.'
J228

Back in Manchester, Ditchley and his maniacal crony watch outside the Fosdyke home...

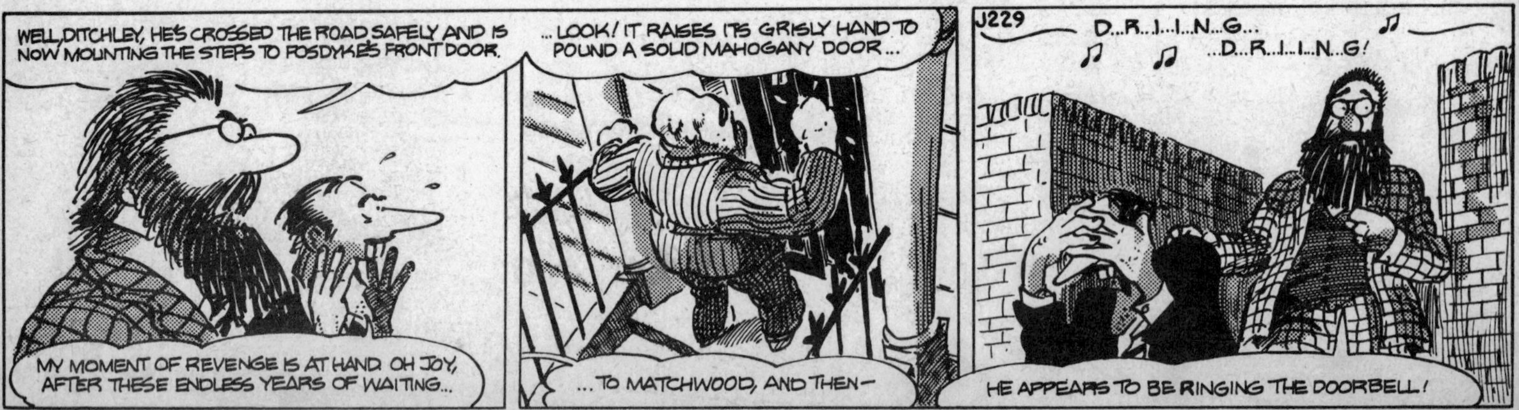
WELL, DITCHLEY, HE'S CROSSED THE ROAD SAFELY AND IS NOW MOUNTING THE STEPS TO FOSDYKE'S FRONT DOOR.
MY MOMENT OF REVENGE IS AT HAND. OH JOY, AFTER THESE ENDLESS YEARS OF WAITING...
... LOOK! IT RAISES ITS GRISLY HAND TO POUND A SOLID MAHOGANY DOOR ...
... TO MATCHWOOD, AND THEN—
J229
D...R...I...I...N...G...
...D...R...I...I...N...G!
HE APPEARS TO BE RINGING THE DOORBELL!

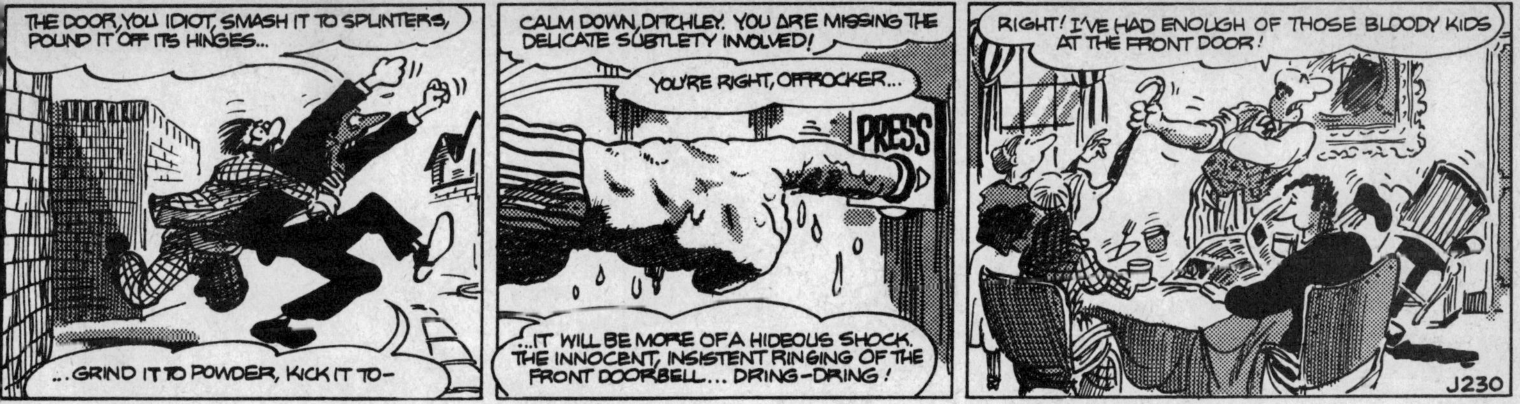
THE DOOR, YOU IDIOT, SMASH IT TO SPLINTERS, POUND IT OFF ITS HINGES...
...GRIND IT TO POWDER, KICK IT TO-
CALM DOWN, DITCHLEY. YOU ARE MISSING THE DELICATE SUBTLETY INVOLVED!
YOU'RE RIGHT, OFFROCKER...
PRESS
...IT WILL BE MORE OF A HIDEOUS SHOCK. THE INNOCENT, INSISTENT RINGING OF THE FRONT DOORBELL... DRING-DRING!
RIGHT! I'VE HAD ENOUGH OF THOSE BLOODY KIDS AT THE FRONT DOOR!
J230

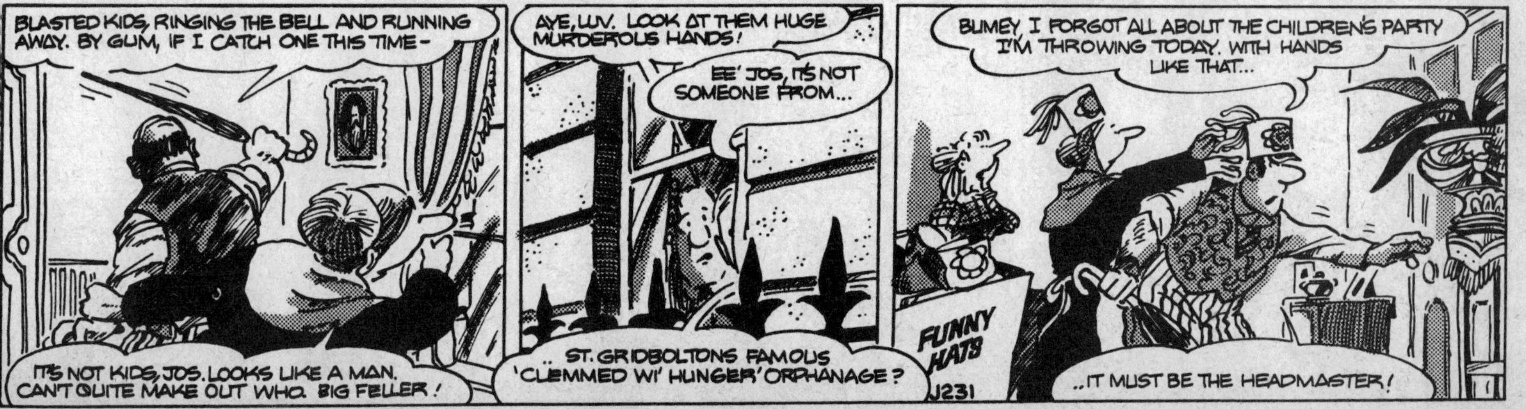
BLASTED KIDS, RINGING THE BELL AND RUNNING AWAY. BY GUM, IF I CATCH ONE THIS TIME-
IT'S NOT KIDS, JOS. LOOKS LIKE A MAN. CAN'T QUITE MAKE OUT WHO. BIG FELLER!
AYE, LUV. LOOK AT THEM HUGE MURDEROUS HANDS!
EE' JOS, IT'S NOT SOMEONE FROM...
.. ST. GRIDBOLTONS FAMOUS 'CLEMMED WI' HUNGER' ORPHANAGE?
BLIMEY, I FORGOT ALL ABOUT THE CHILDREN'S PARTY I'M THROWING TODAY. WITH HANDS LIKE THAT...
FUNNY HATS
..IT MUST BE THE HEADMASTER!
J231

And indeed, round the corner...

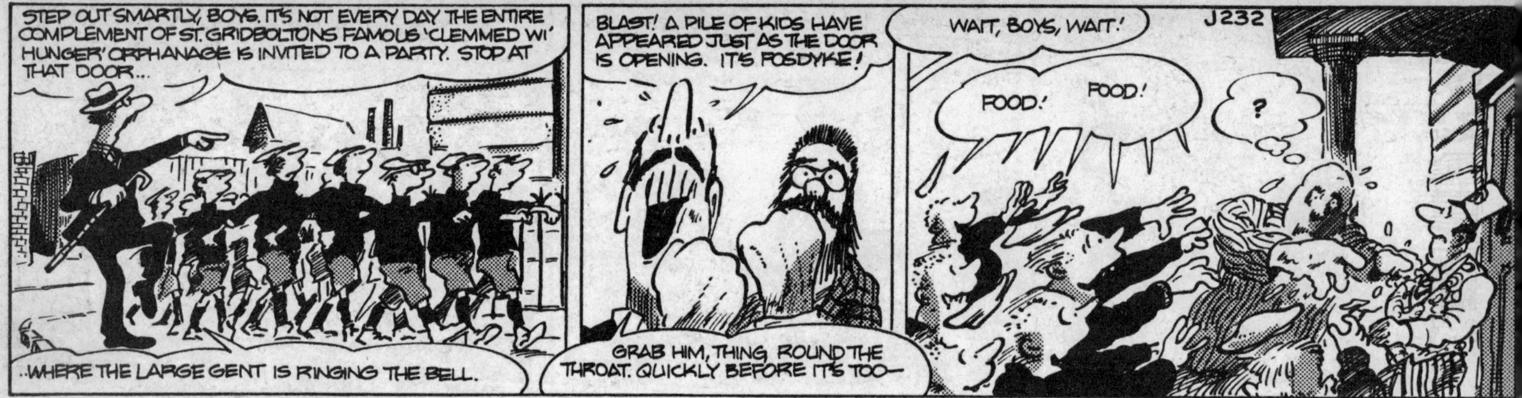
STEP OUT SMARTLY, BOYS. IT'S NOT EVERY DAY THE ENTIRE COMPLEMENT OF ST. GRIDBOLTONS FAMOUS 'CLEMMED WI' HUNGER' ORPHANAGE IS INVITED TO A PARTY. STOP AT THAT DOOR...
..WHERE THE LARGE GENT IS RINGING THE BELL.
BLAST! A PILE OF KIDS HAVE APPEARED JUST AS THE DOOR IS OPENING. IT'S FOSDYKE!
GRAB HIM, THING. ROUND THE THROAT. QUICKLY BEFORE IT'S TOO—
J232
WAIT, BOYS, WAIT!
FOOD! FOOD!
?

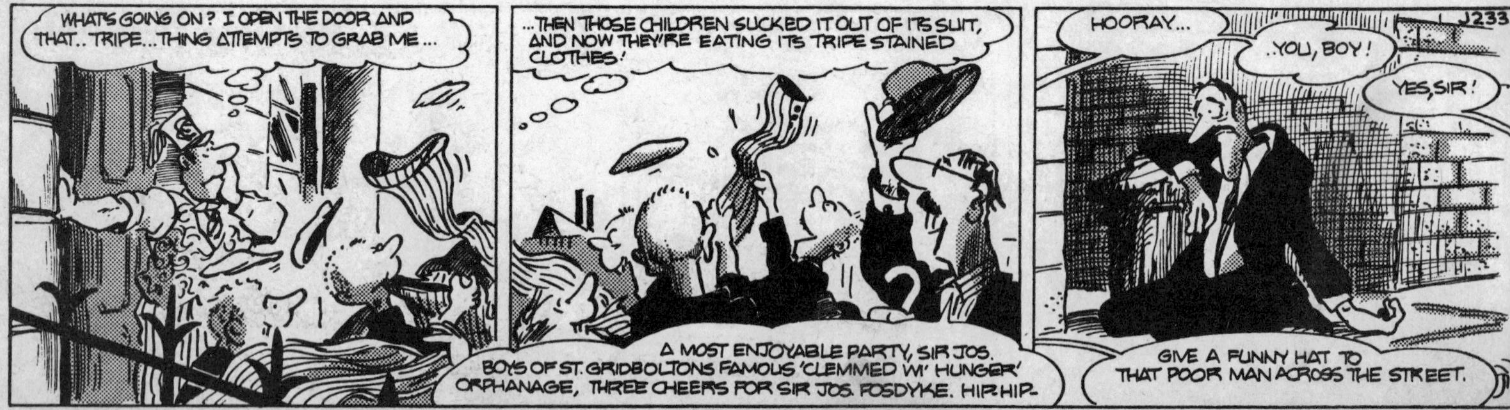
WHAT'S GOING ON? I OPEN THE DOOR AND THAT.. TRIPE... THING ATTEMPTS TO GRAB ME...
...THEN THOSE CHILDREN SUCKED IT OUT OF ITS SUIT, AND NOW THEY'RE EATING ITS TRIPE STAINED CLOTHES!
A MOST ENJOYABLE PARTY, SIR JOS.
BOYS OF ST. GRIDBOLTONS FAMOUS 'CLEMMED WI' HUNGER' ORPHANAGE, THREE CHEERS FOR SIR JOS. FOSDYKE. HIP-HIP-
J233
HOORAY...
..YOU, BOY!
YES, SIR!
GIVE A FUNNY HAT TO THAT POOR MAN ACROSS THE STREET.

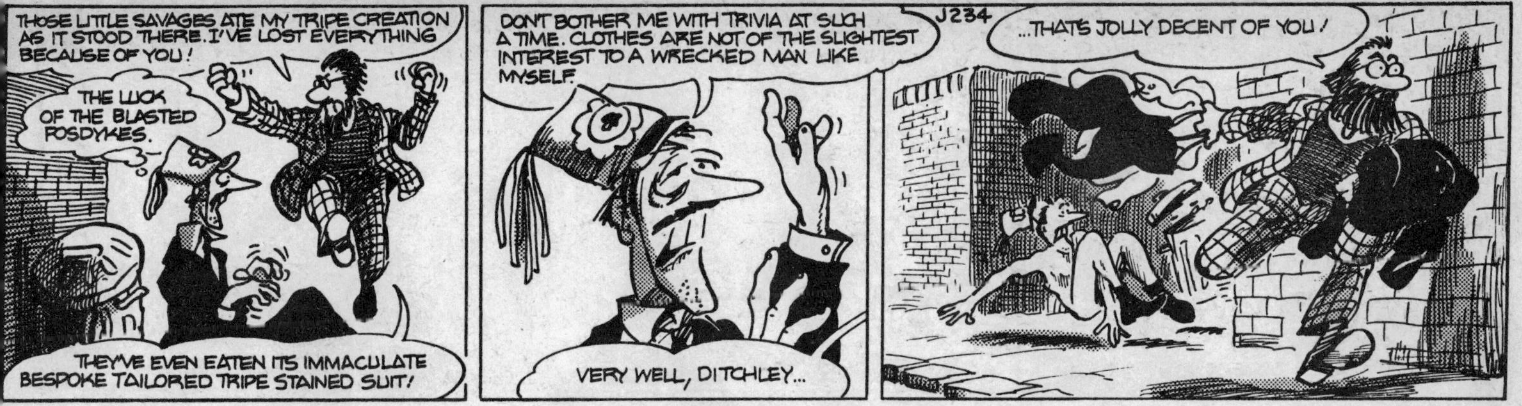
THOSE LITTLE SAVAGES ATE MY TRIPE CREATION AS IT STOOD THERE. I'VE LOST EVERYTHING BECAUSE OF YOU!
THE LUCK OF THE BLASTED FOSDYKES.
THEY'VE EVEN EATEN ITS IMMACULATE BESPOKE TAILORED TRIPE STAINED SUIT!
DON'T BOTHER ME WITH TRIVIA AT SUCH A TIME. CLOTHES ARE NOT OF THE SLIGHTEST INTEREST TO A WRECKED MAN LIKE MYSELF.
VERY WELL, DITCHLEY...
J234
...THAT'S JOLLY DECENT OF YOU!

In a Berlin hotel Tim soothes the trembling white hope of British boxing...

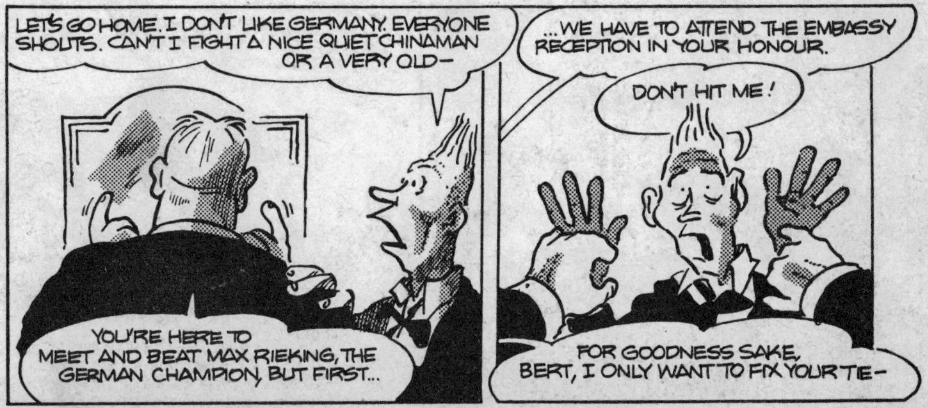
LET'S GO HOME. I DON'T LIKE GERMANY. EVERYONE SHOUTS. CAN'T I FIGHT A NICE QUIET CHINAMAN OR A VERY OLD—
YOU'RE HERE TO MEET AND BEAT MAX RIEKING, THE GERMAN CHAMPION, BUT FIRST...
...WE HAVE TO ATTEND THE EMBASSY RECEPTION IN YOUR HONOUR.
DON'T HIT ME!
FOR GOODNESS SAKE, BERT, I ONLY WANT TO FIX YOUR TIE—

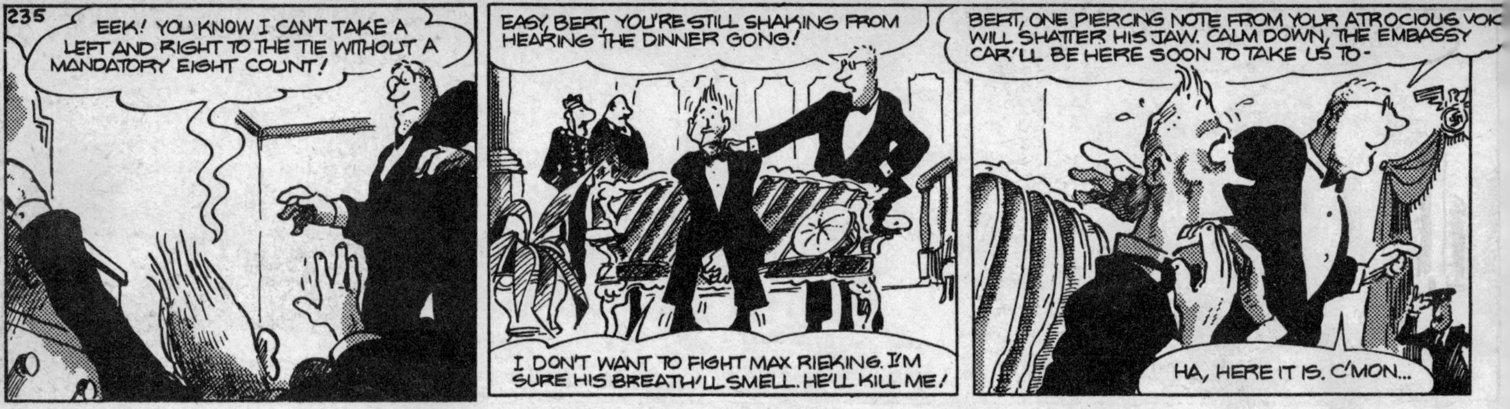

235
EEK! YOU KNOW I CAN'T TAKE A LEFT AND RIGHT TO THE TIE WITHOUT A MANDATORY EIGHT COUNT!
EASY, BERT, YOU'RE STILL SHAKING FROM HEARING THE DINNER GONG!
I DON'T WANT TO FIGHT MAX RIEKING. I'M SURE HIS BREATH'LL SMELL. HE'LL KILL ME!
BERT, ONE PIERCING NOTE FROM YOUR ATROCIOUS VOIC
WILL SHATTER HIS JAW. CALM DOWN, THE EMBASSY CAR'LL BE HERE SOON TO TAKE US TO-
HA, HERE IT IS. C'MON...

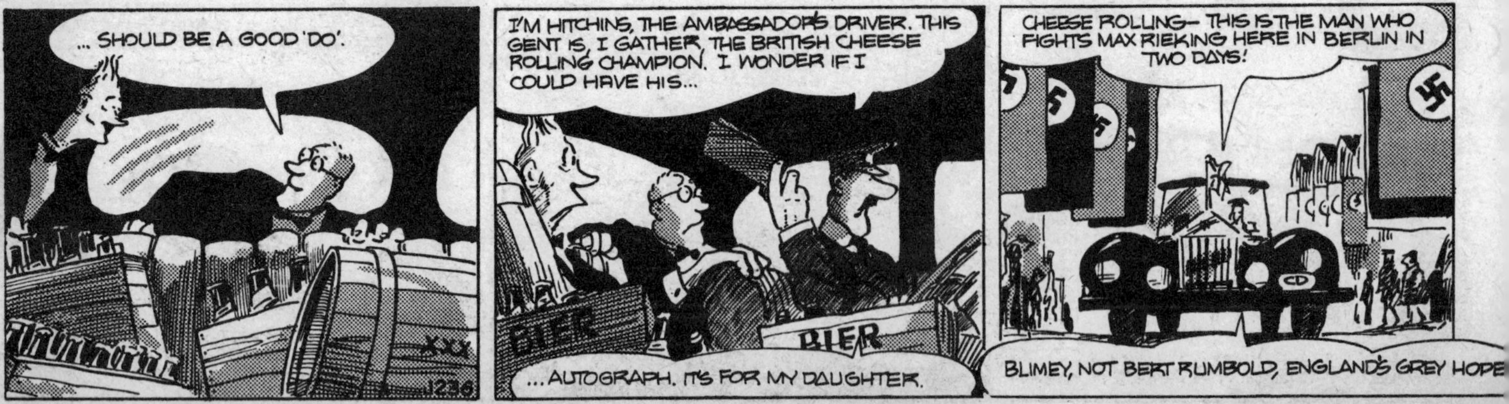

... SHOULD BE A GOOD 'DO'.
1236
I'M HITCHINS, THE AMBASSADOR'S DRIVER. THIS GENT IS, I GATHER, THE BRITISH CHEESE ROLLING CHAMPION. I WONDER IF I COULD HAVE HIS...
BIER
BIER
... AUTOGRAPH. IT'S FOR MY DAUGHTER.
CHEESE ROLLING— THIS IS THE MAN WHO FIGHTS MAX RIEKING HERE IN BERLIN IN TWO DAYS!
CD
BLIMEY, NOT BERT RUMBOLD, ENGLAND'S GREY HOPE

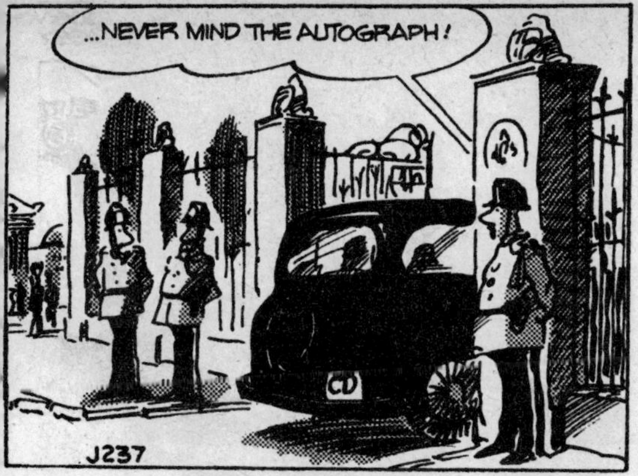
...NEVER MIND THE AUTOGRAPH!
CD
J237

At the reception...

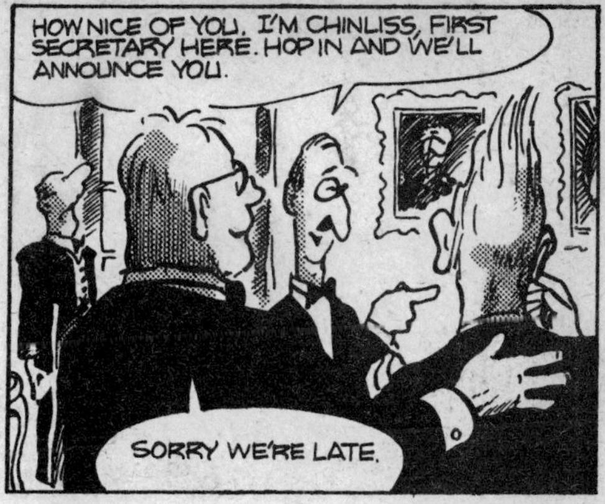
HOW NICE OF YOU. I'M CHINLISS, FIRST SECRETARY HERE. HOP IN AND WE'LL ANNOUNCE YOU.
SORRY WE'RE LATE.

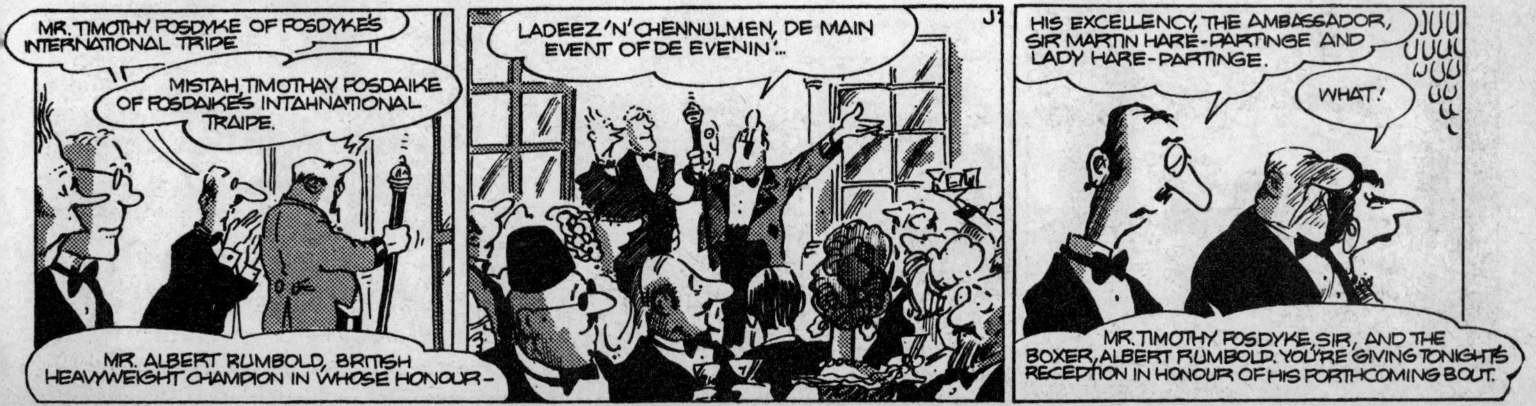
MR. TIMOTHY FOSDYKE OF FOSDYKE'S INTERNATIONAL TRIPE
MISTAH TIMOTHAY FOSDAIKE OF FOSDAIKE'S INTAHNATIONAL TRAIPE.
MR. ALBERT RUMBOLD, BRITISH HEAVYWEIGHT CHAMPION IN WHOSE HONOUR–
LADEEZ 'N' CHENNULMEN, DE MAIN EVENT OF DE EVENIN'...
HIS EXCELLENCY, THE AMBASSADOR, SIR MARTIN HARE-PARTINGE AND LADY HARE-PARTINGE.
WHAT!
MR. TIMOTHY FOSDYKE, SIR, AND THE BOXER, ALBERT RUMBOLD. YOU'RE GIVING TONIGHT'S RECEPTION IN HONOUR OF HIS FORTHCOMING BOUT.

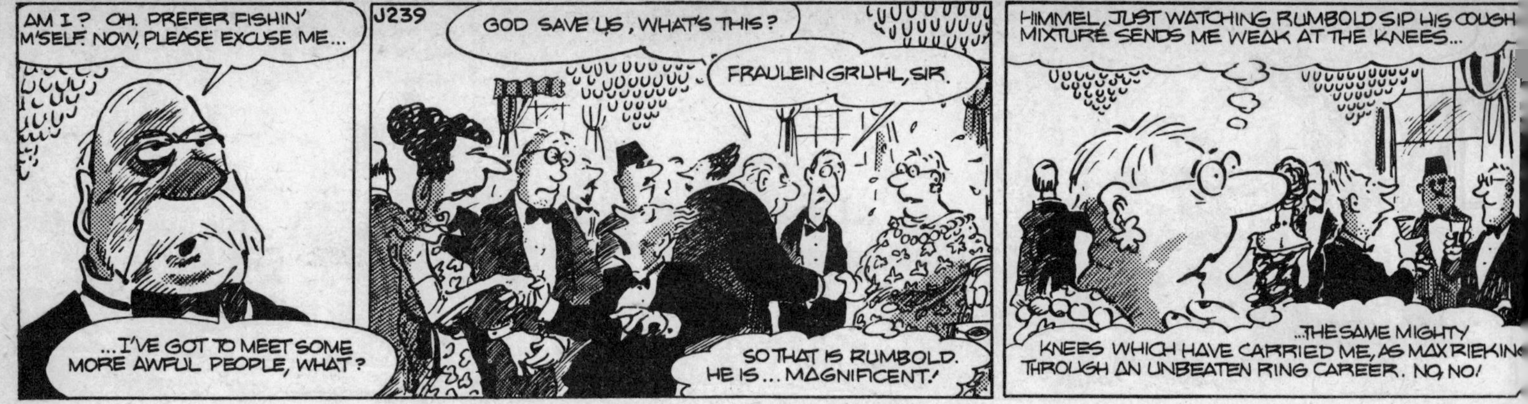
AM I? OH. PREFER FISHIN' M'SELF. NOW, PLEASE EXCUSE ME...
...I'VE GOT TO MEET SOME MORE AWFUL PEOPLE, WHAT?
J239
GOD SAVE US, WHAT'S THIS?
FRAULEIN GRUHL, SIR.
SO THAT IS RUMBOLD. HE IS... MAGNIFICENT!
HIMMEL, JUST WATCHING RUMBOLD SIP HIS COUGH MIXTURE SENDS ME WEAK AT THE KNEES...
...THE SAME MIGHTY KNEES WHICH HAVE CARRIED ME, AS MAX RIEKING
THROUGH AN UNBEATEN RING CAREER. NO, NO!

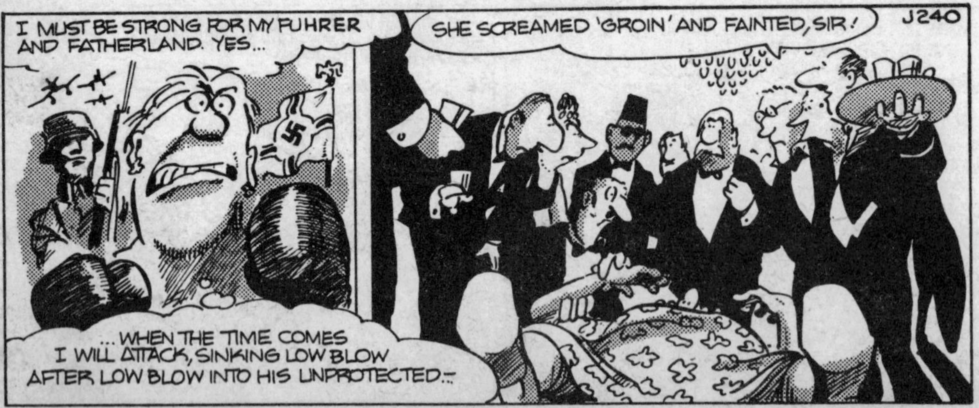
I MUST BE STRONG FOR MY FUHRER AND FATHERLAND. YES...
...WHEN THE TIME COMES I WILL ATTACK, SINKING LOW BLOW AFTER LOW BLOW INTO HIS UNPROTECTED...
SHE SCREAMED 'GROIN' AND FAINTED, SIR!
J240

Meanwhile, in the far-off tropics, Albert regains his support ship.

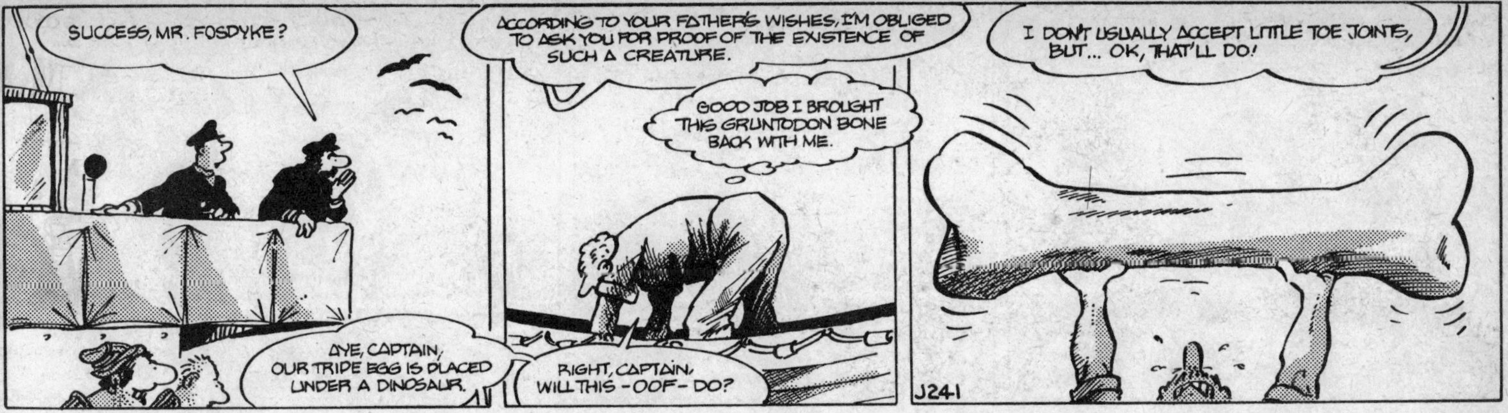
SUCCESS, MR. FOSDYKE?
AYE, CAPTAIN, OUR TRIPE EGG IS PLACED UNDER A DINOSAUR.
ACCORDING TO YOUR FATHER'S WISHES, I'M OBLIGED TO ASK YOU FOR PROOF OF THE EXISTENCE OF SUCH A CREATURE.
GOOD JOB I BROUGHT THIS GRUNTODON BONE BACK WITH ME.
RIGHT, CAPTAIN, WILL THIS -OOF- DO?
I DON'T USUALLY ACCEPT LITTLE TOE JOINTS, BUT... OK, THAT'LL DO!
J241

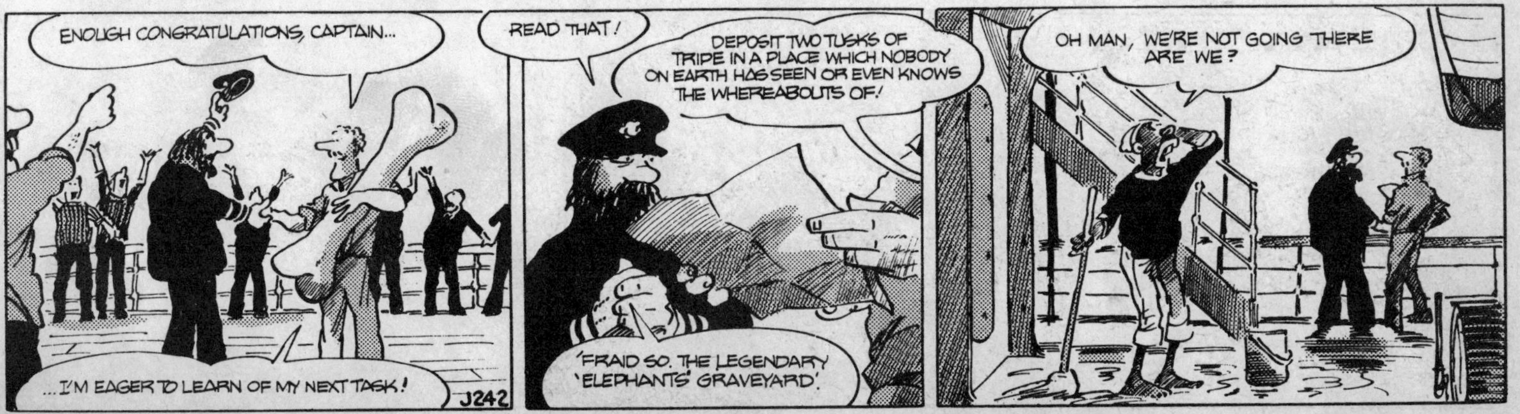
ENOUGH CONGRATULATIONS, CAPTAIN...
...I'M EAGER TO LEARN OF MY NEXT TASK!
J242
READ THAT!
DEPOSIT TWO TUSKS OF TRIPE IN A PLACE WHICH NOBODY ON EARTH HAS SEEN OR EVEN KNOWS THE WHEREABOUTS OF!
'FRAID SO. THE LEGENDARY 'ELEPHANTS' GRAVEYARD'.
OH MAN, WE'RE NOT GOING THERE ARE WE?

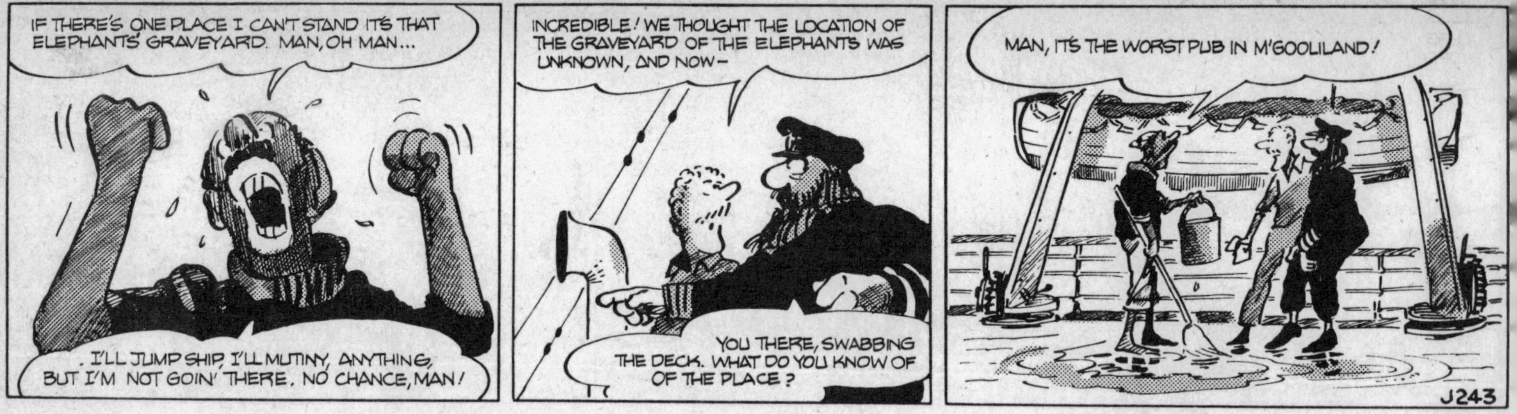
IF THERE'S ONE PLACE I CAN'T STAND IT'S THAT ELEPHANTS' GRAVEYARD. MAN, OH MAN...
. I'LL JUMP SHIP, I'LL MUTINY, ANYTHING, BUT I'M NOT GOIN' THERE. NO CHANCE, MAN!
INCREDIBLE! WE THOUGHT THE LOCATION OF THE GRAVEYARD OF THE ELEPHANTS WAS UNKNOWN, AND NOW –
YOU THERE, SWABBING THE DECK. WHAT DO YOU KNOW OF OF THE PLACE?
MAN, IT'S THE WORST PUB IN M'GOOLILAND!
J243

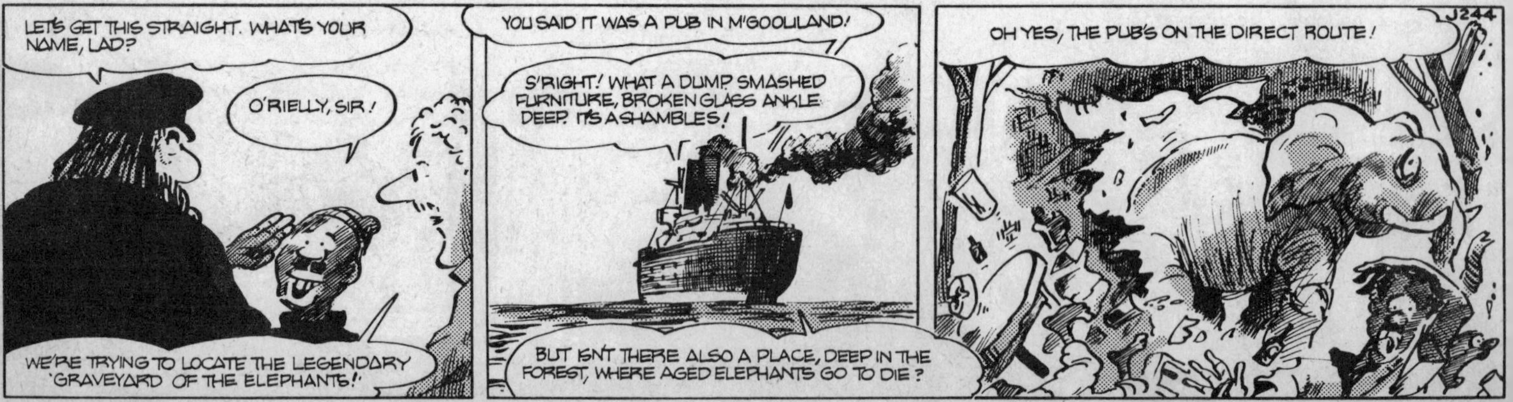
LET'S GET THIS STRAIGHT. WHAT'S YOUR NAME, LAD?
O'RIELLY, SIR!
WE'RE TRYING TO LOCATE THE LEGENDARY 'GRAVEYARD OF THE ELEPHANTS!'
YOU SAID IT WAS A PUB IN M'GOOLILAND!
S'RIGHT! WHAT A DUMP. SMASHED FURNITURE, BROKEN GLASS ANKLE DEEP. IT'S A SHAMBLES!
BUT ISN'T THERE ALSO A PLACE, DEEP IN THE FOREST, WHERE AGED ELEPHANTS GO TO DIE?
J244
OH YES, THE PUB'S ON THE DIRECT ROUTE!

ome weeks later...

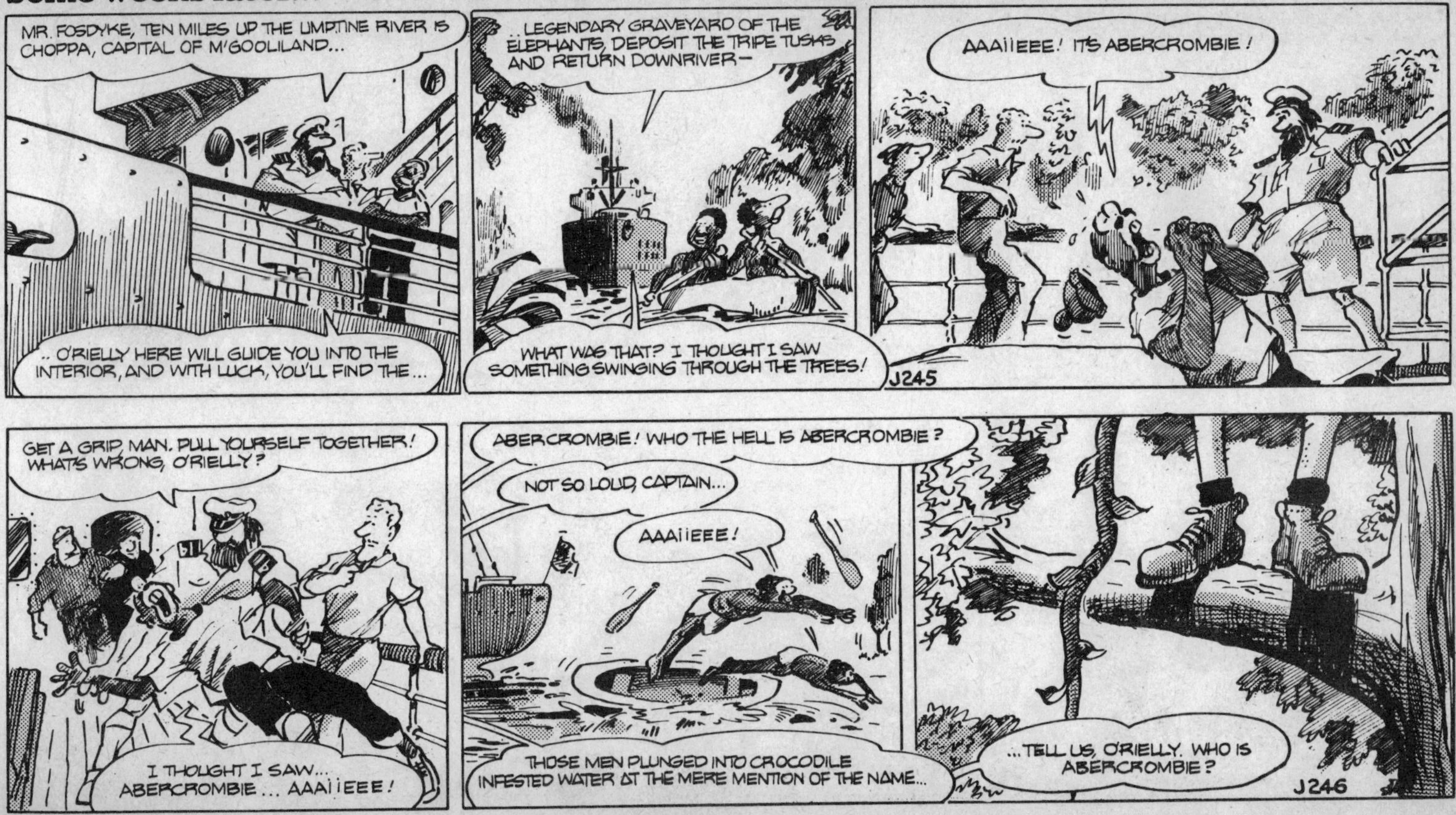

MR. FOSDYKE, TEN MILES UP THE UMPTINE RIVER IS CHOPPA, CAPITAL OF M'GOOLILAND...
.. O'RIELLY HERE WILL GUIDE YOU INTO THE INTERIOR, AND WITH LUCK, YOU'LL FIND THE ...
.. LEGENDARY GRAVEYARD OF THE ELEPHANTS, DEPOSIT THE TRIPE TUSKS AND RETURN DOWNRIVER—
WHAT WAS THAT? I THOUGHT I SAW SOMETHING SWINGING THROUGH THE TREES!
AAAiiEEE! IT'S ABERCROMBIE!
J245
GET A GRIP, MAN. PULL YOURSELF TOGETHER! WHAT'S WRONG, O'RIELLY?
I THOUGHT I SAW... ABERCROMBIE ... AAAiiEEE!
ABERCROMBIE! WHO THE HELL IS ABERCROMBIE?
NOT SO LOUD, CAPTAIN...
AAAiiEEE!
THOSE MEN PLUNGED INTO CROCODILE INFESTED WATER AT THE MERE MENTION OF THE NAME...
...TELL US, O'RIELLY. WHO IS ABERCROMBIE?
J246

And in a Manchester back alley...

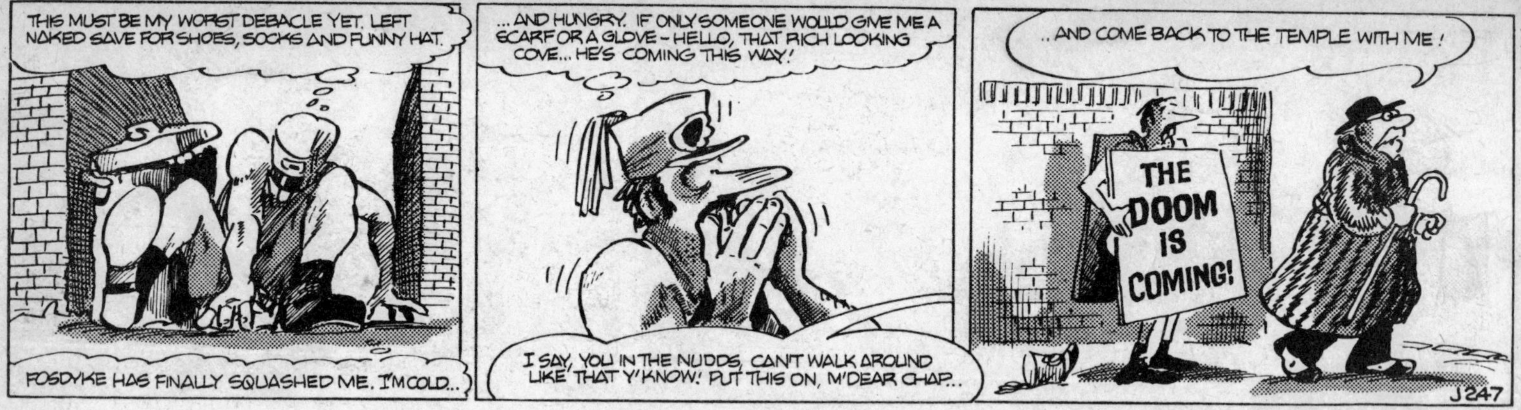
THIS MUST BE MY WORST DEBACLE YET. LEFT NAKED SAVE FOR SHOES, SOCKS AND FUNNY HAT.
FOSDYKE HAS FINALLY SQUASHED ME. I'M COLD...
...AND HUNGRY. IF ONLY SOMEONE WOULD GIVE ME A SCARF OR A GLOVE – HELLO, THAT RICH LOOKING COVE... HE'S COMING THIS WAY!
I SAY, YOU IN THE NUDDS, CAN'T WALK AROUND LIKE THAT Y'KNOW! PUT THIS ON, M'DEAR CHAP...
..AND COME BACK TO THE TEMPLE WITH ME!
THE DOOM IS COMING!
J 247

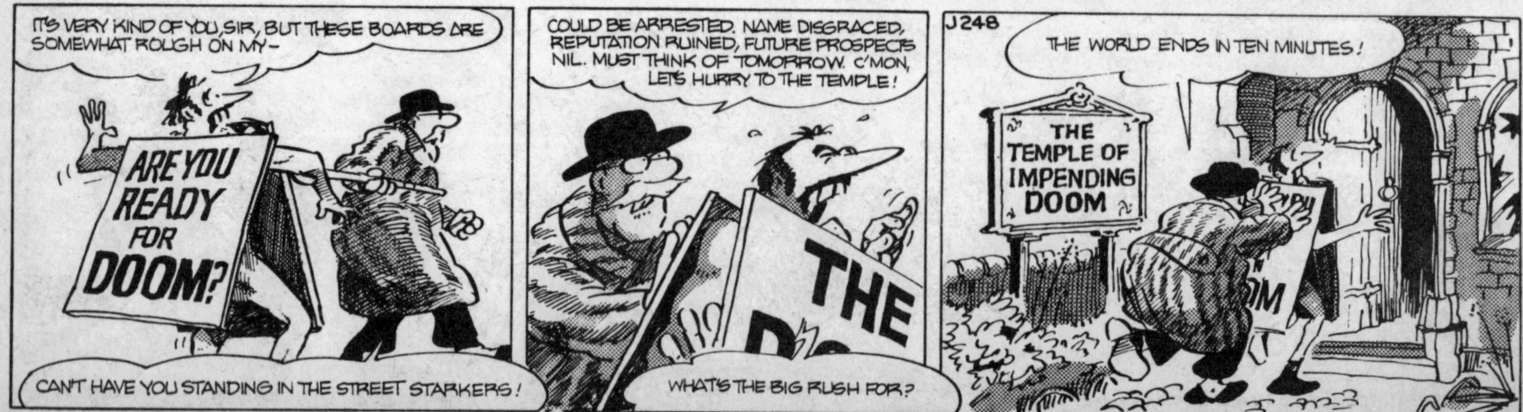
IT'S VERY KIND OF YOU, SIR, BUT THESE BOARDS ARE SOMEWHAT ROUGH ON MY–
ARE YOU READY FOR DOOM?
CAN'T HAVE YOU STANDING IN THE STREET STARKERS!
COULD BE ARRESTED. NAME DISGRACED, REPUTATION RUINED, FUTURE PROSPECTS NIL. MUST THINK OF TOMORROW. C'MON, LET'S HURRY TO THE TEMPLE!
THE
WHAT'S THE BIG RUSH FOR?
J 248
THE WORLD ENDS IN TEN MINUTES!
THE TEMPLE OF IMPENDING DOOM

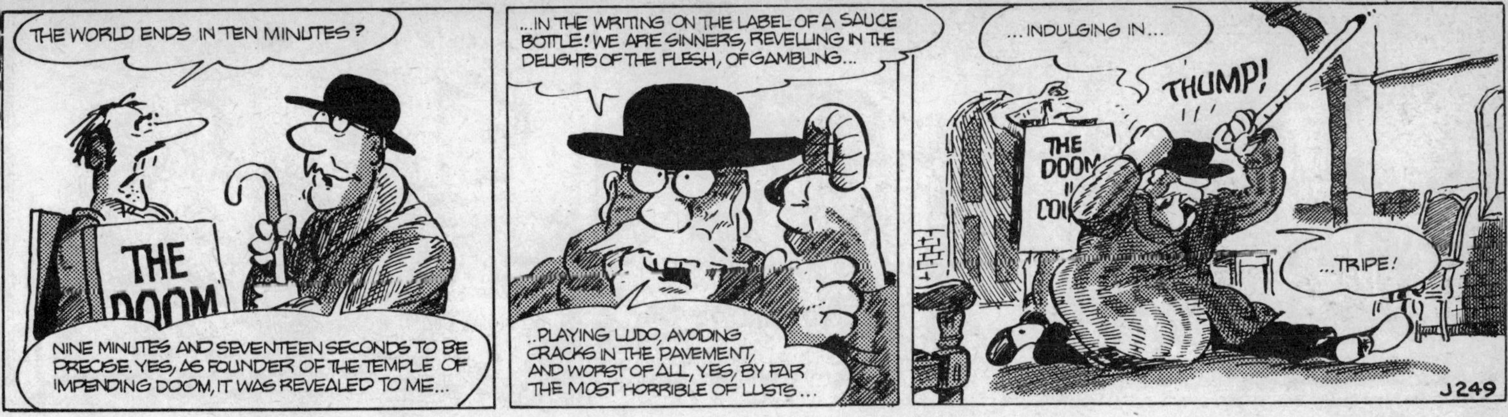
THE WORLD ENDS IN TEN MINUTES?
THE
NINE MINUTES AND SEVENTEEN SECONDS TO BE PRECISE. YES, AS FOUNDER OF THE TEMPLE OF IMPENDING DOOM, IT WAS REVEALED TO ME...
...IN THE WRITING ON THE LABEL OF A SAUCE BOTTLE! WE ARE SINNERS, REVELLING IN THE DELIGHTS OF THE FLESH, OF GAMBLING...
..PLAYING LUDO, AVOIDING CRACKS IN THE PAVEMENT, AND WORST OF ALL, YES, BY FAR THE MOST HORRIBLE OF LUSTS...
... INDULGING IN...
THUMP!
THE
...TRIPE!
J249

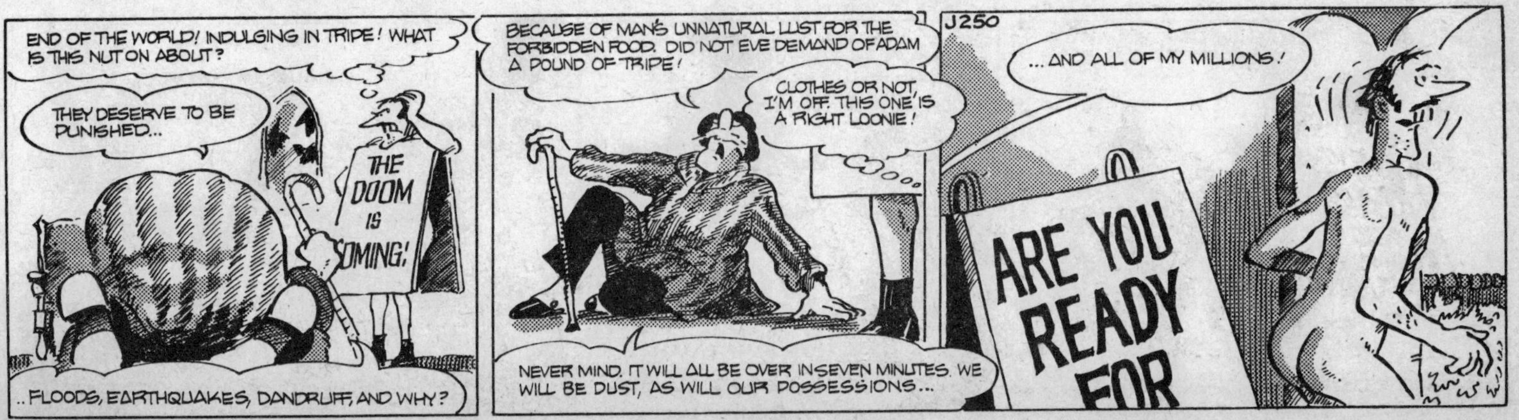
END OF THE WORLD! INDULGING IN TRIPE! WHAT IS THIS NUT ON ABOUT?
THEY DESERVE TO BE PUNISHED...
THE DOOM IS
.. FLOODS, EARTHQUAKES, DANDRUFF, AND WHY?
BECAUSE OF MAN'S UNNATURAL LUST FOR THE FORBIDDEN FOOD. DID NOT EVE DEMAND OF ADAM A POUND OF TRIPE!
CLOTHES OR NOT, I'M OFF. THIS ONE IS A RIGHT LOONIE!
NEVER MIND. IT WILL ALL BE OVER IN SEVEN MINUTES. WE WILL BE DUST, AS WILL OUR POSSESSIONS...
J250
... AND ALL OF MY MILLIONS!
ARE YOU READY

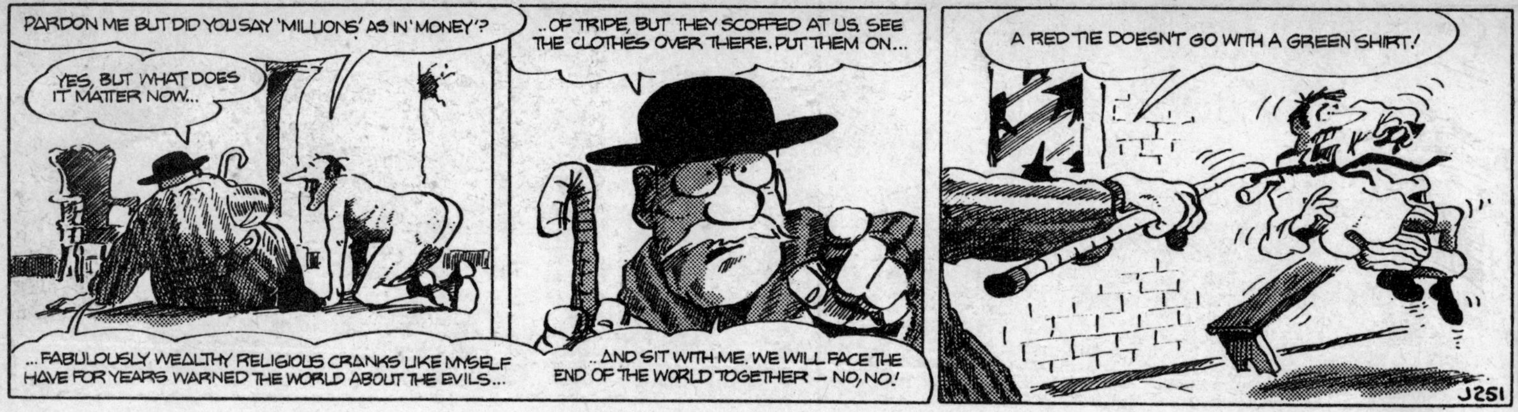
PARDON ME BUT DID YOU SAY 'MILLIONS' AS IN 'MONEY'?
YES, BUT WHAT DOES IT MATTER NOW...
...FABULOUSLY WEALTHY RELIGIOUS CRANKS LIKE MYSELF HAVE FOR YEARS WARNED THE WORLD ABOUT THE EVILS...
..OF TRIPE, BUT THEY SCOFFED AT US. SEE THE CLOTHES OVER THERE. PUT THEM ON...
..AND SIT WITH ME. WE WILL FACE THE END OF THE WORLD TOGETHER – NO, NO!
A RED TIE DOESN'T GO WITH A GREEN SHIRT!
J251

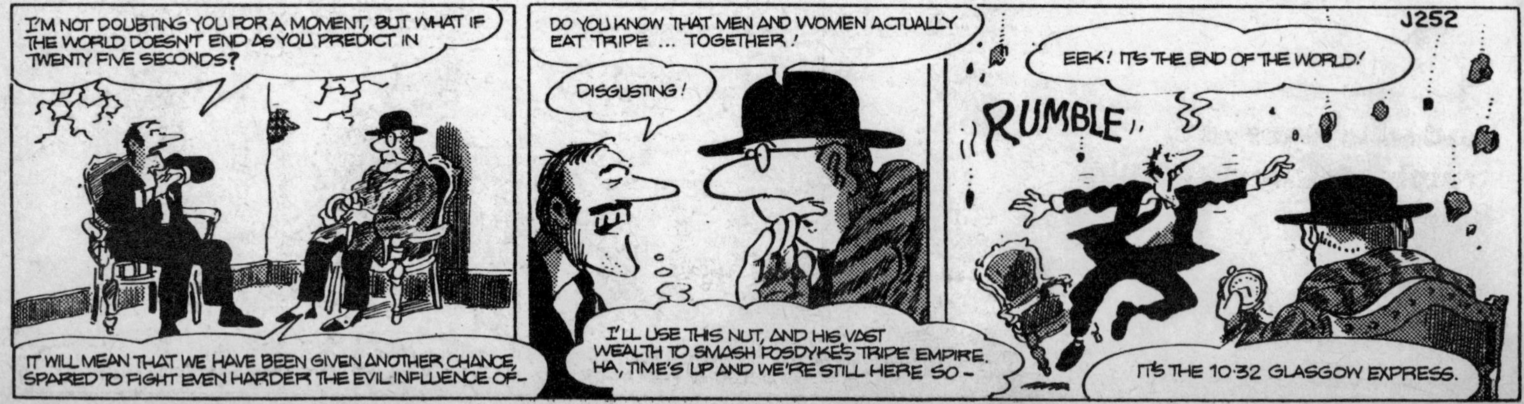
I'M NOT DOUBTING YOU FOR A MOMENT, BUT WHAT IF THE WORLD DOESN'T END AS YOU PREDICT IN TWENTY FIVE SECONDS?
IT WILL MEAN THAT WE HAVE BEEN GIVEN ANOTHER CHANCE, SPARED TO FIGHT EVEN HARDER THE EVIL INFLUENCE OF–
DO YOU KNOW THAT MEN AND WOMEN ACTUALLY EAT TRIPE ... TOGETHER!
DISGUSTING!
I'LL USE THIS NUT, AND HIS VAST WEALTH TO SMASH FOSDYKE'S TRIPE EMPIRE. HA, TIME'S UP AND WE'RE STILL HERE SO–
J252
EEK! IT'S THE END OF THE WORLD!
RUMBLE
IT'S THE 10·32 GLASGOW EXPRESS.

And at the British Embassy in Berlin...

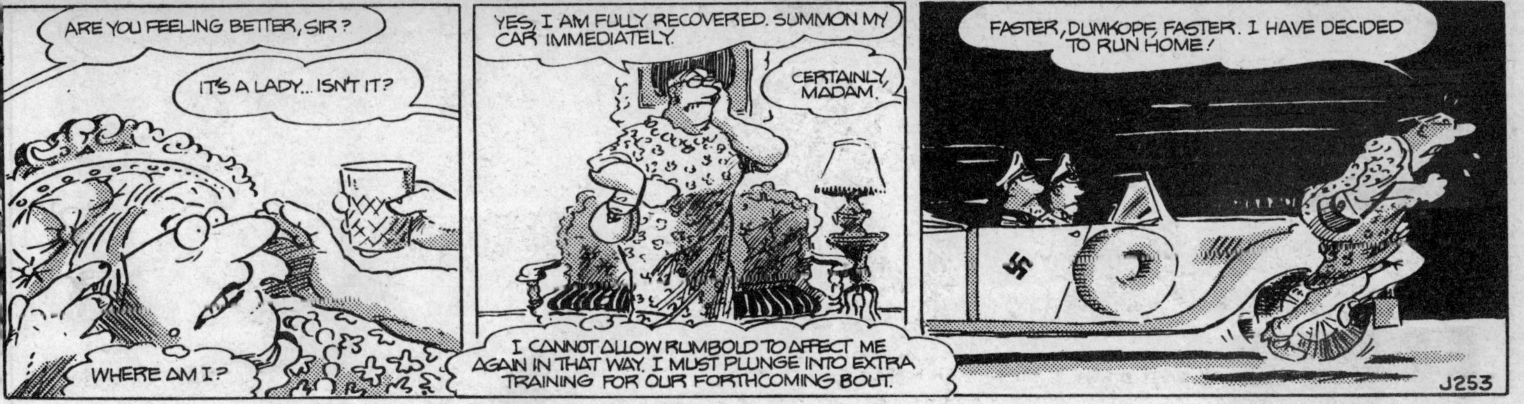
ARE YOU FEELING BETTER, SIR?
IT'S A LADY... ISN'T IT?
WHERE AM I?
YES, I AM FULLY RECOVERED. SUMMON MY CAR IMMEDIATELY.
CERTAINLY, MADAM.
I CANNOT ALLOW RUMBOLD TO AFFECT ME AGAIN IN THAT WAY. I MUST PLUNGE INTO EXTRA TRAINING FOR OUR FORTHCOMING BOUT.
FASTER, DUMKOPF, FASTER. I HAVE DECIDED TO RUN HOME!
J253

And so to rigorous training without further delay...

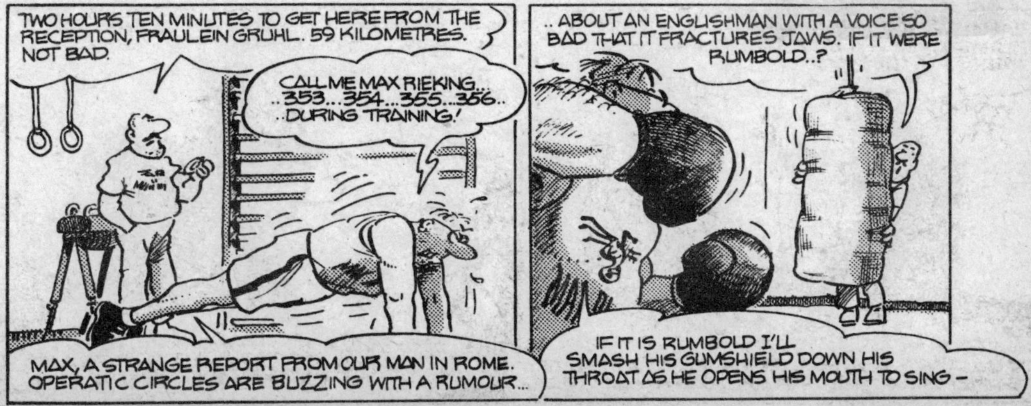
TWO HOURS TEN MINUTES TO GET HERE FROM THE RECEPTION, FRAULEIN GRUHL.. 59 KILOMETRES. NOT BAD.
CALL ME MAX RIEKING... ..353...354...355...356.. ..DURING TRAINING!
MAX, A STRANGE REPORT FROM OUR MAN IN ROME. OPERATIC CIRCLES ARE BUZZING WITH A RUMOUR...
..ABOUT AN ENGLISHMAN WITH A VOICE SO BAD THAT IT FRACTURES JAWS. IF IT WERE RUMBOLD..?
IF IT IS RUMBOLD I'LL SMASH HIS GUMSHIELD DOWN HIS THROAT AS HE OPENS HIS MOUTH TO SING –

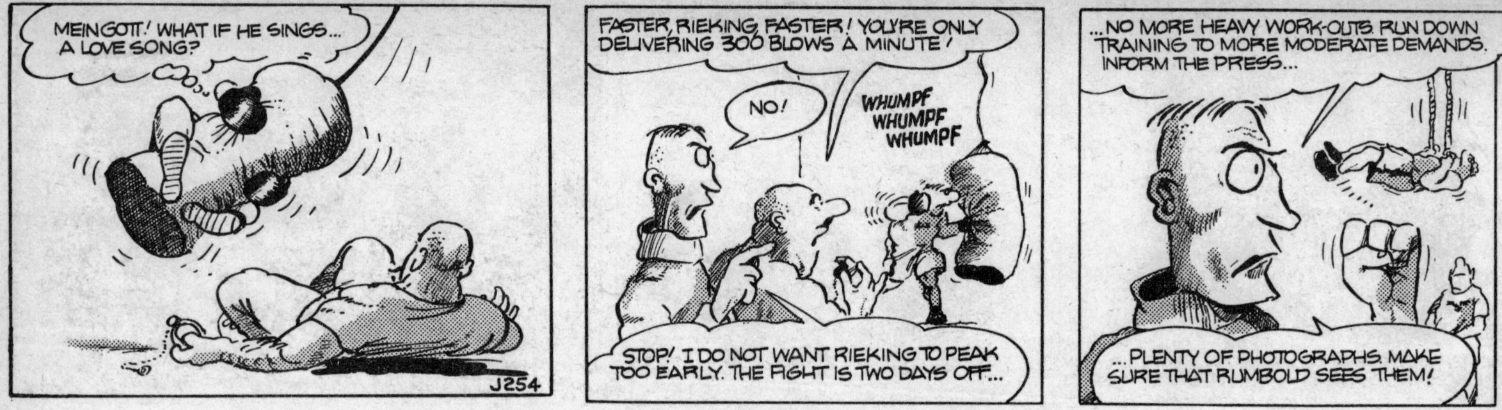
MEIN GOTT! WHAT IF HE SINGS... A LOVE SONG?
J254
FASTER, RIEKING, FASTER! YOU'RE ONLY DELIVERING 300 BLOWS A MINUTE!
NO!
WHUMPF WHUMPF WHUMPF
STOP! I DO NOT WANT RIEKING TO PEAK TOO EARLY. THE FIGHT IS TWO DAYS OFF...
...NO MORE HEAVY WORK-OUTS. RUN DOWN TRAINING TO MORE MODERATE DEMANDS. INFORM THE PRESS...
...PLENTY OF PHOTOGRAPHS. MAKE SURE THAT RUMBOLD SEES THEM!

In the Fosdyke hotel suite next morning...

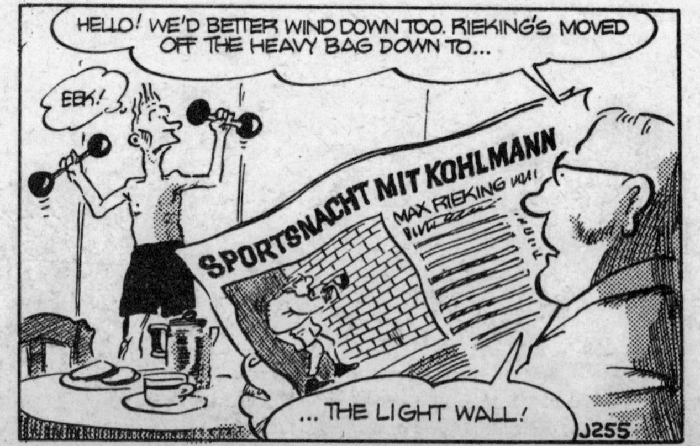
HELLO! WE'D BETTER WIND DOWN TOO. RIEKING'S MOVED OFF THE HEAVY BAG DOWN TO...
EEK!
SPORTSNACHT MIT KOHLMANN
MAX RIEKING
... THE LIGHT WALL!
J255

And so the excitement mounts...

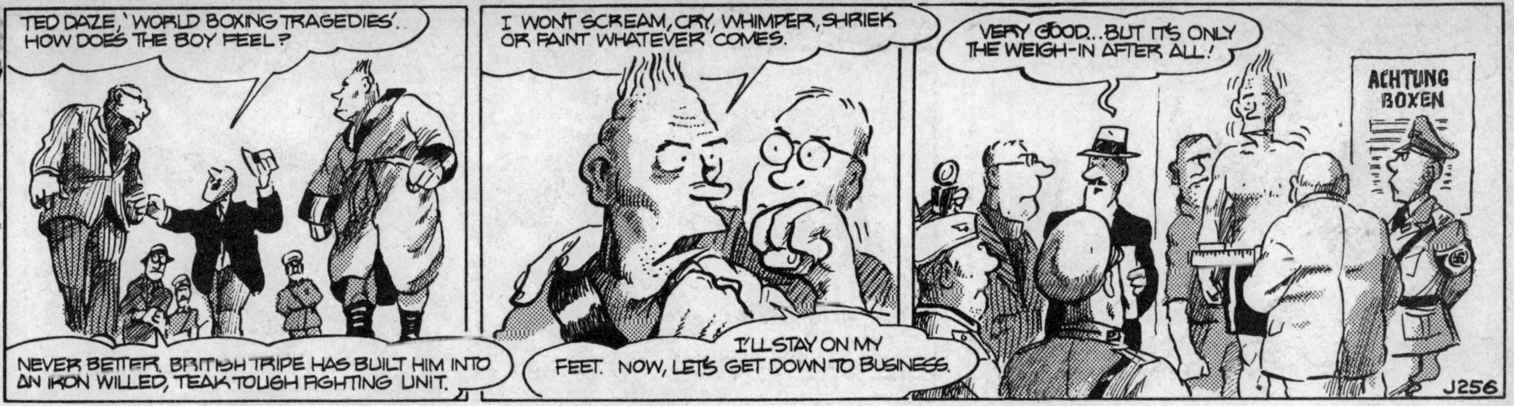
TED DAZE, 'WORLD BOXING TRAGEDIES'. HOW DOES THE BOY FEEL?
NEVER BETTER. BRITISH TRIPE HAS BUILT HIM INTO AN IRON WILLED, TEAK TOUGH FIGHTING UNIT.
I WON'T SCREAM, CRY, WHIMPER, SHRIEK OR FAINT WHATEVER COMES.
I'LL STAY ON MY FEET. NOW, LET'S GET DOWN TO BUSINESS.
VERY GOOD... BUT IT'S ONLY THE WEIGH-IN AFTER ALL!
ACHTUNG BOXEN
J256

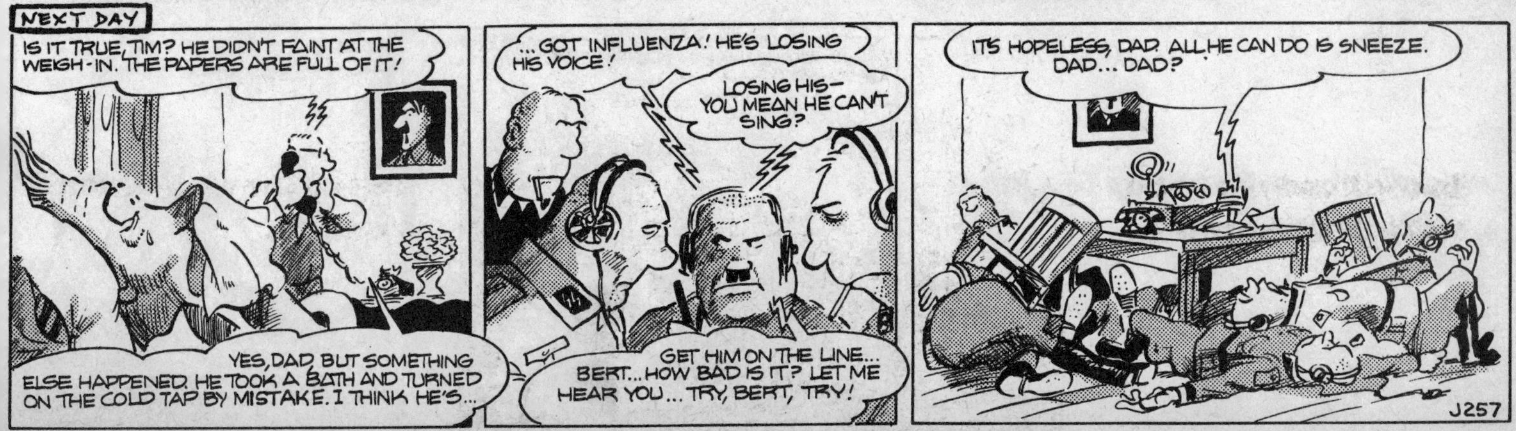
NEXT DAY
IS IT TRUE, TIM? HE DIDN'T FAINT AT THE WEIGH-IN. THE PAPERS ARE FULL OF IT!
YES, DAD. BUT SOMETHING ELSE HAPPENED. HE TOOK A BATH AND TURNED ON THE COLD TAP BY MISTAKE. I THINK HE'S...
...GOT INFLUENZA! HE'S LOSING HIS VOICE!
LOSING HIS— YOU MEAN HE CAN'T SING?
GET HIM ON THE LINE... BERT... HOW BAD IS IT? LET ME HEAR YOU... TRY, BERT, TRY!
IT'S HOPELESS, DAD. ALL HE CAN DO IS SNEEZE. DAD... DAD?
J257

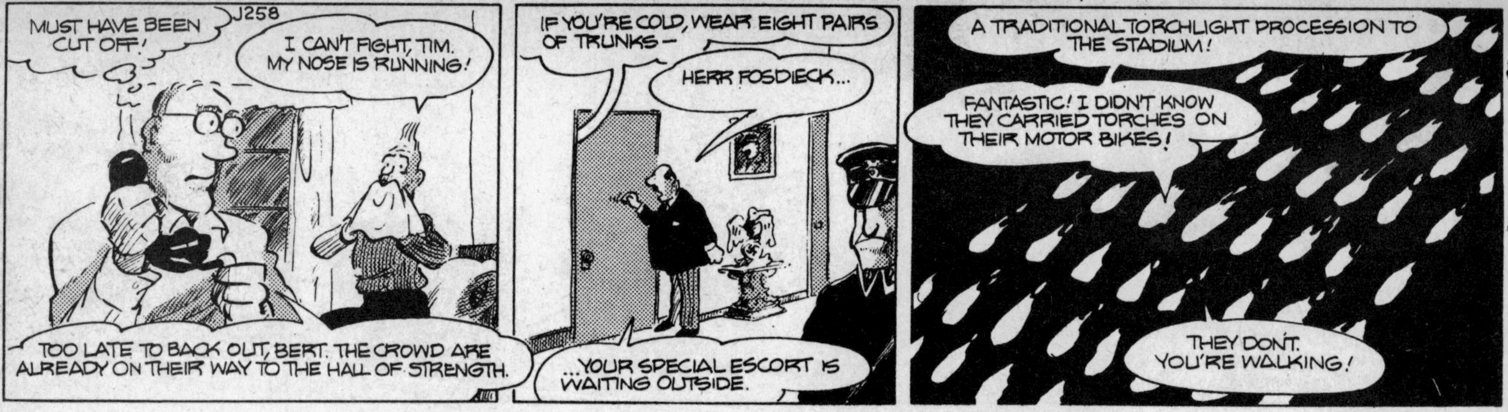
J258
MUST HAVE BEEN CUT OFF!
I CAN'T FIGHT, TIM. MY NOSE IS RUNNING!
TOO LATE TO BACK OUT, BERT. THE CROWD ARE ALREADY ON THEIR WAY TO THE HALL OF STRENGTH.
IF YOU'RE COLD, WEAR EIGHT PAIRS OF TRUNKS —
HERR FOSDIECK...
...YOUR SPECIAL ESCORT IS WAITING OUTSIDE.
A TRADITIONAL TORCHLIGHT PROCESSION TO THE STADIUM!
FANTASTIC! I DIDN'T KNOW THEY CARRIED TORCHES ON THEIR MOTOR BIKES!
THEY DON'T. YOU'RE WALKING!

Meanwhile, cruising up the jungle-clad Umptine River...

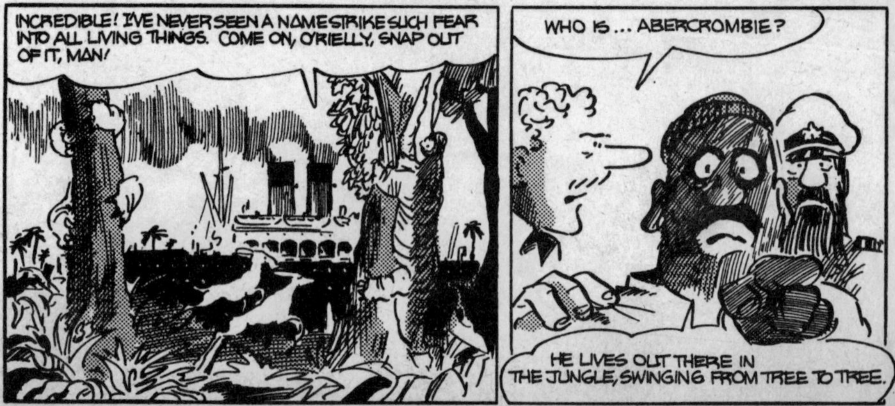
INCREDIBLE! I'VE NEVER SEEN A NAME STRIKE SUCH FEAR INTO ALL LIVING THINGS. COME ON, O'RIELLY, SNAP OUT OF IT, MAN!
WHO IS ... ABERCROMBIE?
HE LIVES OUT THERE IN THE JUNGLE, SWINGING FROM TREE TO TREE.

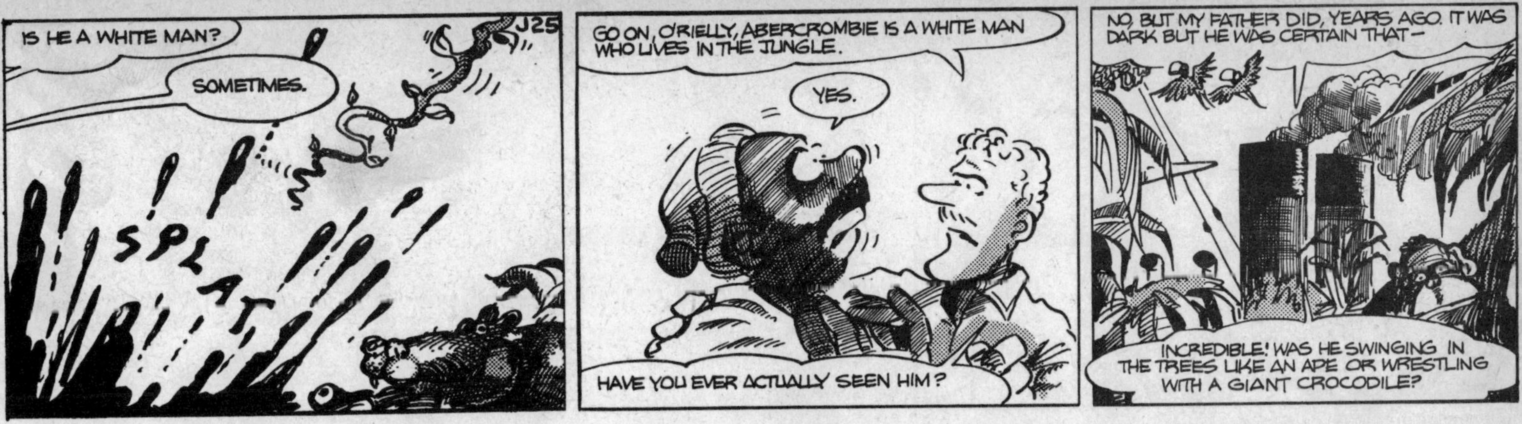
J25
IS HE A WHITE MAN?
SOMETIMES.
SPLAT
GO ON, O'RIELLY, ABERCROMBIE IS A WHITE MAN WHO LIVES IN THE JUNGLE.
YES.
HAVE YOU EVER ACTUALLY SEEN HIM?
NO, BUT MY FATHER DID, YEARS AGO. IT WAS DARK BUT HE WAS CERTAIN THAT—
INCREDIBLE! WAS HE SWINGING IN THE TREES LIKE AN APE OR WRESTLING WITH A GIANT CROCODILE?

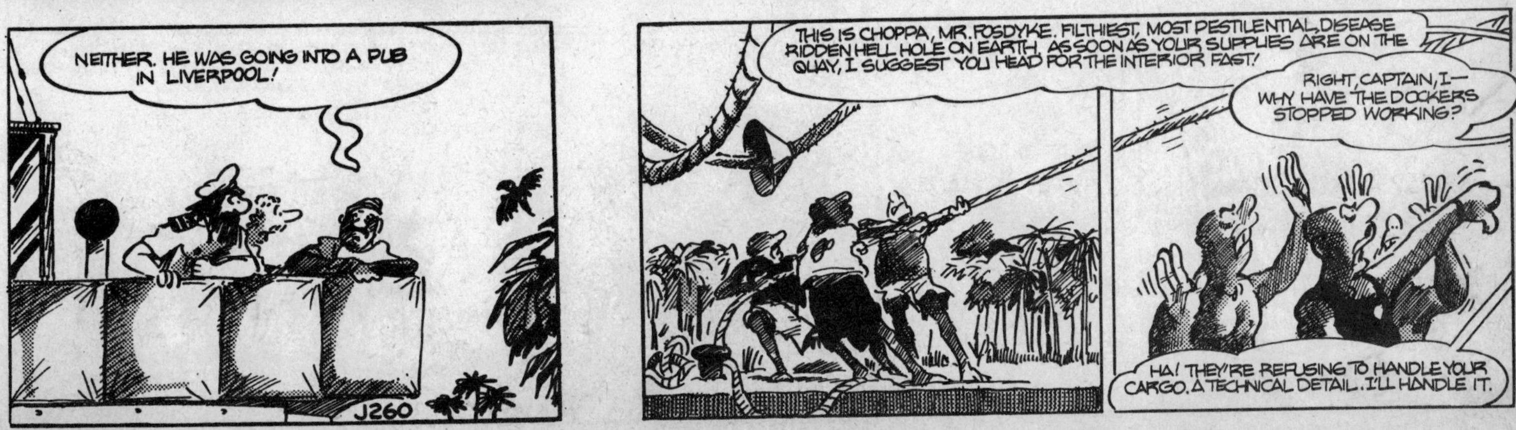
NEITHER. HE WAS GOING INTO A PUB IN LIVERPOOL!
J260
THIS IS CHOPPA, MR. FOSDYKE. FILTHIEST, MOST PESTILENTIAL, DISEASE RIDDEN HELL HOLE ON EARTH. AS SOON AS YOUR SUPPLIES ARE ON THE QUAY, I SUGGEST YOU HEAD FOR THE INTERIOR FAST!
RIGHT, CAPTAIN, I— WHY HAVE THE DOCKERS STOPPED WORKING?
HA! THEY'RE REFUSING TO HANDLE YOUR CARGO. A TECHNICAL DETAIL. I'LL HANDLE IT.

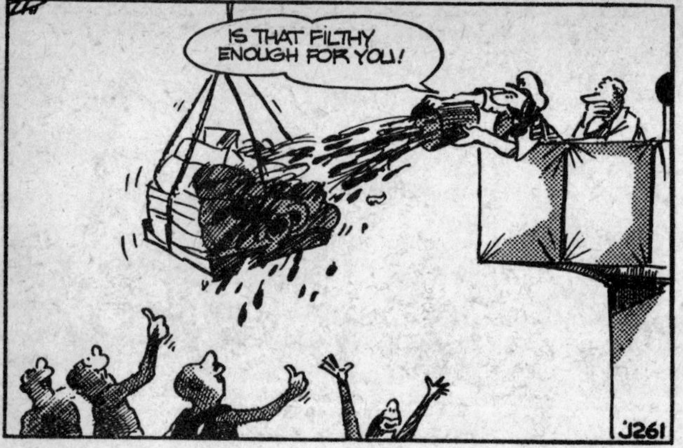
IS THAT FILTHY ENOUGH FOR YOU!
J261

Some hours later…

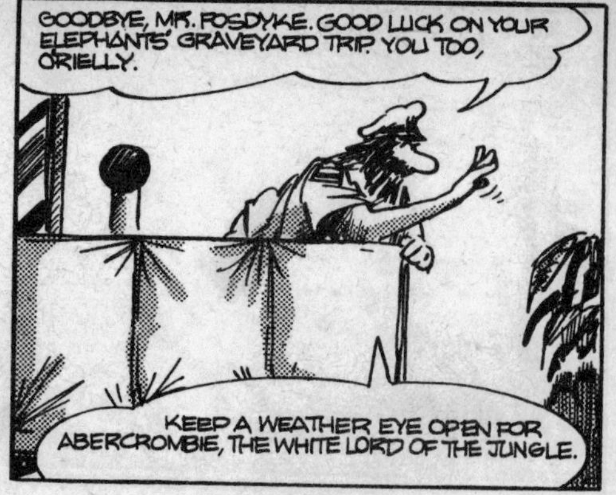
GOODBYE, MR. FOSDYKE. GOOD LUCK ON YOUR ELEPHANTS' GRAVEYARD TRIP. YOU TOO, O'RIELLY.
KEEP A WEATHER EYE OPEN FOR ABERCROMBIE, THE WHITE LORD OF THE JUNGLE.

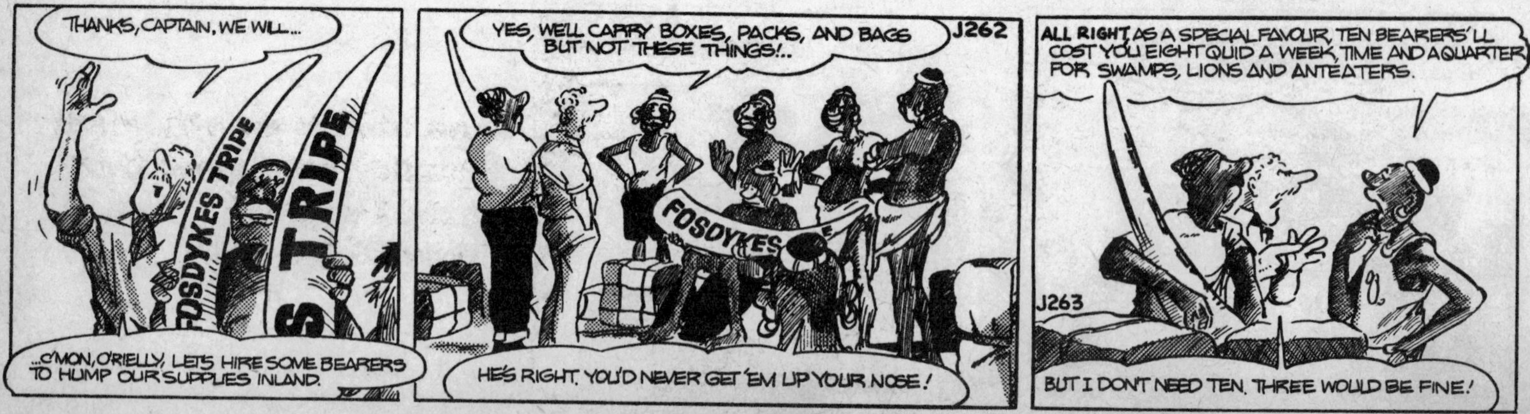
THANKS, CAPTAIN, WE WILL...
FOSDYKES TRIPE
…C'MON, O'RIELLY, LET'S HIRE SOME BEARERS TO HUMP OUR SUPPLIES INLAND.
J262
YES, WELL CARRY BOXES, PACKS, AND BAGS BUT NOT THESE THINGS!..
FOSDYKES
HE'S RIGHT. YOU'D NEVER GET 'EM UP YOUR NOSE!
ALL RIGHT, AS A SPECIAL FAVOUR, TEN BEARERS'LL COST YOU EIGHT QUID A WEEK, TIME AND A QUARTER FOR SWAMPS, LIONS AND ANTEATERS.
J263
BUT I DON'T NEED TEN. THREE WOULD BE FINE!

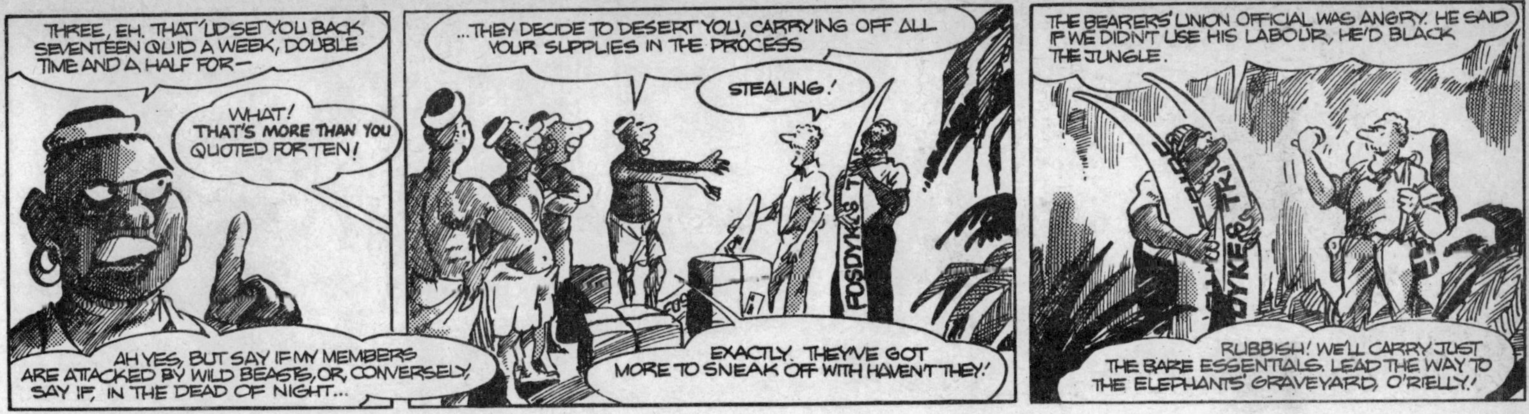
THREE, EH. THAT'UD SET YOU BACK SEVENTEEN QUID A WEEK, DOUBLE TIME AND A HALF FOR—
WHAT! THAT'S MORE THAN YOU QUOTED FOR TEN!
AH YES, BUT SAY IF MY MEMBERS ARE ATTACKED BY WILD BEASTS, OR, CONVERSELY, SAY IF, IN THE DEAD OF NIGHT...
...THEY DECIDE TO DESERT YOU, CARRYING OFF ALL YOUR SUPPLIES IN THE PROCESS
STEALING!
EXACTLY. THEY'VE GOT MORE TO SNEAK OFF WITH HAVEN'T THEY!
THE BEARERS' UNION OFFICIAL WAS ANGRY. HE SAID IF WE DIDN'T USE HIS LABOUR, HE'D BLACK THE JUNGLE.
RUBBISH! WE'LL CARRY JUST THE BARE ESSENTIALS. LEAD THE WAY TO THE ELEPHANTS' GRAVEYARD, O'RIELLY!

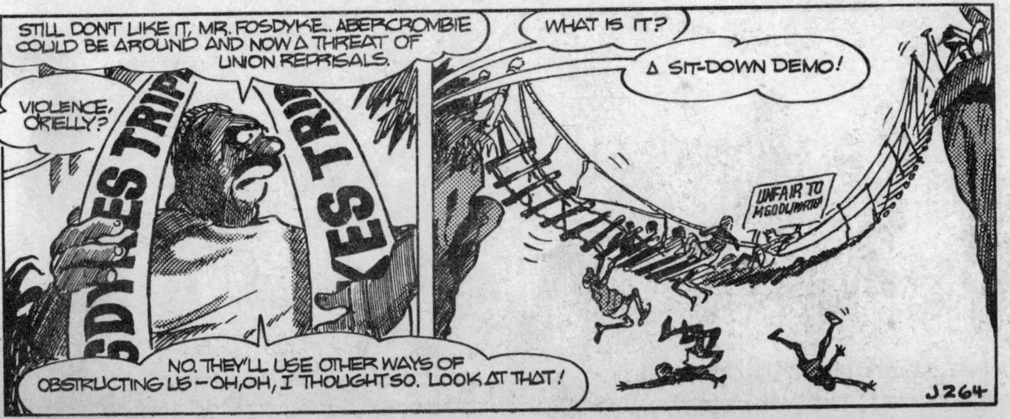
STILL DON'T LIKE IT, MR. FOSDYKE.. ABERCROMBIE COULD BE AROUND AND NOW A THREAT OF UNION REPRISALS.
VIOLENCE, O'RIELLY?
NO. THEY'LL USE OTHER WAYS OF OBSTRUCTING US — OH, OH, I THOUGHT SO. LOOK AT THAT!
WHAT IS IT?
A SIT-DOWN DEMO!
UNFAIR TO
J264

And what of the villainous Ditchley, scheming afresh in the Temple of Impending Doom?

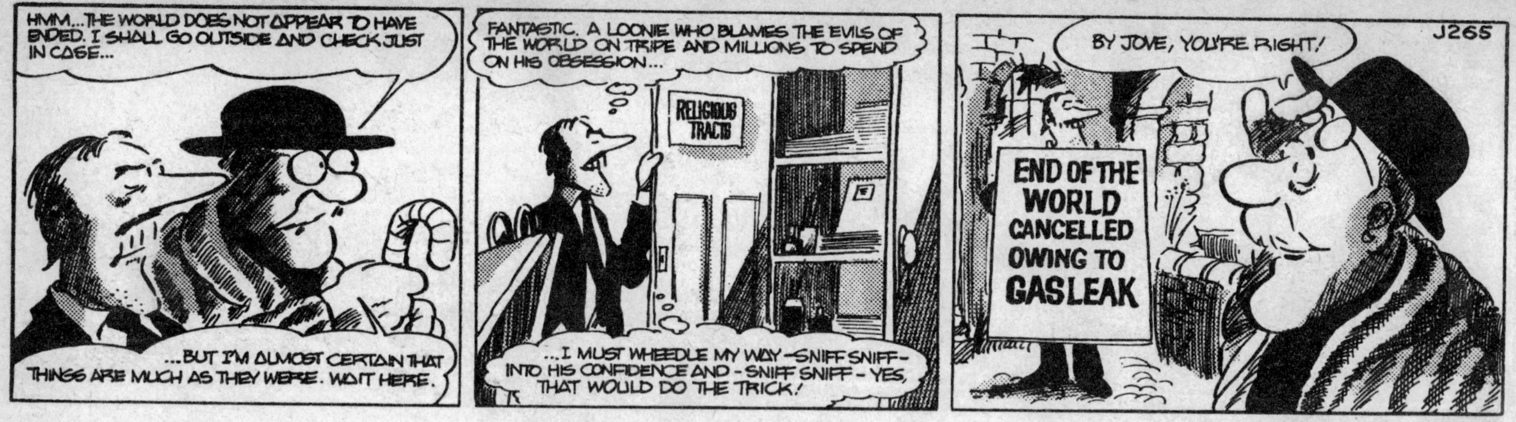
HMM... THE WORLD DOES NOT APPEAR TO HAVE ENDED. I SHALL GO OUTSIDE AND CHECK JUST IN CASE...
...BUT I'M ALMOST CERTAIN THAT THINGS ARE MUCH AS THEY WERE. WAIT HERE.
FANTASTIC. A LOONIE WHO BLAMES THE EVILS OF THE WORLD ON TRIPE AND MILLIONS TO SPEND ON HIS OBSESSION...
RELIGIOUS TRACTS
...I MUST WHEEDLE MY WAY —SNIFF SNIFF— INTO HIS CONFIDENCE AND - SNIFF SNIFF - YES, THAT WOULD DO THE TRICK!
BY JOVE, YOU'RE RIGHT!
J265
END OF THE WORLD CANCELLED OWING TO GAS LEAK

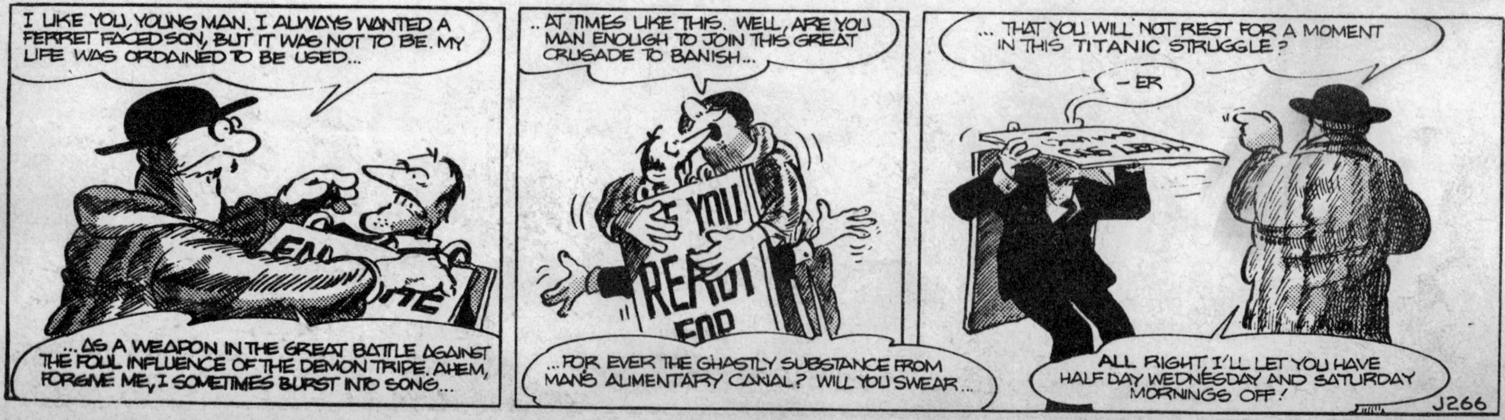
I LIKE YOU, YOUNG MAN. I ALWAYS WANTED A FERRET FACED SON, BUT IT WAS NOT TO BE. MY LIFE WAS ORDAINED TO BE USED...
...AS A WEAPON IN THE GREAT BATTLE AGAINST THE FOUL INFLUENCE OF THE DEMON TRIPE. AHEM, FORGIVE ME, I SOMETIMES BURST INTO SONG...
..AT TIMES LIKE THIS. WELL, ARE YOU MAN ENOUGH TO JOIN THIS GREAT CRUSADE TO BANISH...
...FOR EVER THE GHASTLY SUBSTANCE FROM MAN'S ALIMENTARY CANAL? WILL YOU SWEAR...
... THAT YOU WILL NOT REST FOR A MOMENT IN THIS TITANIC STRUGGLE?
- ER
ALL RIGHT, I'LL LET YOU HAVE HALF DAY WEDNESDAY AND SATURDAY MORNINGS OFF!
J266

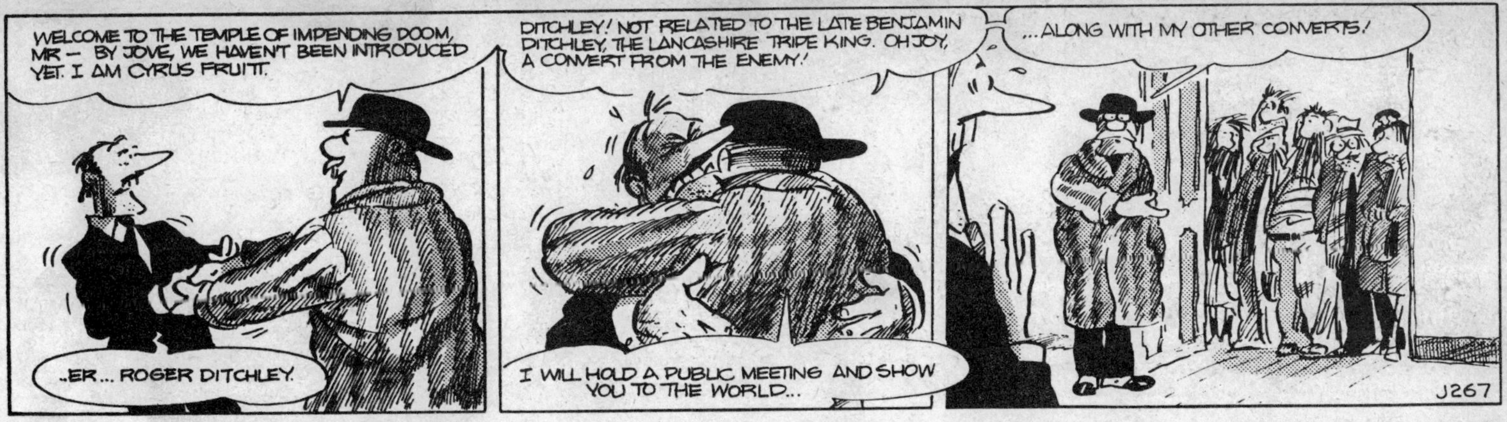
WELCOME TO THE TEMPLE OF IMPENDING DOOM, MR — BY JOVE, WE HAVEN'T BEEN INTRODUCED YET. I AM CYRUS FRUITT.
..ER... ROGER DITCHLEY.
DITCHLEY! NOT RELATED TO THE LATE BENJAMIN DITCHLEY, THE LANCASHIRE TRIPE KING. OH JOY, A CONVERT FROM THE ENEMY!
I WILL HOLD A PUBLIC MEETING AND SHOW YOU TO THE WORLD...
...ALONG WITH MY OTHER CONVERTS!
J267

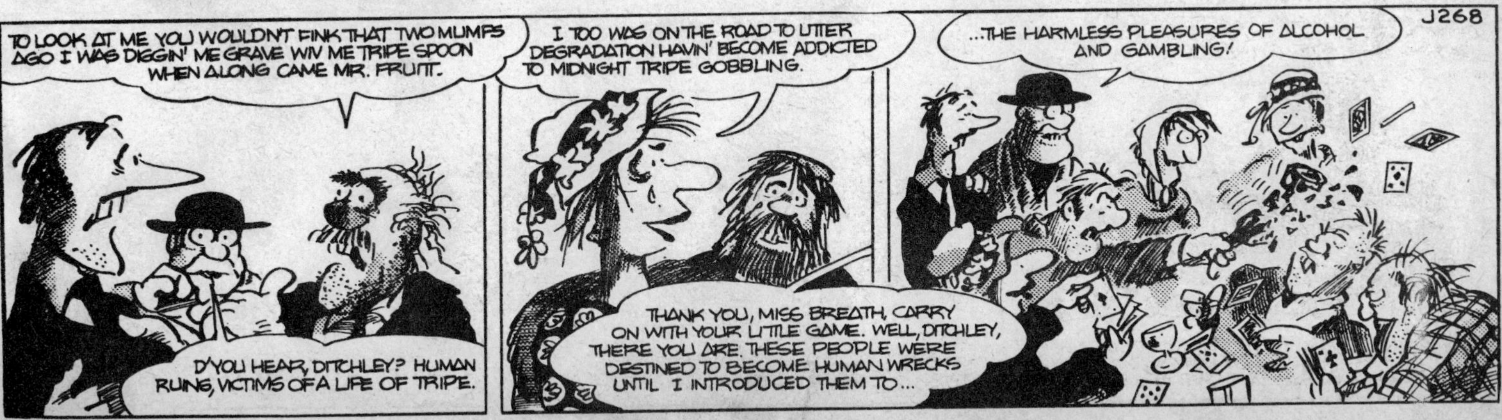
J268
TO LOOK AT ME YOU WOULDN'T FINK THAT TWO MUMFS AGO I WAS DIGGIN' ME GRAVE WIV ME TRIPE SPOON WHEN ALONG CAME MR. FRUITT.
D'YOU HEAR, DITCHLEY? HUMAN RUINS, VICTIMS OF A LIFE OF TRIPE.
I TOO WAS ON THE ROAD TO UTTER DEGRADATION HAVIN' BECOME ADDICTED TO MIDNIGHT TRIPE GOBBLING.
THANK YOU, MISS BREATH, CARRY ON WITH YOUR LITTLE GAME. WELL, DITCHLEY, THERE YOU ARE. THESE PEOPLE WERE DESTINED TO BECOME HUMAN WRECKS UNTIL I INTRODUCED THEM TO...
...THE HARMLESS PLEASURES OF ALCOHOL AND GAMBLING!

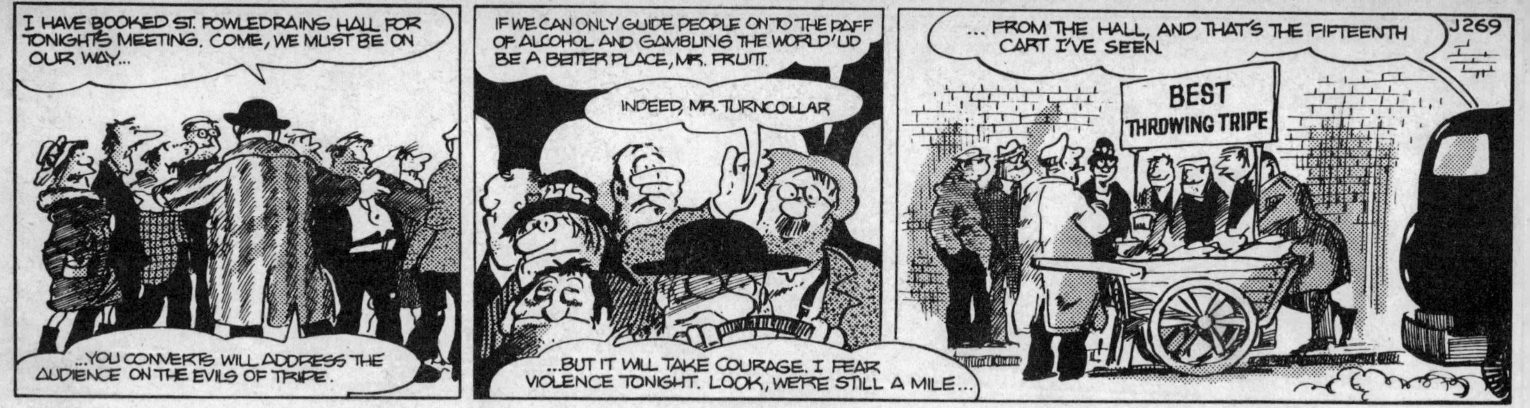
I HAVE BOOKED ST. POWLEDRAINS HALL FOR TONIGHT'S MEETING. COME, WE MUST BE ON OUR WAY...
...YOU CONVERTS WILL ADDRESS THE AUDIENCE ON THE EVILS OF TRIPE.
IF WE CAN ONLY GUIDE PEOPLE ON TO THE PAFF OF ALCOHOL AND GAMBLING THE WORLD'UD BE A BETTER PLACE, MR. FRUITT.
INDEED, MR. TURNCOLLAR
...BUT IT WILL TAKE COURAGE. I FEAR VIOLENCE TONIGHT. LOOK, WE'RE STILL A MILE...
... FROM THE HALL, AND THAT'S THE FIFTEENTH CART I'VE SEEN.
J269
BEST THROWING TRIPE

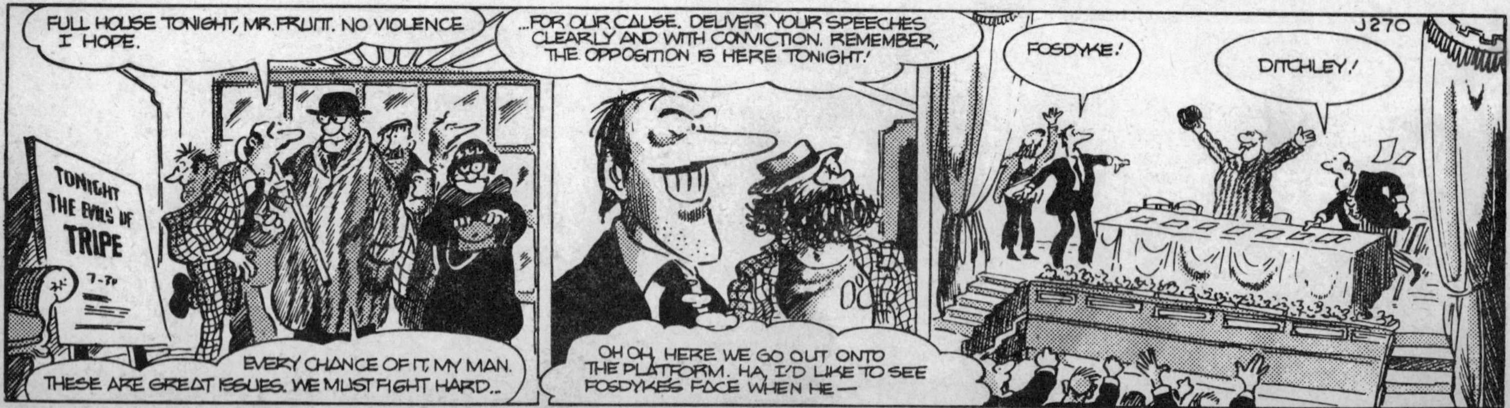
FULL HOUSE TONIGHT, MR. FRUITT. NO VIOLENCE I HOPE.
TONIGHT THE EVILS OF TRIPE
EVERY CHANCE OF IT, MY MAN. THESE ARE GREAT ISSUES. WE MUST FIGHT HARD..
...FOR OUR CAUSE. DELIVER YOUR SPEECHES CLEARLY AND WITH CONVICTION. REMEMBER, THE OPPOSITION IS HERE TONIGHT!
OH OH, HERE WE GO OUT ONTO THE PLATFORM. HA, I'D LIKE TO SEE FOSDYKE'S FACE WHEN HE—
J270
FOSDYKE!
DITCHLEY!

And at the Berlin Hall of Strength...

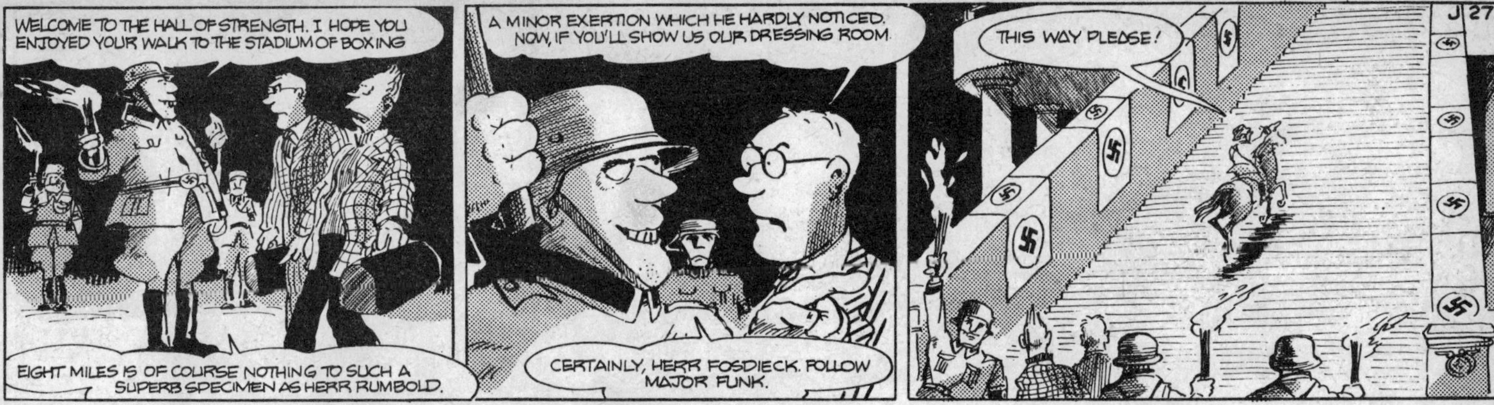
WELCOME TO THE HALL OF STRENGTH. I HOPE YOU ENJOYED YOUR WALK TO THE STADIUM OF BOXING
EIGHT MILES IS OF COURSE NOTHING TO SUCH A SUPERB SPECIMEN AS HERR RUMBOLD.
A MINOR EXERTION WHICH HE HARDLY NOTICED. NOW, IF YOU'LL SHOW US OUR DRESSING ROOM.
CERTAINLY, HERR FOSDIECK. FOLLOW MAJOR FUNK.
J 271
THIS WAY PLEASE!

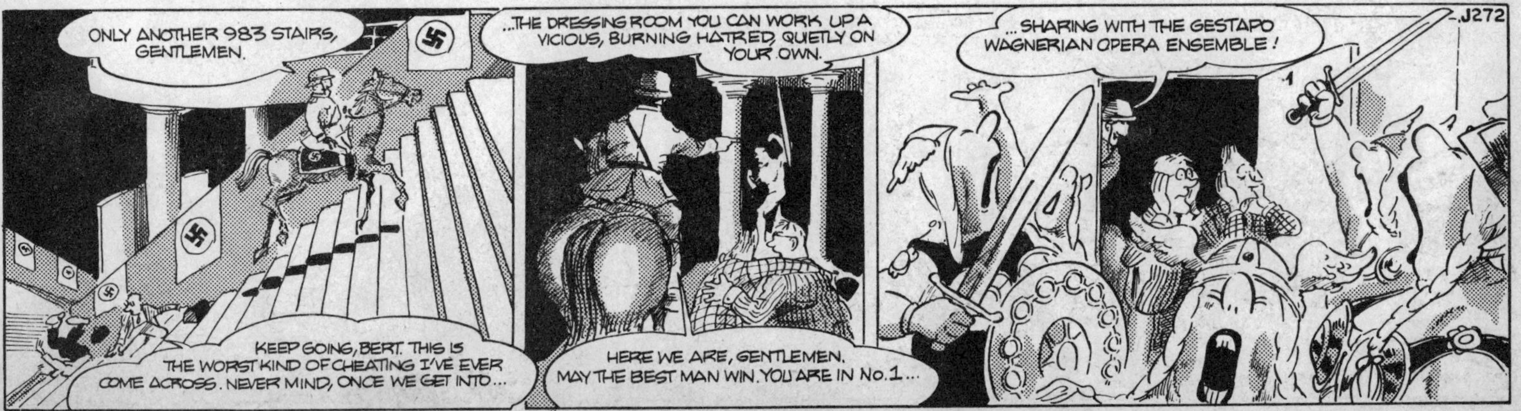
J272
ONLY ANOTHER 983 STAIRS, GENTLEMEN.
KEEP GOING, BERT. THIS IS THE WORST KIND OF CHEATING I'VE EVER COME ACROSS. NEVER MIND, ONCE WE GET INTO...
...THE DRESSING ROOM YOU CAN WORK UP A VICIOUS, BURNING HATRED, QUIETLY ON YOUR OWN.
HERE WE ARE, GENTLEMEN. MAY THE BEST MAN WIN. YOU ARE IN No.1...
1
...SHARING WITH THE GESTAPO WAGNERIAN OPERA ENSEMBLE!

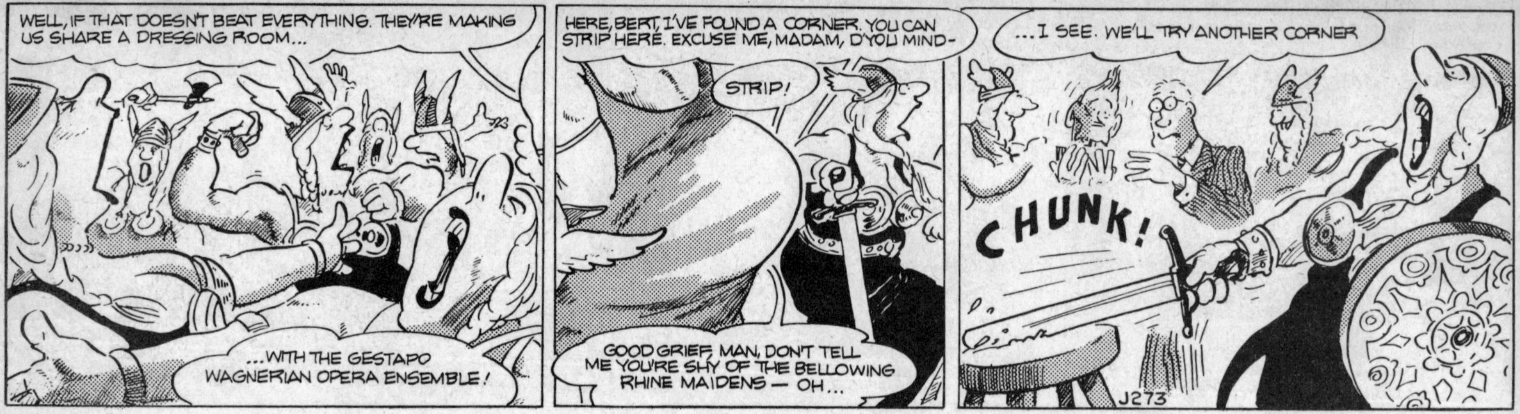
WELL, IF THAT DOESN'T BEAT EVERYTHING. THEY'RE MAKING US SHARE A DRESSING ROOM...
...WITH THE GESTAPO WAGNERIAN OPERA ENSEMBLE!
HERE, BERT, I'VE FOUND A CORNER. YOU CAN STRIP HERE. EXCUSE ME, MADAM, D'YOU MIND-
STRIP!
GOOD GRIEF, MAN, DON'T TELL ME YOU'RE SHY OF THE BELLOWING RHINE MAIDENS — OH...
...I SEE. WE'LL TRY ANOTHER CORNER
CHUNK!
J273

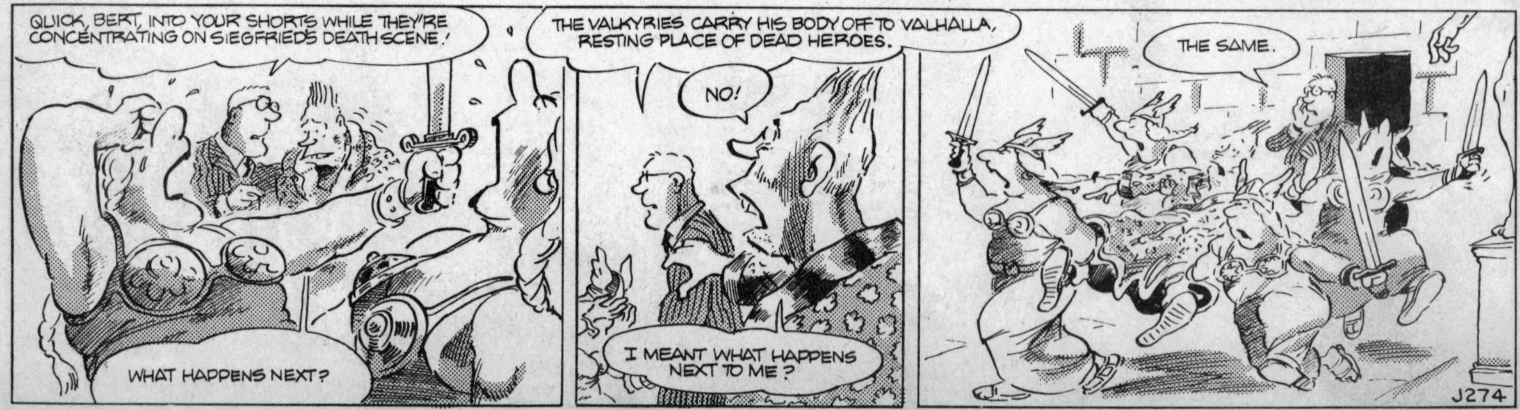
QUICK, BERT, INTO YOUR SHORTS WHILE THEY'RE CONCENTRATING ON SIEGFRIED'S DEATH SCENE!
WHAT HAPPENS NEXT?
THE VALKYRIES CARRY HIS BODY OFF TO VALHALLA, RESTING PLACE OF DEAD HEROES.
NO!
I MEANT WHAT HAPPENS NEXT TO ME?
THE SAME.
J274

In the boxing arena...

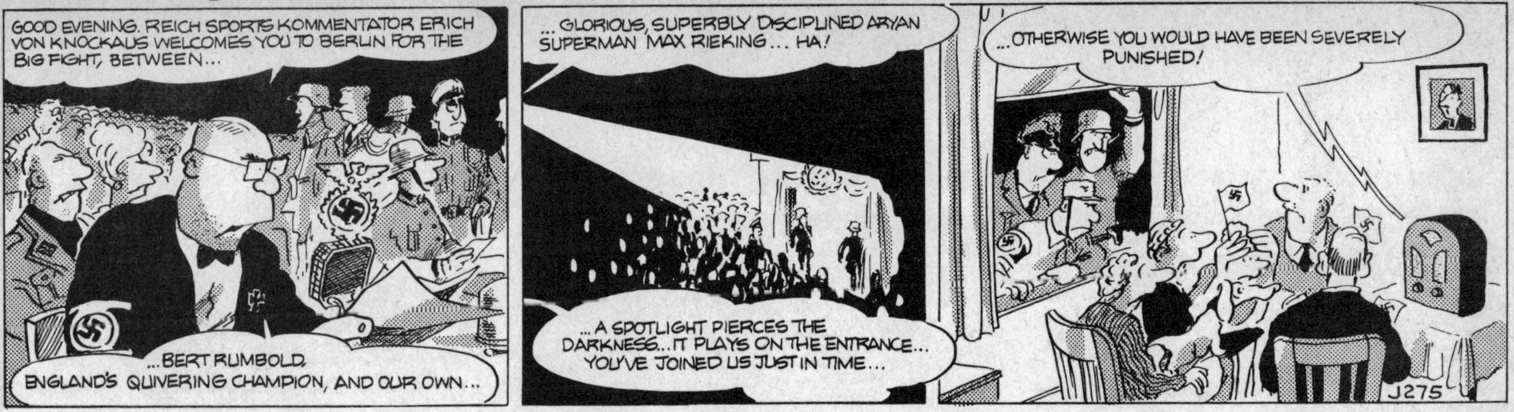
GOOD EVENING. REICH SPORTS KOMMENTATOR ERICH VON KNOCKAUS WELCOMES YOU TO BERLIN FOR THE BIG FIGHT, BETWEEN...
...BERT RUMBOLD, ENGLAND'S QUIVERING CHAMPION, AND OUR OWN...
...GLORIOUS, SUPERBLY DISCIPLINED ARYAN SUPERMAN MAX RIEKING... HA!
...A SPOTLIGHT PIERCES THE DARKNESS...IT PLAYS ON THE ENTRANCE... YOU'VE JOINED US JUST IN TIME...
...OTHERWISE YOU WOULD HAVE BEEN SEVERELY PUNISHED!
J275

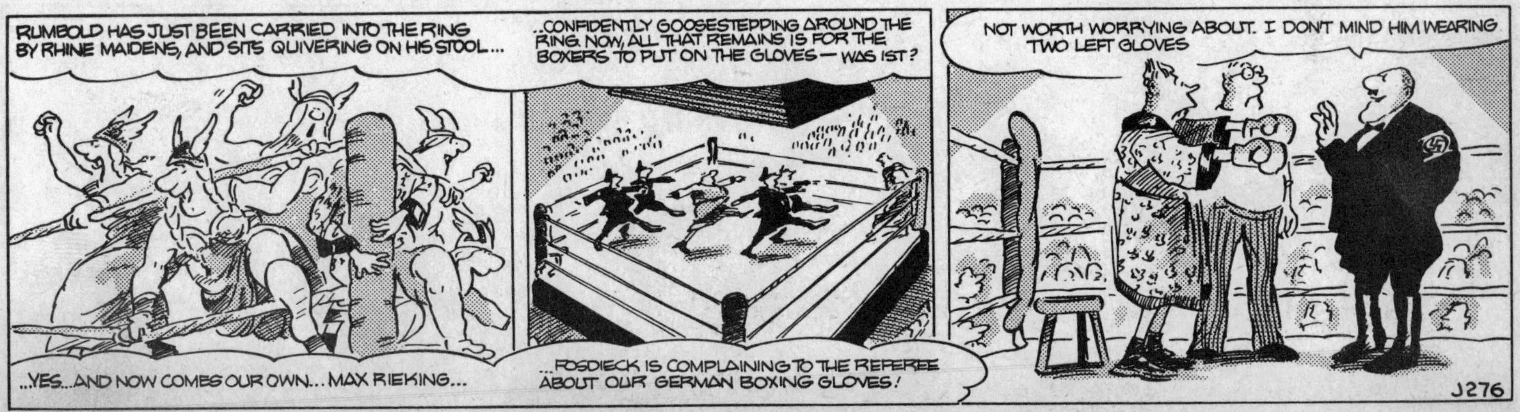
RUMBOLD HAS JUST BEEN CARRIED INTO THE RING BY RHINE MAIDENS, AND SITS QUIVERING ON HIS STOOL...
...YES...AND NOW COMES OUR OWN... MAX RIEKING...
...CONFIDENTLY GOOSESTEPPING AROUND THE RING. NOW, ALL THAT REMAINS IS FOR THE BOXERS TO PUT ON THE GLOVES — WAS IST?
...FOSDIECK IS COMPLAINING TO THE REFEREE ABOUT OUR GERMAN BOXING GLOVES!
NOT WORTH WORRYING ABOUT. I DON'T MIND HIM WEARING TWO LEFT GLOVES
J276

Meanwhile, Albert and O'Rielly are forging through the African jungle, beset by foes and unseen terrors, bent on an impossible goal.

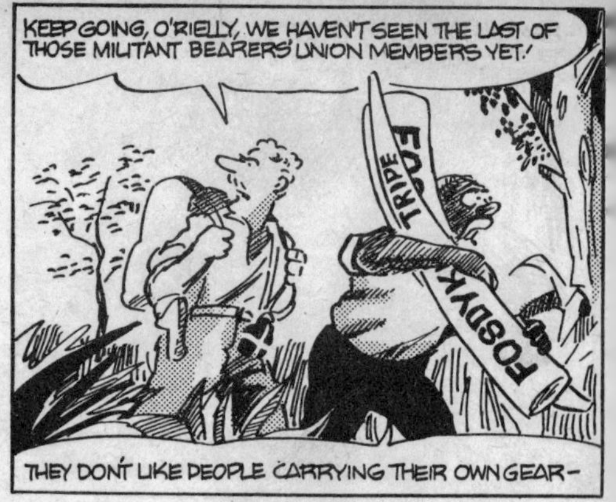

KEEP GOING, O'RIELLY, WE HAVEN'T SEEN THE LAST OF THOSE MILITANT BEARERS' UNION MEMBERS YET!
TRIPE
THEY DON'T LIKE PEOPLE CARRYING THEIR OWN GEAR–

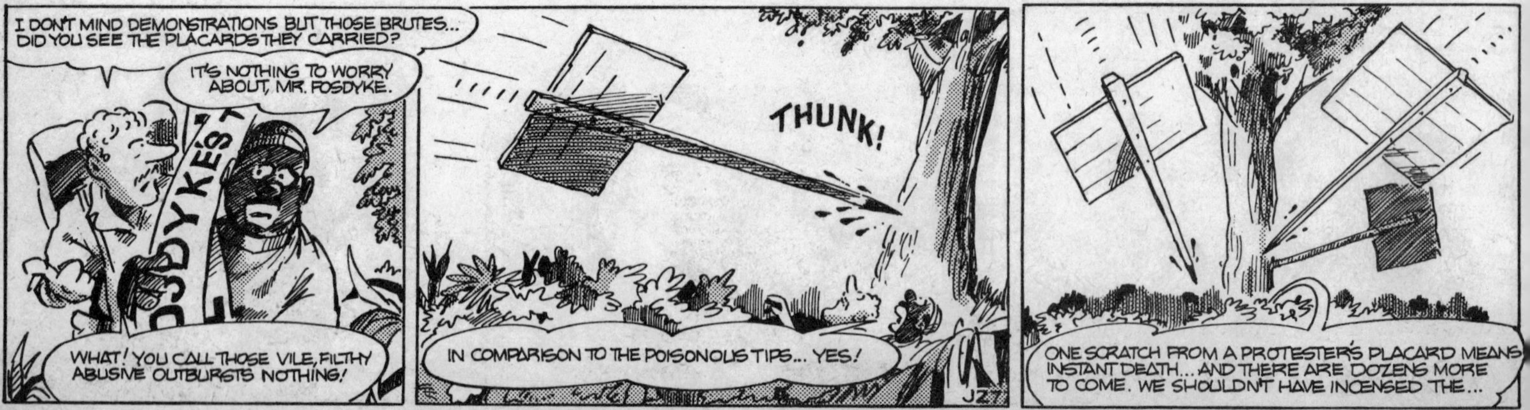

I DON'T MIND DEMONSTRATIONS BUT THOSE BRUTES... DID YOU SEE THE PLACARDS THEY CARRIED?
IT'S NOTHING TO WORRY ABOUT, MR. FOSDYKE.
WHAT! YOU CALL THOSE VILE, FILTHY ABUSIVE OUTBURSTS NOTHING!
THUNK!
IN COMPARISON TO THE POISONOUS TIPS... YES!
ONE SCRATCH FROM A PROTESTER'S PLACARD MEANS INSTANT DEATH... AND THERE ARE DOZENS MORE TO COME. WE SHOULDN'T HAVE INCENSED THE...

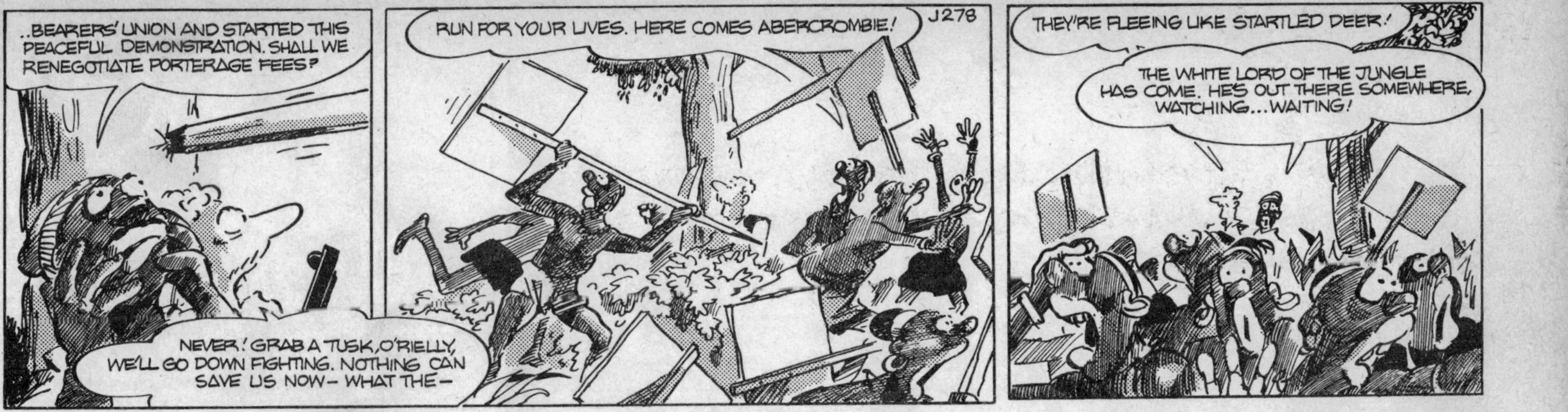

..BEARERS' UNION AND STARTED THIS PEACEFUL DEMONSTRATION. SHALL WE RENEGOTIATE PORTERAGE FEES?
NEVER! GRAB A TUSK, O'RIELLY, WE'LL GO DOWN FIGHTING. NOTHING CAN SAVE US NOW— WHAT THE—
RUN FOR YOUR LIVES. HERE COMES ABERCROMBIE!
J278
THEY'RE FLEEING LIKE STARTLED DEER!
THE WHITE LORD OF THE JUNGLE HAS COME. HE'S OUT THERE SOMEWHERE, WATCHING... WAITING!

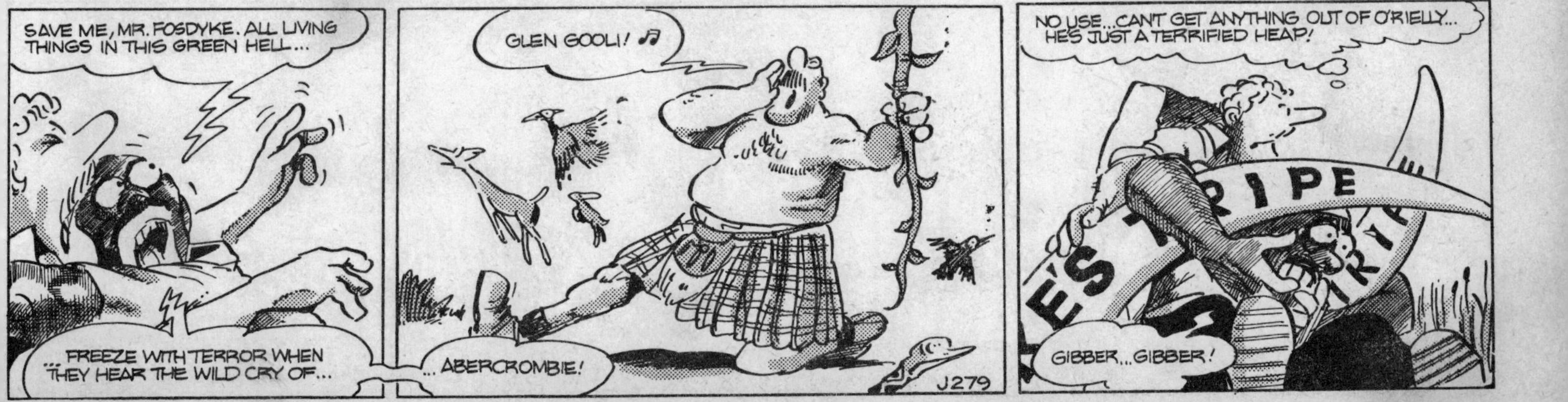

SAVE ME, MR. FOSDYKE. ALL LIVING THINGS IN THIS GREEN HELL...
... FREEZE WITH TERROR WHEN THEY HEAR THE WILD CRY OF...
GLEN GOOLI!
... ABERCROMBIE!
J279
NO USE... CAN'T GET ANYTHING OUT OF O'RIELLY... HE'S JUST A TERRIFIED HEAP!
TRIPE
GIBBER... GIBBER!

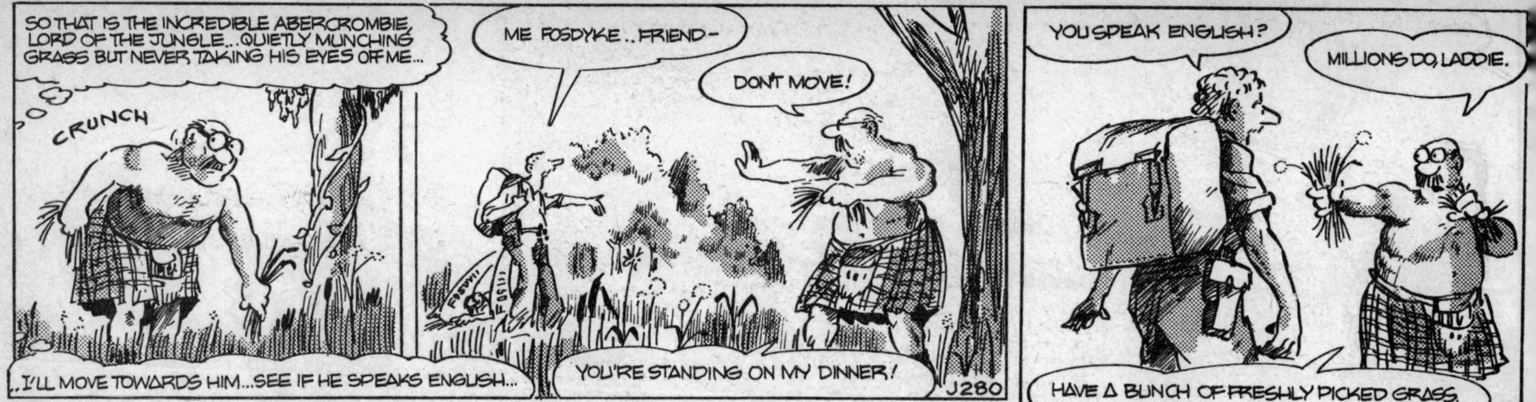
SO THAT IS THE INCREDIBLE ABERCROMBIE, LORD OF THE JUNGLE.. QUIETLY MUNCHING GRASS BUT NEVER TAKING HIS EYES OFF ME...
CRUNCH
..I'LL MOVE TOWARDS HIM...SEE IF HE SPEAKS ENGLISH...
ME FOSDYKE.. FRIEND-
DON'T MOVE!
YOU'RE STANDING ON MY DINNER!
J280
YOU SPEAK ENGLISH?
MILLIONS DO, LADDIE.
HAVE A BUNCH OF FRESHLY PICKED GRASS.

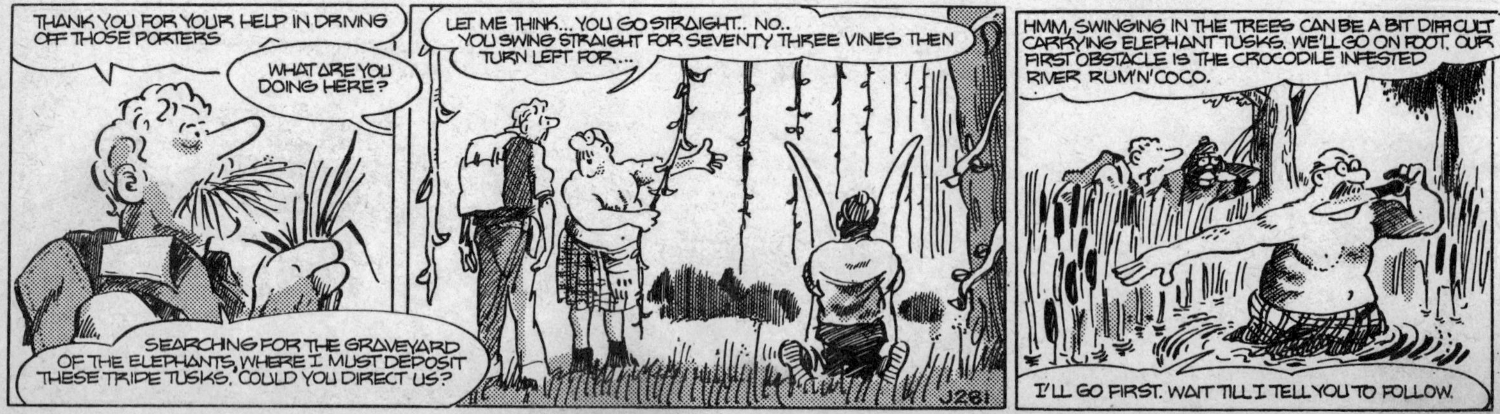
THANK YOU FOR YOUR HELP IN DRIVING OFF THOSE PORTERS
WHAT ARE YOU DOING HERE?
SEARCHING FOR THE GRAVEYARD OF THE ELEPHANTS, WHERE I MUST DEPOSIT THESE TRIPE TUSKS, COULD YOU DIRECT US?
LET ME THINK... YOU GO STRAIGHT.. NO.. YOU SWING STRAIGHT FOR SEVENTY THREE VINES THEN TURN LEFT FOR....
J281
HMM, SWINGING IN THE TREES CAN BE A BIT DIFFICULT CARRYING ELEPHANT TUSKS. WE'LL GO ON FOOT. OUR FIRST OBSTACLE IS THE CROCODILE INFESTED RIVER RUM'N'COCO.
I'LL GO FIRST. WAIT TILL I TELL YOU TO FOLLOW.

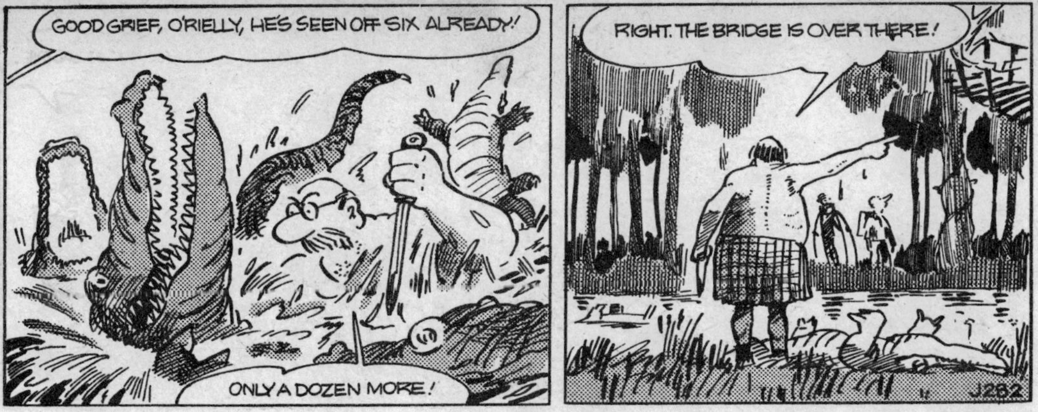
GOOD GRIEF, O'RIELLY, HE'S SEEN OFF SIX ALREADY!
ONLY A DOZEN MORE!
RIGHT. THE BRIDGE IS OVER THERE!
J282

And at St. Fowledrain's Hall, Manchester...

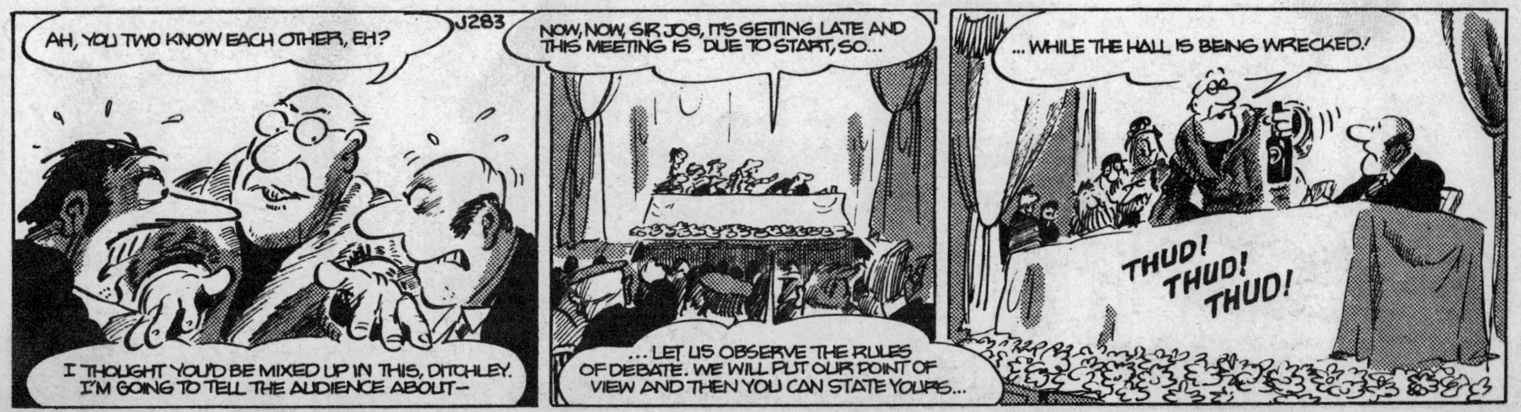
J283
AH, YOU TWO KNOW EACH OTHER, EH?
I THOUGHT YOU'D BE MIXED UP IN THIS, DITCHLEY. I'M GOING TO TELL THE AUDIENCE ABOUT–
NOW, NOW, SIR JOS, IT'S GETTING LATE AND THIS MEETING IS DUE TO START, SO...
... LET US OBSERVE THE RULES OF DEBATE. WE WILL PUT OUR POINT OF VIEW AND THEN YOU CAN STATE YOURS...
... WHILE THE HALL IS BEING WRECKED!
THUD! THUD! THUD!

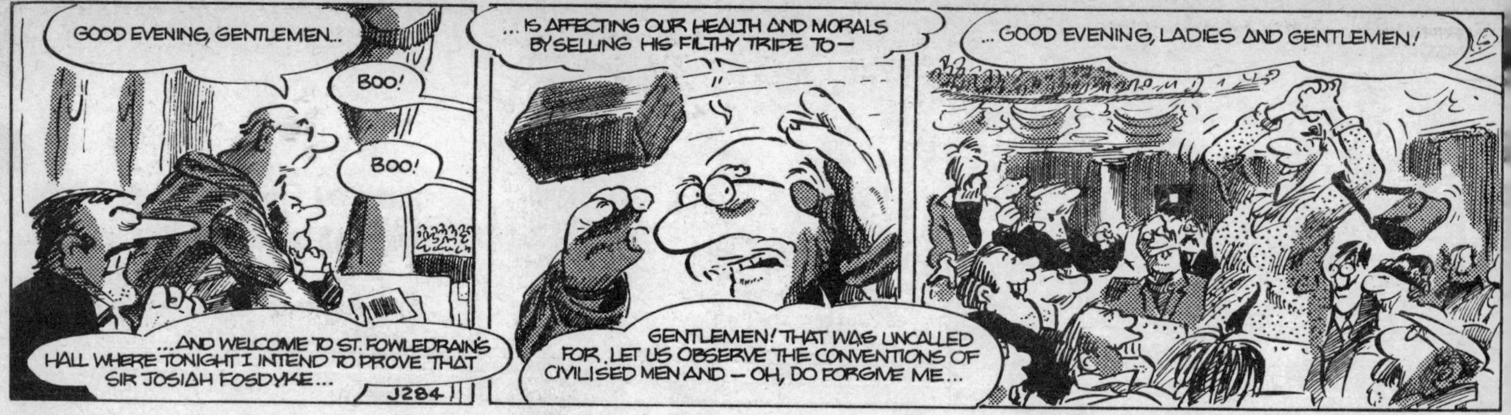
GOOD EVENING, GENTLEMEN...
BOO!
BOO!
...AND WELCOME TO ST. FOWLEDRAIN'S HALL WHERE TONIGHT I INTEND TO PROVE THAT SIR JOSIAH FOSDYKE...
J284
... IS AFFECTING OUR HEALTH AND MORALS BY SELLING HIS FILTHY TRIPE TO —
GENTLEMEN! THAT WAS UNCALLED FOR, LET US OBSERVE THE CONVENTIONS OF CIVILISED MEN AND — OH, DO FORGIVE ME...
... GOOD EVENING, LADIES AND GENTLEMEN!

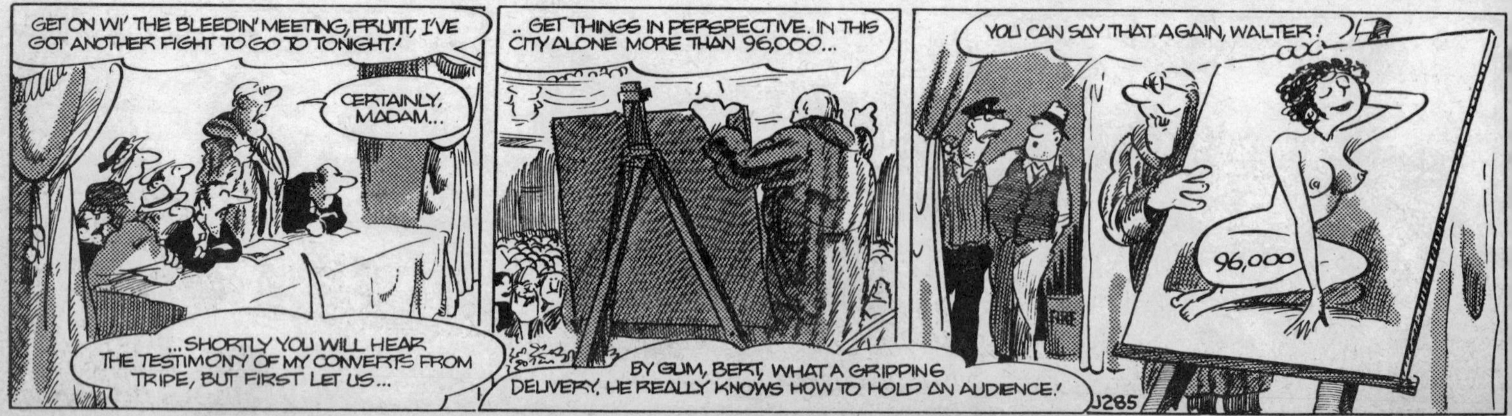
GET ON WI' THE BLEEDIN' MEETING, FRUIT, I'VE GOT ANOTHER FIGHT TO GO TO TONIGHT!
CERTAINLY, MADAM...
...SHORTLY YOU WILL HEAR THE TESTIMONY OF MY CONVERTS FROM TRIPE, BUT FIRST LET US...
.. GET THINGS IN PERSPECTIVE. IN THIS CITY ALONE MORE THAN 96,000...
BY GUM, BERT, WHAT A GRIPPING DELIVERY. HE REALLY KNOWS HOW TO HOLD AN AUDIENCE!
YOU CAN SAY THAT AGAIN, WALTER!
FIRE
96,000
J285

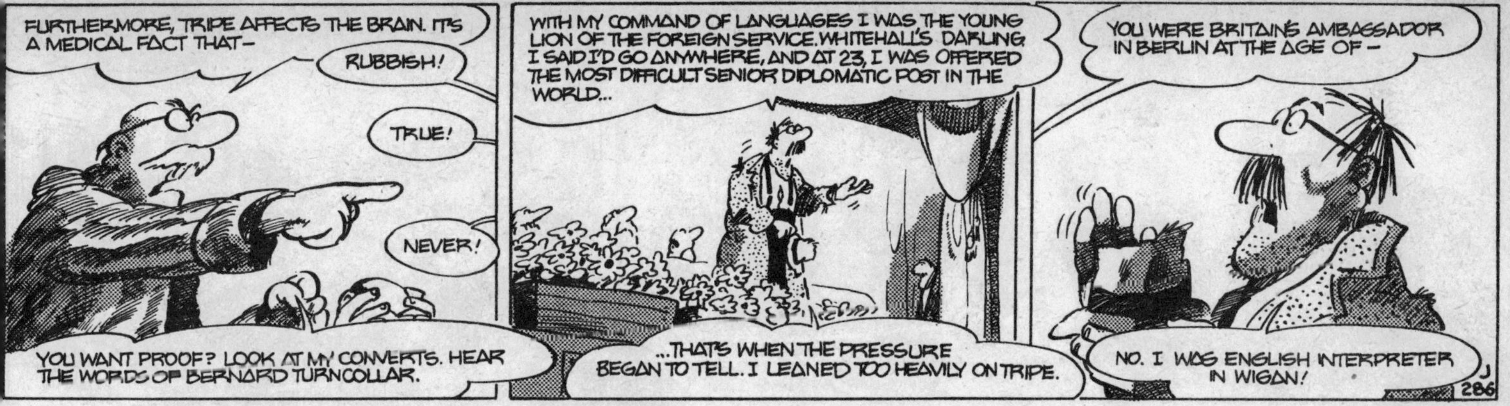
FURTHERMORE, TRIPE AFFECTS THE BRAIN. IT'S A MEDICAL FACT THAT–
RUBBISH!
TRUE!
NEVER!
YOU WANT PROOF? LOOK AT MY CONVERTS. HEAR THE WORDS OF BERNARD TURNCOLLAR.
WITH MY COMMAND OF LANGUAGES I WAS THE YOUNG LION OF THE FOREIGN SERVICE. WHITEHALL'S DARLING. I SAID I'D GO ANYWHERE, AND AT 23, I WAS OFFERED THE MOST DIFFICULT SENIOR DIPLOMATIC POST IN THE WORLD...
...THAT'S WHEN THE PRESSURE BEGAN TO TELL. I LEANED TOO HEAVILY ON TRIPE.
YOU WERE BRITAIN'S AMBASSADOR IN BERLIN AT THE AGE OF –
NO. I WAS ENGLISH INTERPRETER IN WIGAN!
J 286

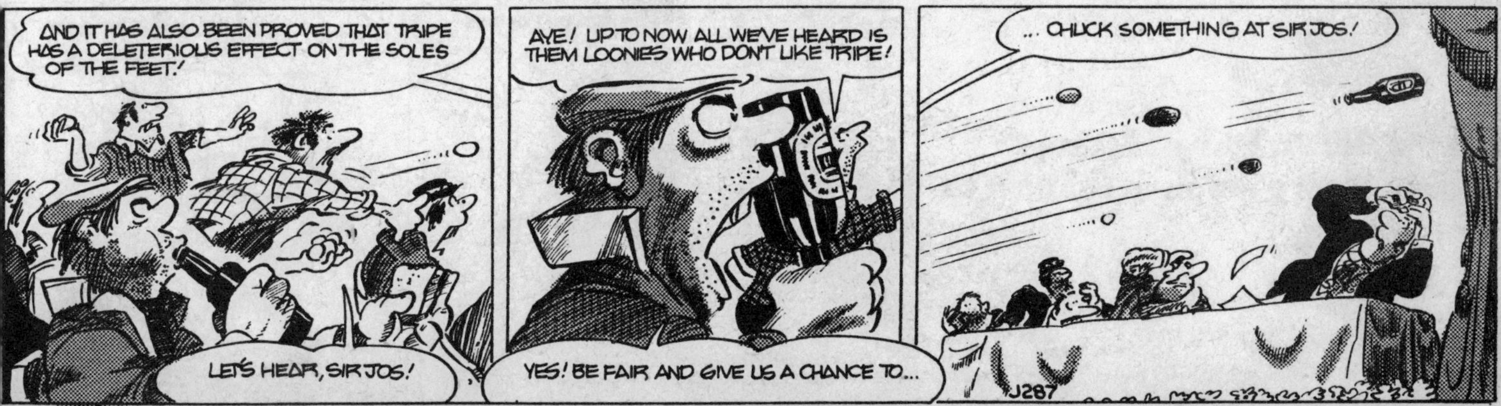
AND IT HAS ALSO BEEN PROVED THAT TRIPE HAS A DELETERIOUS EFFECT ON THE SOLES OF THE FEET!
LET'S HEAR, SIR JOS!
AYE! UP TO NOW ALL WE'VE HEARD IS THEM LOONIES WHO DON'T LIKE TRIPE!
YES! BE FAIR AND GIVE US A CHANCE TO...
... CHUCK SOMETHING AT SIR JOS!
J287

Behind the scenes...

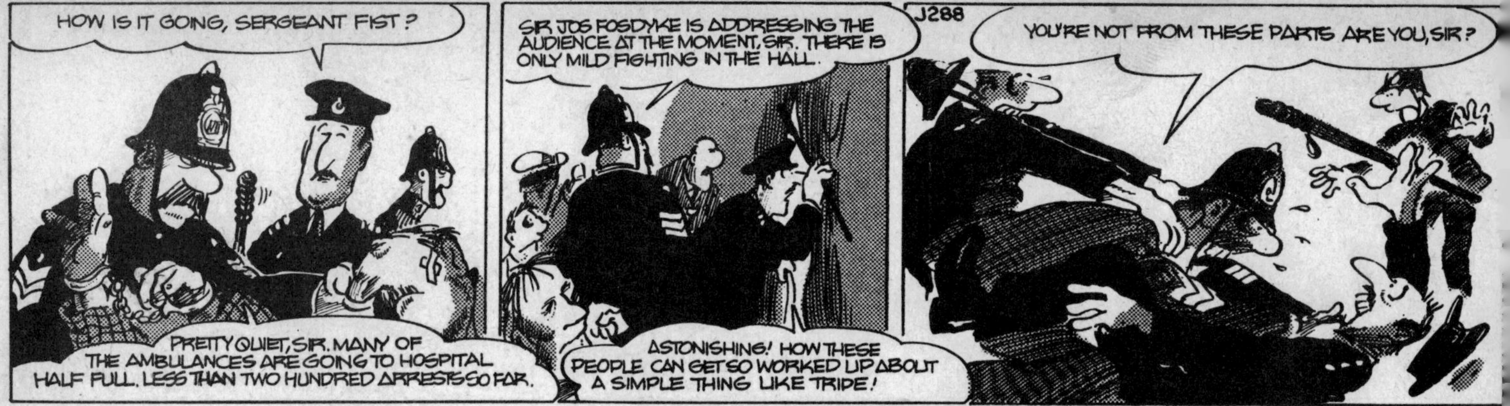
HOW IS IT GOING, SERGEANT FIST ?
PRETTY QUIET, SIR. MANY OF THE AMBULANCES ARE GOING TO HOSPITAL HALF FULL. LESS THAN TWO HUNDRED ARRESTS SO FAR.
SIR JOS FOSDYKE IS ADDRESSING THE AUDIENCE AT THE MOMENT, SIR. THERE IS ONLY MILD FIGHTING IN THE HALL.
ASTONISHING! HOW THESE PEOPLE CAN GET SO WORKED UP ABOUT A SIMPLE THING LIKE TRIPE!
J288
YOU'RE NOT FROM THESE PARTS ARE YOU, SIR ?

In the Berlin Hall of Strength a duel of more moment is about to commence.

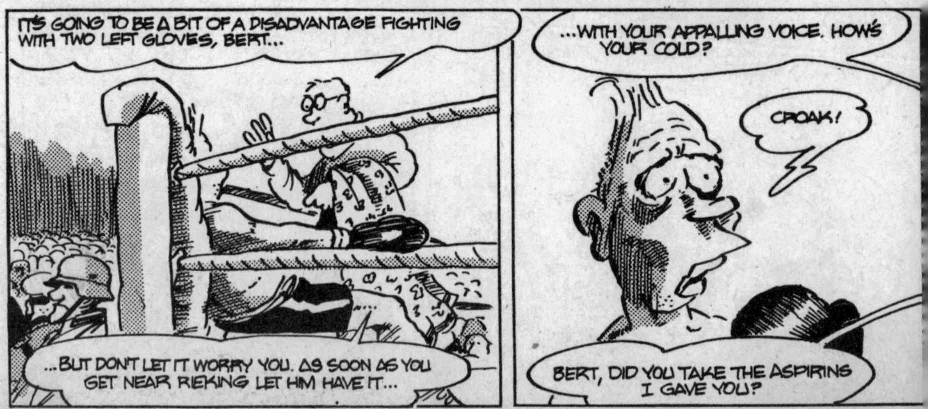
IT'S GOING TO BE A BIT OF A DISADVANTAGE FIGHTING WITH TWO LEFT GLOVES, BERT...
...BUT DON'T LET IT WORRY YOU. AS SOON AS YOU GET NEAR RIEKING LET HIM HAVE IT...
...WITH YOUR APPALLING VOICE. HOW'S YOUR COLD?
CROAK!
BERT, DID YOU TAKE THE ASPIRINS I GAVE YOU?

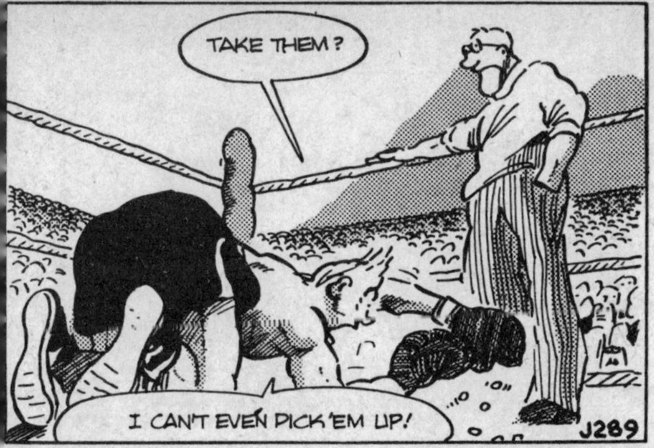
TAKE THEM ?
I CAN'T EVEN PICK 'EM UP!
J289

And during the preliminary formalities...

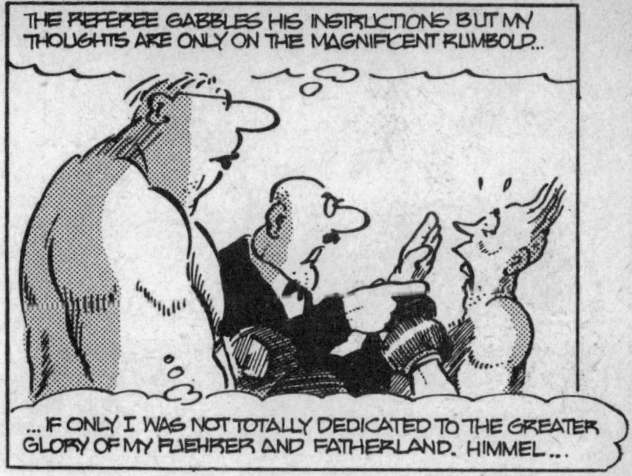
THE REFEREE GABBLES HIS INSTRUCTIONS BUT MY THOUGHTS ARE ONLY ON THE MAGNIFICENT RUMBOLD...
... IF ONLY I WAS NOT TOTALLY DEDICATED TO THE GREATER GLORY OF MY FUEHRER AND FATHERLAND. HIMMEL...

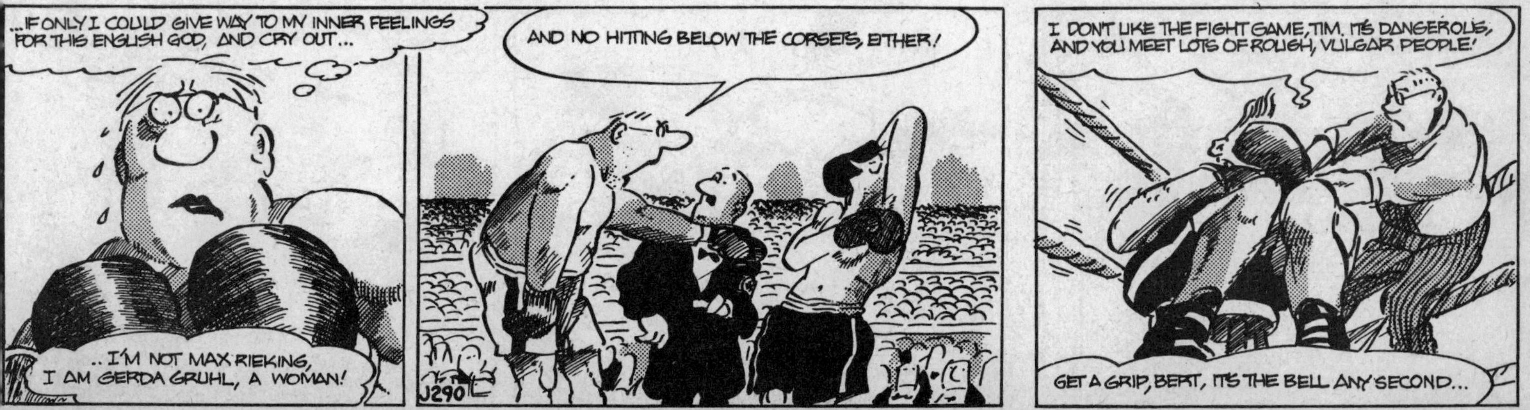
...IF ONLY I COULD GIVE WAY TO MY INNER FEELINGS FOR THIS ENGLISH GOD, AND CRY OUT...
.. I'M NOT MAX RIEKING, I AM GERDA GRUHL, A WOMAN!
AND NO HITTING BELOW THE CORSETS, EITHER!
J290
I DON'T LIKE THE FIGHT GAME, TIM. IT'S DANGEROUS, AND YOU MEET LOTS OF ROUGH, VULGAR PEOPLE!
GET A GRIP, BERT, IT'S THE BELL ANY SECOND...

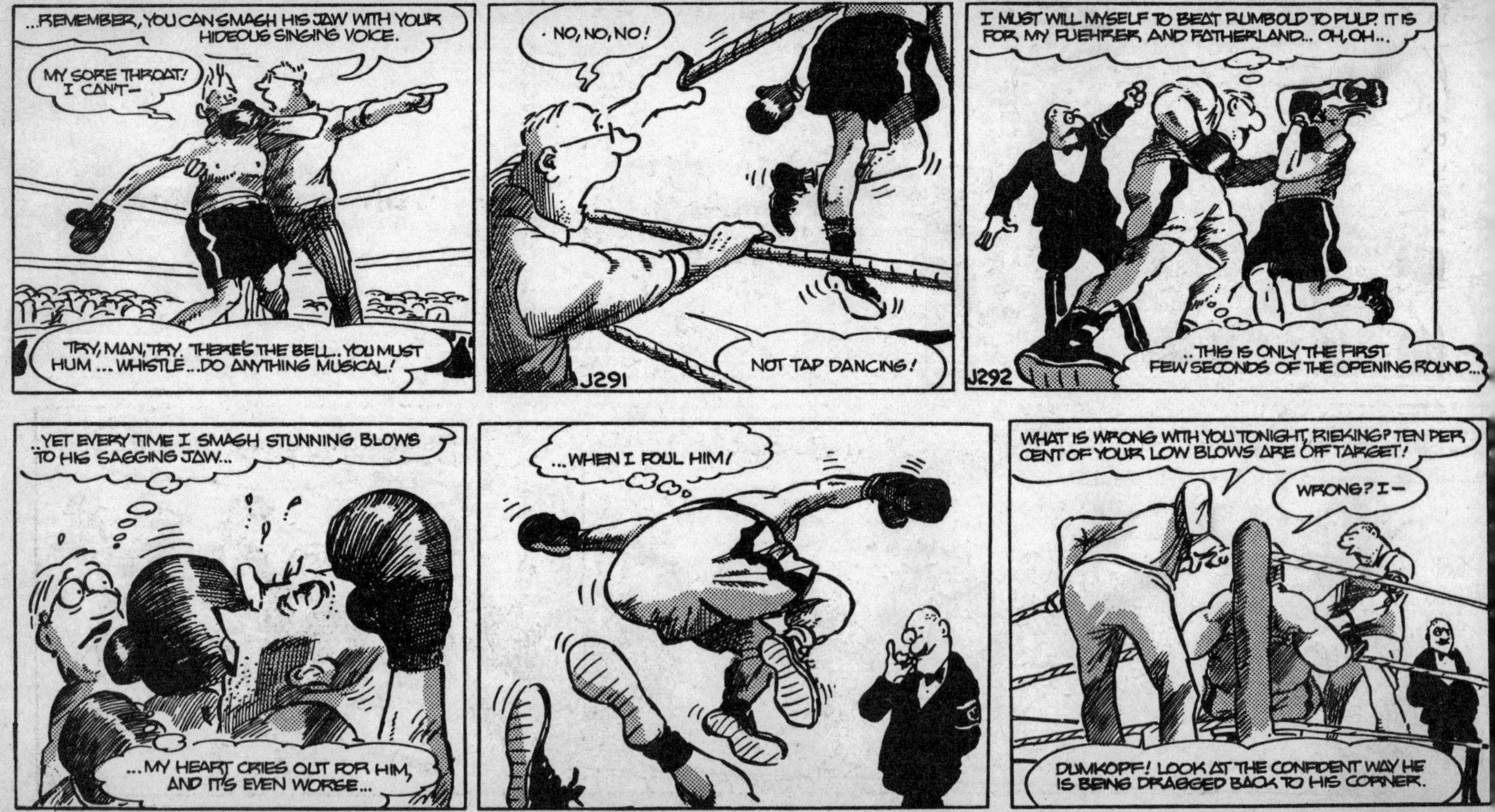

...REMEMBER, YOU CAN SMASH HIS JAW WITH YOUR HIDEOUS SINGING VOICE.
MY SORE THROAT! I CAN'T—
TRY, MAN, TRY. THERE'S THE BELL... YOU MUST HUM ... WHISTLE... DO ANYTHING MUSICAL!
· NO, NO, NO!
NOT TAP DANCING!
J291
I MUST WILL MYSELF TO BEAT RUMBOLD TO PULP. IT IS FOR MY FUEHRER AND FATHERLAND... OH, OH...
...THIS IS ONLY THE FIRST FEW SECONDS OF THE OPENING ROUND...
J292
..YET EVERY TIME I SMASH STUNNING BLOWS TO HIS SAGGING JAW...
...MY HEART CRIES OUT FOR HIM, AND IT'S EVEN WORSE...
...WHEN I FOUL HIM!
WHAT IS WRONG WITH YOU TONIGHT, RIEKING? TEN PER CENT OF YOUR LOW BLOWS ARE OFF TARGET!
WRONG? I—
DUMKOPF! LOOK AT THE CONFIDENT WAY HE IS BEING DRAGGED BACK TO HIS CORNER.

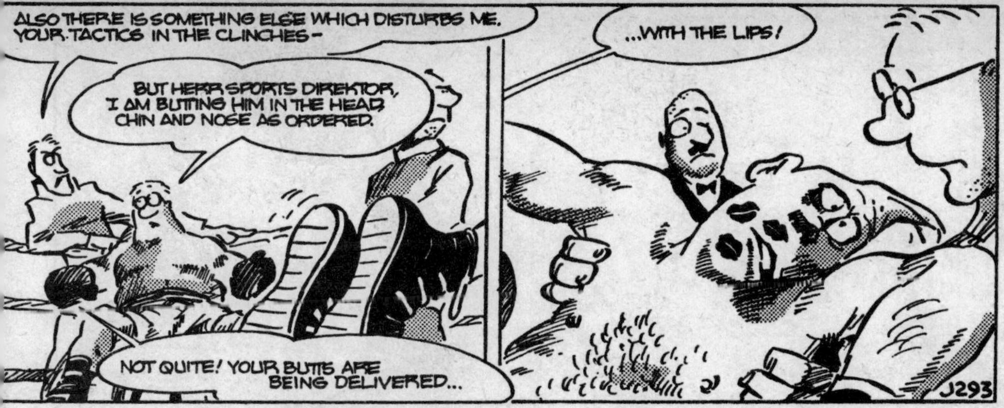
ALSO THERE IS SOMETHING ELSE WHICH DISTURBS ME. YOUR TACTICS IN THE CLINCHES –
BUT HERR SPORTS DIREKTOR, I AM BUTTING HIM IN THE HEAD, CHIN AND NOSE AS ORDERED.
NOT QUITE! YOUR BUTTS ARE BEING DELIVERED...
...WITH THE LIPS!
J293

A few rounds later...

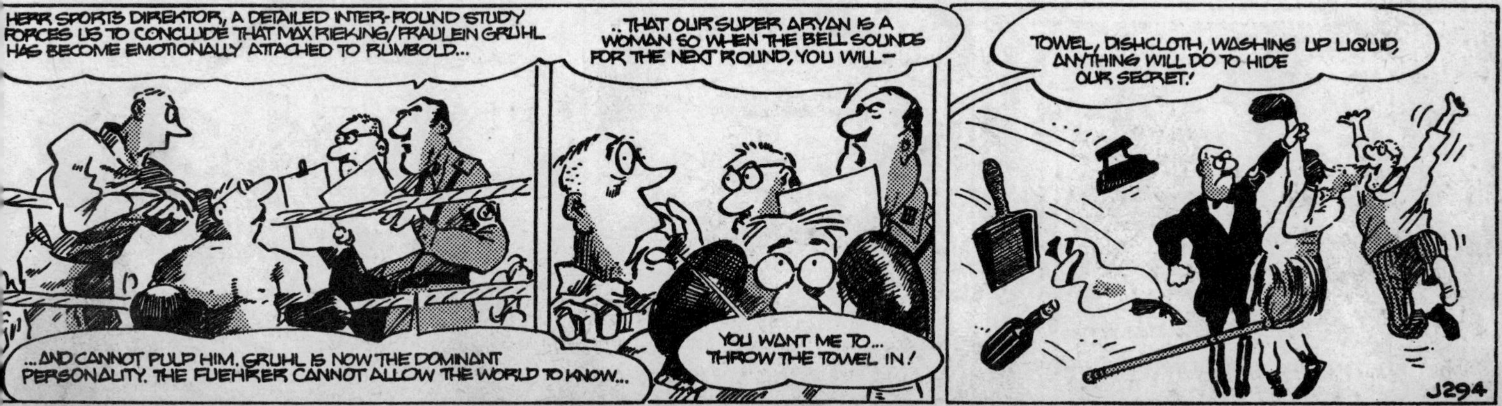
HERR SPORTS DIREKTOR, A DETAILED INTER-ROUND STUDY FORCES US TO CONCLUDE THAT MAX RIEKING/FRAULEIN GRUHL HAS BECOME EMOTIONALLY ATTACHED TO RUMBOLD...
...AND CANNOT PULP HIM. GRUHL IS NOW THE DOMINANT PERSONALITY. THE FUEHRER CANNOT ALLOW THE WORLD TO KNOW...
..THAT OUR SUPER ARYAN IS A WOMAN SO WHEN THE BELL SOUNDS FOR THE NEXT ROUND, YOU WILL –
YOU WANT ME TO... THROW THE TOWEL IN!
TOWEL, DISHCLOTH, WASHING UP LIQUID, ANYTHING WILL DO TO HIDE OUR SECRET!
J294

In the African jungle...

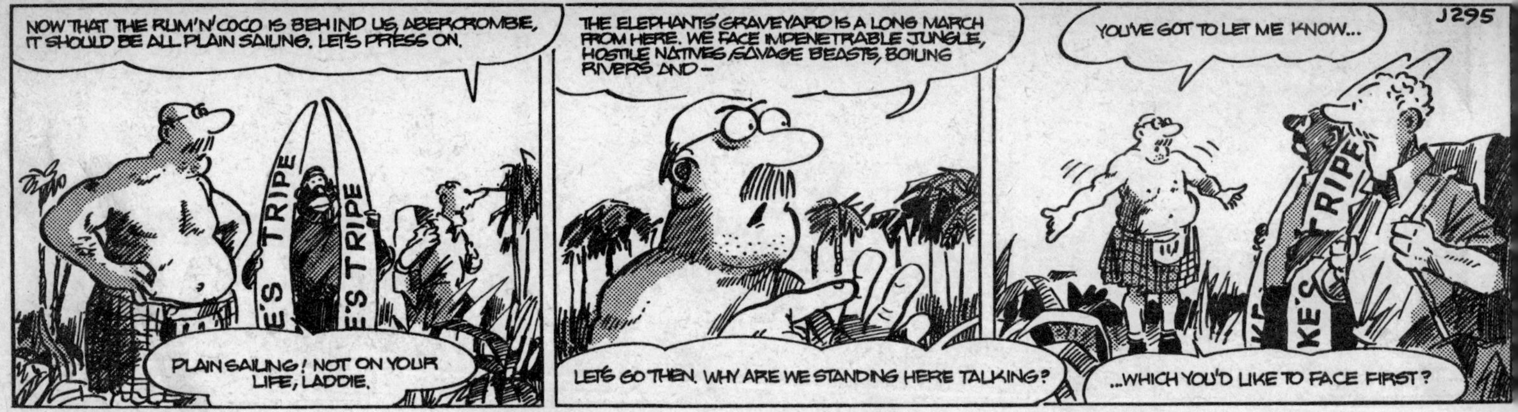
J295
NOW THAT THE RUM'N'COCO IS BEHIND US, ABERCROMBIE, IT SHOULD BE ALL PLAIN SAILING. LET'S PRESS ON.
PLAIN SAILING! NOT ON YOUR LIFE, LADDIE.
THE ELEPHANTS' GRAVEYARD IS A LONG MARCH FROM HERE. WE FACE IMPENETRABLE JUNGLE, HOSTILE NATIVES, SAVAGE BEASTS, BOILING RIVERS AND—
LET'S GO THEN. WHY ARE WE STANDING HERE TALKING?
YOU'VE GOT TO LET ME KNOW...
...WHICH YOU'D LIKE TO FACE FIRST?

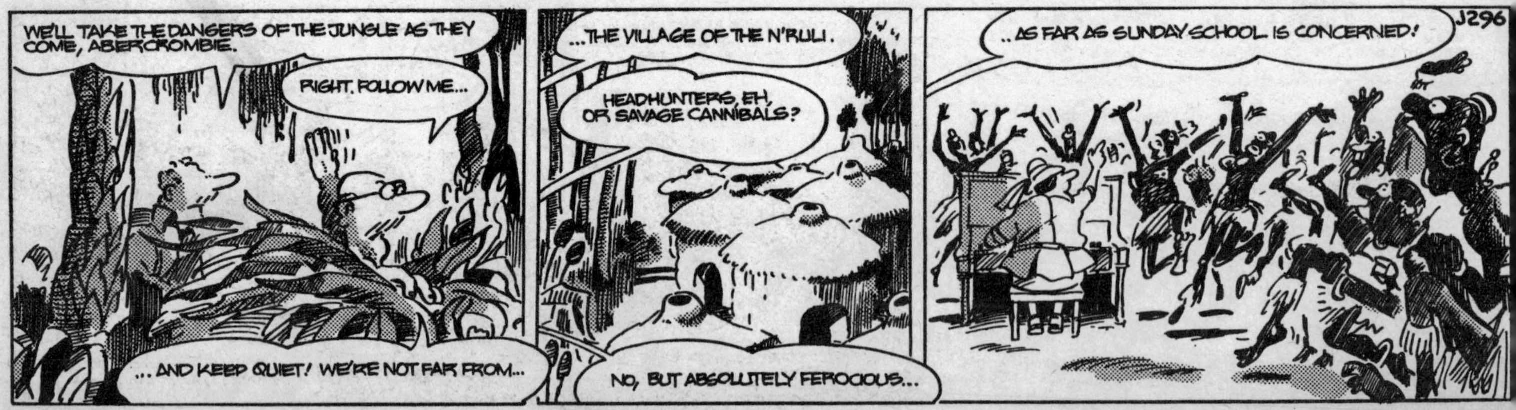
J296
WE'LL TAKE THE DANGERS OF THE JUNGLE AS THEY COME, ABERCROMBIE.
RIGHT. FOLLOW ME...
... AND KEEP QUIET! WE'RE NOT FAR FROM...
...THE VILLAGE OF THE N'RULI.
HEADHUNTERS, EH, OR SAVAGE CANNIBALS?
NO, BUT ABSOLUTELY FEROCIOUS...
...AS FAR AS SUNDAY SCHOOL IS CONCERNED!

Some hours later...

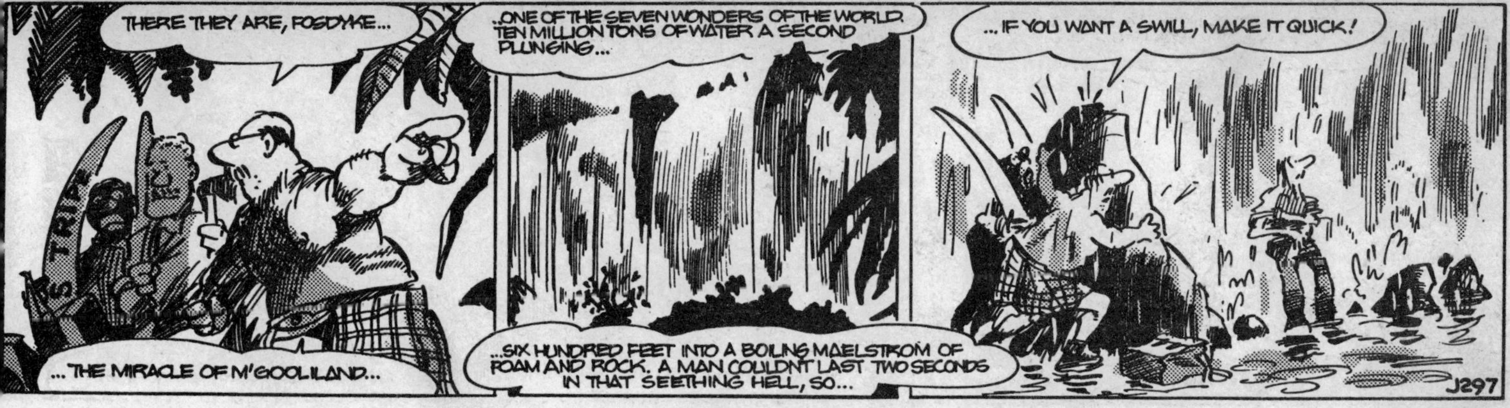
THERE THEY ARE, FOSDYKE...
... THE MIRACLE OF M'GOOLILAND...
..ONE OF THE SEVEN WONDERS OF THE WORLD. TEN MILLION TONS OF WATER A SECOND PLUNGING...
...SIX HUNDRED FEET INTO A BOILING MAELSTROM OF FOAM AND ROCK. A MAN COULDN'T LAST TWO SECONDS IN THAT SEETHING HELL, SO...
... IF YOU WANT A SWILL, MAKE IT QUICK!
J297

And after another long march...

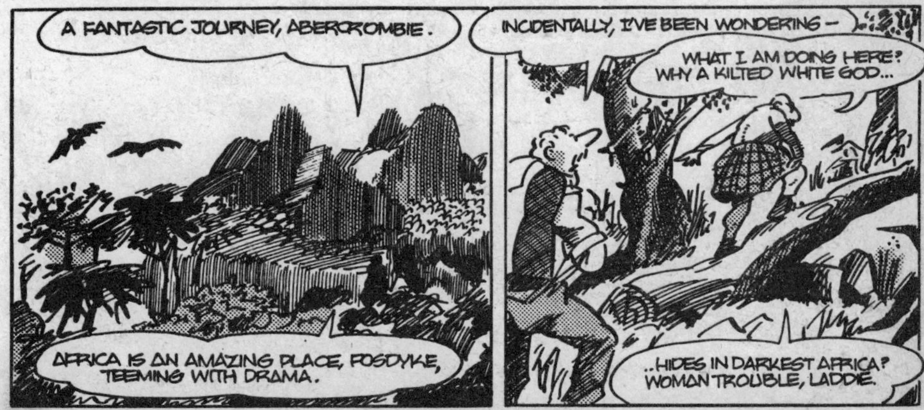
A FANTASTIC JOURNEY, ABERCROMBIE.
AFRICA IS AN AMAZING PLACE, FOSDYKE, TEEMING WITH DRAMA.
INCIDENTALLY, I'VE BEEN WONDERING –
WHAT I AM DOING HERE? WHY A KILTED WHITE GOD...
..HIDES IN DARKEST AFRICA? WOMAN TROUBLE, LADDIE.

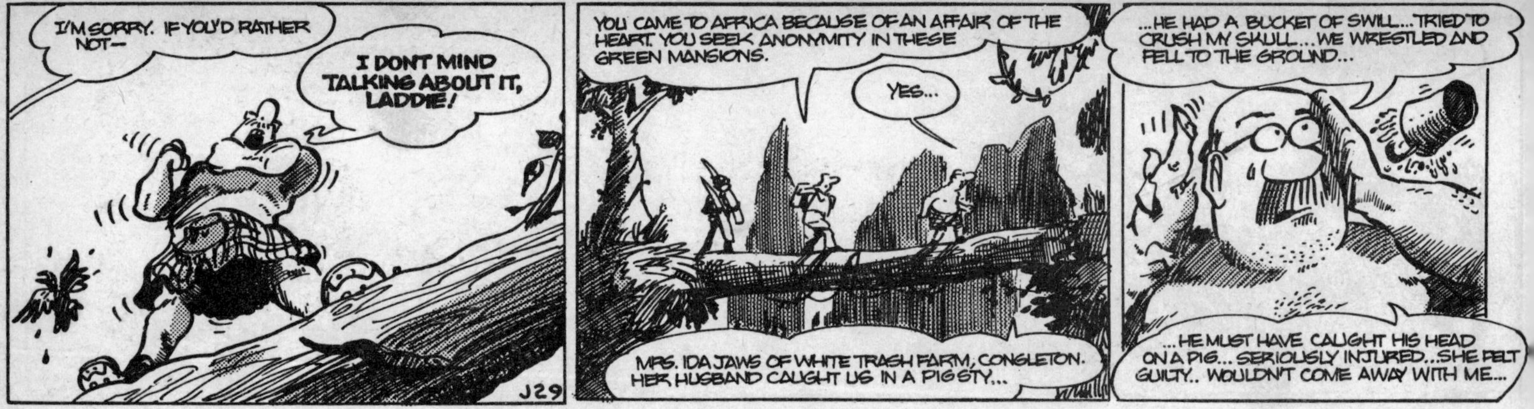
I'M SORRY. IF YOU'D RATHER NOT—
I DONT MIND TALKING ABOUT IT, LADDIE!
YOU CAME TO AFRICA BECAUSE OF AN AFFAIR OF THE HEART. YOU SEEK ANONYMITY IN THESE GREEN MANSIONS.
YES...
MRS. IDA JAWS OF WHITE TRASH FARM, CONGLETON. HER HUSBAND CAUGHT US IN A PIGSTY...
...HE HAD A BUCKET OF SWILL...TRIED TO CRUSH MY SKULL...WE WRESTLED AND FELL TO THE GROUND...
...HE MUST HAVE CAUGHT HIS HEAD ON A PIG... SERIOUSLY INJURED...SHE FELT GUILTY.. WOULDN'T COME AWAY WITH ME...

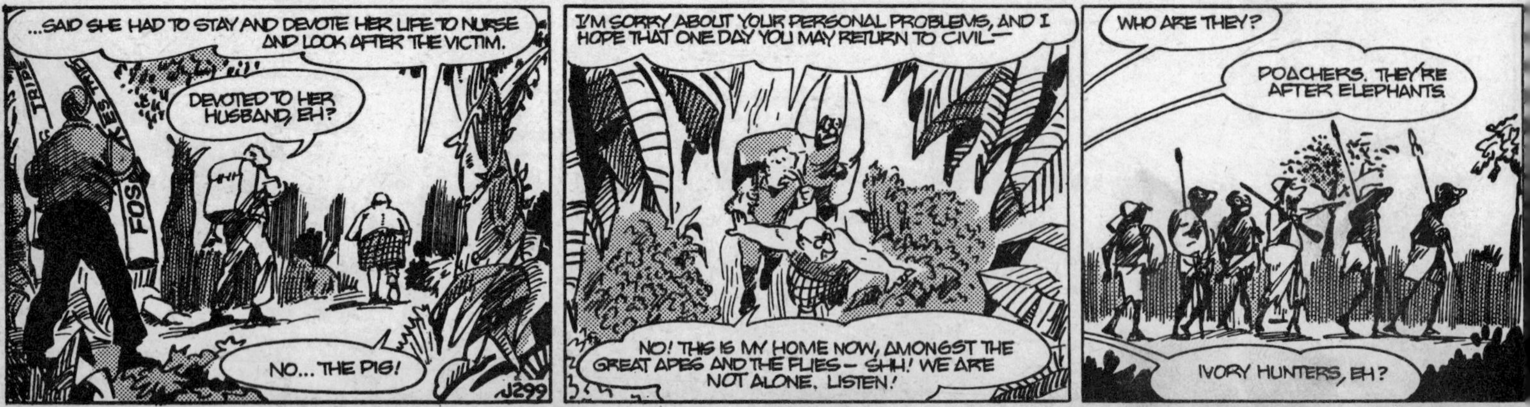
...SAID SHE HAD TO STAY AND DEVOTE HER LIFE TO NURSE AND LOOK AFTER THE VICTIM.
DEVOTED TO HER HUSBAND, EH?
NO... THE PIG!
I'M SORRY ABOUT YOUR PERSONAL PROBLEMS, AND I HOPE THAT ONE DAY YOU MAY RETURN TO CIVIL—
NO! THIS IS MY HOME NOW, AMONGST THE GREAT APES AND THE FLIES— SHH! WE ARE NOT ALONE. LISTEN!
WHO ARE THEY?
POACHERS. THEY'RE AFTER ELEPHANTS.
IVORY HUNTERS, EH?

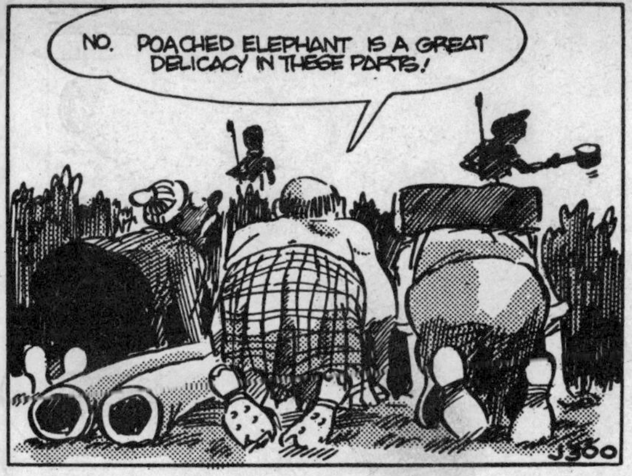
NO. POACHED ELEPHANT IS A GREAT DELICACY IN THESE PARTS!
J300

Meanwhile Sir Jos addresses the heckling hordes in St. Fowledrain's Hall...

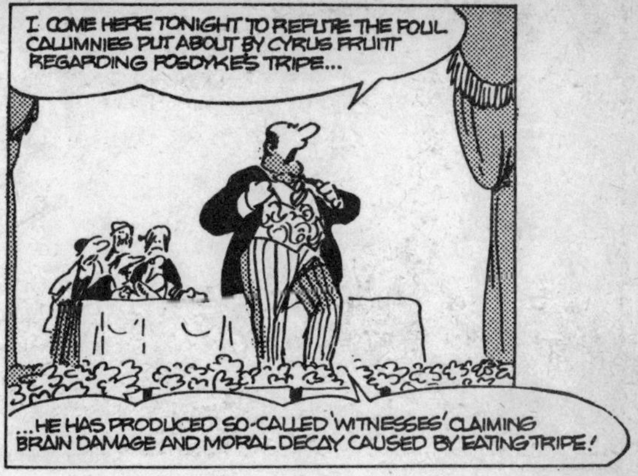
I COME HERE TONIGHT TO REFUTE THE FOUL CALUMNIES PUT ABOUT BY CYRUS FRUITT REGARDING FOSDYKE'S TRIPE...
...HE HAS PRODUCED SO-CALLED 'WITNESSES' CLAIMING BRAIN DAMAGE AND MORAL DECAY CAUSED BY EATING TRIPE!

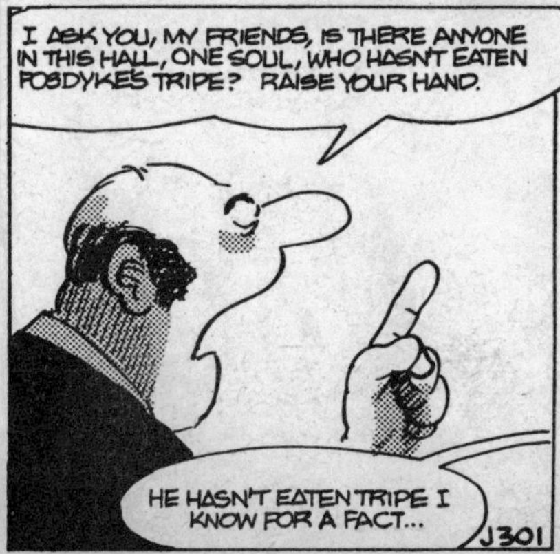
I ASK YOU, MY FRIENDS, IS THERE ANYONE IN THIS HALL, ONE SOUL, WHO HASN'T EATEN FOSDYKE'S TRIPE? RAISE YOUR HAND.
HE HASN'T EATEN TRIPE I KNOW FOR A FACT...
J301

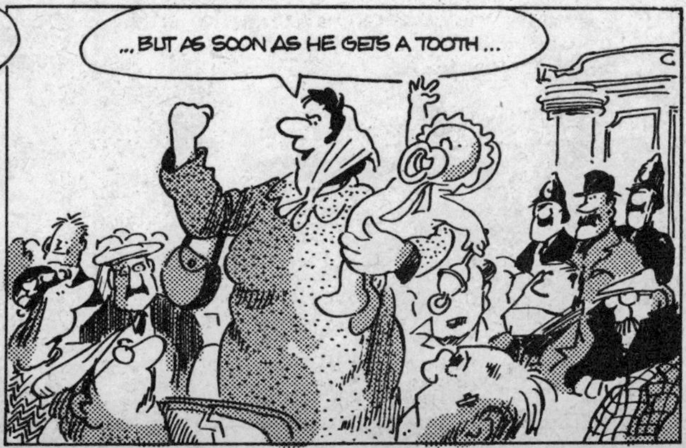
...BUT AS SOON AS HE GETS A TOOTH...

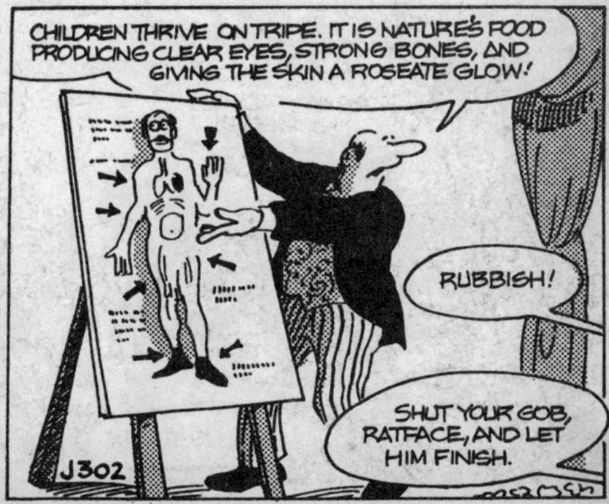
CHILDREN THRIVE ON TRIPE. IT IS NATURE'S FOOD PRODUCING CLEAR EYES, STRONG BONES, AND GIVING THE SKIN A ROSEATE GLOW!
RUBBISH!
SHUT YOUR GOB, RATFACE, AND LET HIM FINISH.
J302

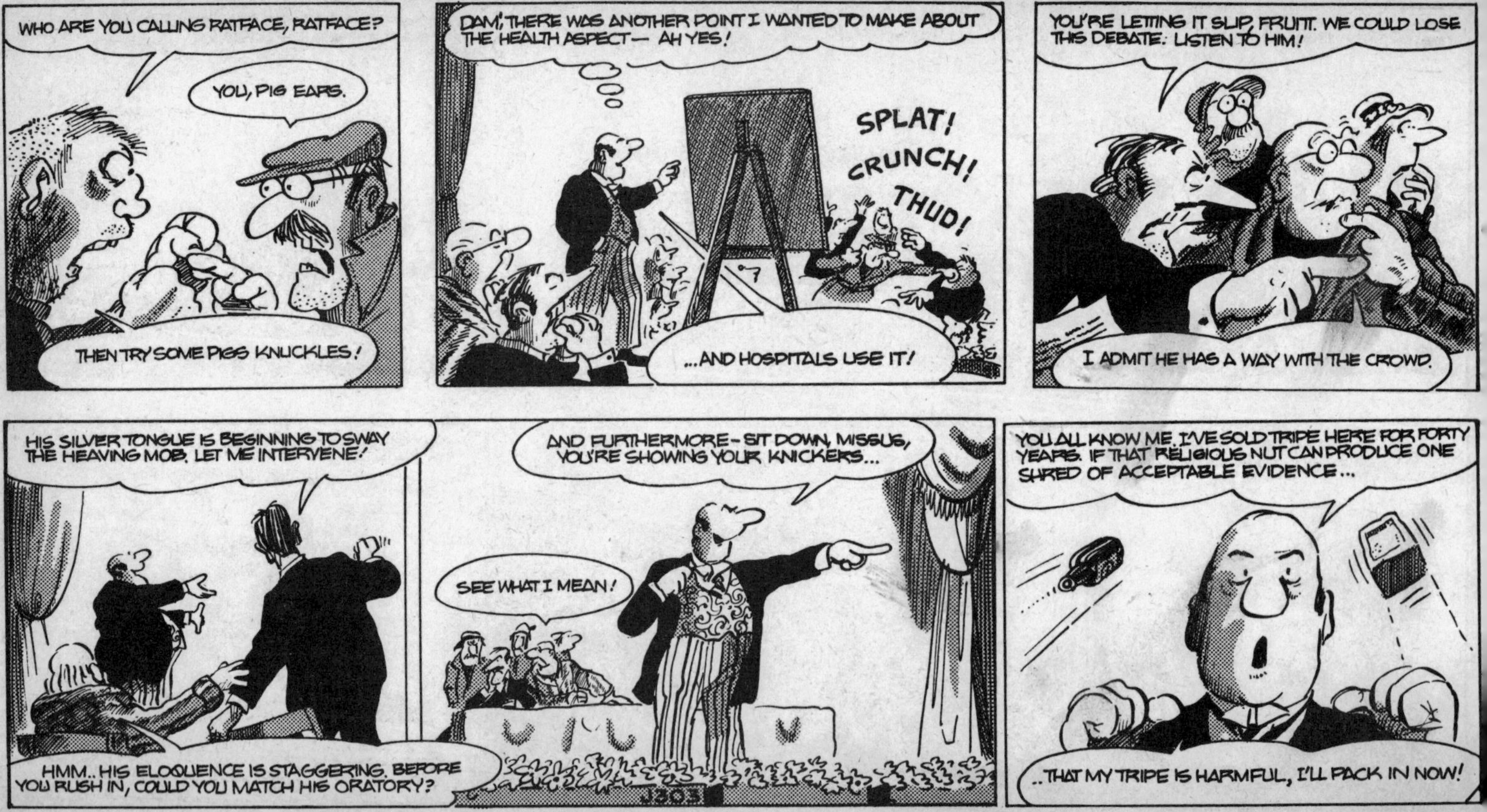
WHO ARE YOU CALLING RATFACE, RATFACE?
YOU, PIG EARS.
THEN TRY SOME PIGS KNUCKLES!
DAM'; THERE WAS ANOTHER POINT I WANTED TO MAKE ABOUT THE HEALTH ASPECT— AH YES!
SPLAT!
CRUNCH!
THUD!
...AND HOSPITALS USE IT!
YOU'RE LETTING IT SLIP, FRUITT. WE COULD LOSE THIS DEBATE. LISTEN TO HIM!
I ADMIT HE HAS A WAY WITH THE CROWD.
HIS SILVER TONGUE IS BEGINNING TO SWAY THE HEAVING MOB. LET ME INTERVENE!
HMM.. HIS ELOQUENCE IS STAGGERING. BEFORE YOU RUSH IN, COULD YOU MATCH HIS ORATORY?
AND FURTHERMORE – SIT DOWN, MISSUS, YOU'RE SHOWING YOUR KNICKERS...
SEE WHAT I MEAN!
J303
YOU ALL KNOW ME. I'VE SOLD TRIPE HERE FOR FORTY YEARS. IF THAT RELIGIOUS NUT CAN PRODUCE ONE SHRED OF ACCEPTABLE EVIDENCE...
..THAT MY TRIPE IS HARMFUL, I'LL PACK IN NOW!

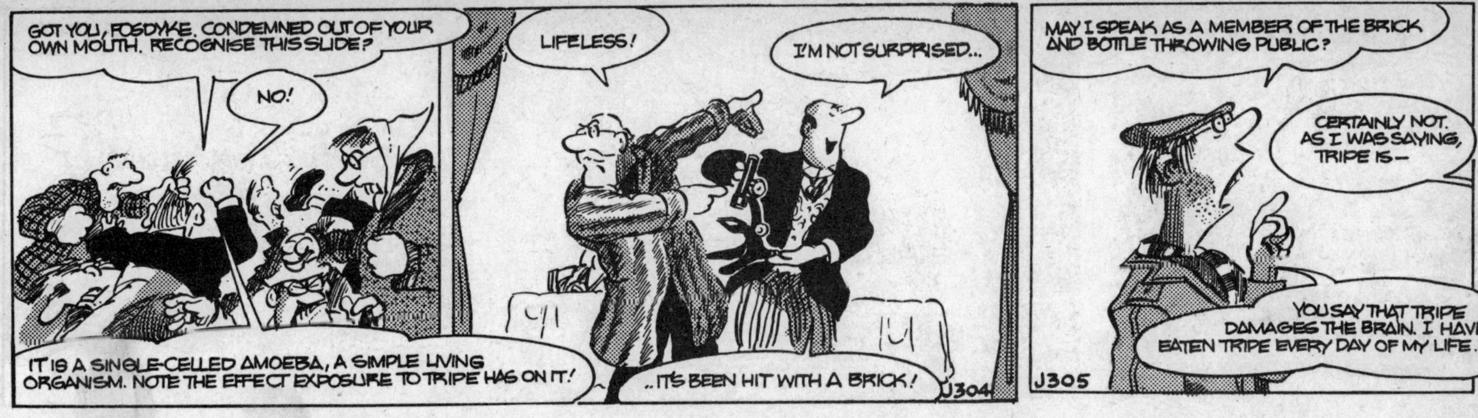
GOT YOU, FOSDYKE. CONDEMNED OUT OF YOUR OWN MOUTH. RECOGNISE THIS SLIDE?
NO!
IT IS A SINGLE-CELLED AMOEBA, A SIMPLE LIVING ORGANISM. NOTE THE EFFECT EXPOSURE TO TRIPE HAS ON IT!
LIFELESS!
I'M NOT SURPRISED...
..IT'S BEEN HIT WITH A BRICK!
J304
MAY I SPEAK AS A MEMBER OF THE BRICK AND BOTTLE THROWING PUBLIC?
CERTAINLY NOT. AS I WAS SAYING, TRIPE IS—
YOU SAY THAT TRIPE DAMAGES THE BRAIN. I HAVE EATEN TRIPE EVERY DAY OF MY LIFE...
J305

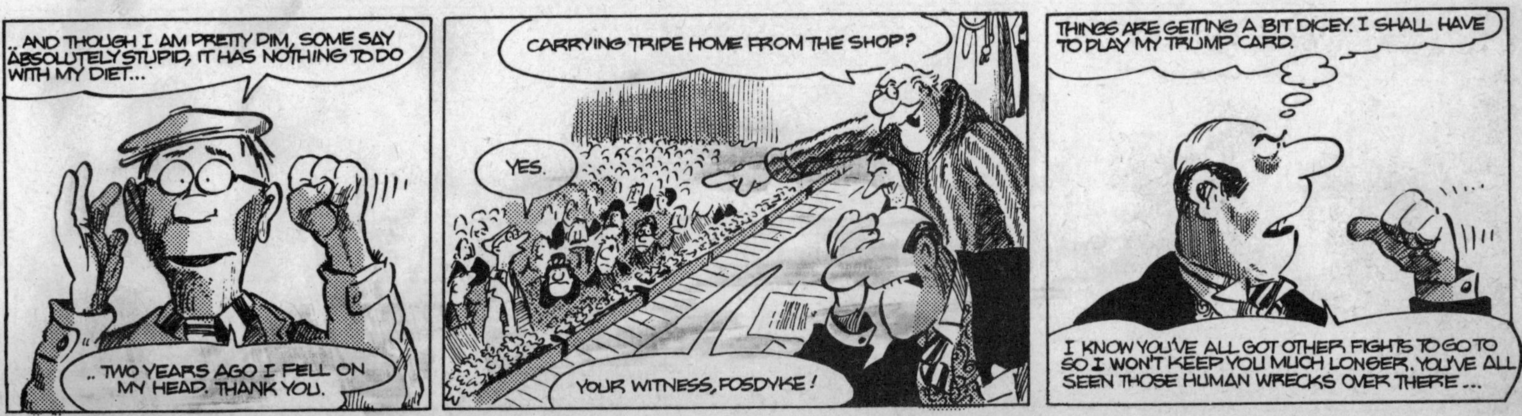
..AND THOUGH I AM PRETTY DIM, SOME SAY ABSOLUTELY STUPID, IT HAS NOTHING TO DO WITH MY DIET...
..TWO YEARS AGO I FELL ON MY HEAD. THANK YOU.
CARRYING TRIPE HOME FROM THE SHOP?
YES.
YOUR WITNESS, FOSDYKE!
THINGS ARE GETTING A BIT DICEY. I SHALL HAVE TO PLAY MY TRUMP CARD.
I KNOW YOU'VE ALL GOT OTHER FIGHTS TO GO TO SO I WON'T KEEP YOU MUCH LONGER. YOU'VE ALL SEEN THOSE HUMAN WRECKS OVER THERE...

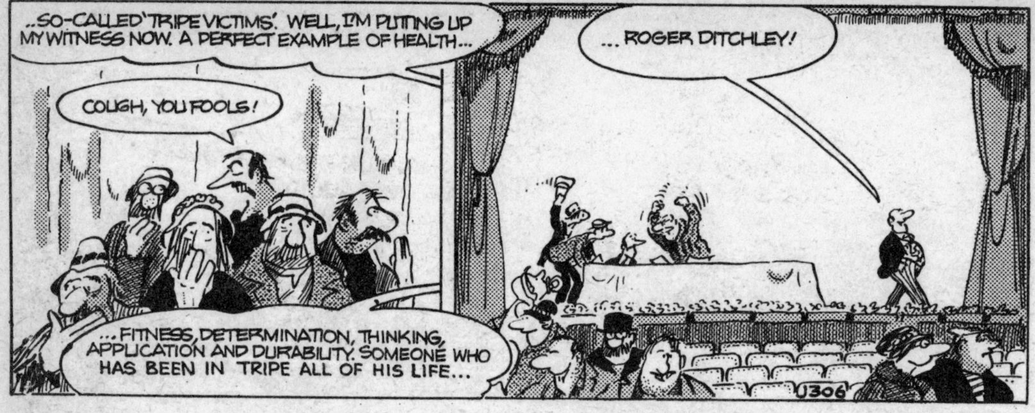
..SO-CALLED 'TRIPE VICTIMS'. WELL, I'M PUTTING UP MY WITNESS NOW. A PERFECT EXAMPLE OF HEALTH...
COUGH, YOU FOOLS!
...FITNESS, DETERMINATION, THINKING, APPLICATION AND DURABILITY. SOMEONE WHO HAS BEEN IN TRIPE ALL OF HIS LIFE...
...ROGER DITCHLEY!
J306

In Berlin Tim and the victorious Bert are bundled out to the airport...

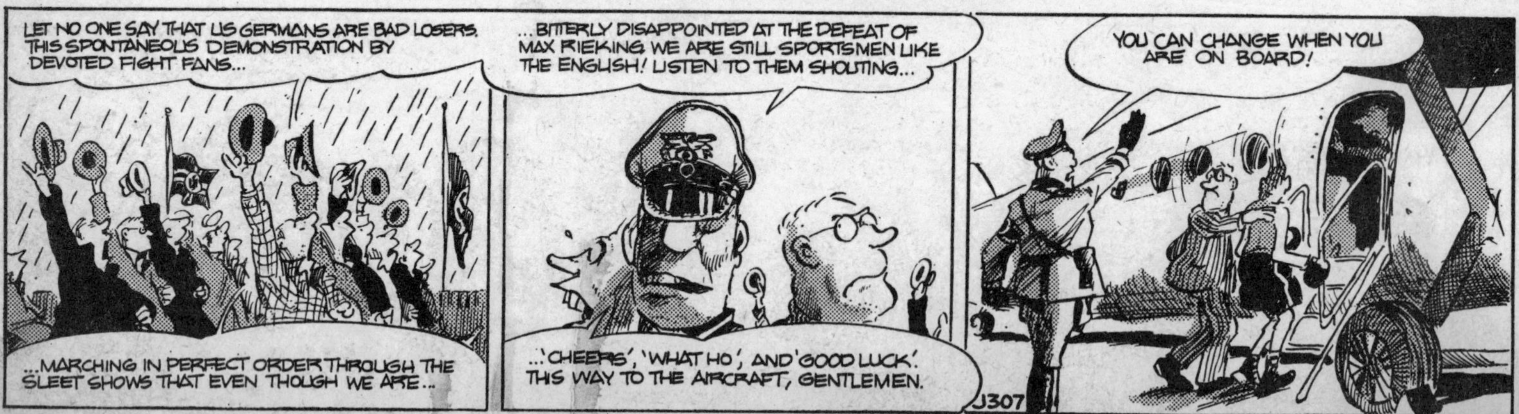
LET NO ONE SAY THAT US GERMANS ARE BAD LOSERS. THIS SPONTANEOUS DEMONSTRATION BY DEVOTED FIGHT FANS...
...MARCHING IN PERFECT ORDER THROUGH THE SLEET SHOWS THAT EVEN THOUGH WE ARE...
...BITTERLY DISAPPOINTED AT THE DEFEAT OF MAX RIEKING WE ARE STILL SPORTSMEN LIKE THE ENGLISH! LISTEN TO THEM SHOUTING...
...'CHEERS', 'WHAT HO', AND 'GOOD LUCK'. THIS WAY TO THE AIRCRAFT, GENTLEMEN.
YOU CAN CHANGE WHEN YOU ARE ON BOARD!
J307

And so back to Manchester...

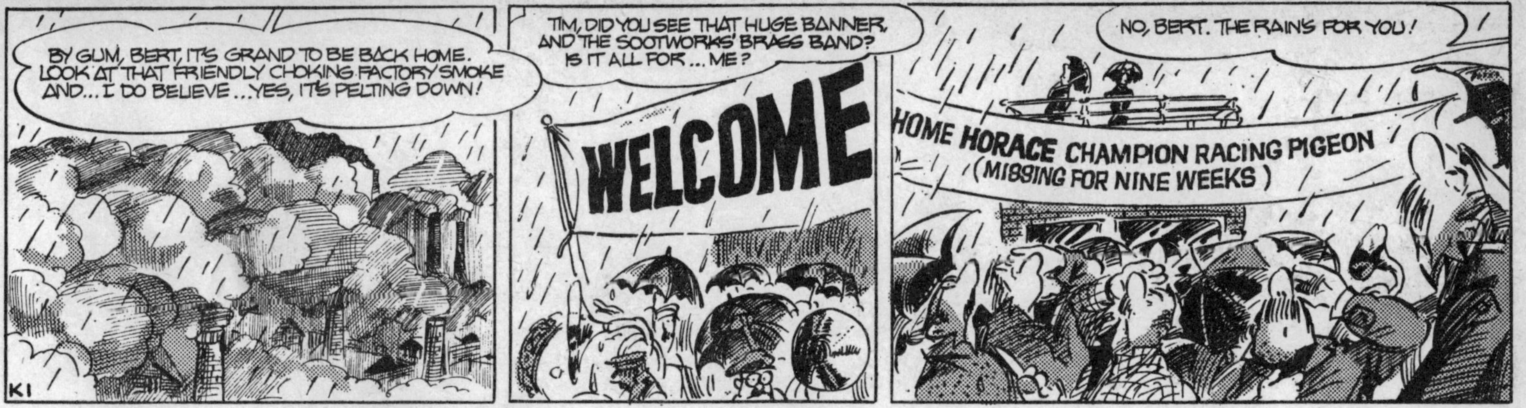

BY GUM, BERT, IT'S GRAND TO BE BACK HOME. LOOK AT THAT FRIENDLY CHOKING FACTORY SMOKE AND... I DO BELIEVE ...YES, IT'S PELTING DOWN!
K1
TIM, DID YOU SEE THAT HUGE BANNER, AND THE SOOTWORKS' BRASS BAND? IS IT ALL FOR ... ME?
WELCOME
NO, BERT. THE RAIN'S FOR YOU!
HOME HORACE CHAMPION RACING PIGEON
(MISSING FOR NINE WEEKS)

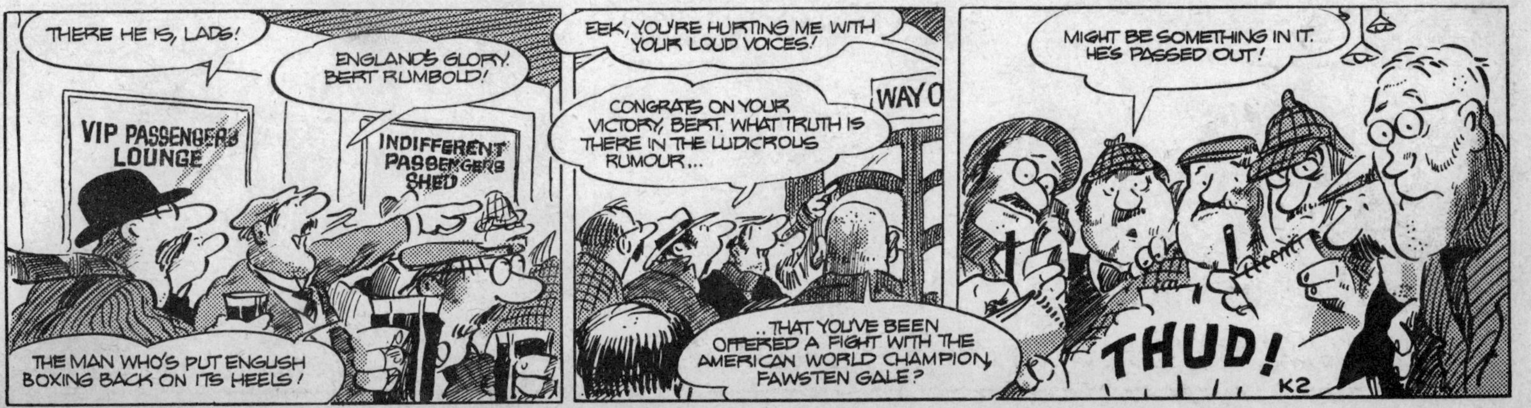

THERE HE IS, LADS!
ENGLAND'S GLORY. BERT RUMBOLD!
VIP PASSENGERS LOUNGE
INDIFFERENT PASSENGERS SHED
THE MAN WHO'S PUT ENGLISH BOXING BACK ON ITS HEELS!
EEK, YOU'RE HURTING ME WITH YOUR LOUD VOICES!
CONGRATS ON YOUR VICTORY, BERT. WHAT TRUTH IS THERE IN THE LUDICROUS RUMOUR...
..THAT YOU'VE BEEN OFFERED A FIGHT WITH THE AMERICAN WORLD CHAMPION, FAWSTEN GALE?
MIGHT BE SOMETHING IN IT. HE'S PASSED OUT!
THUD!
K2

And on the steps of the Fosdyke home...

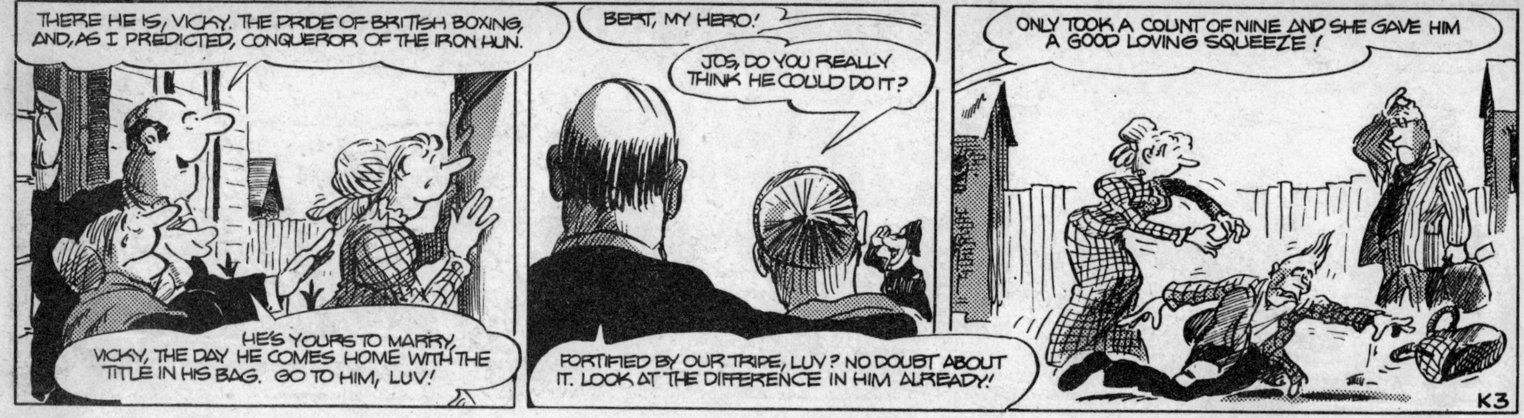
THERE HE IS, VICKY. THE PRIDE OF BRITISH BOXING, AND, AS I PREDICTED, CONQUEROR OF THE IRON HUN.
HE'S YOURS TO MARRY, VICKY, THE DAY HE COMES HOME WITH THE TITLE IN HIS BAG. GO TO HIM, LUV!
BERT, MY HERO!
JOS, DO YOU REALLY THINK HE COULD DO IT?
FORTIFIED BY OUR TRIPE, LUV? NO DOUBT ABOUT IT. LOOK AT THE DIFFERENCE IN HIM ALREADY!
ONLY TOOK A COUNT OF NINE AND SHE GAVE HIM A GOOD LOVING SQUEEZE!
K3

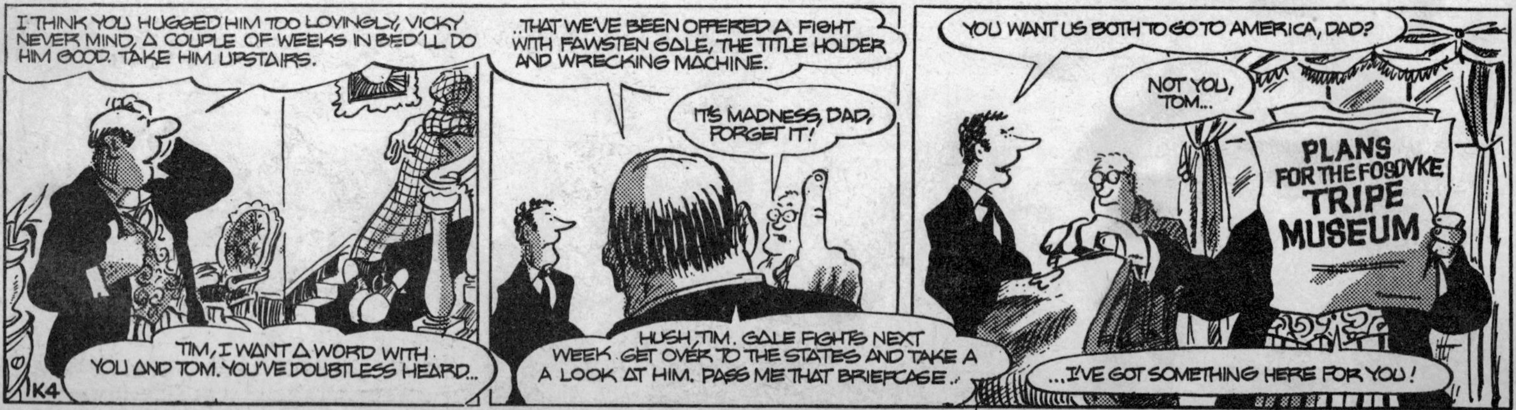
I THINK YOU HUGGED HIM TOO LOVINGLY, VICKY. NEVER MIND, A COUPLE OF WEEKS IN BED'LL DO HIM GOOD. TAKE HIM UPSTAIRS.
TIM, I WANT A WORD WITH YOU AND TOM. YOU'VE DOUBTLESS HEARD...
K4
...THAT WE'VE BEEN OFFERED A FIGHT WITH FAWSTEN GALE, THE TITLE HOLDER AND WRECKING MACHINE.
IT'S MADNESS, DAD, FORGET IT!
HUSH, TIM. GALE FIGHTS NEXT WEEK. GET OVER TO THE STATES AND TAKE A LOOK AT HIM. PASS ME THAT BRIEFCASE..
YOU WANT US BOTH TO GO TO AMERICA, DAD?
NOT YOU, TOM...
PLANS FOR THE FOSDYKE TRIPE MUSEUM
...I'VE GOT SOMETHING HERE FOR YOU!

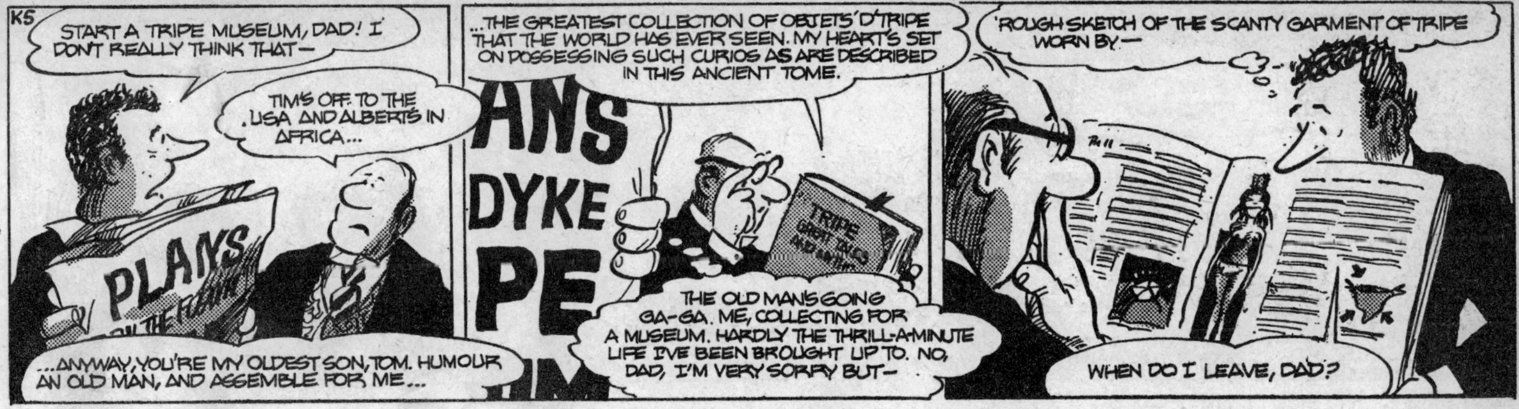
K5
START A TRIPE MUSEUM, DAD! I DON'T REALLY THINK THAT—
TIM'S OFF TO THE USA AND ALBERT'S IN AFRICA...
...ANYWAY, YOU'RE MY OLDEST SON, TOM. HUMOUR AN OLD MAN, AND ASSEMBLE FOR ME...
PLANS
...THE GREATEST COLLECTION OF OBJETS' D'TRIPE THAT THE WORLD HAS EVER SEEN. MY HEART'S SET ON POSSESSING SUCH CURIOS AS ARE DESCRIBED IN THIS ANCIENT TOME.
ANS
DYKE
PE
TRIPE
THE OLD MAN'S GOING GA-GA. ME, COLLECTING FOR A MUSEUM. HARDLY THE THRILL-A-MINUTE LIFE I'VE BEEN BROUGHT UP TO. NO, DAD, I'M VERY SORRY BUT—
'ROUGH SKETCH OF THE SCANTY GARMENT OF TRIPE WORN BY—
WHEN DO I LEAVE, DAD?

Far away in the fetid undergrowth of the African jungle...

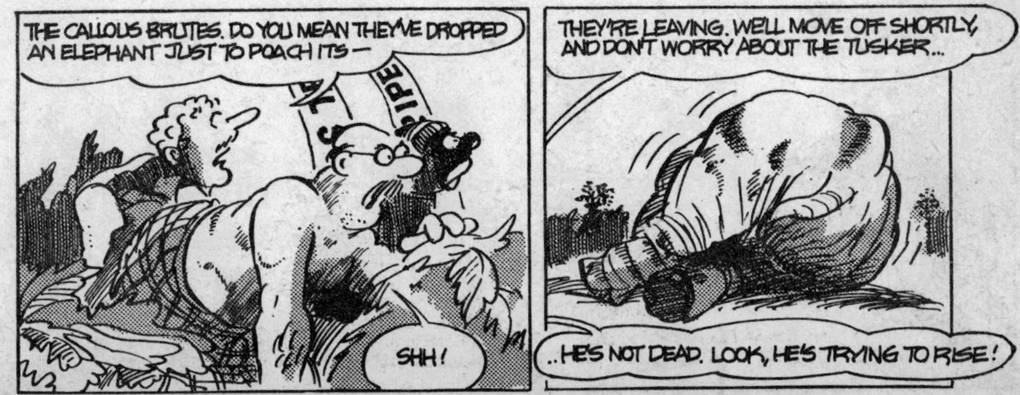
THE CALLOUS BRUTES. DO YOU MEAN THEY'VE DROPPED AN ELEPHANT JUST TO POACH ITS—
SHH!
THEY'RE LEAVING. WE'LL MOVE OFF SHORTLY, AND DON'T WORRY ABOUT THE TUSKER...
..HE'S NOT DEAD. LOOK, HE'S TRYING TO RISE!

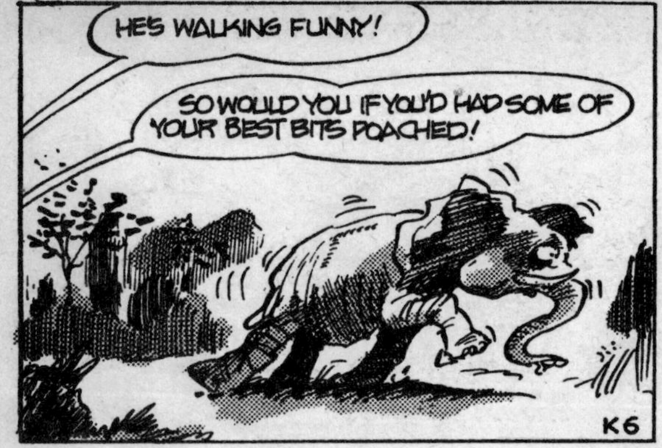
HE'S WALKING FUNNY!
SO WOULD YOU IF YOU'D HAD SOME OF YOUR BEST BITS POACHED!
K6

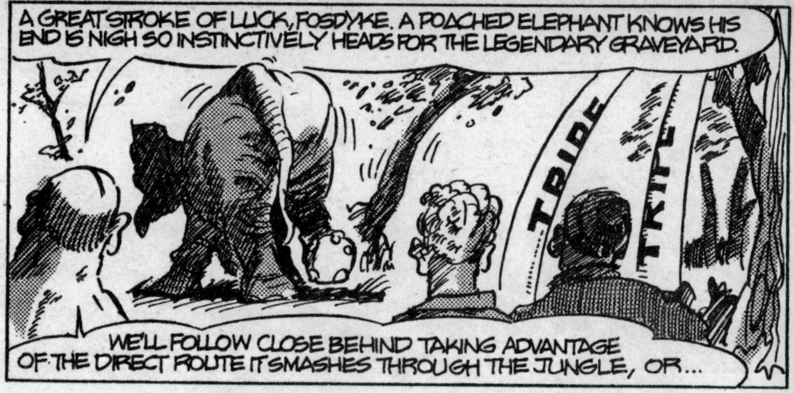
A GREAT STROKE OF LUCK, FOSDYKE. A POACHED ELEPHANT KNOWS HIS END IS NIGH SO INSTINCTIVELY HEADS FOR THE LEGENDARY GRAVEYARD.
TRIPE
TRIPE
WE'LL FOLLOW CLOSE BEHIND TAKING ADVANTAGE OF THE DIRECT ROUTE IT SMASHES THROUGH THE JUNGLE, OR...

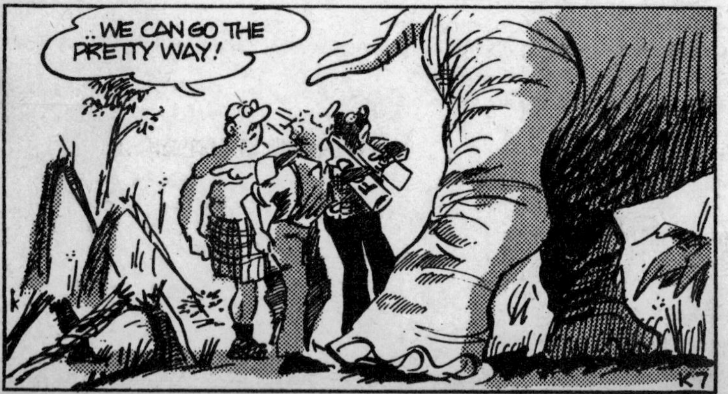
..WE CAN GO THE PRETTY WAY!
K7

Some time later...

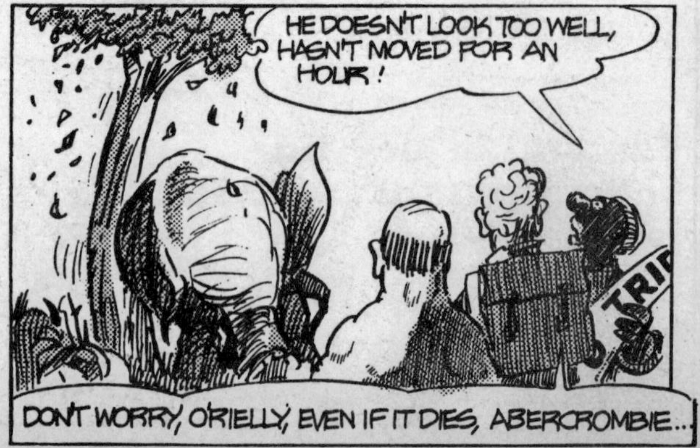
HE DOESN'T LOOK TOO WELL, HASN'T MOVED FOR AN HOUR!
DON'T WORRY, O'RIELLY, EVEN IF IT DIES, ABERCROMBIE...

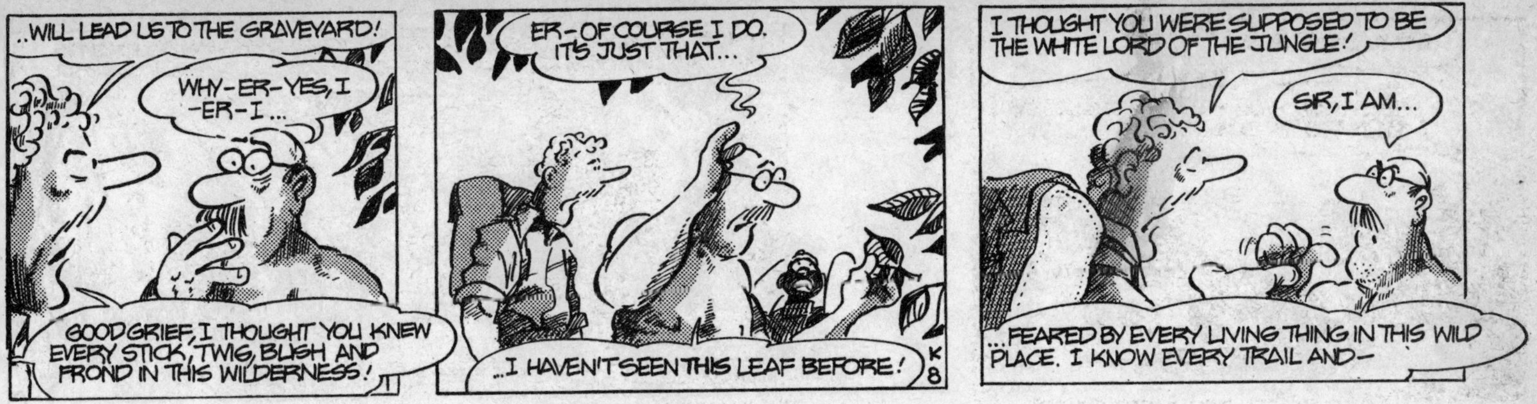
..WILL LEAD US TO THE GRAVEYARD!
WHY-ER-YES, I -ER-I...
GOOD GRIEF, I THOUGHT YOU KNEW EVERY STICK, TWIG, BUSH AND FROND IN THIS WILDERNESS!
ER-OF COURSE I DO. IT'S JUST THAT...
...I HAVEN'T SEEN THIS LEAF BEFORE!
K 8
I THOUGHT YOU WERE SUPPOSED TO BE THE WHITE LORD OF THE JUNGLE!
SIR, I AM...
...FEARED BY EVERY LIVING THING IN THIS WILD PLACE. I KNOW EVERY TRAIL AND-

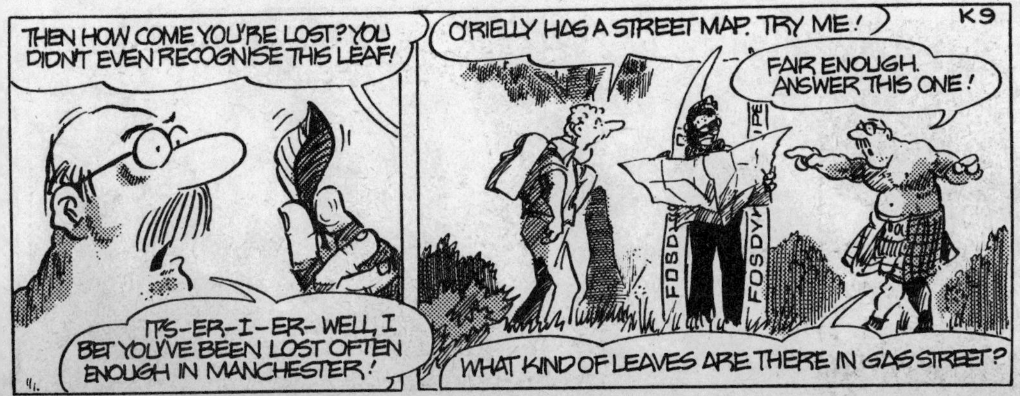
THEN HOW COME YOU'RE LOST? YOU DIDN'T EVEN RECOGNISE THIS LEAF!
IT'S-ER-I-ER-WELL, I BET YOU'VE BEEN LOST OFTEN ENOUGH IN MANCHESTER!
K9
O'RIELLY HAS A STREET MAP. TRY ME!
FAIR ENOUGH. ANSWER THIS ONE!
WHAT KIND OF LEAVES ARE THERE IN GAS STREET?

But time passes...

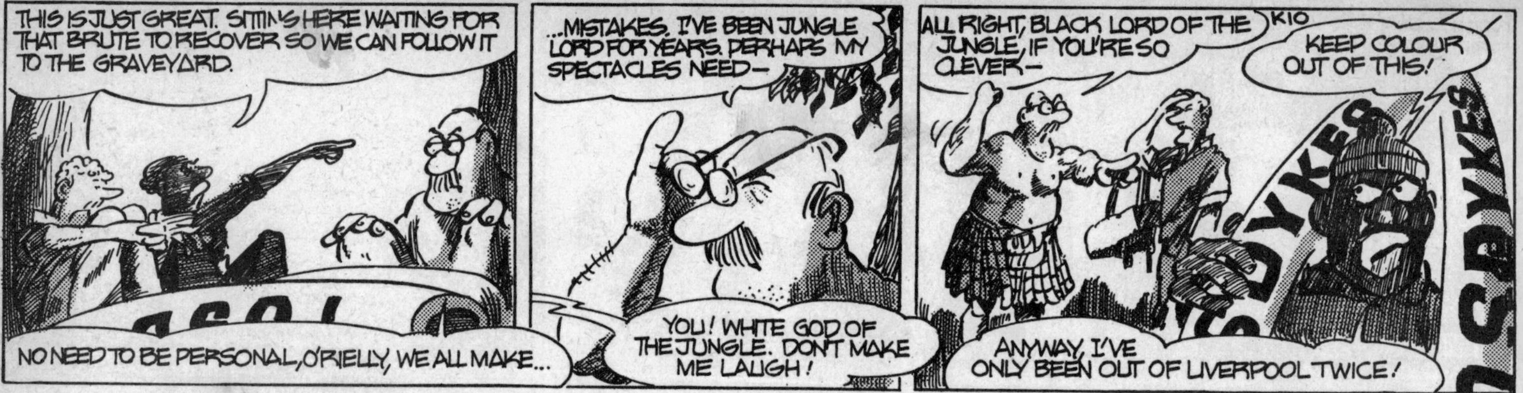
THIS IS JUST GREAT. SITTIN'S HERE WAITING FOR THAT BRUTE TO RECOVER SO WE CAN FOLLOW IT TO THE GRAVEYARD.
NO NEED TO BE PERSONAL, O'RIELLY, WE ALL MAKE...
...MISTAKES. I'VE BEEN JUNGLE LORD FOR YEARS. PERHAPS MY SPECTACLES NEED—
YOU! WHITE GOD OF THE JUNGLE. DON'T MAKE ME LAUGH!
ALL RIGHT, BLACK LORD OF THE JUNGLE, IF YOU'RE SO CLEVER—
K10
KEEP COLOUR OUT OF THIS!
ANYWAY, I'VE ONLY BEEN OUT OF LIVERPOOL TWICE!

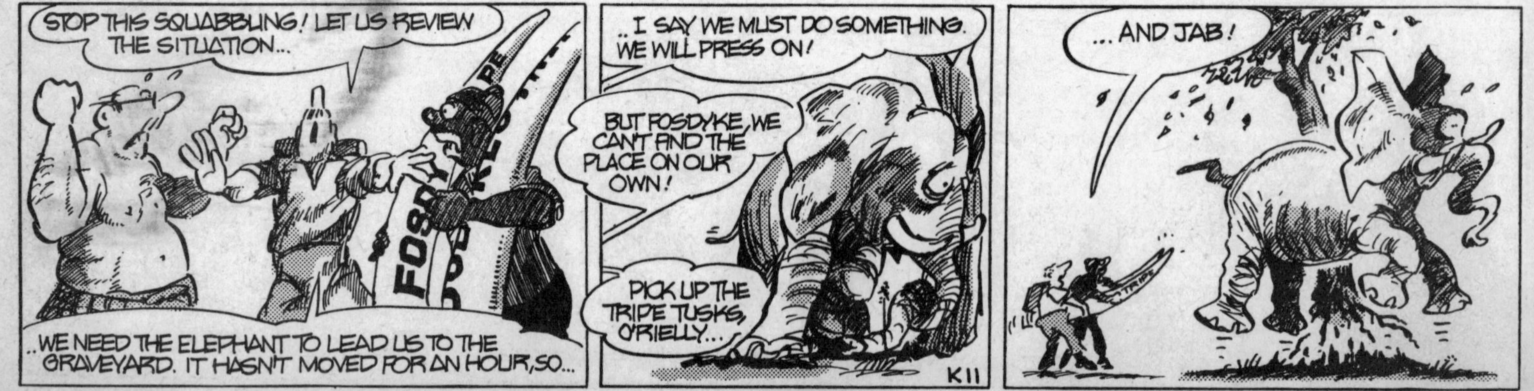
STOP THIS SQUABBLING! LET US REVIEW THE SITUATION...
...WE NEED THE ELEPHANT TO LEAD US TO THE GRAVEYARD. IT HASN'T MOVED FOR AN HOUR, SO...
.. I SAY WE MUST DO SOMETHING. WE WILL PRESS ON!
BUT FOSDYKE, WE CAN'T FIND THE PLACE ON OUR OWN!
PICK UP THE TRIPE TUSKS, O'RIELLY...
K11
... AND JAB!

Back home in Manchester...

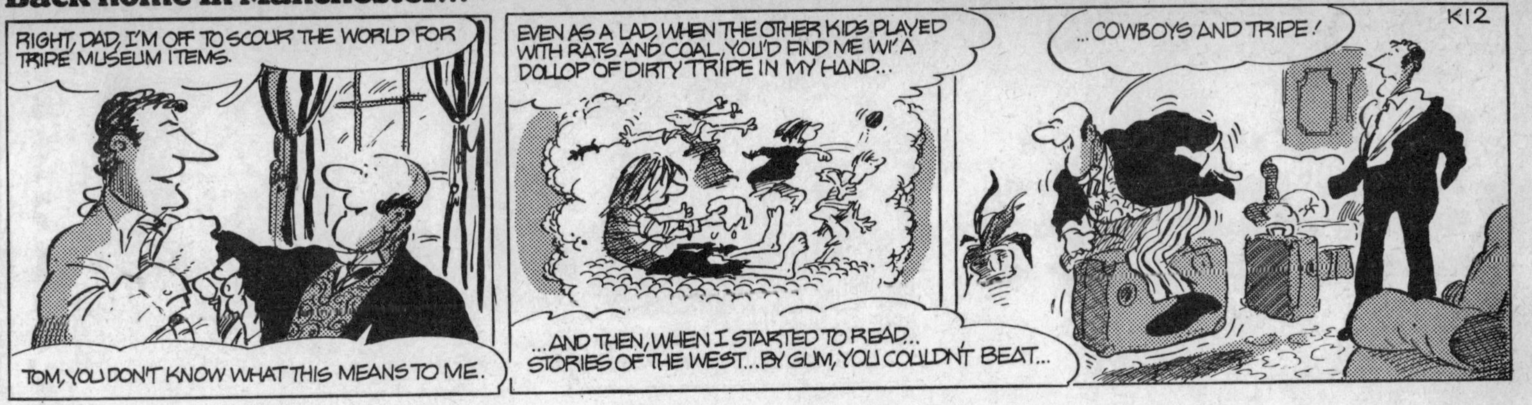

RIGHT, DAD, I'M OFF TO SCOUR THE WORLD FOR TRIPE MUSEUM ITEMS.
TOM, YOU DON'T KNOW WHAT THIS MEANS TO ME.
EVEN AS A LAD, WHEN THE OTHER KIDS PLAYED WITH RATS AND COAL, YOU'D FIND ME WI' A DOLLOP OF DIRTY TRIPE IN MY HAND...
...AND THEN, WHEN I STARTED TO READ... STORIES OF THE WEST... BY GUM, YOU COULDN'T BEAT...
...COWBOYS AND TRIPE!
K12

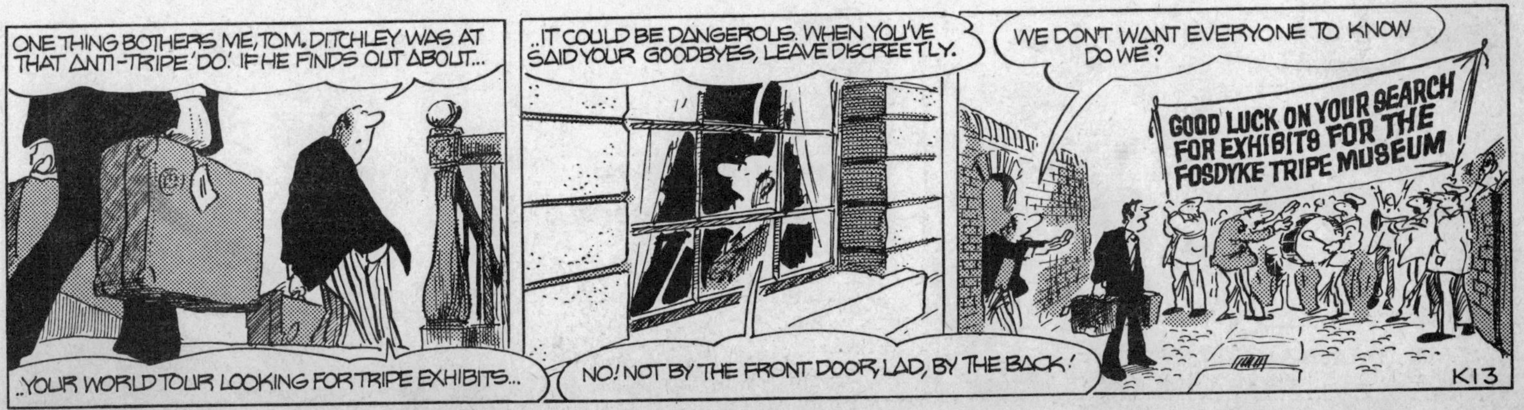

ONE THING BOTHERS ME, TOM. DITCHLEY WAS AT THAT ANTI-TRIPE 'DO'. IF HE FINDS OUT ABOUT...
..YOUR WORLD TOUR LOOKING FOR TRIPE EXHIBITS...
..IT COULD BE DANGEROUS. WHEN YOU'VE SAID YOUR GOODBYES, LEAVE DISCREETLY.
NO! NOT BY THE FRONT DOOR, LAD, BY THE BACK!
WE DON'T WANT EVERYONE TO KNOW DO WE?
GOOD LUCK ON YOUR SEARCH FOR EXHIBITS FOR THE FOSDYKE TRIPE MUSEUM
K13

Meanwhile, skulking in the Temple of Impending Doom, Ditchley and his latest partner in crime nurse their injured pride...

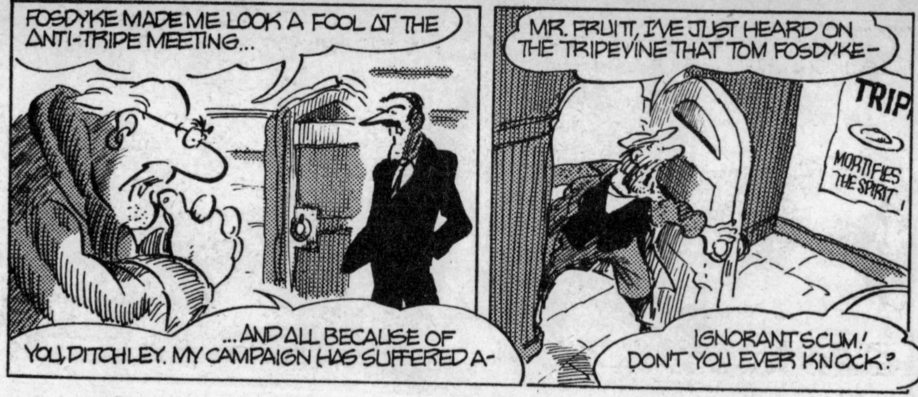
FOSDYKE MADE ME LOOK A FOOL AT THE ANTI-TRIPE MEETING...
...AND ALL BECAUSE OF YOU, DITCHLEY. MY CAMPAIGN HAS SUFFERED A-
MR. FRUITT, I'VE JUST HEARD ON THE TRIPEVINE THAT TOM FOSDYKE-
TRIP
MORTIFIES THE SPIRIT!
IGNORANT SCUM! DON'T YOU EVER KNOCK?

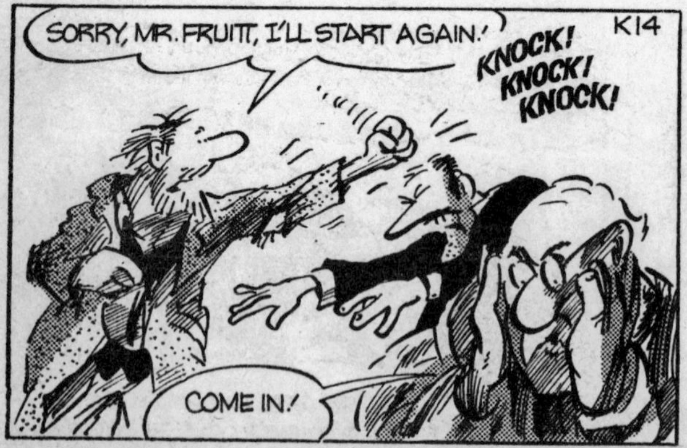
SORRY, MR. FRUITT, I'LL START AGAIN!
K14
KNOCK! KNOCK! KNOCK!
COME IN!

And when the stupendous news has been imparted...

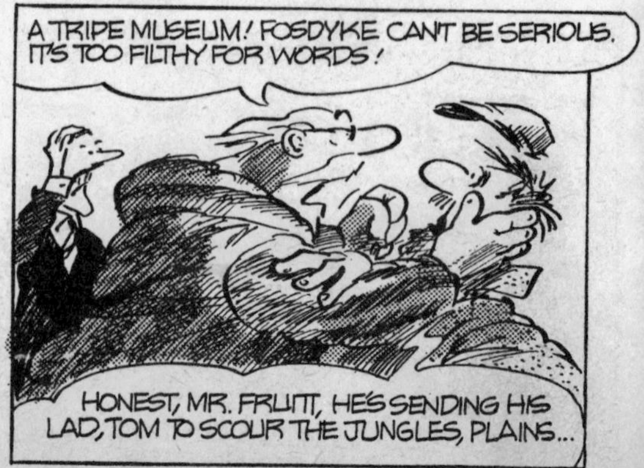
A TRIPE MUSEUM! FOSDYKE CAN'T BE SERIOUS. IT'S TOO FILTHY FOR WORDS!
HONEST, MR. FRUITT, HE'S SENDING HIS LAD, TOM TO SCOUR THE JUNGLES, PLAINS...

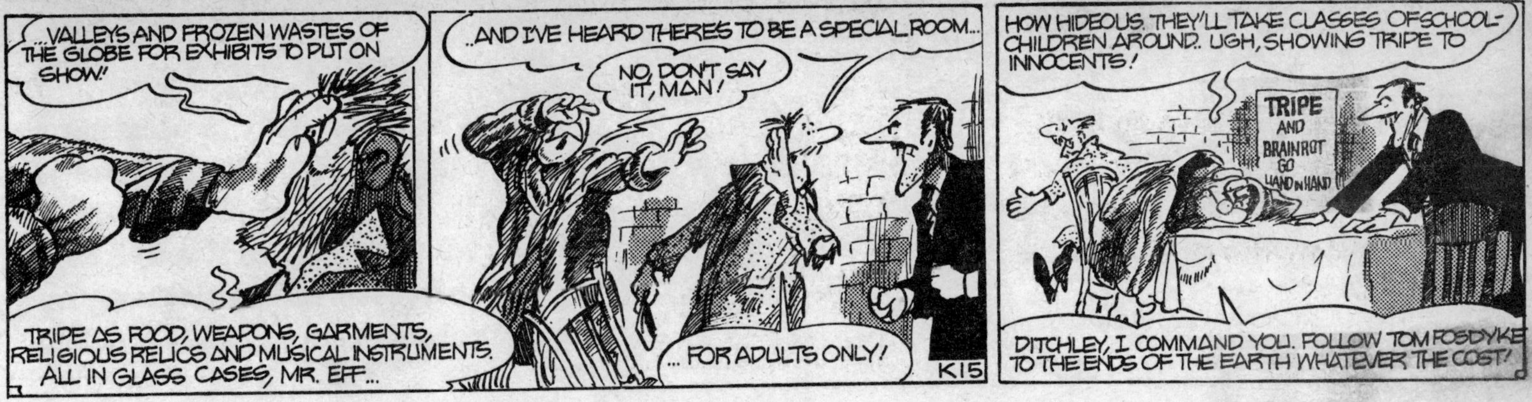
...VALLEYS AND FROZEN WASTES OF THE GLOBE FOR EXHIBITS TO PUT ON SHOW!
TRIPE AS FOOD, WEAPONS, GARMENTS, RELIGIOUS RELICS AND MUSICAL INSTRUMENTS. ALL IN GLASS CASES, MR. EFF...
...AND I'VE HEARD THERE'S TO BE A SPECIAL ROOM...
NO, DON'T SAY IT, MAN!
...FOR ADULTS ONLY!
K15
HOW HIDEOUS. THEY'LL TAKE CLASSES OF SCHOOL-CHILDREN AROUND.. UGH, SHOWING TRIPE TO INNOCENTS!
TRIPE AND BRAINROT GO HAND IN HAND
DITCHLEY, I COMMAND YOU. FOLLOW TOM FOSDYKE TO THE ENDS OF THE EARTH WHATEVER THE COST!

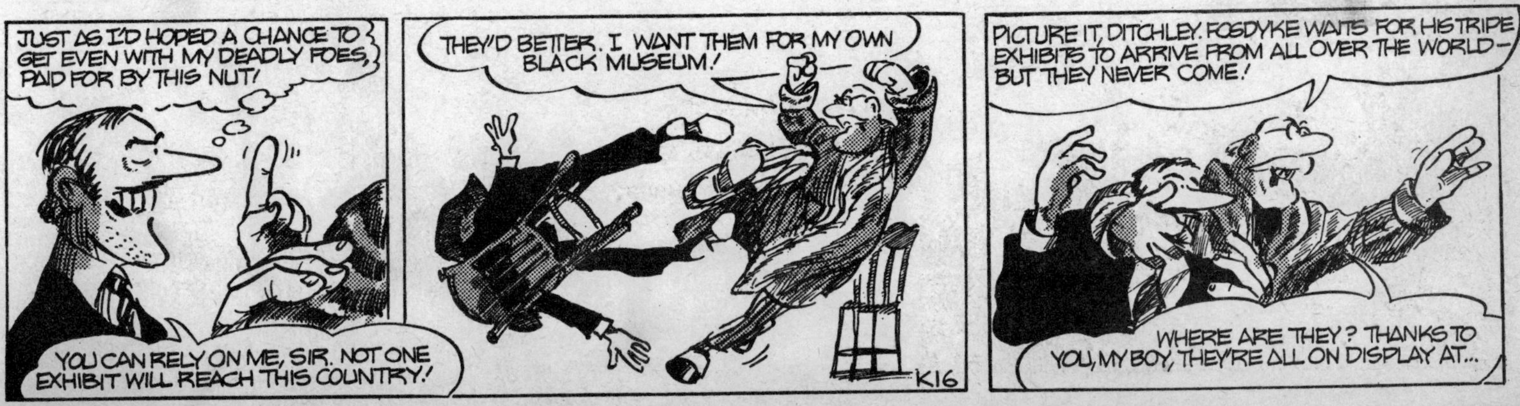
JUST AS I'D HOPED A CHANCE TO GET EVEN WITH MY DEADLY FOES, PAID FOR BY THIS NUT!
YOU CAN RELY ON ME, SIR. NOT ONE EXHIBIT WILL REACH THIS COUNTRY!
THEY'D BETTER. I WANT THEM FOR MY OWN BLACK MUSEUM!
K16
PICTURE IT, DITCHLEY. FOSDYKE WAITS FOR HIS TRIPE EXHIBITS TO ARRIVE FROM ALL OVER THE WORLD- BUT THEY NEVER COME!
WHERE ARE THEY? THANKS TO YOU, MY BOY, THEY'RE ALL ON DISPLAY AT...

...FRUITTS BLACK MUSEUM, 273 BILE STREET...
...WITH A FRANTIC, BIASED COMMENTARY IN EIGHTEEN LANGUAGES OVER HEADSETS, SHRIEKING OUT—
K17
COULDN'T THE MUSEUM GUARDS DO THE COMMENTARY?
FOOL! THEY'LL BE FULLY OCCUPIED
FRUITTS BLACK MUSEUM
...ENCOURAGING VISITORS TO DAMAGE THE EXHIBITS!

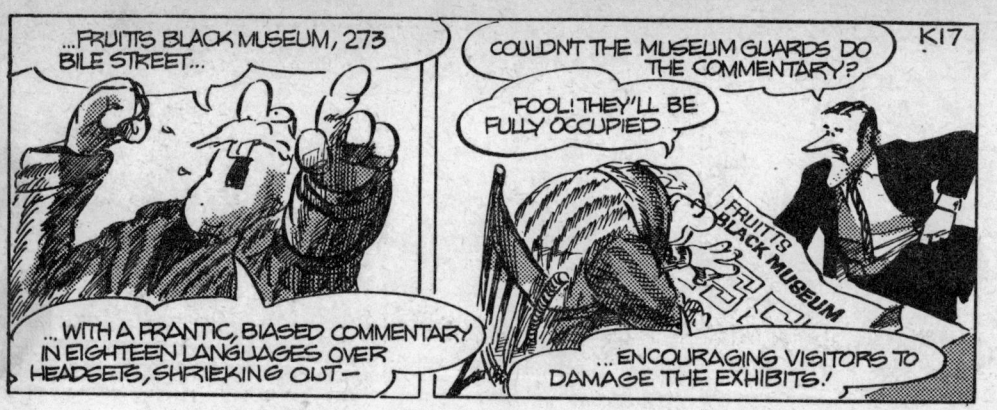

While Ditchley is plotting further devilries for the discomfort of his old adversary, the Fosdykes, oblivious of Tom's danger, relax in their quiet home...

HOUSE SEEMS EMPTY WITHOUT THE LADS, JOS. ALBERT UP THE CONGO—
RUM N' COCO, MOTHER!
..AND TOM AWAY HUNTING FOR ODD BITS OF TRIPE.
I WONDER HOW TIM'S DOING IN THE U.S.A? HE'S RUNNING THE RULE OVER FAWSTEN GALE, MY BELOVED'S NEXT OPPONENT.
AYE, VICKY, I HOPE HE SPOTS A WEAKNESS.

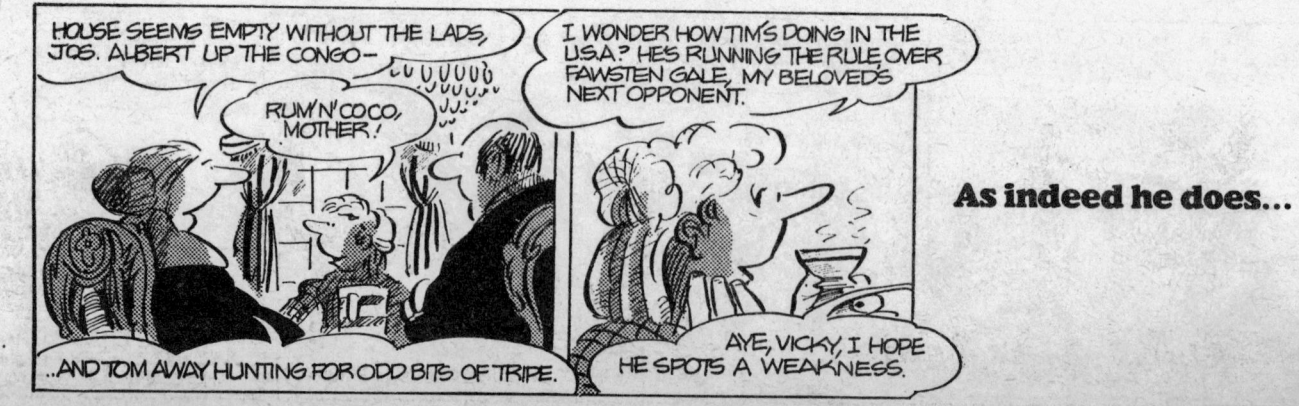

As indeed he does...

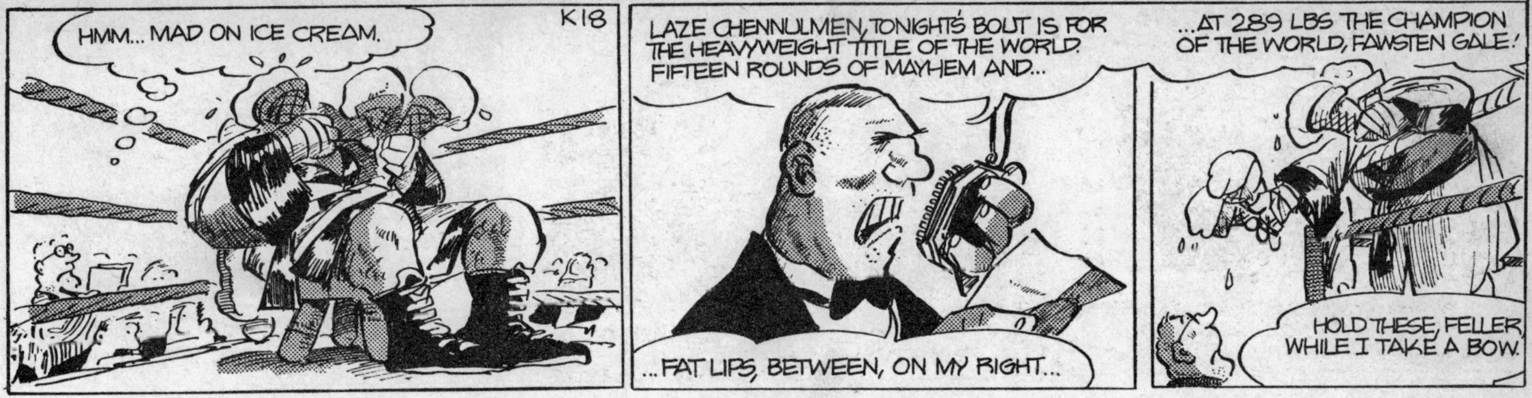
HMM... MAD ON ICE CREAM.
K18
LAZE CHENNULMEN, TONIGHT'S BOUT IS FOR THE HEAVYWEIGHT TITLE OF THE WORLD. FIFTEEN ROUNDS OF MAYHEM AND...
...FAT LIPS, BETWEEN, ON MY RIGHT...
...AT 289 LBS THE CHAMPION OF THE WORLD, FAWSTEN GALE!
HOLD THESE, FELLER WHILE I TAKE A BOW.

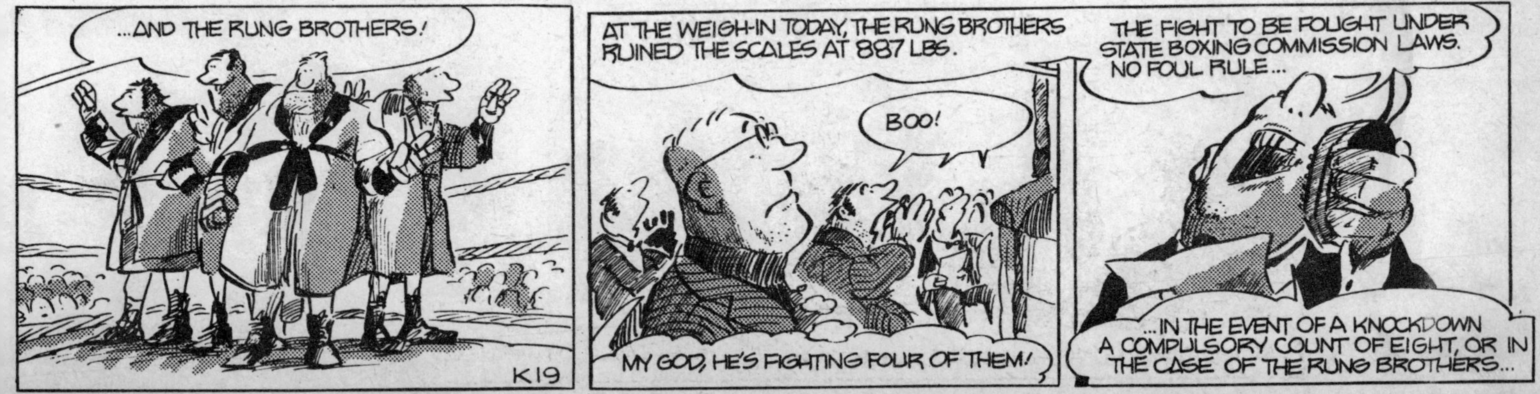
...AND THE RUNG BROTHERS!
K19
AT THE WEIGH-IN TODAY, THE RUNG BROTHERS RUINED THE SCALES AT 887 LBS.
BOO!
MY GOD, HE'S FIGHTING FOUR OF THEM!
THE FIGHT TO BE FOUGHT UNDER STATE BOXING COMMISSION LAWS. NO FOUL RULE...
...IN THE EVENT OF A KNOCKDOWN A COMPULSORY COUNT OF EIGHT, OR IN THE CASE OF THE RUNG BROTHERS...

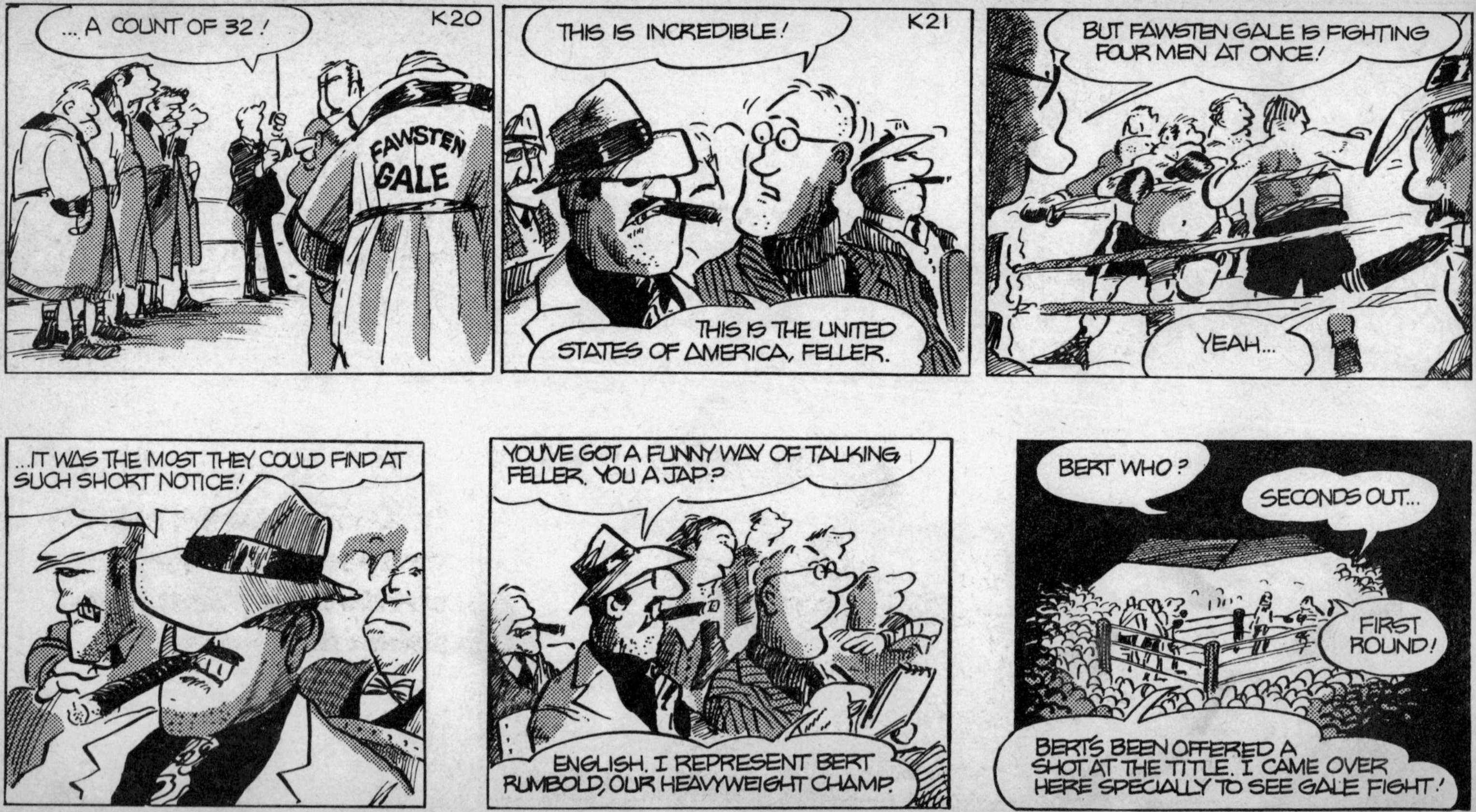
K20
... A COUNT OF 32 !
FAWSTEN GALE
K21
THIS IS INCREDIBLE !
THIS IS THE UNITED STATES OF AMERICA, FELLER.
BUT FAWSTEN GALE IS FIGHTING FOUR MEN AT ONCE !
YEAH...
...IT WAS THE MOST THEY COULD FIND AT SUCH SHORT NOTICE !
YOU'VE GOT A FUNNY WAY OF TALKING, FELLER. YOU A JAP ?
ENGLISH. I REPRESENT BERT RUMBOLD, OUR HEAVYWEIGHT CHAMP.
BERT WHO ?
SECONDS OUT...
FIRST ROUND !
BERT'S BEEN OFFERED A SHOT AT THE TITLE. I CAME OVER HERE SPECIALLY TO SEE GALE FIGHT !

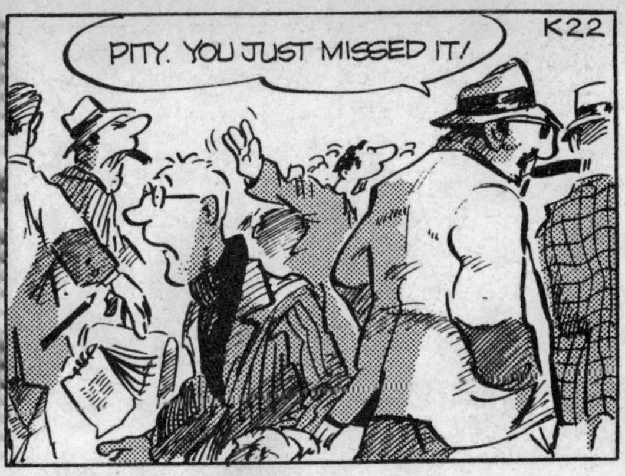
K22
PITY. YOU JUST MISSED IT!

And a few seconds later...

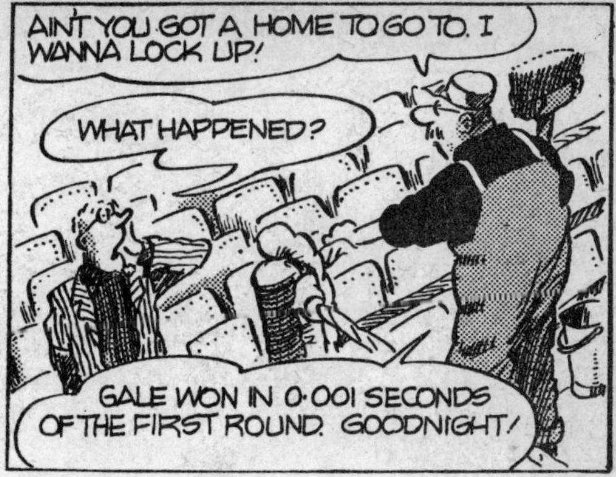
AIN'T YOU GOT A HOME TO GO TO. I WANNA LOCK UP!
WHAT HAPPENED?
GALE WON IN 0·001 SECONDS OF THE FIRST ROUND. GOODNIGHT!

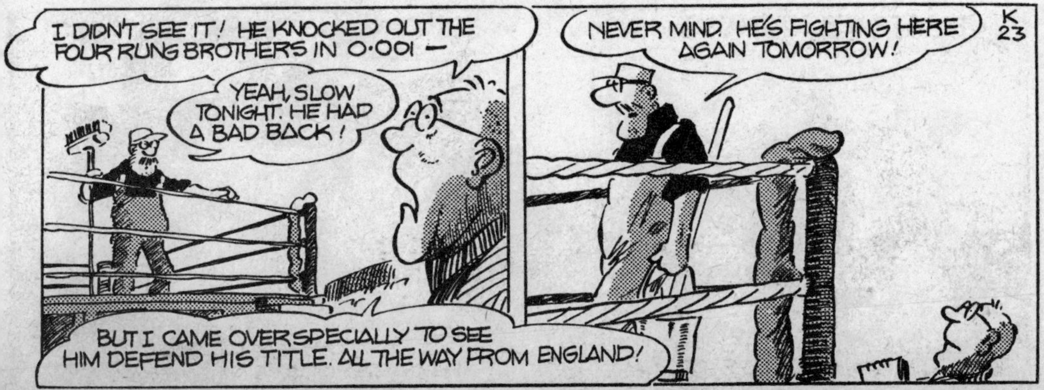
I DIDN'T SEE IT! HE KNOCKED OUT THE FOUR RUNG BROTHERS IN 0·001 –
YEAH, SLOW TONIGHT. HE HAD A BAD BACK!
BUT I CAME OVER SPECIALLY TO SEE HIM DEFEND HIS TITLE. ALL THE WAY FROM ENGLAND!
NEVER MIND. HE'S FIGHTING HERE AGAIN TOMORROW!
K
23

In Africa , Albert and his companions usher the stricken elephant to its final resting place...

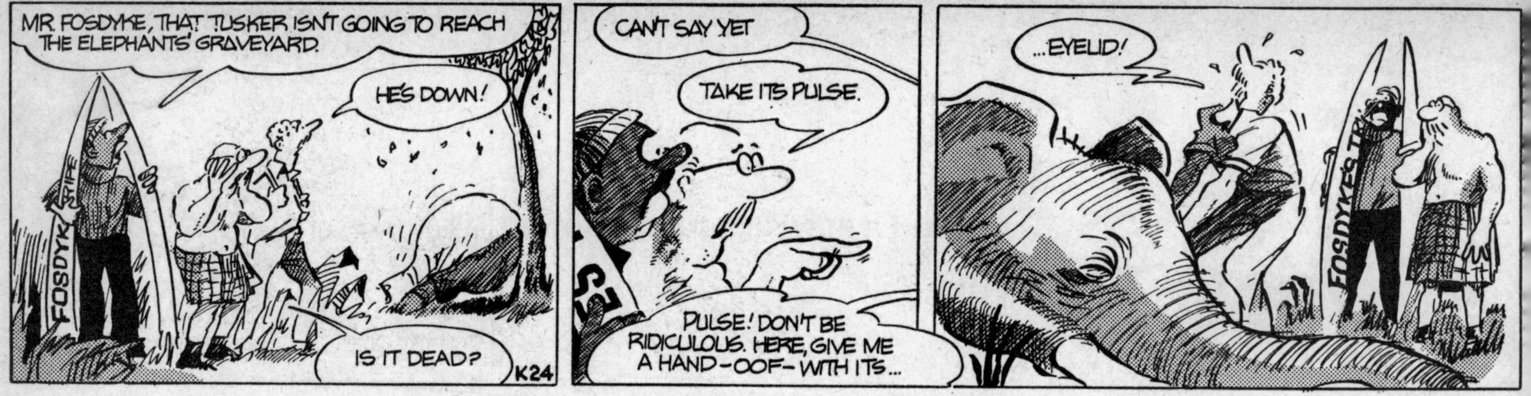
MR. FOSDYKE, THAT TUSKER ISN'T GOING TO REACH THE ELEPHANTS' GRAVEYARD.
HE'S DOWN!
IS IT DEAD?
K24
CAN'T SAY YET
TAKE ITS PULSE.
PULSE! DON'T BE RIDICULOUS. HERE, GIVE ME A HAND-OOF-WITH ITS...
...EYELID!

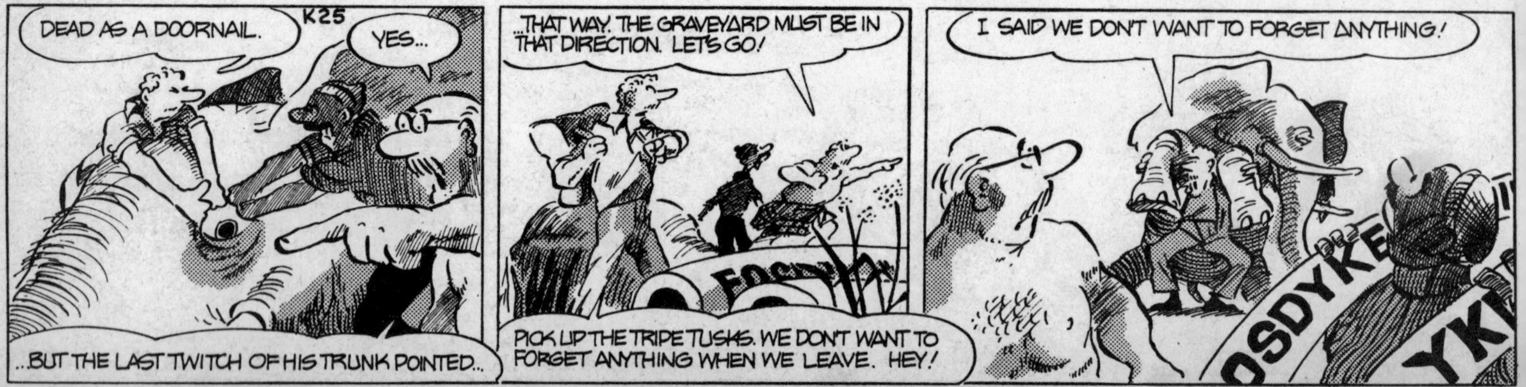
DEAD AS A DOORNAIL.
K25
YES...
...BUT THE LAST TWITCH OF HIS TRUNK POINTED...
...THAT WAY. THE GRAVEYARD MUST BE IN THAT DIRECTION. LET'S GO!
PICK UP THE TRIPE TUSKS. WE DON'T WANT TO FORGET ANYTHING WHEN WE LEAVE. HEY!
I SAID WE DON'T WANT TO FORGET ANYTHING!

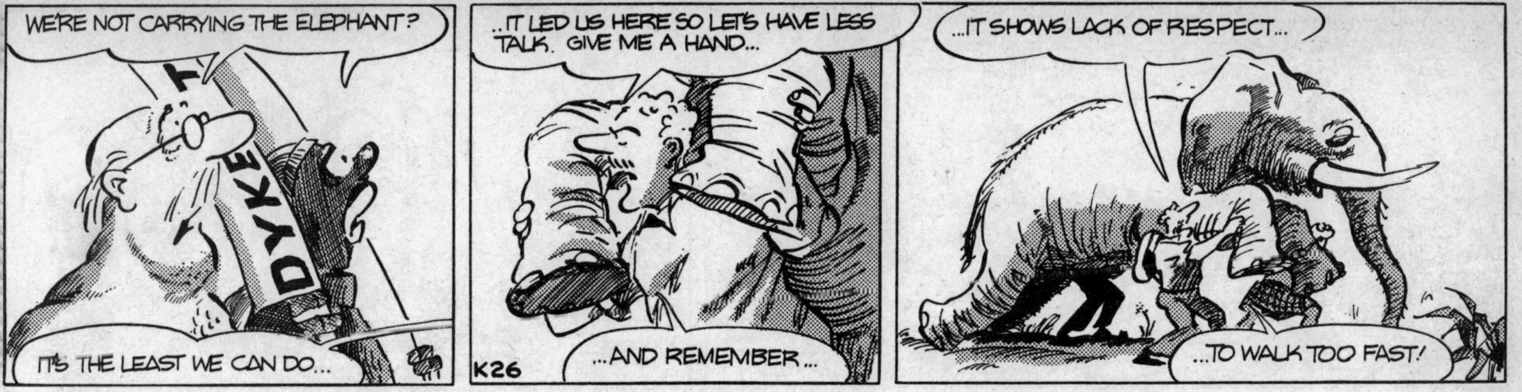
WE'RE NOT CARRYING THE ELEPHANT?
DYKE
IT'S THE LEAST WE CAN DO...
...IT LED US HERE SO LET'S HAVE LESS TALK. GIVE ME A HAND...
...AND REMEMBER...
K26
...IT SHOWS LACK OF RESPECT...
...TO WALK TOO FAST!

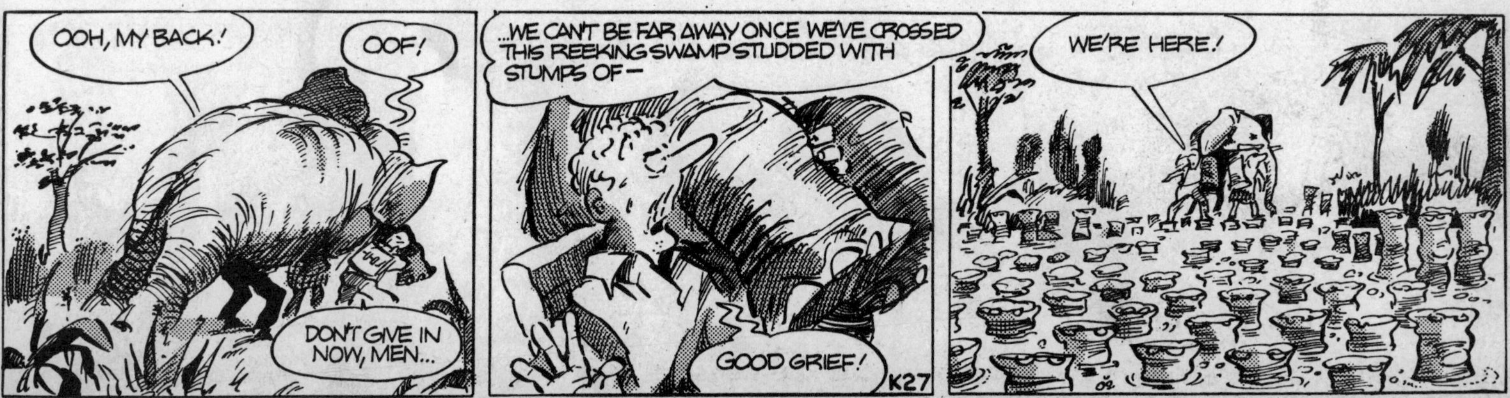
OOH, MY BACK!
OOF!
DON'T GIVE IN NOW, MEN...
...WE CAN'T BE FAR AWAY ONCE WE'VE CROSSED THIS REEKING SWAMP STUDDED WITH STUMPS OF –
GOOD GRIEF!
K27
WE'RE HERE!

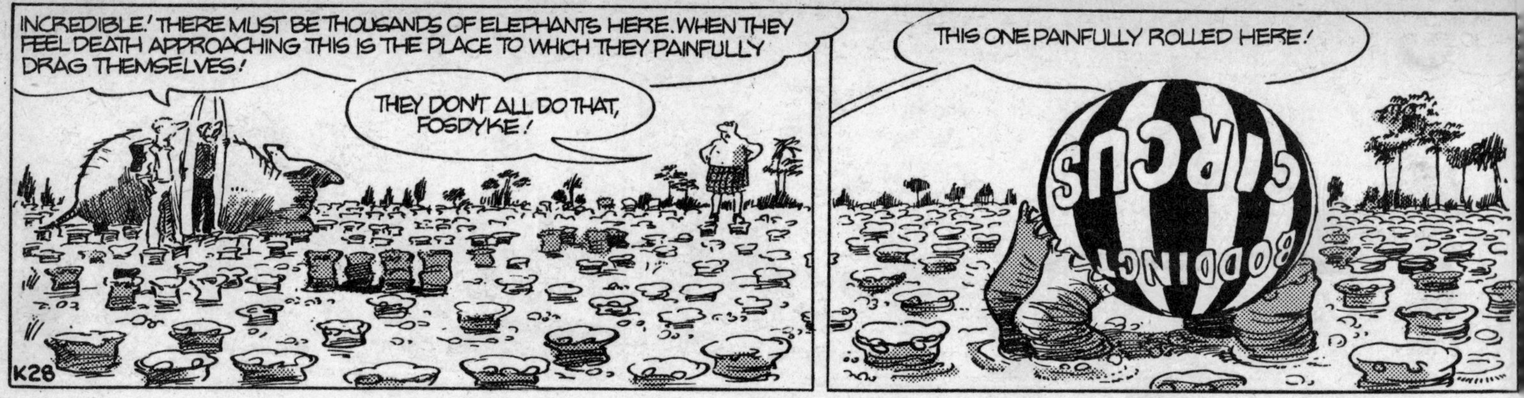
INCREDIBLE! THERE MUST BE THOUSANDS OF ELEPHANTS HERE. WHEN THEY FEEL DEATH APPROACHING THIS IS THE PLACE TO WHICH THEY PAINFULLY DRAG THEMSELVES!
THEY DON'T ALL DO THAT, FOSDYKE!
K28
THIS ONE PAINFULLY ROLLED HERE!
CIRCUS
BODINGT

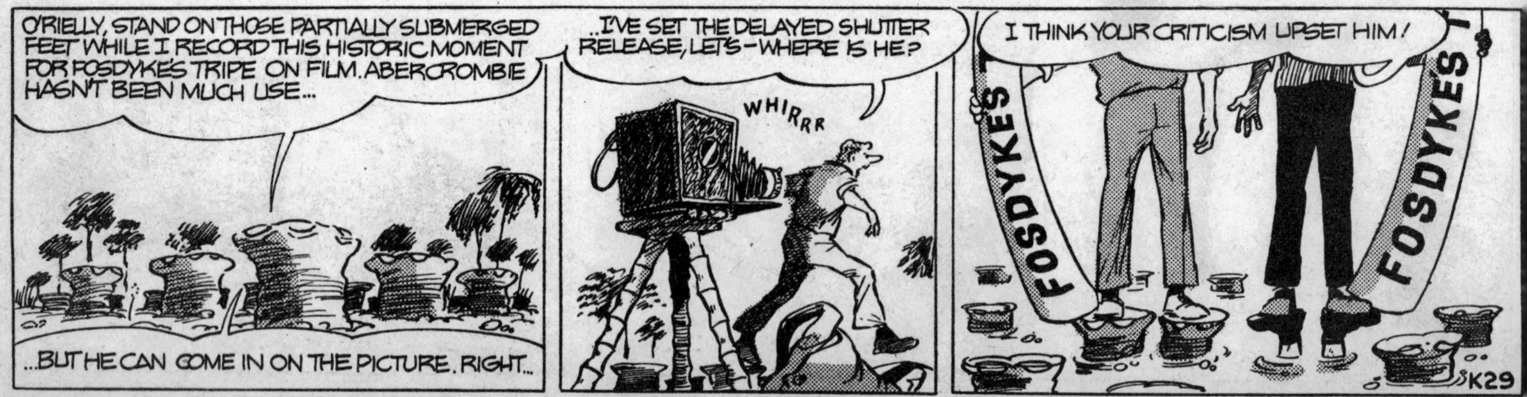
O'RIELLY, STAND ON THOSE PARTIALLY SUBMERGED FEET WHILE I RECORD THIS HISTORIC MOMENT FOR FOSDYKE'S TRIPE ON FILM. ABERCROMBIE HASN'T BEEN MUCH USE...
...BUT HE CAN COME IN ON THE PICTURE. RIGHT...
...I'VE SET THE DELAYED SHUTTER RELEASE, LET'S – WHERE IS HE?
WHIRRR
I THINK YOUR CRITICISM UPSET HIM!
FOSDYKES T
FOSDYKE'S T
K29

Back at Cyrus Fruitt's headquarters...

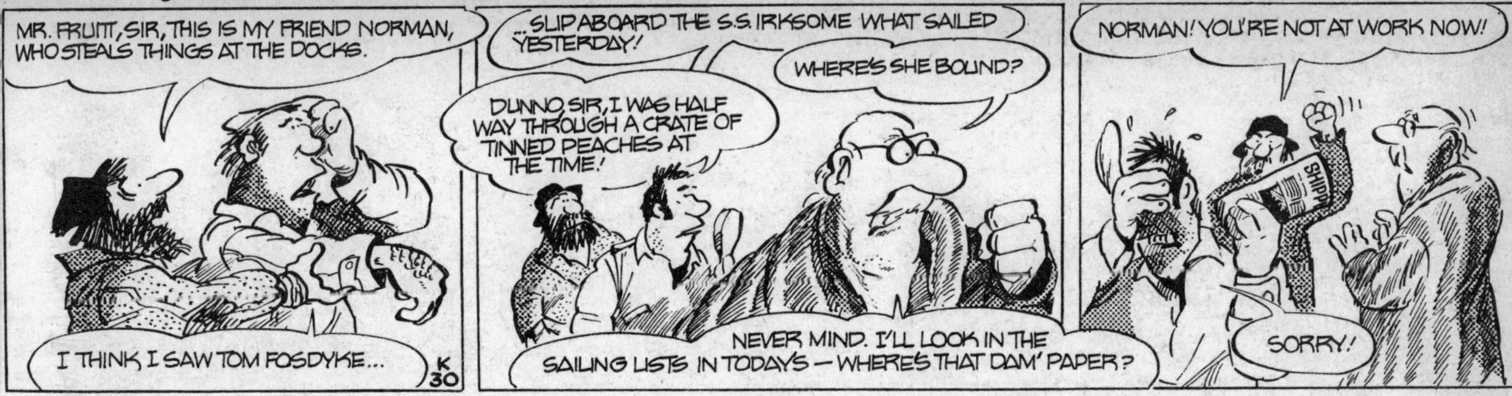
MR. FRUITT, SIR, THIS IS MY FRIEND NORMAN, WHO STEALS THINGS AT THE DOCKS.
I THINK I SAW TOM FOSDYKE...
K 30
...SLIP ABOARD THE S.S. IRKSOME WHAT SAILED YESTERDAY!
WHERE'S SHE BOUND?
DUNNO, SIR, I WAS HALF WAY THROUGH A CRATE OF TINNED PEACHES AT THE TIME!
NEVER MIND. I'LL LOOK IN THE SAILING LISTS IN TODAY'S — WHERE'S THAT DAM' PAPER?
NORMAN! YOU'RE NOT AT WORK NOW!
SORRY!

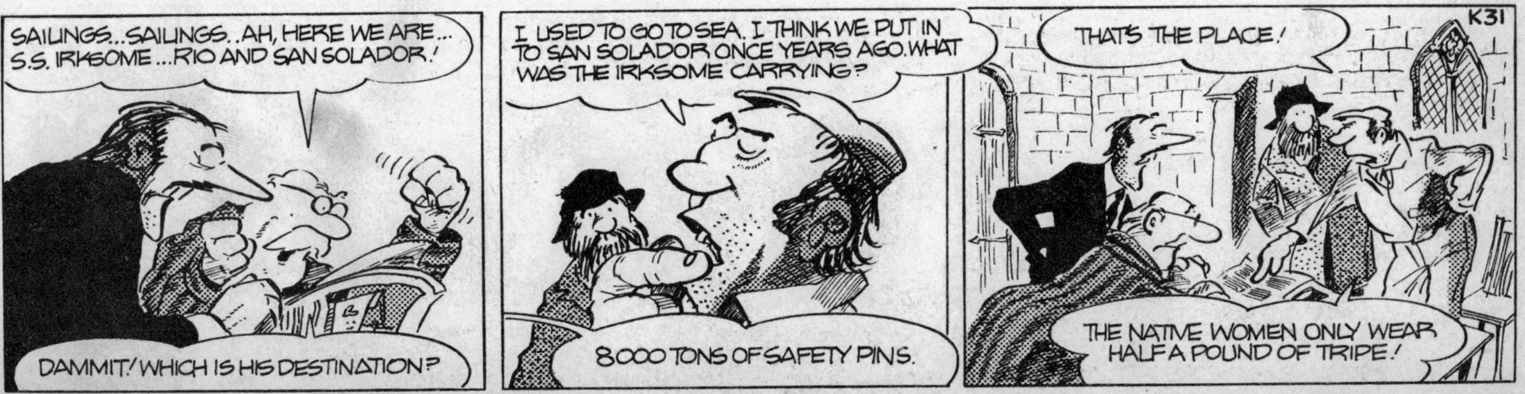
SAILINGS...SAILINGS..AH, HERE WE ARE... S.S. IRKSOME...RIO AND SAN SOLADOR!
DAMMIT! WHICH IS HIS DESTINATION?
I USED TO GO TO SEA. I THINK WE PUT IN TO SAN SOLADOR ONCE YEARS AGO. WHAT WAS THE IRKSOME CARRYING?
8000 TONS OF SAFETY PINS.
K31
THAT'S THE PLACE!
THE NATIVE WOMEN ONLY WEAR HALF A POUND OF TRIPE!

A few hours later...

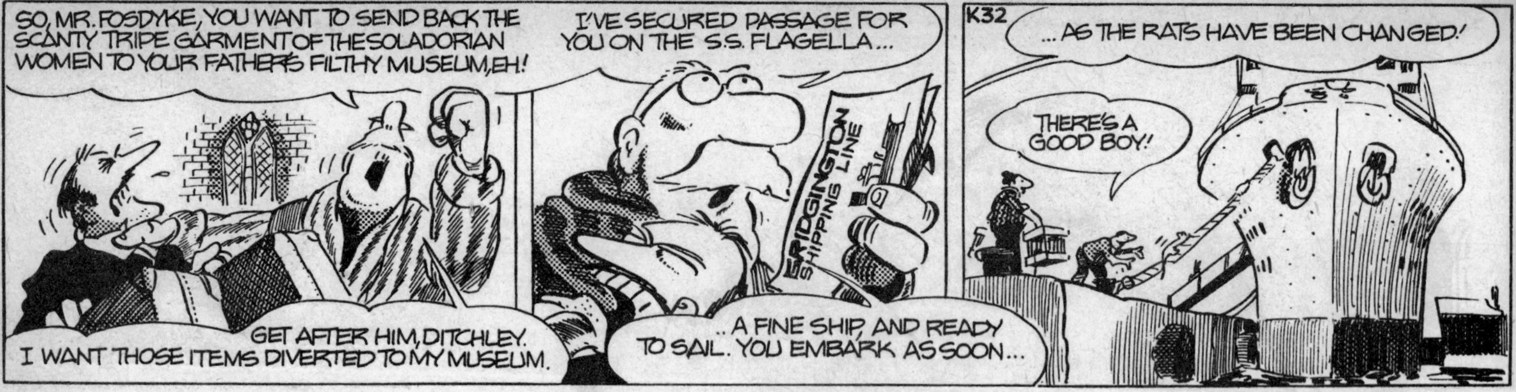
SO, MR. FOSDYKE, YOU WANT TO SEND BACK THE SCANTY TRIPE GARMENT OF THE SOLADORIAN WOMEN TO YOUR FATHER'S FILTHY MUSEUM, EH!
GET AFTER HIM, DITCHLEY. I WANT THOSE ITEMS DIVERTED TO MY MUSEUM.
I'VE SECURED PASSAGE FOR YOU ON THE S.S. FLAGELLA...
BRIDGINGTON SHIPPING LINE
.. A FINE SHIP, AND READY TO SAIL. YOU EMBARK AS SOON...
K32
... AS THE RATS HAVE BEEN CHANGED!
THERE'S A GOOD BOY!

Shortly afterwards...

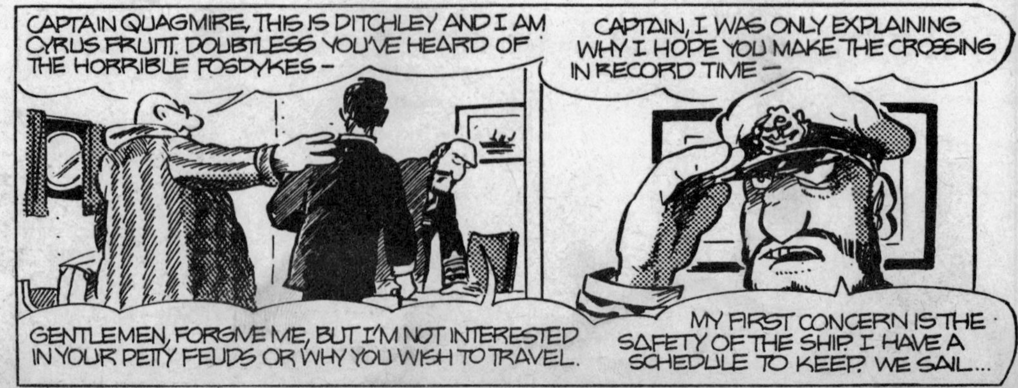
CAPTAIN QUAGMIRE, THIS IS DITCHLEY AND I AM CYRUS FRUITT. DOUBTLESS YOU'VE HEARD OF THE HORRIBLE FOSDYKES –
GENTLEMEN, FORGIVE ME, BUT I'M NOT INTERESTED IN YOUR PETTY FEUDS OR WHY YOU WISH TO TRAVEL.
CAPTAIN, I WAS ONLY EXPLAINING WHY I HOPE YOU MAKE THE CROSSING IN RECORD TIME –
MY FIRST CONCERN IS THE SAFETY OF THE SHIP. I HAVE A SCHEDULE TO KEEP. WE SAIL...

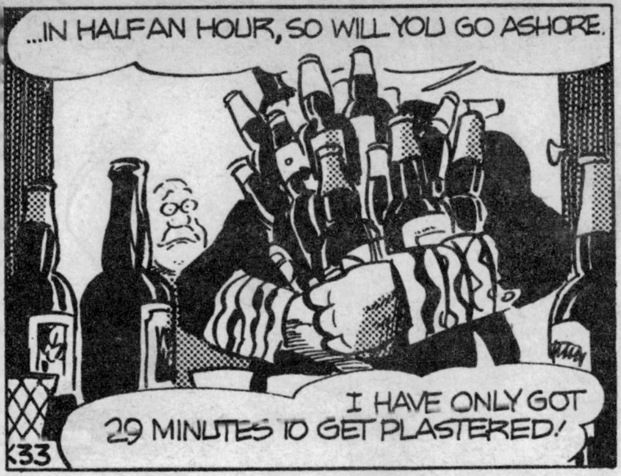
...IN HALF AN HOUR, SO WILL YOU GO ASHORE.
I HAVE ONLY GOT 29 MINUTES TO GET PLASTERED!
K33

And when the ship is some way out to sea...

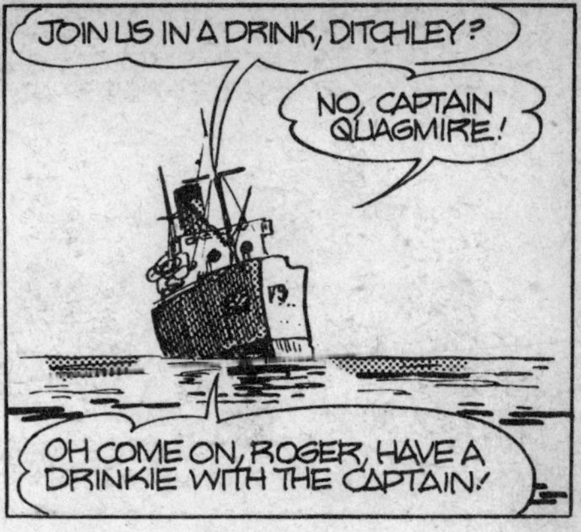
JOIN US IN A DRINK, DITCHLEY?
NO, CAPTAIN QUAGMIRE!
OH COME ON, ROGER, HAVE A DRINKIE WITH THE CAPTAIN!

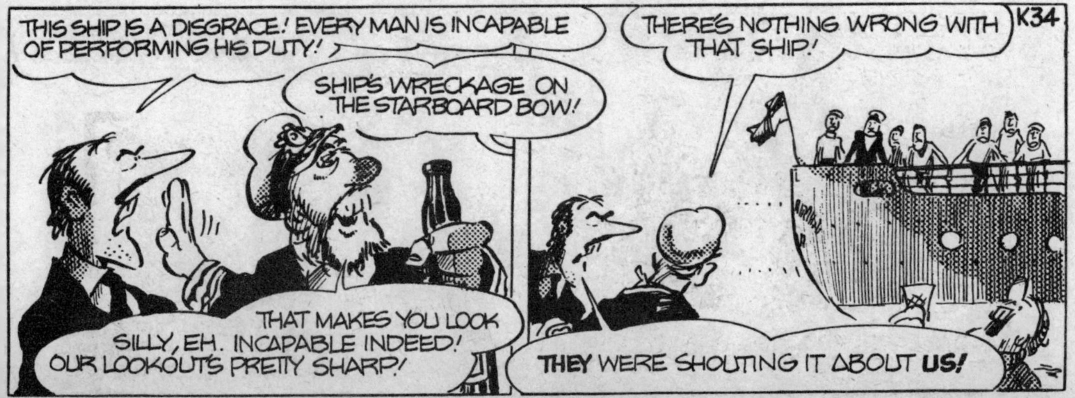
THIS SHIP IS A DISGRACE! EVERY MAN IS INCAPABLE OF PERFORMING HIS DUTY!
SHIP'S WRECKAGE ON THE STARBOARD BOW!
THAT MAKES YOU LOOK SILLY, EH. INCAPABLE INDEED! OUR LOOKOUT'S PRETTY SHARP!
K34
THERE'S NOTHING WRONG WITH THAT SHIP!
THEY WERE SHOUTING IT ABOUT US!

And after days of alcoholic cruising...

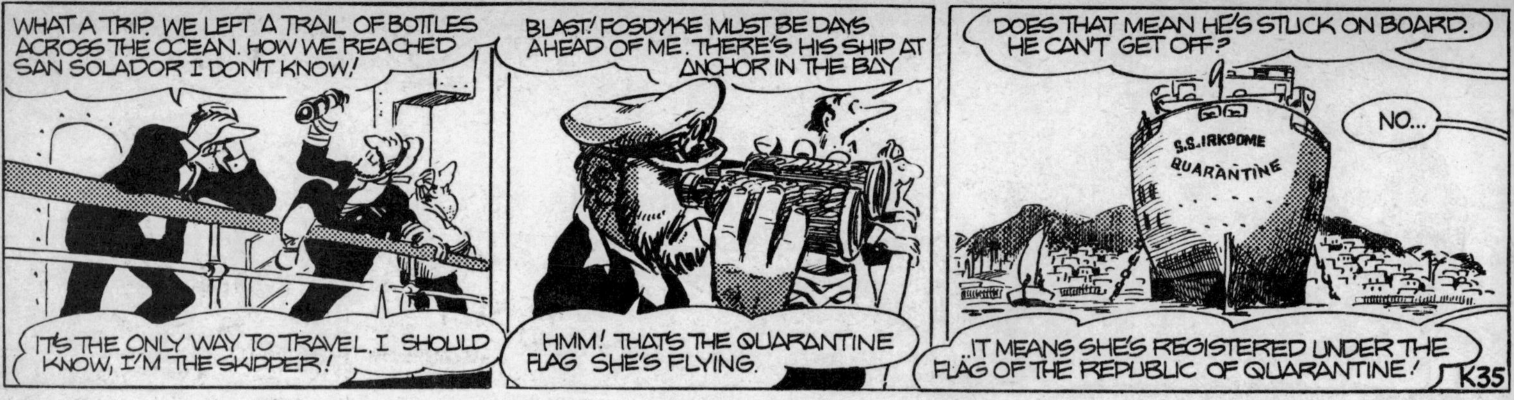
WHAT A TRIP. WE LEFT A TRAIL OF BOTTLES ACROSS THE OCEAN. HOW WE REACHED SAN SOLADOR I DON'T KNOW!
IT'S THE ONLY WAY TO TRAVEL. I SHOULD KNOW, I'M THE SKIPPER!
BLAST! FOSDYKE MUST BE DAYS AHEAD OF ME. THERE'S HIS SHIP AT ANCHOR IN THE BAY
HMM! THAT'S THE QUARANTINE FLAG SHE'S FLYING.
DOES THAT MEAN HE'S STUCK ON BOARD. HE CAN'T GET OFF?
S.S. IRKBOME
QUARANTINE
NO...
...IT MEANS SHE'S REGISTERED UNDER THE FLAG OF THE REPUBLIC OF QUARANTINE!
K35

Meanwhile, in a New York hotel room...

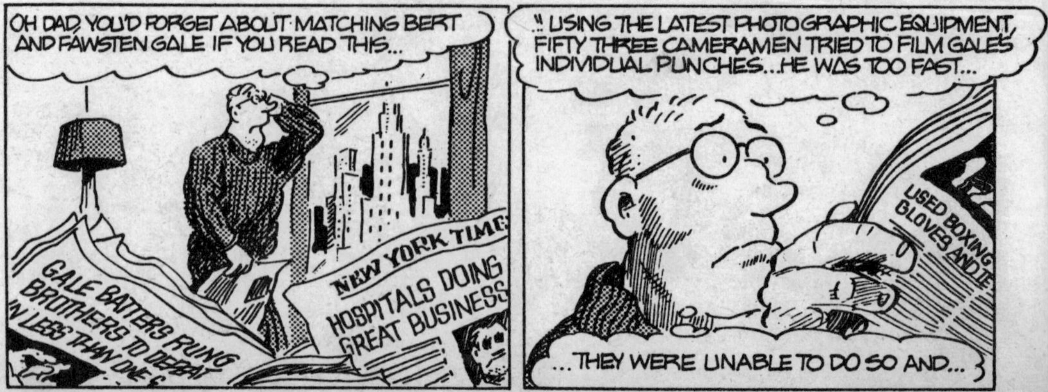
OH DAD, YOU'D FORGET ABOUT MATCHING BERT AND FAWSTEN GALE IF YOU READ THIS...
GALE BATTERS RUING BROTHERS TO DEFEAT IN LESS THAN ONE
NEW YORK TIME
HOSPITALS DOING GREAT BUSINESS
...USING THE LATEST PHOTOGRAPHIC EQUIPMENT, FIFTY THREE CAMERAMEN TRIED TO FILM GALE'S INDIVIDUAL PUNCHES...HE WAS TOO FAST...
USED BOXING GLOVES AND IT
...THEY WERE UNABLE TO DO SO AND...

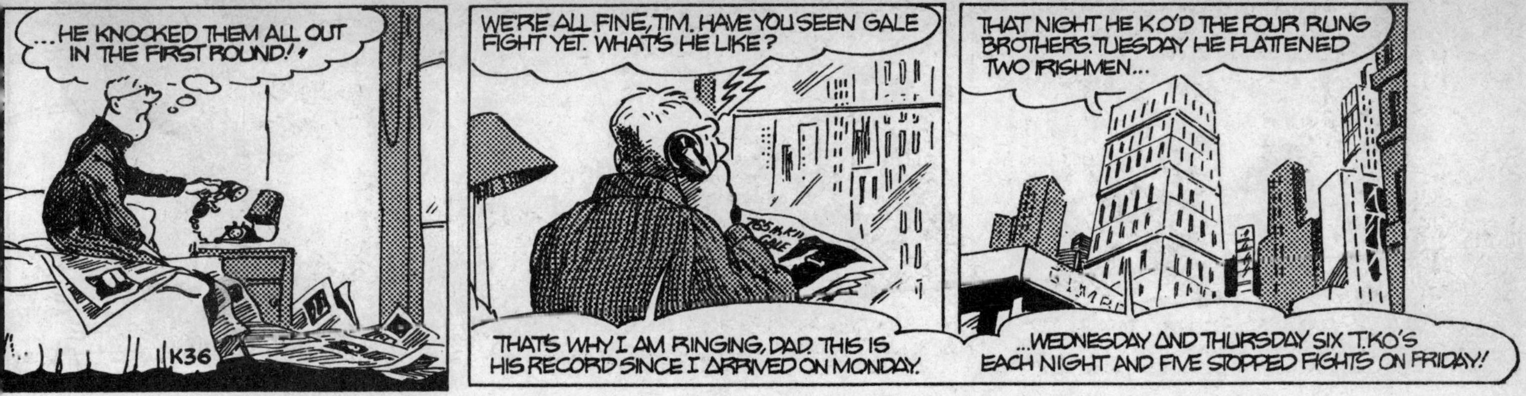
...HE KNOCKED THEM ALL OUT IN THE FIRST ROUND!
K36
WE'RE ALL FINE, TIM. HAVE YOU SEEN GALE FIGHT YET. WHAT'S HE LIKE?
THAT'S WHY I AM RINGING, DAD. THIS IS HIS RECORD SINCE I ARRIVED ON MONDAY.
THAT NIGHT HE K.O'D THE FOUR RUNG BROTHERS. TUESDAY HE FLATTENED TWO IRISHMEN...
...WEDNESDAY AND THURSDAY SIX T.KO'S EACH NIGHT AND FIVE STOPPED FIGHTS ON FRIDAY!

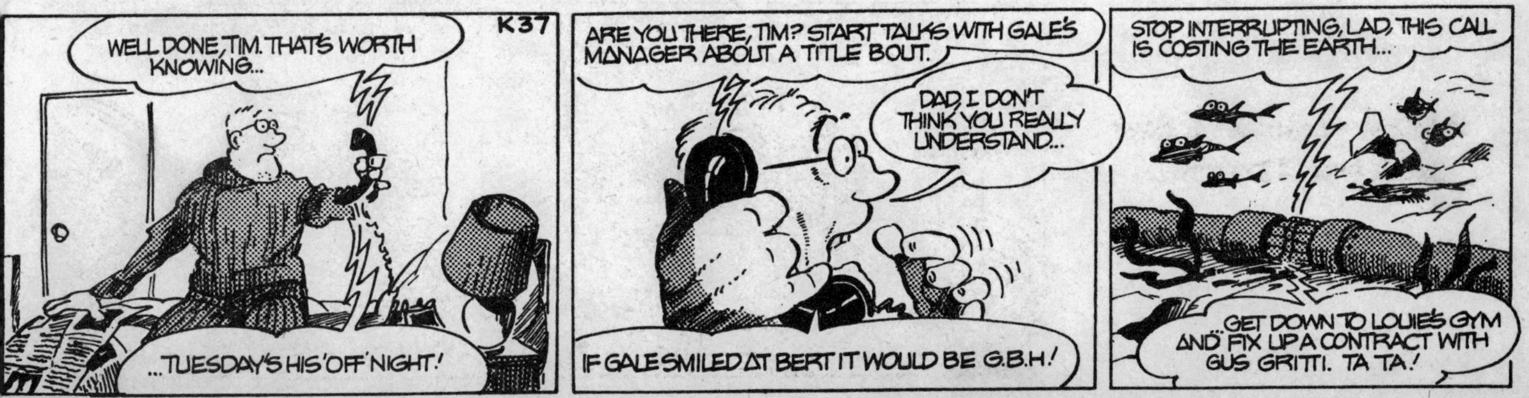
K37
WELL DONE, TIM. THAT'S WORTH KNOWING...
...TUESDAY'S HIS 'OFF' NIGHT!
ARE YOU THERE, TIM? START TALKS WITH GALE'S MANAGER ABOUT A TITLE BOUT.
DAD, I DON'T THINK YOU REALLY UNDERSTAND...
IF GALE SMILED AT BERT IT WOULD BE G.B.H!
STOP INTERRUPTING, LAD, THIS CALL IS COSTING THE EARTH...
...GET DOWN TO LOUIE'S GYM AND FIX UP A CONTRACT WITH GUS GRITTI. TA TA!

A little later...

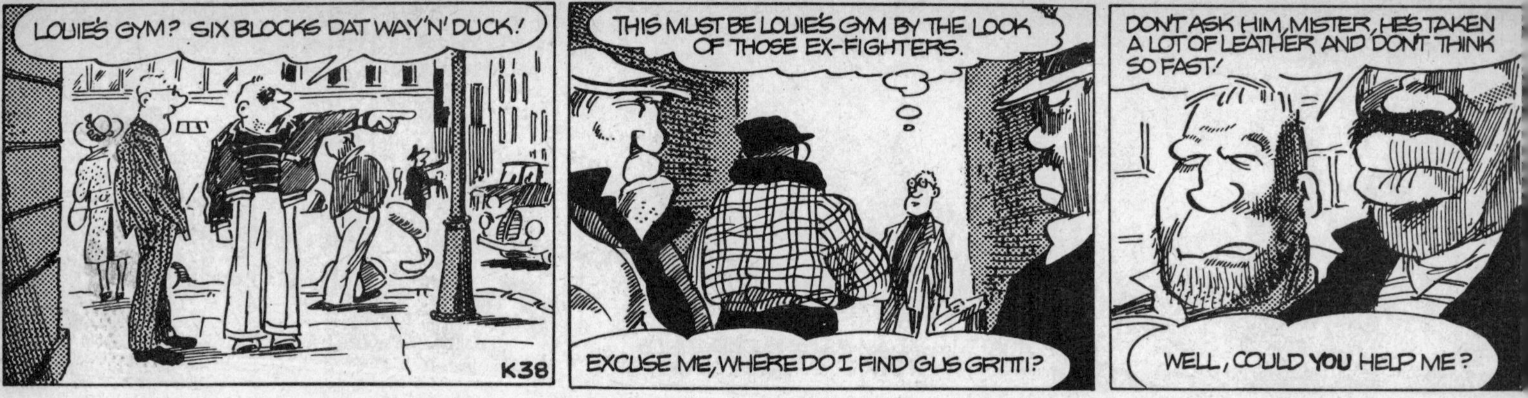

LOUIE'S GYM? SIX BLOCKS DAT WAY'N' DUCK!
K38
THIS MUST BE LOUIE'S GYM BY THE LOOK OF THOSE EX-FIGHTERS.
EXCUSE ME, WHERE DO I FIND GUS GRITTI?
DON'T ASK HIM, MISTER, HE'S TAKEN A LOT OF LEATHER AND DON'T THINK SO FAST!
WELL, COULD **YOU** HELP ME?

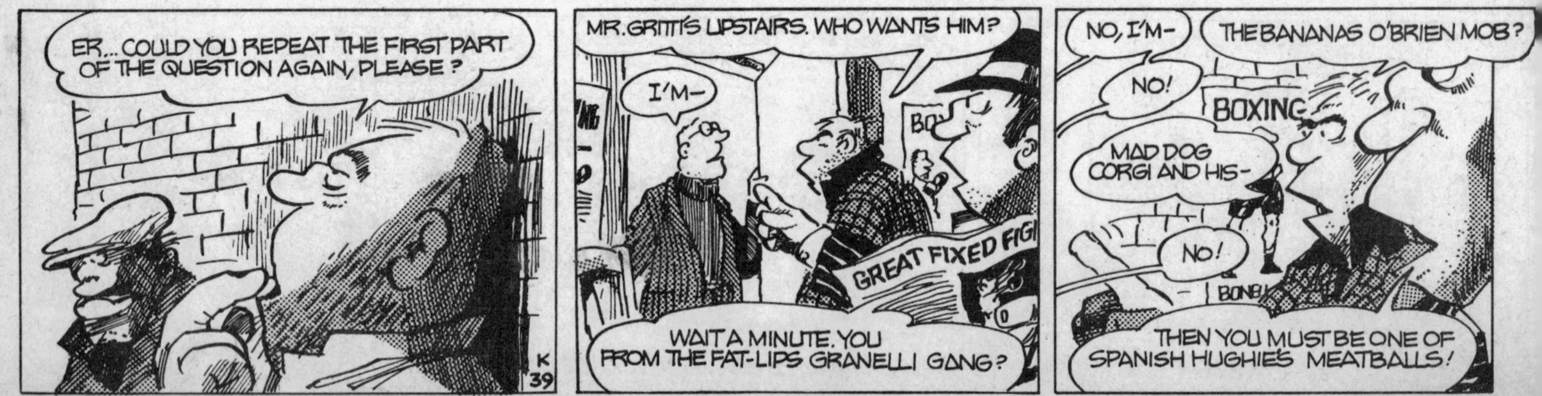

ER... COULD YOU REPEAT THE FIRST PART OF THE QUESTION AGAIN, PLEASE?
K 39
MR. GRITTI'S UPSTAIRS. WHO WANTS HIM?
I'M-
WAIT A MINUTE. YOU FROM THE FAT-LIPS GRANELLI GANG?
GREAT FIXED FIG
NO, I'M-
THE BANANAS O'BRIEN MOB?
NO!
BOXING
MAD DOG CORGI AND HIS-
NO!
THEN YOU MUST BE ONE OF SPANISH HUGHIE'S MEATBALLS!

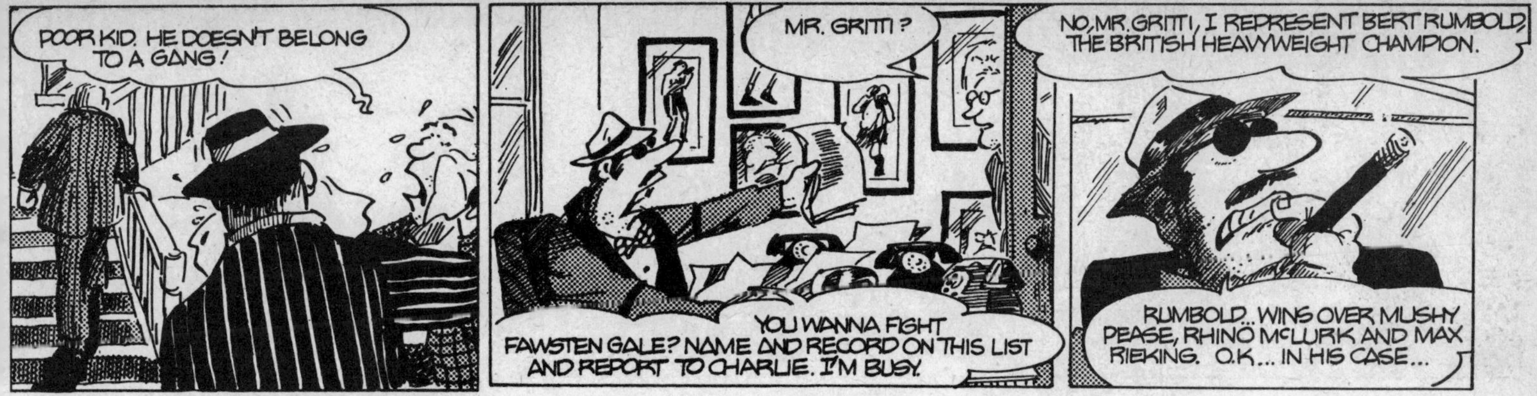
POOR KID. HE DOESN'T BELONG TO A GANG!
MR. GRITTI ?
YOU WANNA FIGHT FAWSTEN GALE? NAME AND RECORD ON THIS LIST AND REPORT TO CHARLIE. I'M BUSY.
NO, MR. GRITTI, I REPRESENT BERT RUMBOLD, THE BRITISH HEAVYWEIGHT CHAMPION.
RUMBOLD... WINS OVER MUSHY PEASE, RHINÖ McLURK AND MAX RIEKING. O.K... IN HIS CASE...

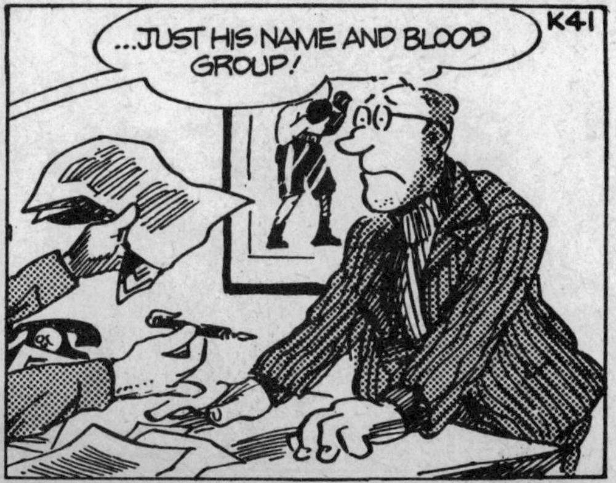
...JUST HIS NAME AND BLOOD GROUP!
K41

And at home in Manchester…

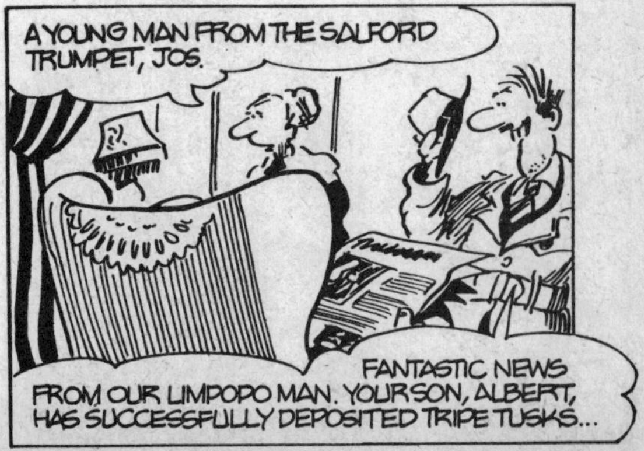
A YOUNG MAN FROM THE SALFORD TRUMPET, JOS.
FANTASTIC NEWS FROM OUR LIMPOPO MAN. YOUR SON, ALBERT, HAS SUCCESSFULLY DEPOSITED TRIPE TUSKS...

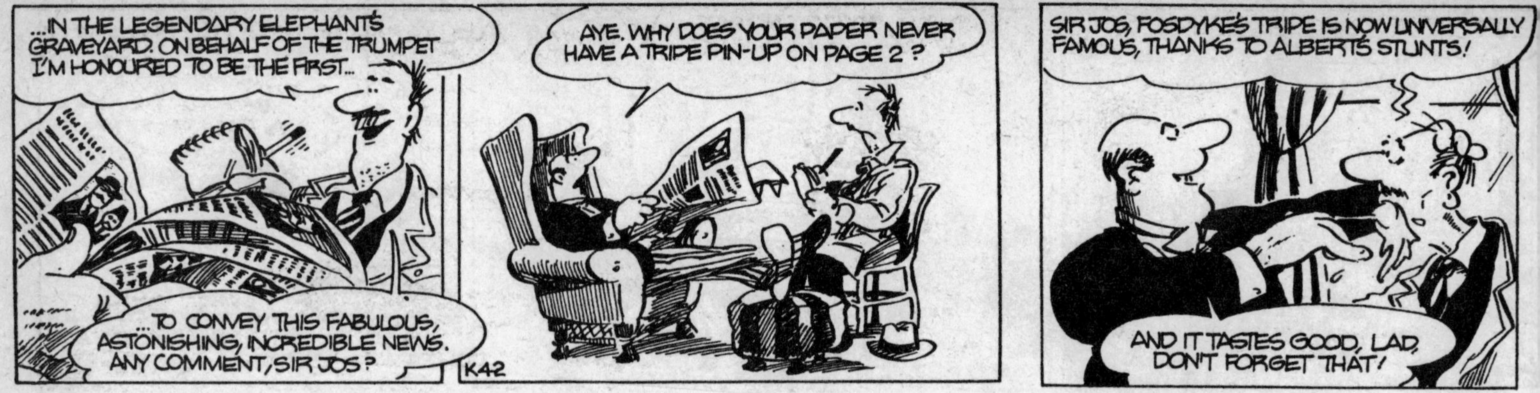
...IN THE LEGENDARY ELEPHANT'S GRAVEYARD. ON BEHALF OF THE TRUMPET I'M HONOURED TO BE THE FIRST...
...TO CONVEY THIS FABULOUS, ASTÖNISHING, INCREDIBLE NEWS. ANY COMMENT, SIR JOS?
AYE. WHY DOES YOUR PAPER NEVER HAVE A TRIPE PIN-UP ON PAGE 2 ?
K42
SIR JOS, FOSDYKE'S TRIPE IS NOW UNIVERSALLY FAMOUS, THANKS TO ALBERT'S STUNTS!
AND IT TASTES GOOD, LAD, DON'T FORGET THAT!

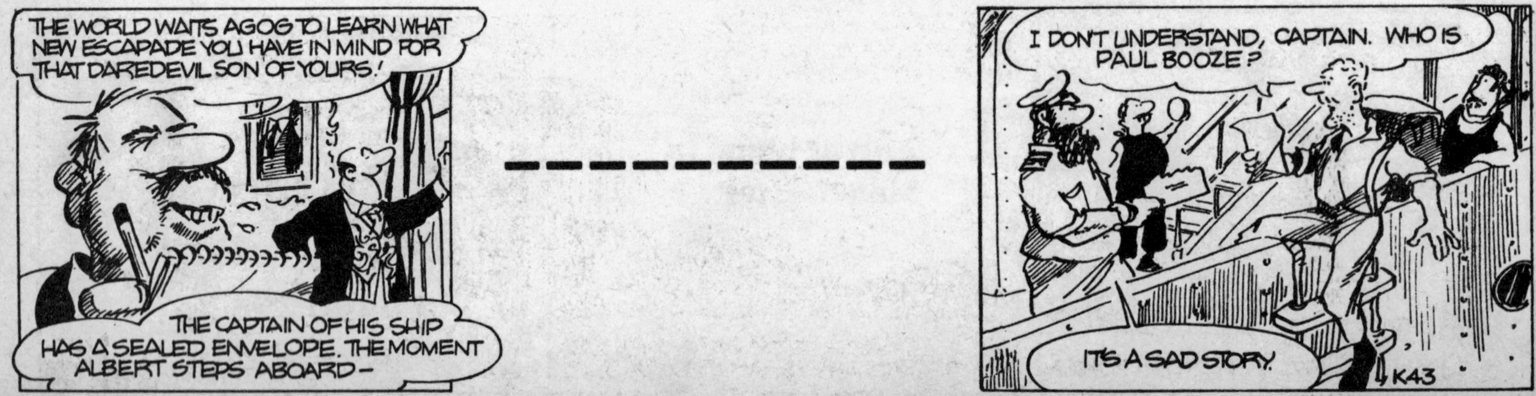
THE WORLD WAITS AGOG TO LEARN WHAT NEW ESCAPADE YOU HAVE IN MIND FOR THAT DAREDEVIL SON OF YOURS!
THE CAPTAIN OF HIS SHIP HAS A SEALED ENVELOPE. THE MOMENT ALBERT STEPS ABOARD –
I DON'T UNDERSTAND, CAPTAIN. WHO IS PAUL BOOZE ?
IT'S A SAD STORY.
K43

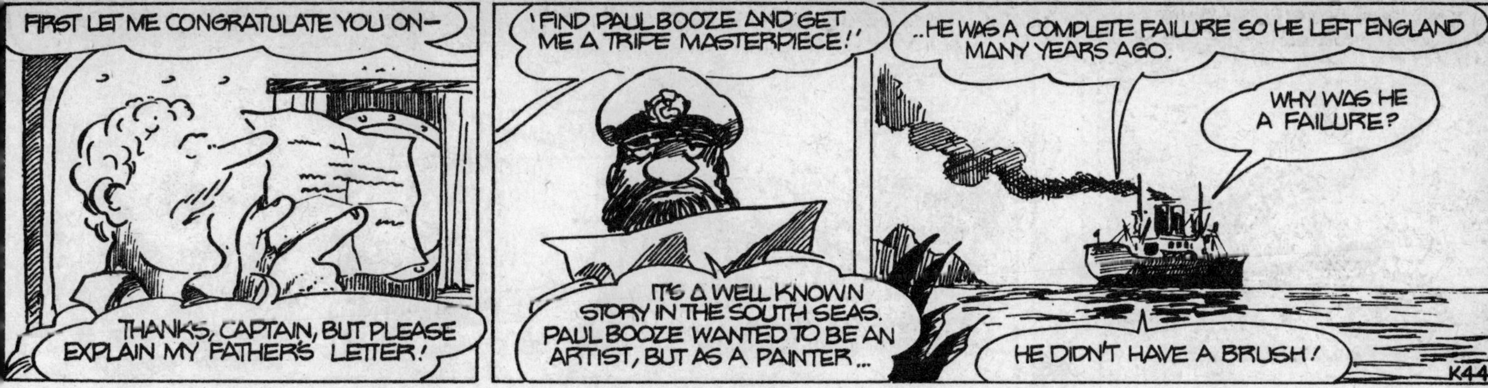
FIRST LET ME CONGRATULATE YOU ON—
THANKS, CAPTAIN, BUT PLEASE EXPLAIN MY FATHER'S LETTER!
'FIND PAUL BOOZE AND GET ME A TRIPE MASTERPIECE!'
IT'S A WELL KNOWN STORY IN THE SOUTH SEAS. PAUL BOOZE WANTED TO BE AN ARTIST, BUT AS A PAINTER...
..HE WAS A COMPLETE FAILURE SO HE LEFT ENGLAND MANY YEARS AGO.
WHY WAS HE A FAILURE?
HE DIDN'T HAVE A BRUSH!
K44

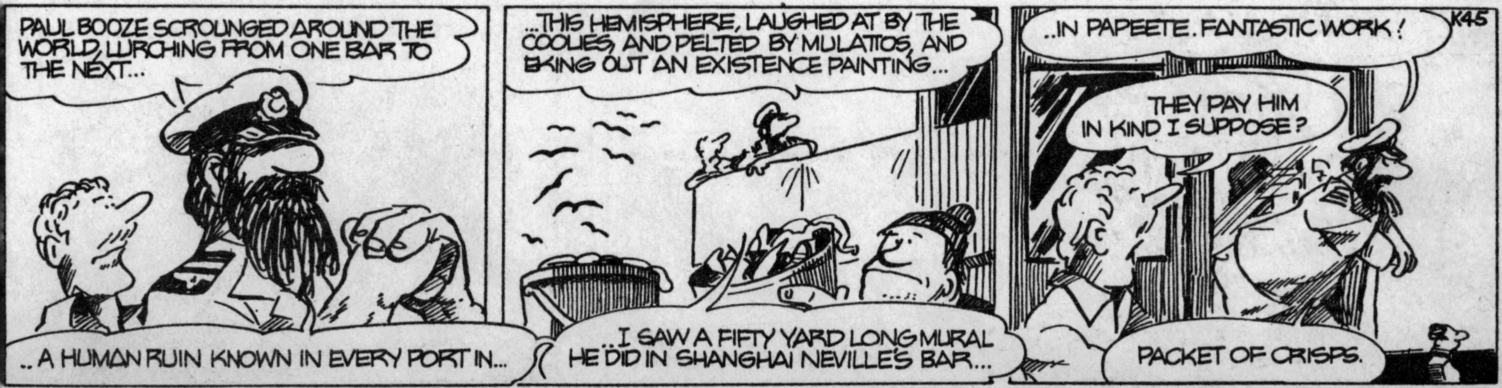
PAUL BOOZE SCROUNGED AROUND THE WORLD, LURCHING FROM ONE BAR TO THE NEXT...
.. A HUMAN RUIN KNOWN IN EVERY PORT IN...
...THIS HEMISPHERE, LAUGHED AT BY THE COOLIES, AND PELTED BY MULATTOS, AND EKING OUT AN EXISTENCE PAINTING...
...I SAW A FIFTY YARD LONG MURAL HE DID IN SHANGHAI NEVILLE'S BAR...
..IN PAPEETE. FANTASTIC WORK!
THEY PAY HIM IN KIND I SUPPOSE?
PACKET OF CRISPS.
K45

And after a voyage to the South Sea Islands...

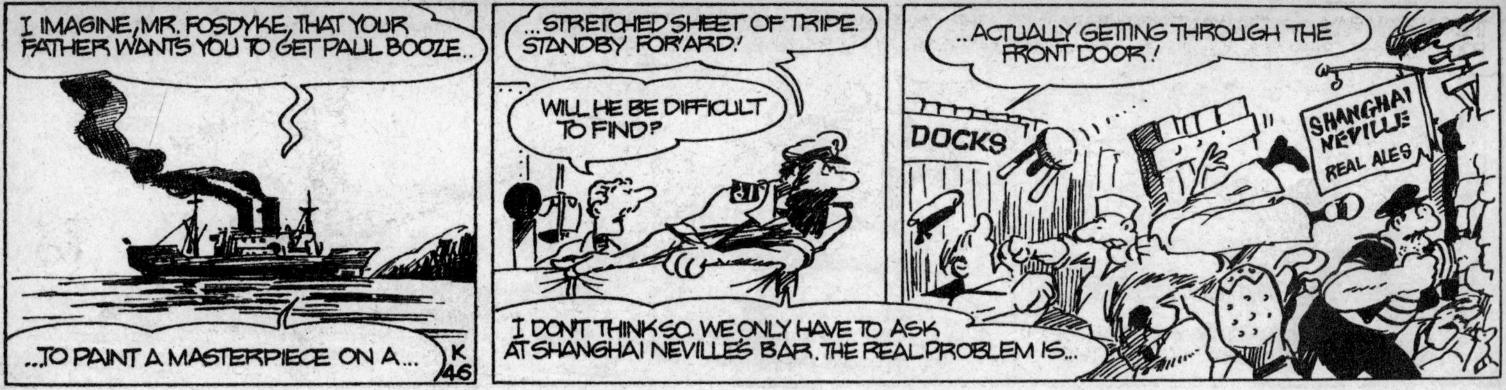
I IMAGINE, MR. FOSDYKE, THAT YOUR FATHER WANTS YOU TO GET PAUL BOOZE..
...TO PAINT A MASTERPIECE ON A...
K 46
...STRETCHED SHEET OF TRIPE. STANDBY FOR'ARD!
WILL HE BE DIFFICULT TO FIND?
I DON'T THINK SO. WE ONLY HAVE TO ASK AT SHANGHAI NEVILLE'S BAR. THE REAL PROBLEM IS...
...ACTUALLY GETTING THROUGH THE FRONT DOOR!
DOCKS
SHANGHAI NEVILLE
REAL ALES

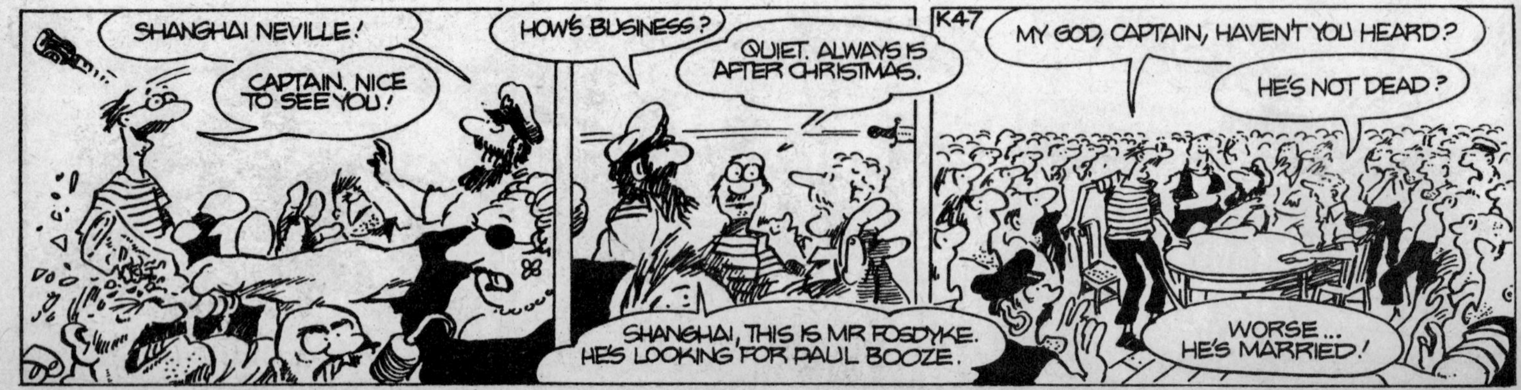
SHANGHAI NEVILLE!
CAPTAIN. NICE TO SEE YOU!
HOW'S BUSINESS?
QUIET. ALWAYS IS AFTER CHRISTMAS.
SHANGHAI, THIS IS MR FOSDYKE. HE'S LOOKING FOR PAUL BOOZE.
K47
MY GOD, CAPTAIN, HAVEN'T YOU HEARD?
HE'S NOT DEAD?
WORSE... HE'S MARRIED!

In the harbour of San Solador...

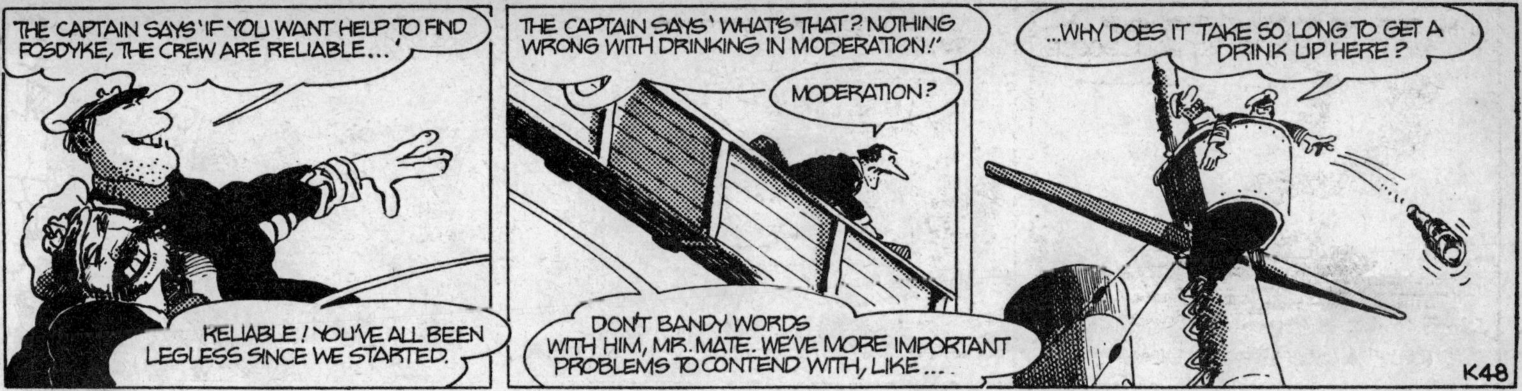
THE CAPTAIN SAYS 'IF YOU WANT HELP TO FIND FOSDYKE, THE CREW ARE RELIABLE...'
RELIABLE! YOU'VE ALL BEEN LEGLESS SINCE WE STARTED.
THE CAPTAIN SAYS 'WHAT'S THAT? NOTHING WRONG WITH DRINKING IN MODERATION!'
MODERATION?
DON'T BANDY WORDS WITH HIM, MR. MATE. WE'VE MORE IMPORTANT PROBLEMS TO CONTEND WITH, LIKE...
...WHY DOES IT TAKE SO LONG TO GET A DRINK UP HERE?
K48

Later, at passport control...

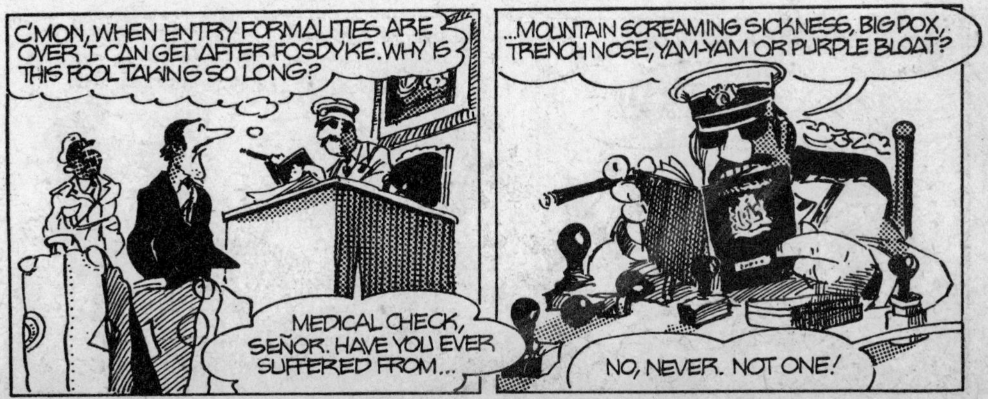
C'MON, WHEN ENTRY FORMALITIES ARE OVER I CAN GET AFTER FOSDYKE. WHY IS THIS FOOL TAKING SO LONG?
MEDICAL CHECK, SEÑOR. HAVE YOU EVER SUFFERED FROM...
...MOUNTAIN SCREAMING SICKNESS, BIG POX, TRENCH NOSE, YAM-YAM OR PURPLE BLOAT?
NO, NEVER. NOT ONE!

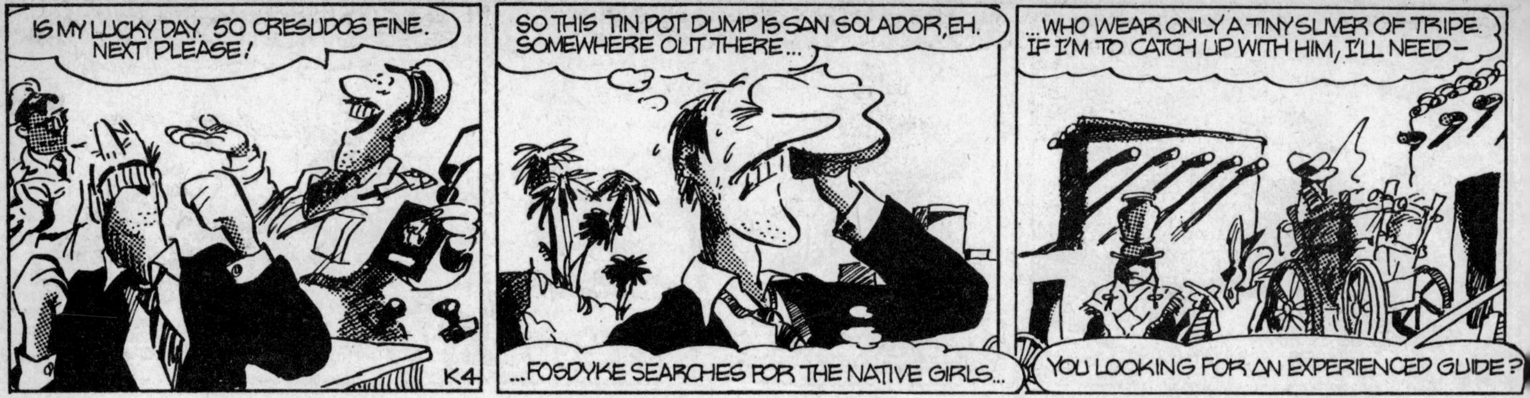
IS MY LUCKY DAY. 50 CRESUDOS FINE. NEXT PLEASE!
K4
SO THIS TIN POT DUMP IS SAN SOLADOR, EH. SOMEWHERE OUT THERE...
...FOSDYKE SEARCHES FOR THE NATIVE GIRLS...
...WHO WEAR ONLY A TINY SLIVER OF TRIPE. IF I'M TO CATCH UP WITH HIM, I'LL NEED—
YOU LOOKING FOR AN EXPERIENCED GUIDE?

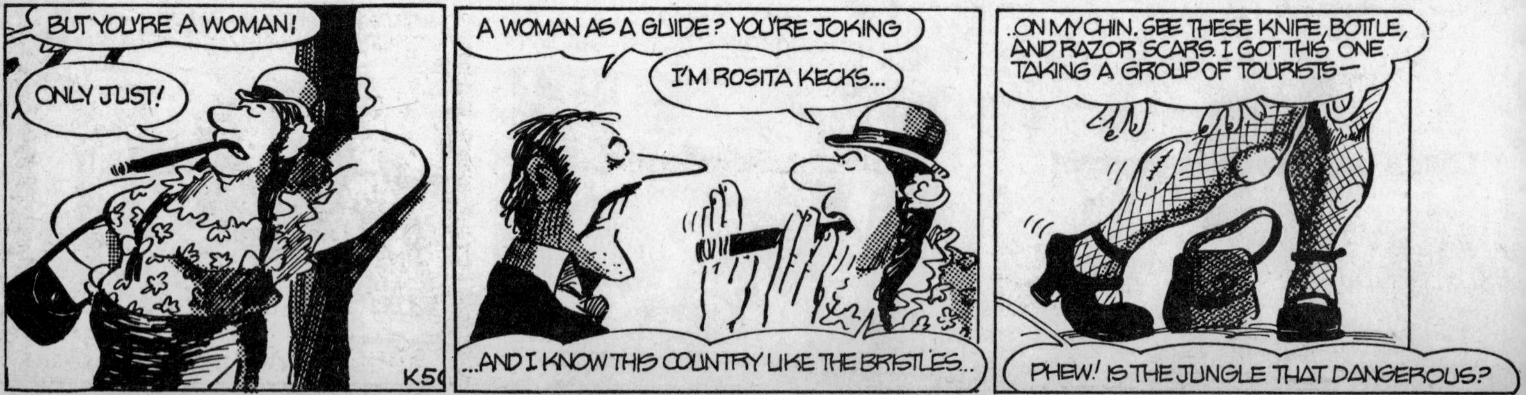
BUT YOU'RE A WOMAN!
ONLY JUST!
K5
A WOMAN AS A GUIDE? YOU'RE JOKING
I'M ROSITA KECKS...
...AND I KNOW THIS COUNTRY LIKE THE BRISTLES...
..ON MY CHIN. SEE THESE KNIFE, BOTTLE, AND RAZOR SCARS. I GOT THIS ONE TAKING A GROUP OF TOURISTS—
PHEW! IS THE JUNGLE THAT DANGEROUS?

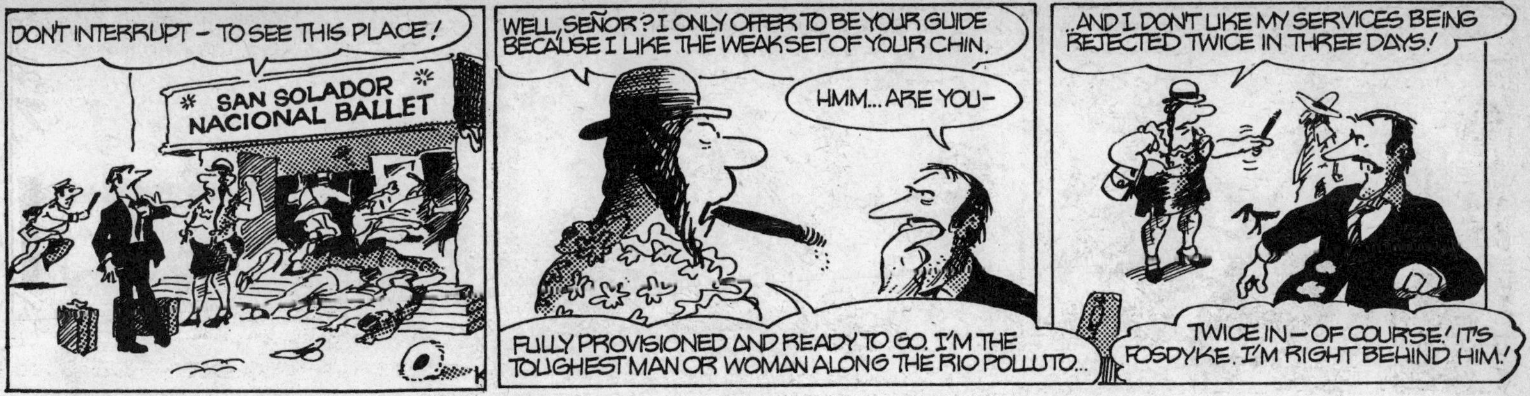
DON'T INTERRUPT – TO SEE THIS PLACE!
SAN SOLADOR NACIONAL BALLET
WELL, SEÑOR? I ONLY OFFER TO BE YOUR GUIDE BECAUSE I LIKE THE WEAK SET OF YOUR CHIN.
HMM... ARE YOU–
FULLY PROVISIONED AND READY TO GO. I'M THE TOUGHEST MAN OR WOMAN ALONG THE RIO POLLUTO...
...AND I DON'T LIKE MY SERVICES BEING REJECTED TWICE IN THREE DAYS!
TWICE IN – OF COURSE! IT'S FOSDYKE. I'M RIGHT BEHIND HIM!

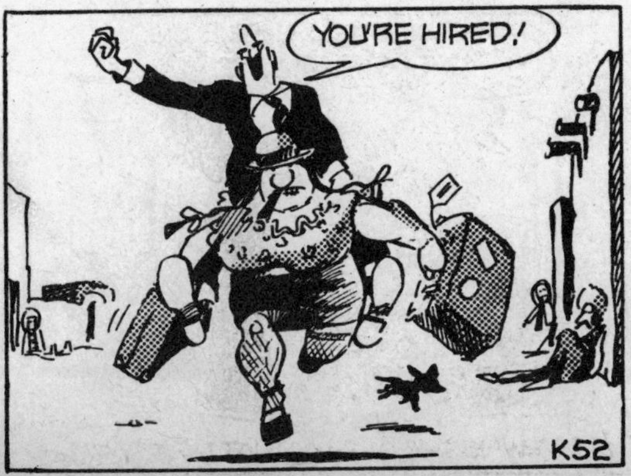
YOU'RE HIRED!
K52

Some days later...

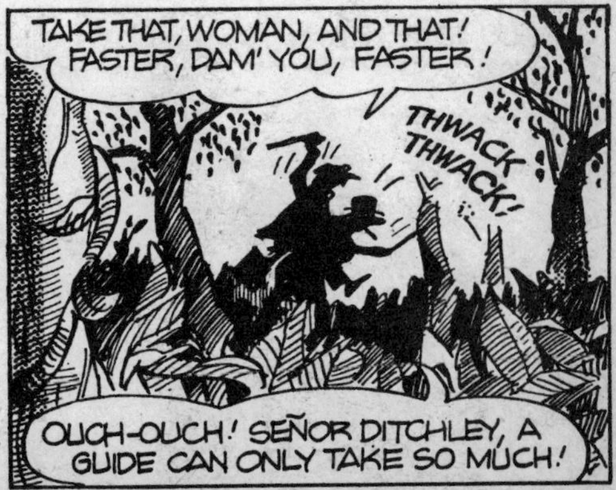
TAKE THAT, WOMAN, AND THAT! FASTER, DAM' YOU, FASTER!
THWACK
THWACK!
OUCH-OUCH! SEÑOR DITCHLEY, A GUIDE CAN ONLY TAKE SO MUCH!

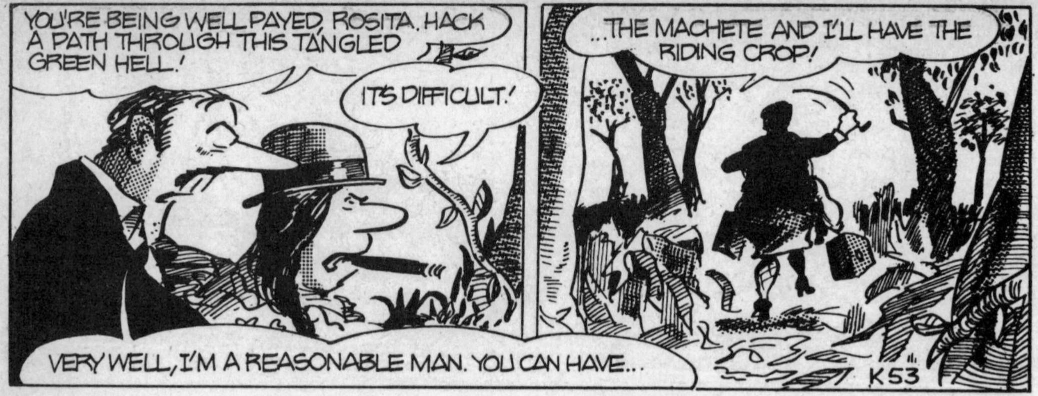
YOU'RE BEING WELL PAYED, ROSITA. HACK A PATH THROUGH THIS TANGLED GREEN HELL!
IT'S DIFFICULT!
VERY WELL, I'M A REASONABLE MAN. YOU CAN HAVE...
...THE MACHETE AND I'LL HAVE THE RIDING CROP!
K53

Meanwhile Tim negotiates contract terms with Fawsten Gale's manager, Gus Gritti...

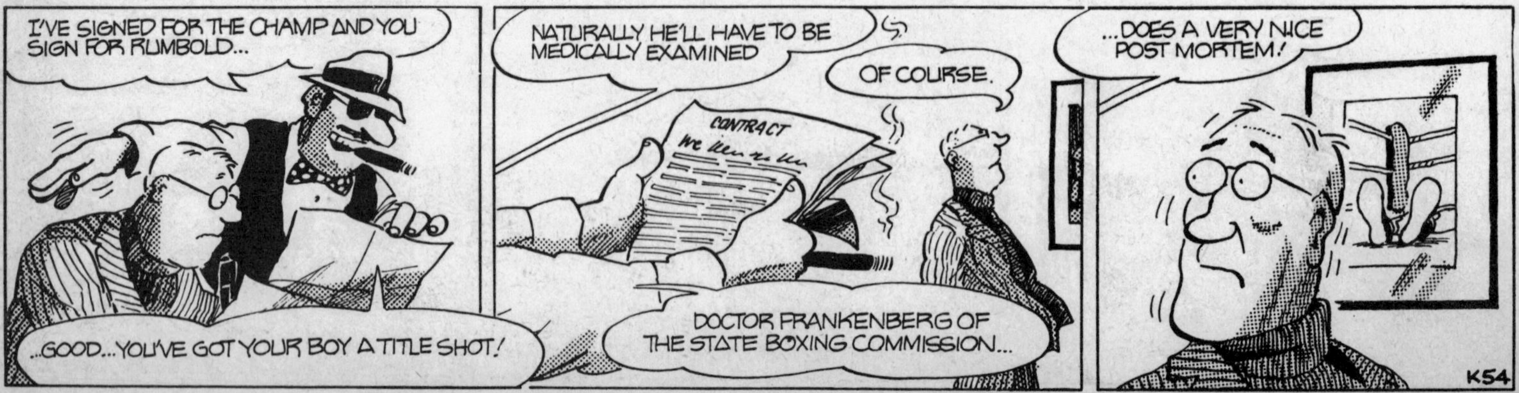
I'VE SIGNED FOR THE CHAMP AND YOU SIGN FOR RUMBOLD...
...GOOD...YOU'VE GOT YOUR BOY A TITLE SHOT!
NATURALLY HE'LL HAVE TO BE MEDICALLY EXAMINED
OF COURSE.
CONTRACT
DOCTOR FRANKENBERG OF THE STATE BOXING COMMISSION...
...DOES A VERY NICE POST MORTEM!
K54

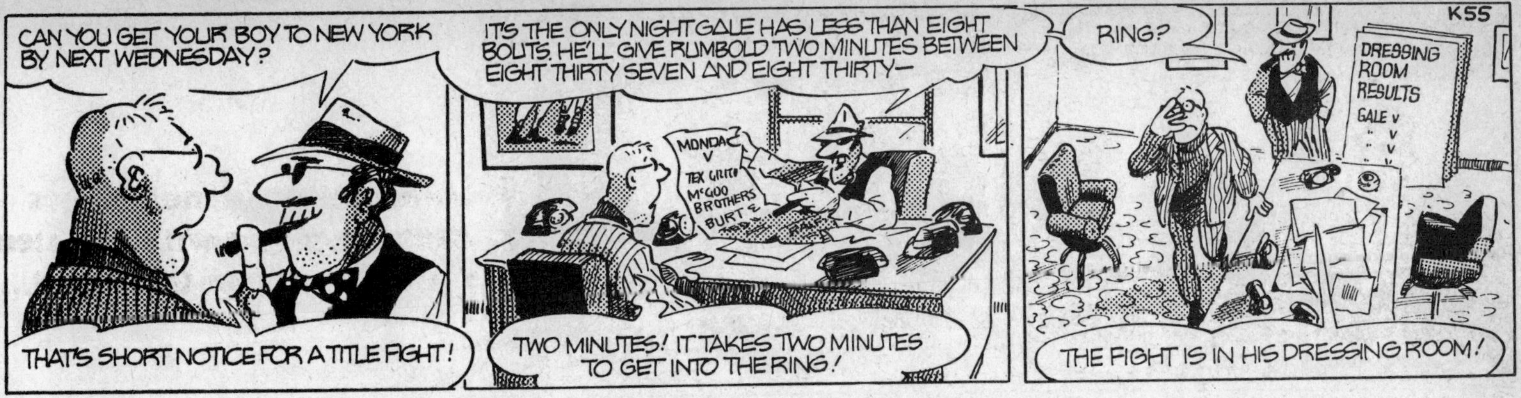
K55
CAN YOU GET YOUR BOY TO NEW YORK BY NEXT WEDNESDAY?
THAT'S SHORT NOTICE FOR A TITLE FIGHT!
IT'S THE ONLY NIGHT GALE HAS LESS THAN EIGHT BOUTS. HE'LL GIVE RUMBOLD TWO MINUTES BETWEEN EIGHT THIRTY SEVEN AND EIGHT THIRTY—
TWO MINUTES! IT TAKES TWO MINUTES TO GET INTO THE RING!
RING?
DRESSING ROOM RESULTS
GALE V
THE FIGHT IS IN HIS DRESSING ROOM!

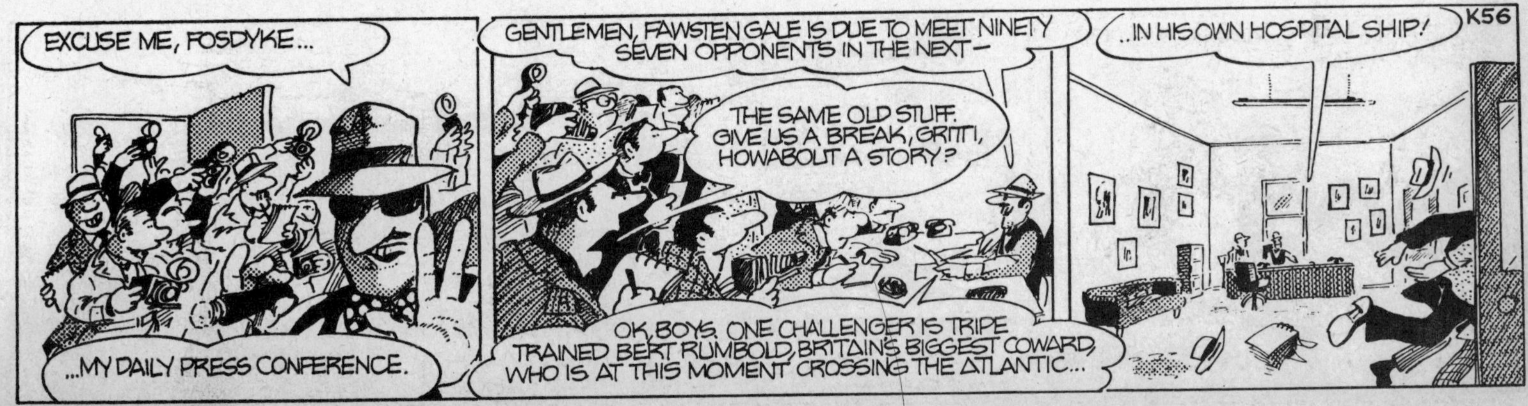
K56
EXCUSE ME, FOSDYKE...
...MY DAILY PRESS CONFERENCE.
GENTLEMEN, FAWSTEN GALE IS DUE TO MEET NINETY SEVEN OPPONENTS IN THE NEXT—
THE SAME OLD STUFF. GIVE US A BREAK, GRITTI, HOW ABOUT A STORY?
OK, BOYS. ONE CHALLENGER IS TRIPE TRAINED BERT RUMBOLD, BRITAIN'S BIGGEST COWARD, WHO IS AT THIS MOMENT CROSSING THE ATLANTIC...
...IN HIS OWN HOSPITAL SHIP!

And steaming into harbour...

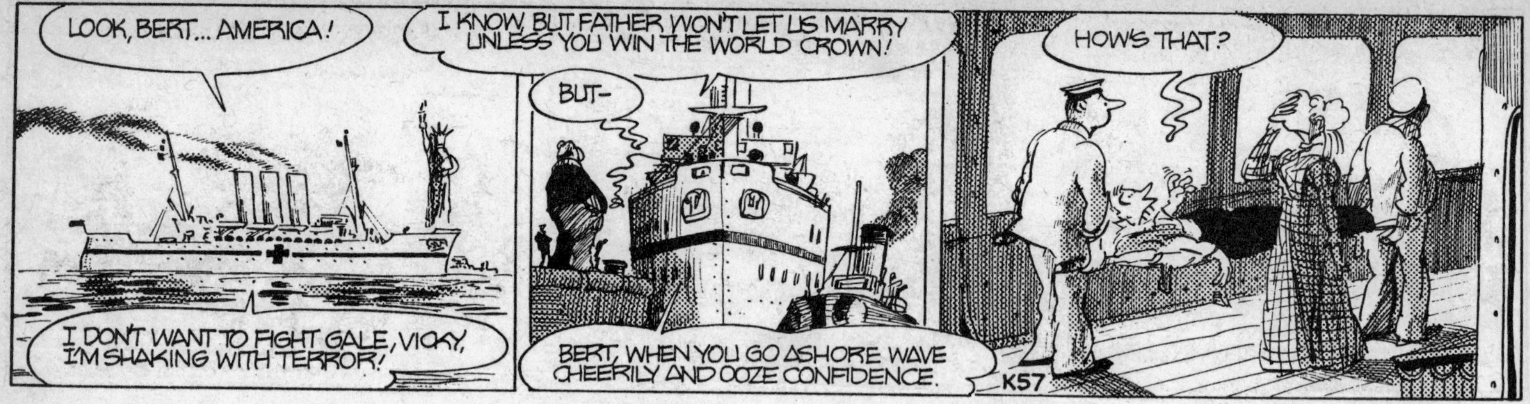
LOOK, BERT... AMERICA!
I DON'T WANT TO FIGHT GALE, VICKY, I'M SHAKING WITH TERROR!
I KNOW, BUT FATHER WON'T LET US MARRY UNLESS YOU WIN THE WORLD CROWN!
BUT-
BERT, WHEN YOU GO ASHORE WAVE CHEERILY AND OOZE CONFIDENCE.
HOW'S THAT?
K57

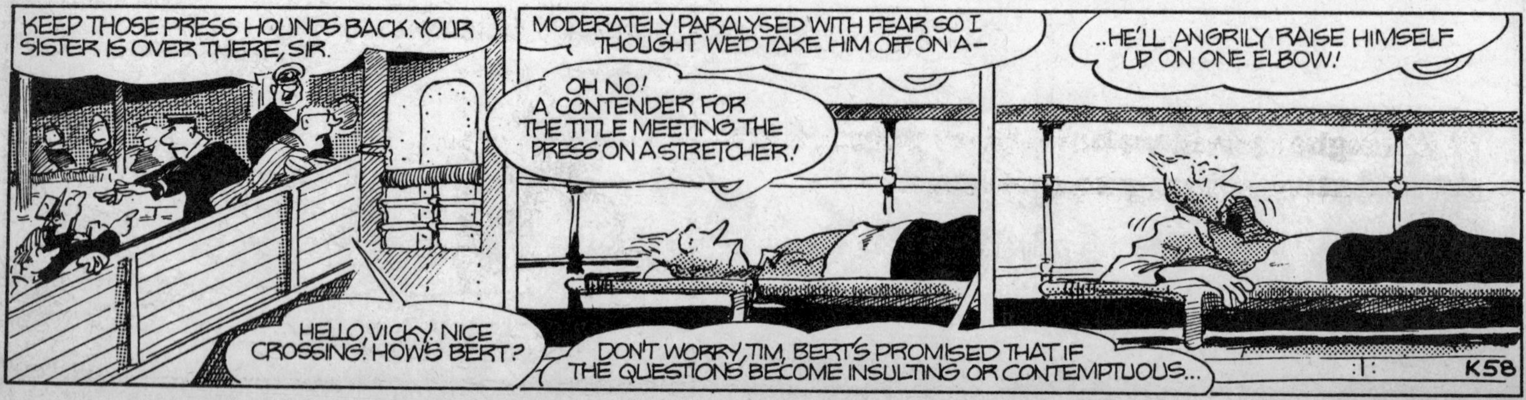
KEEP THOSE PRESS HOUNDS BACK. YOUR SISTER IS OVER THERE, SIR.
HELLO, VICKY. NICE CROSSING. HOW'S BERT?
MODERATELY PARALYSED WITH FEAR SO I THOUGHT WE'D TAKE HIM OFF ON A-
OH NO! A CONTENDER FOR THE TITLE MEETING THE PRESS ON A STRETCHER!
DON'T WORRY, TIM, BERT'S PROMISED THAT IF THE QUESTIONS BECOME INSULTING OR CONTEMPTUOUS...
...HE'LL ANGRILY RAISE HIMSELF UP ON ONE ELBOW!
K58

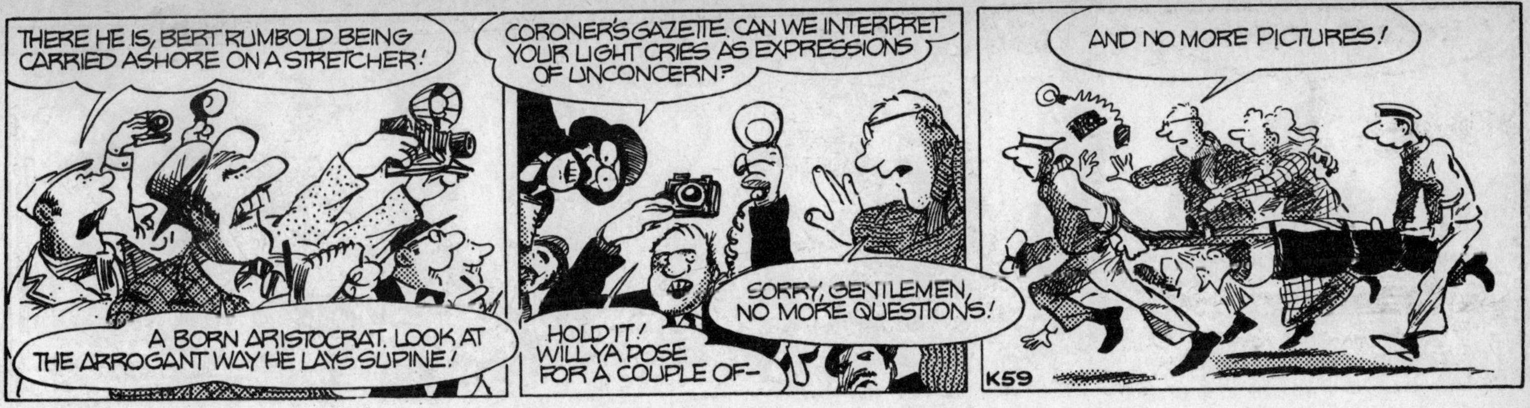
THERE HE IS, BERT RUMBOLD BEING CARRIED ASHORE ON A STRETCHER!
A BORN ARISTOCRAT. LOOK AT THE ARROGANT WAY HE LAYS SUPINE!
CORONER'S GAZETTE. CAN WE INTERPRET YOUR LIGHT CRIES AS EXPRESSIONS OF UNCONCERN?
HOLD IT! WILL YA POSE FOR A COUPLE OF–
SORRY, GENTLEMEN, NO MORE QUESTIONS!
AND NO MORE PICTURES!
K59

In Shanghai Neville's bar Albert pursues his latest extraordinary commission.

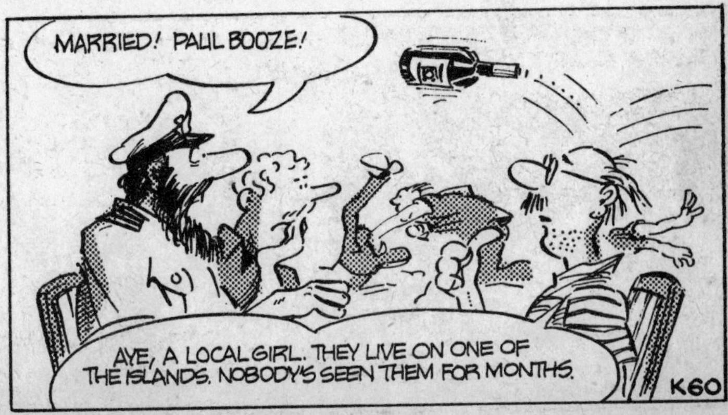
MARRIED! PAUL BOOZE!
AYE, A LOCAL GIRL. THEY LIVE ON ONE OF THE ISLANDS. NOBODY'S SEEN THEM FOR MONTHS.
K60

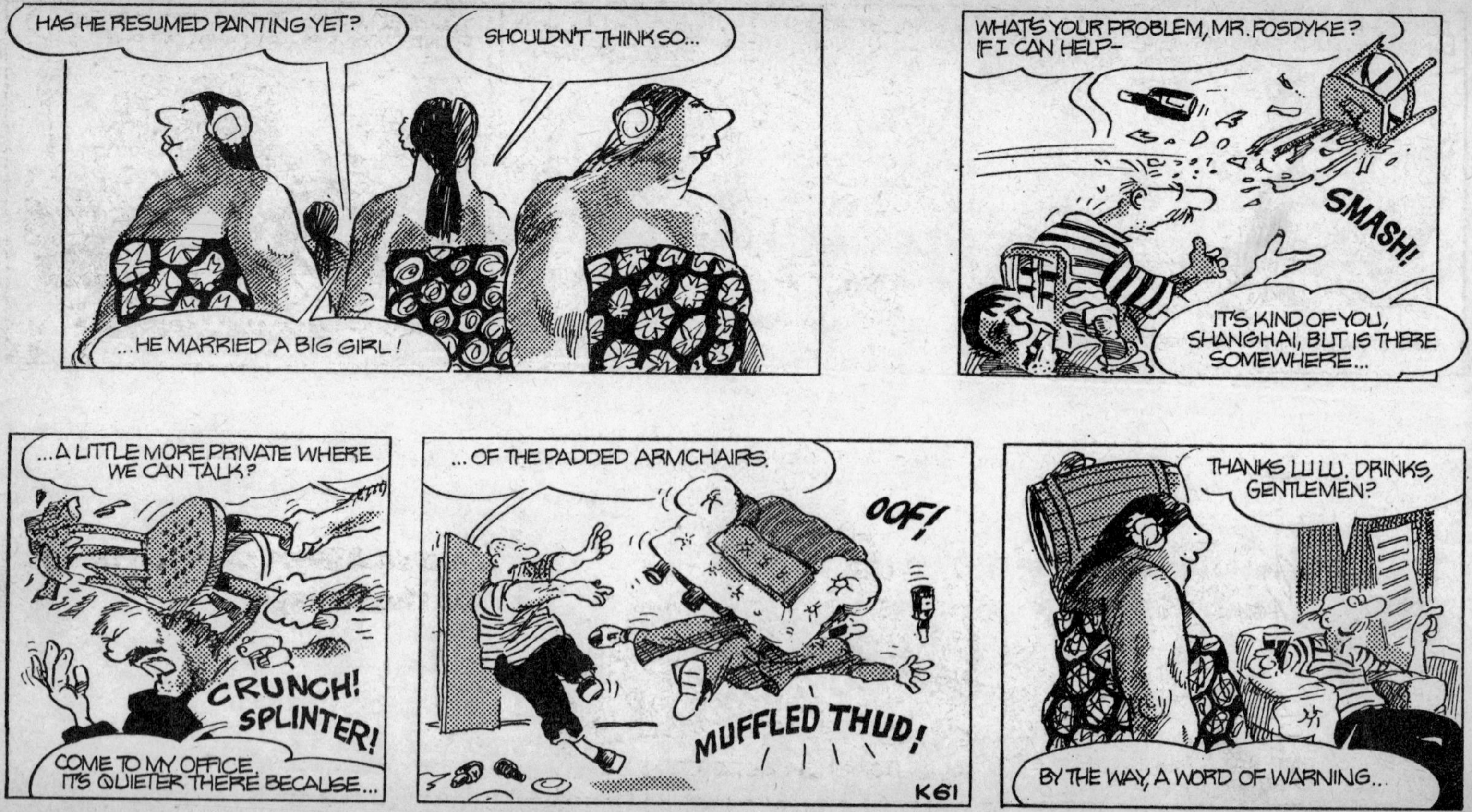
HAS HE RESUMED PAINTING YET?
SHOULDN'T THINK SO...
...HE MARRIED A BIG GIRL!
WHAT'S YOUR PROBLEM, MR. FOSDYKE? IF I CAN HELP–
SMASH!
IT'S KIND OF YOU, SHANGHAI, BUT IS THERE SOMEWHERE...
...A LITTLE MORE PRIVATE WHERE WE CAN TALK?
CRUNCH! SPLINTER!
COME TO MY OFFICE. IT'S QUIETER THERE BECAUSE...
...OF THE PADDED ARMCHAIRS.
OOF!
MUFFLED THUD!
K61
THANKS LULU. DRINKS, GENTLEMEN?
BY THE WAY, A WORD OF WARNING...

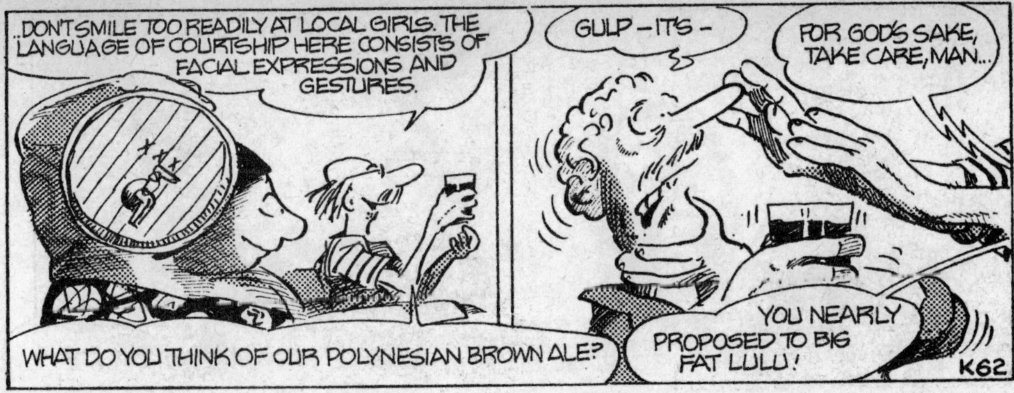
..DON'T SMILE TOO READILY AT LOCAL GIRLS. THE LANGUAGE OF COURTSHIP HERE CONSISTS OF FACIAL EXPRESSIONS AND GESTURES.
WHAT DO YOU THINK OF OUR POLYNESIAN BROWN ALE?
GULP – IT'S –
FOR GOD'S SAKE, TAKE CARE, MAN...
YOU NEARLY PROPOSED TO BIG FAT LULU!
K62

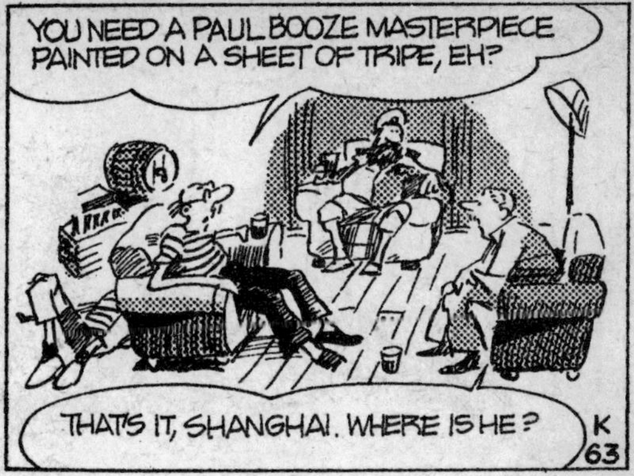
YOU NEED A PAUL BOOZE MASTERPIECE PAINTED ON A SHEET OF TRIPE, EH?
THAT'S IT, SHANGHAI. WHERE IS HE?
K 63

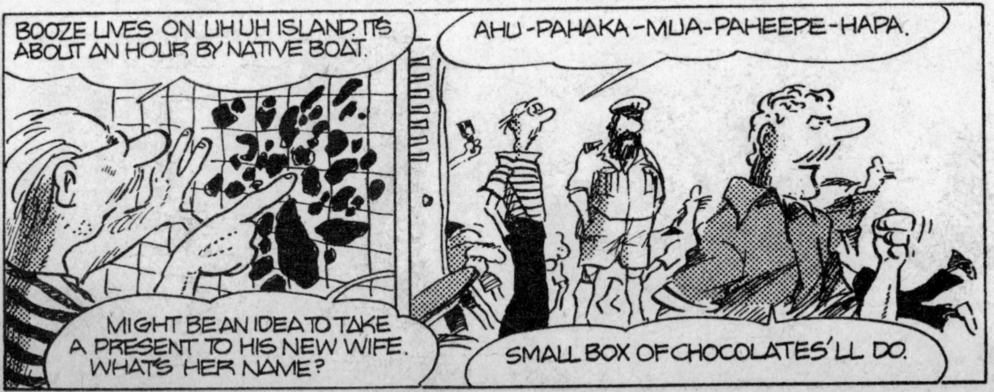
BOOZE LIVES ON UH UH ISLAND. IT'S ABOUT AN HOUR BY NATIVE BOAT.
MIGHT BE AN IDEA TO TAKE A PRESENT TO HIS NEW WIFE. WHAT'S HER NAME?
AHU-PAHAKA-MUA-PAHEEPE-HAPA.
SMALL BOX OF CHOCOLATES'LL DO.

And so Albert makes ready for the voyage...

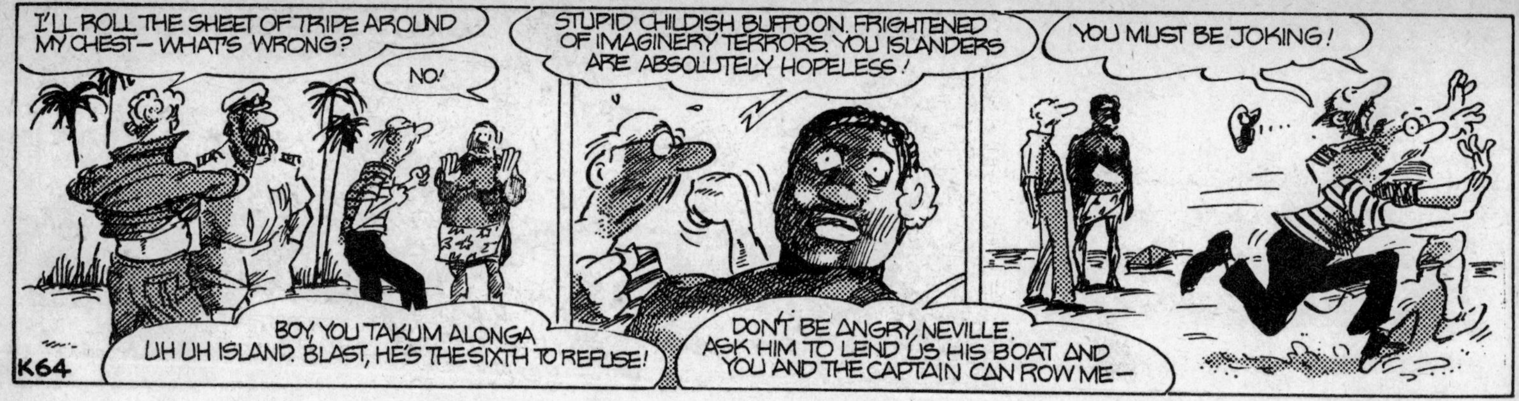
I'LL ROLL THE SHEET OF TRIPE AROUND MY CHEST— WHAT'S WRONG?
NO!
BOY, YOU TAKUM ALONGA UH UH ISLAND. BLAST, HE'S THE SIXTH TO REFUSE!
K64
STUPID CHILDISH BUFFOON. FRIGHTENED OF IMAGINERY TERRORS. YOU ISLANDERS ARE ABSOLUTELY HOPELESS!
DON'T BE ANGRY, NEVILLE. ASK HIM TO LEND US HIS BOAT AND YOU AND THE CAPTAIN CAN ROW ME—
YOU MUST BE JOKING!

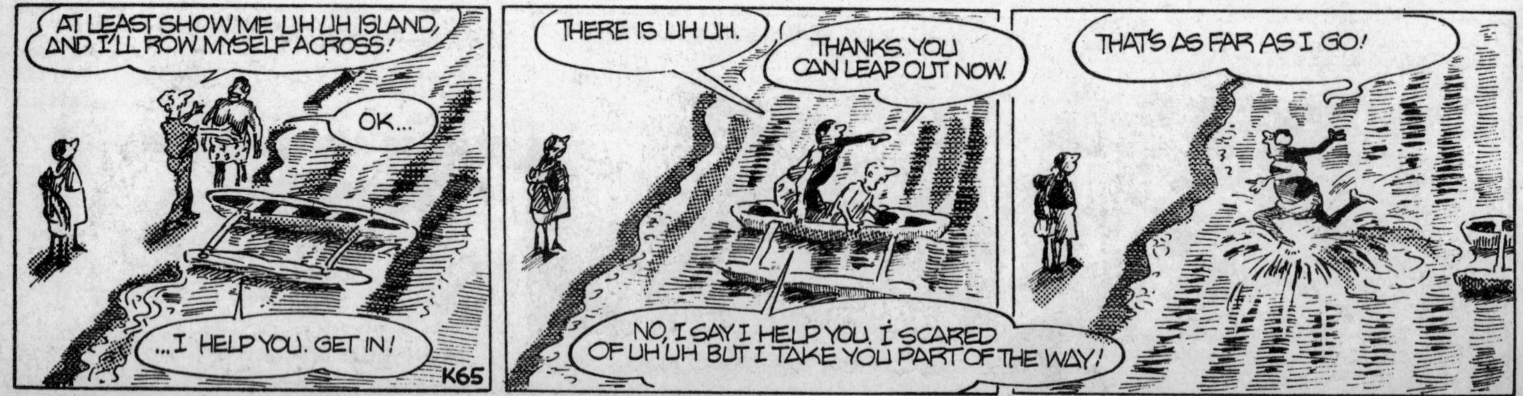
AT LEAST SHOW ME UH UH ISLAND, AND I'LL ROW MYSELF ACROSS!
OK...
...I HELP YOU. GET IN!
K65
THERE IS UH UH.
THANKS. YOU CAN LEAP OUT NOW.
NO, I SAY I HELP YOU. I SCARED OF UH UH BUT I TAKE YOU PART OF THE WAY!
THAT'S AS FAR AS I GO!

Deep in the Soladorian jungle Rosita Kecks carries Ditchley in hot pursuit of his prey...

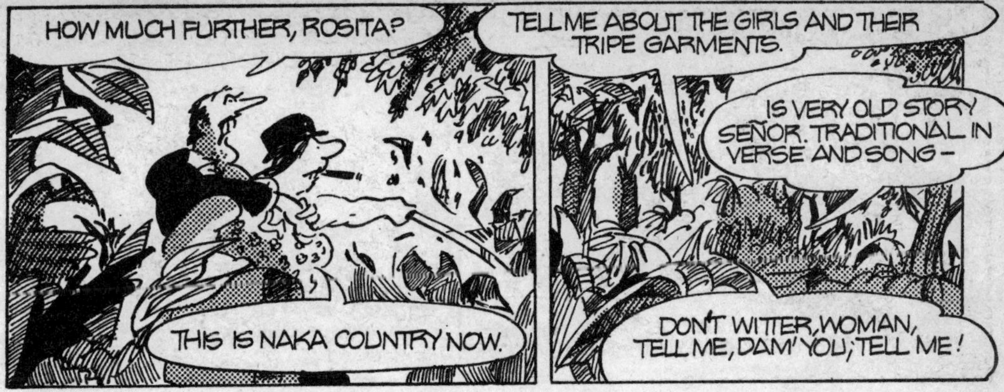

HOW MUCH FURTHER, ROSITA?
THIS IS NAKA COUNTRY NOW.
TELL ME ABOUT THE GIRLS AND THEIR TRIPE GARMENTS.
IS VERY OLD STORY SEÑOR. TRADITIONAL IN VERSE AND SONG –
DON'T WITTER, WOMAN, TELL ME, DAM' YOU; TELL ME!

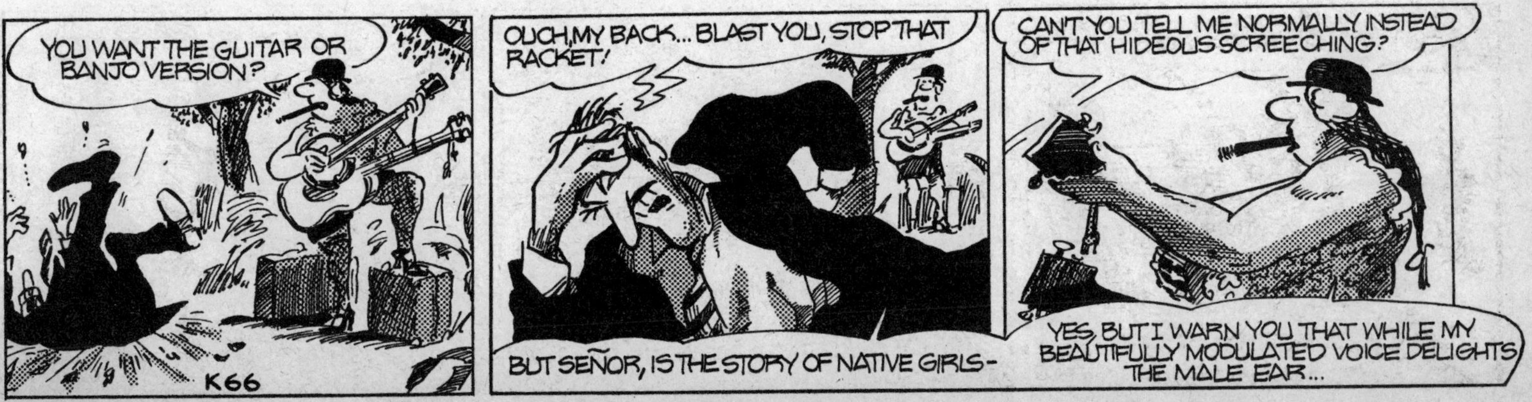

YOU WANT THE GUITAR OR BANJO VERSION?
K66
OUCH, MY BACK... BLAST YOU, STOP THAT RACKET!
BUT SEÑOR, IS THE STORY OF NATIVE GIRLS –
CAN'T YOU TELL ME NORMALLY INSTEAD OF THAT HIDEOUS SCREECHING?
YES, BUT I WARN YOU THAT WHILE MY BEAUTIFULLY MODULATED VOICE DELIGHTS THE MALE EAR...

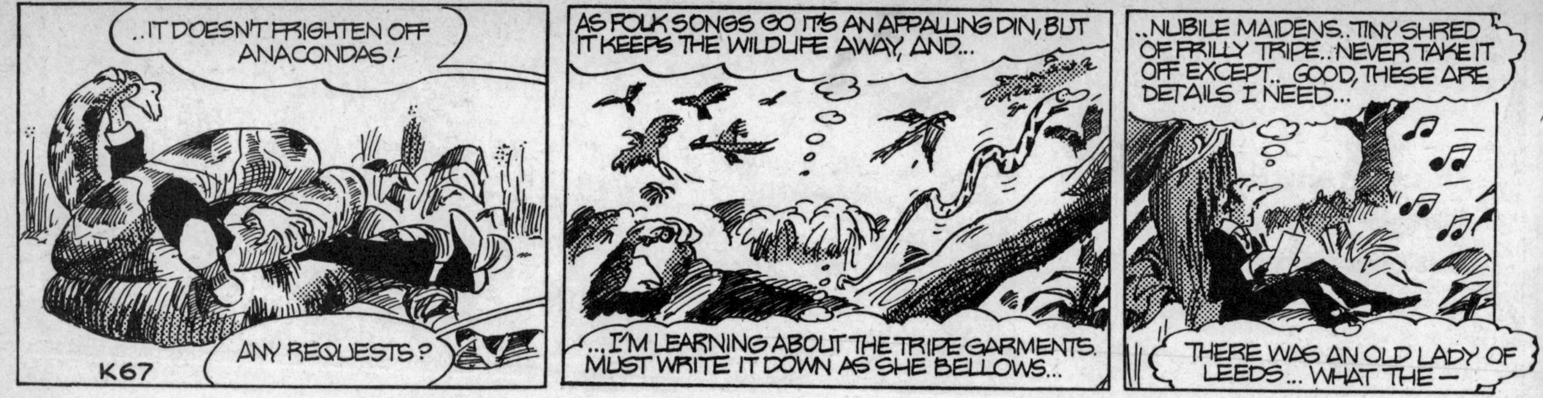
..IT DOESN'T FRIGHTEN OFF ANACONDAS!
ANY REQUESTS?
K67
AS FOLK SONGS GO IT'S AN APPALLING DIN, BUT IT KEEPS THE WILDLIFE AWAY, AND...
...I'M LEARNING ABOUT THE TRIPE GARMENTS. MUST WRITE IT DOWN AS SHE BELLOWS...
..NUBILE MAIDENS..TINY SHRED OF FRILLY TRIPE..NEVER TAKE IT OFF EXCEPT.. GOOD, THESE ARE DETAILS I NEED...
THERE WAS AN OLD LADY OF LEEDS... WHAT THE —

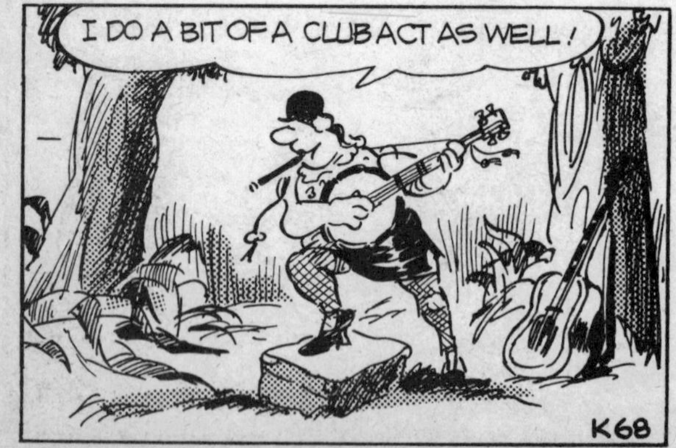
I DO A BIT OF A CLUB ACT AS WELL!
K68

Some hours later...

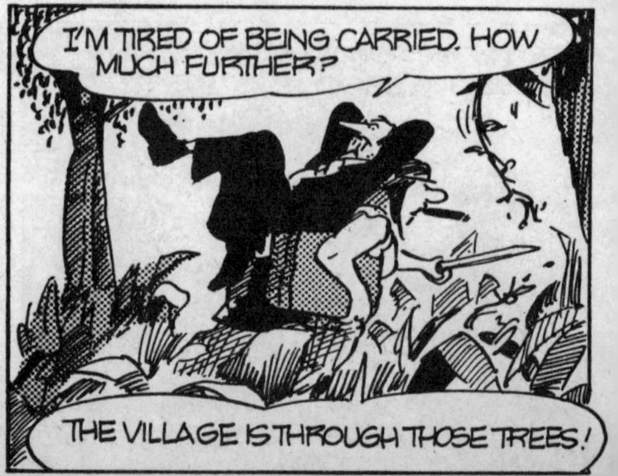
I'M TIRED OF BEING CARRIED. HOW MUCH FURTHER?
THE VILLAGE IS THROUGH THOSE TREES!

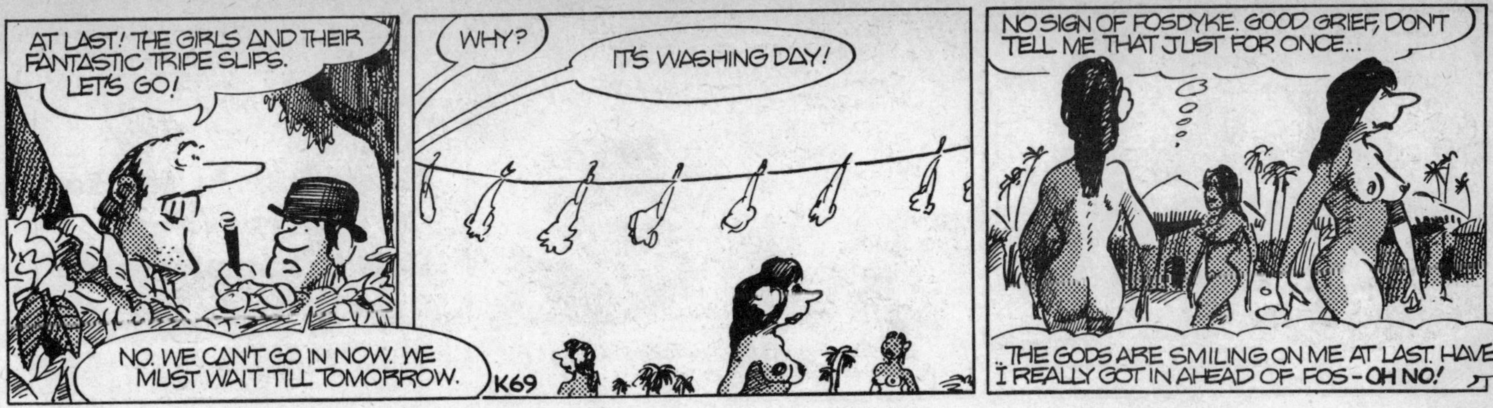
AT LAST! THE GIRLS AND THEIR FANTASTIC TRIPE SLIPS. LET'S GO!
NO. WE CAN'T GO IN NOW. WE MUST WAIT TILL TOMORROW.
WHY?
IT'S WASHING DAY!
K69
NO SIGN OF FOSDYKE. GOOD GRIEF, DON'T TELL ME THAT JUST FOR ONCE...
..THE GODS ARE SMILING ON ME AT LAST. HAVE I REALLY GOT IN AHEAD OF FOS-**OH NO!**

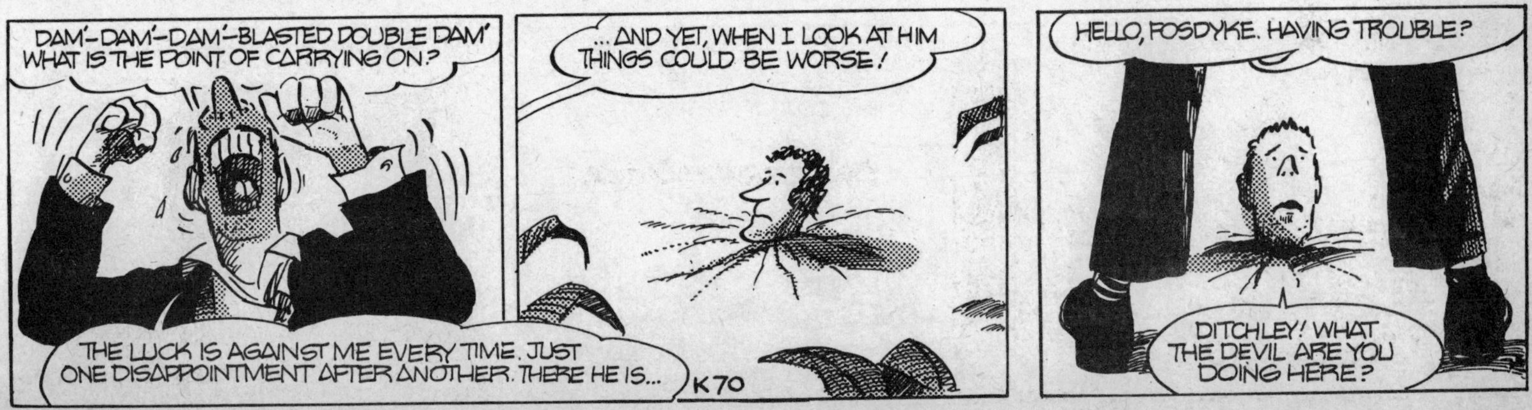
DAM'-DAM'-DAM'-BLASTED DOUBLE DAM' WHAT IS THE POINT OF CARRYING ON?
THE LUCK IS AGAINST ME EVERY TIME. JUST ONE DISAPPOINTMENT AFTER ANOTHER. THERE HE IS...
...AND YET, WHEN I LOOK AT HIM THINGS COULD BE WORSE!
K70
HELLO, FOSDYKE. HAVING TROUBLE?
DITCHLEY! WHAT THE DEVIL ARE YOU DOING HERE?

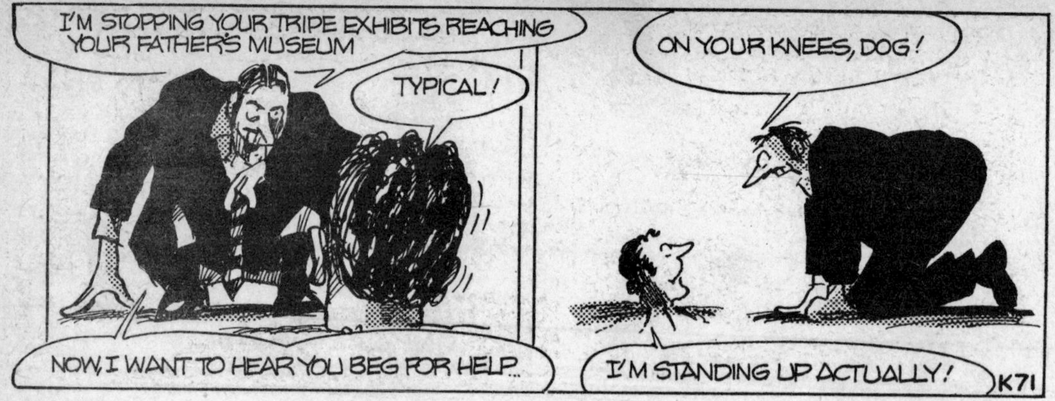
I'M STOPPING YOUR TRIPE EXHIBITS REACHING YOUR FATHER'S MUSEUM
TYPICAL!
NOW, I WANT TO HEAR YOU BEG FOR HELP...
ON YOUR KNEES, DOG!
I'M STANDING UP ACTUALLY!
K71

Meanwhile, in New York the Fosdykes await Bert's championship fight...

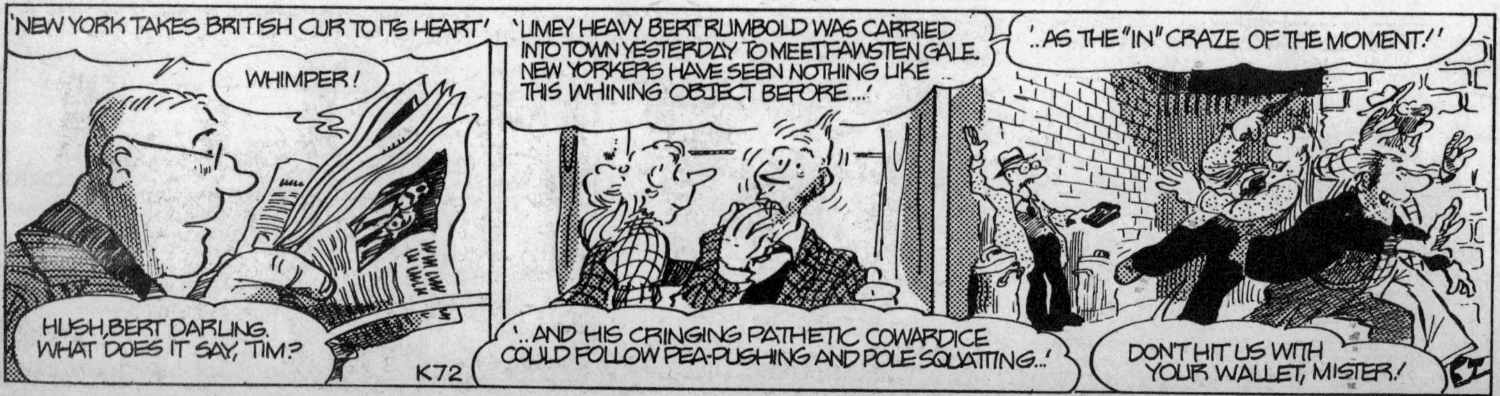
'NEW YORK TAKES BRITISH CUR TO ITS HEART'
WHIMPER!
HUSH, BERT DARLING. WHAT DOES IT SAY, TIM?
K72
'LIMEY HEAVY BERT RUMBOLD WAS CARRIED INTO TOWN YESTERDAY TO MEET FAWSTEN GALE. NEW YORKERS HAVE SEEN NOTHING LIKE THIS WHINING OBJECT BEFORE...'
'...AND HIS CRINGING PATHETIC COWARDICE COULD FOLLOW PEA-PUSHING AND POLE SQUATTING..!'
'...AS THE "IN" CRAZE OF THE MOMENT!'
DON'T HIT US WITH YOUR WALLET, MISTER!

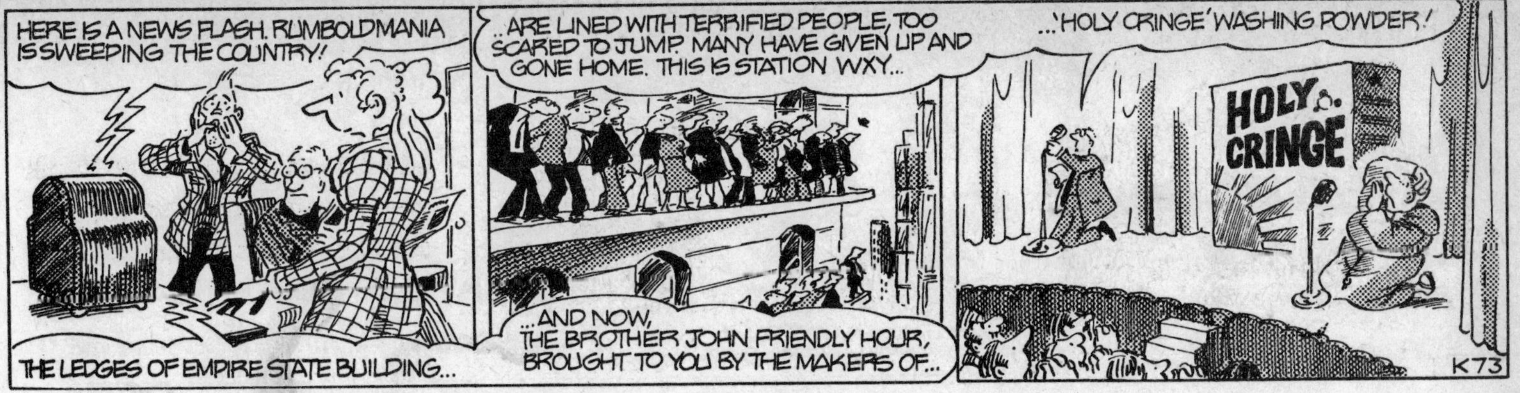
HERE IS A NEWS FLASH. RUMBOLDMANIA IS SWEEPING THE COUNTRY!
THE LEDGES OF EMPIRE STATE BUILDING...
..ARE LINED WITH TERRIFIED PEOPLE, TOO SCARED TO JUMP. MANY HAVE GIVEN UP AND GONE HOME. THIS IS STATION WXY...
...AND NOW, THE BROTHER JOHN FRIENDLY HOUR, BROUGHT TO YOU BY THE MAKERS OF...
...'HOLY CRINGE' WASHING POWDER!
HOLY CRINGE
K73

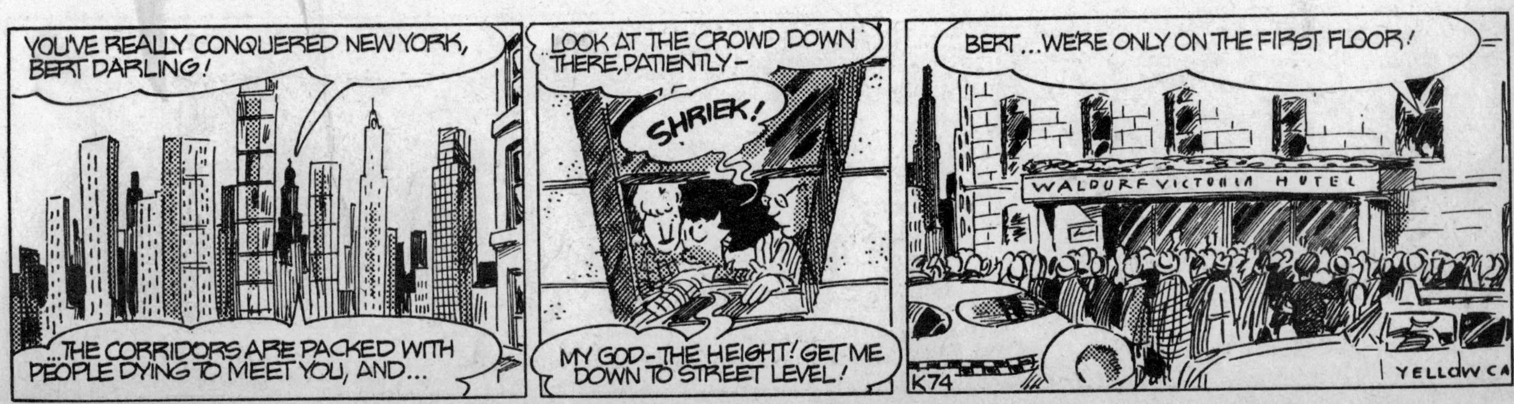
YOU'VE REALLY CONQUERED NEW YORK, BERT DARLING!
...THE CORRIDORS ARE PACKED WITH PEOPLE DYING TO MEET YOU, AND...
...LOOK AT THE CROWD DOWN THERE, PATIENTLY–
SHRIEK!
MY GOD–THE HEIGHT! GET ME DOWN TO STREET LEVEL!
BERT...WE'RE ONLY ON THE FIRST FLOOR!
WALDURF VICTORIA HOTEL
YELLOW CA
K74

And still the hysteria grows...

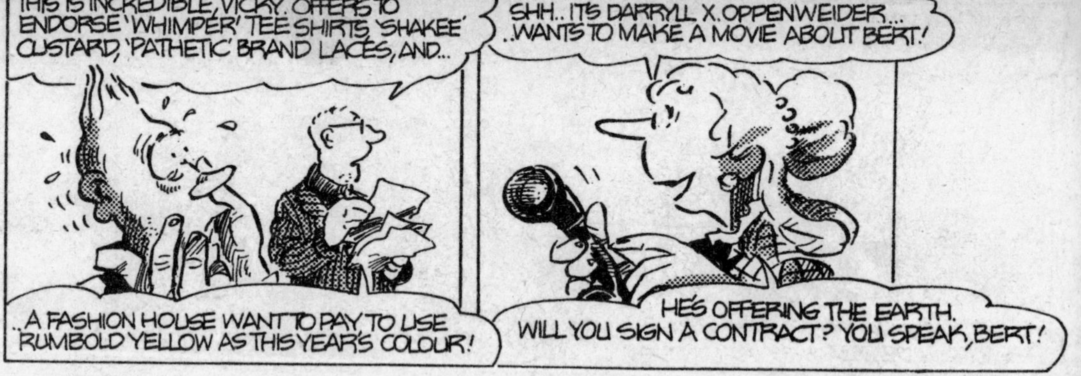
THIS IS INCREDIBLE, VICKY. OFFERS TO ENDORSE 'WHIMPER' TEE SHIRTS, 'SHAKEE' CUSTARD, 'PATHETIC' BRAND LACES, AND...
..A FASHION HOUSE WANT TO PAY TO USE RUMBOLD YELLOW AS THIS YEAR'S COLOUR!
SHH.. IT'S DARRYLL X. OPPENWEIDER... ..WANTS TO MAKE A MOVIE ABOUT BERT!
HE'S OFFERING THE EARTH. WILL YOU SIGN A CONTRACT? YOU SPEAK, BERT!

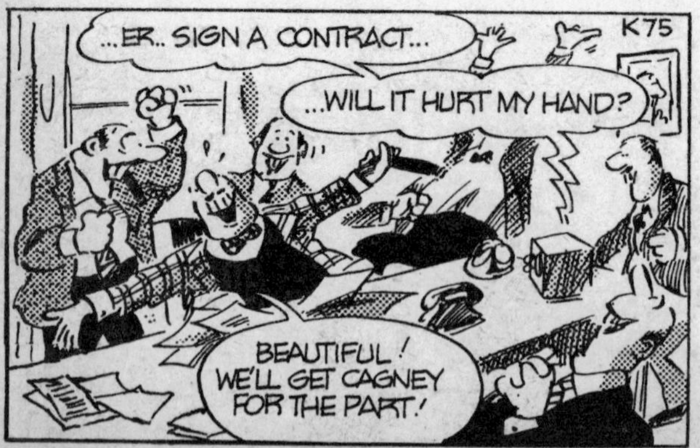
K75
...ER.. SIGN A CONTRACT...
...WILL IT HURT MY HAND?
BEAUTIFUL! WE'LL GET CAGNEY FOR THE PART!

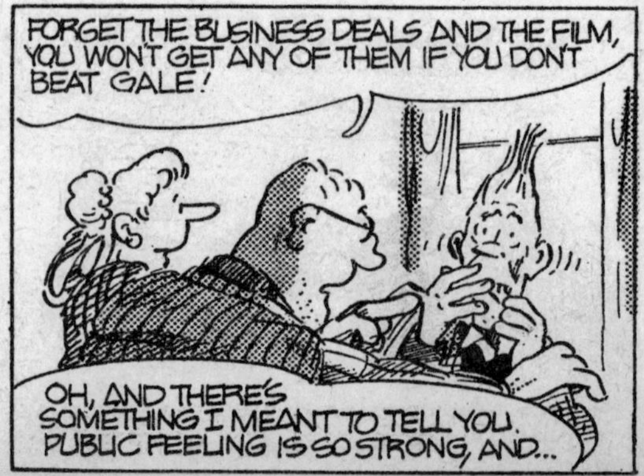
FORGET THE BUSINESS DEALS AND THE FILM, YOU WON'T GET ANY OF THEM IF YOU DON'T BEAT GALE!
OH, AND THERE'S SOMETHING I MEANT TO TELL YOU. PUBLIC FEELING IS SO STRONG, AND...

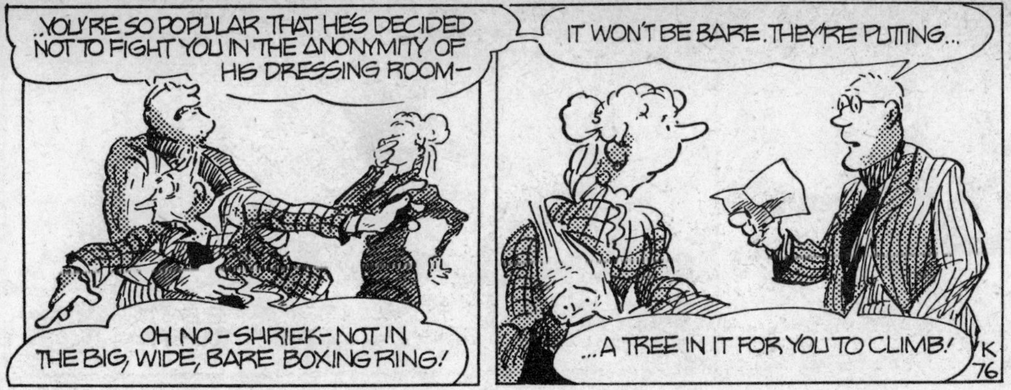
..YOU'RE SO POPULAR THAT HE'S DECIDED NOT TO FIGHT YOU IN THE ANONYMITY OF HIS DRESSING ROOM-
OH NO - SHRIEK- NOT IN THE BIG, WIDE, BARE BOXING RING!
IT WON'T BE BARE. THEY'RE PUTTING...
...A TREE IN IT FOR YOU TO CLIMB!
K 76

And as the day draws near...

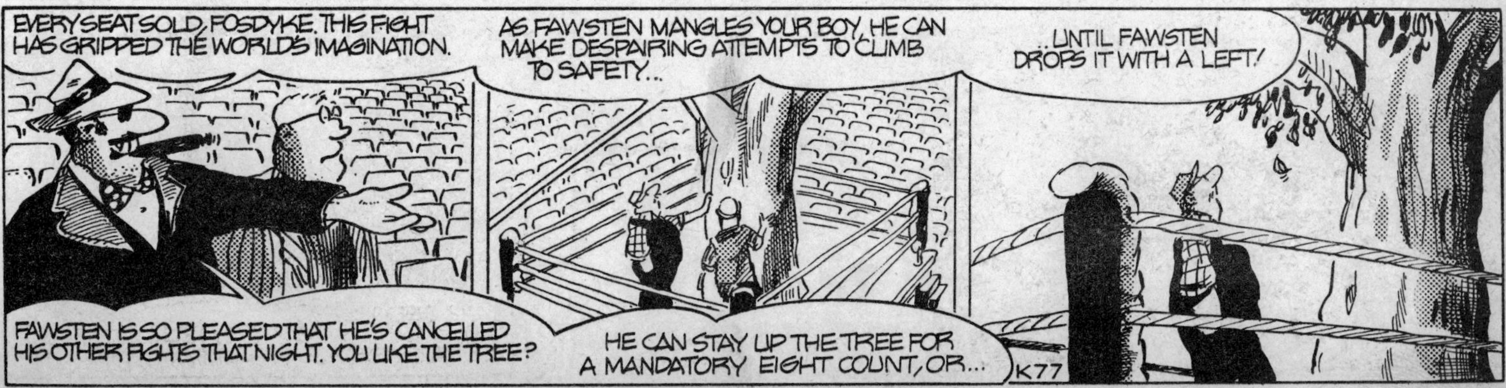
EVERY SEAT SOLD, FOSDYKE. THIS FIGHT HAS GRIPPED THE WORLD'S IMAGINATION.
FAWSTEN IS SO PLEASED THAT HE'S CANCELLED HIS OTHER FIGHTS THAT NIGHT. YOU LIKE THE TREE?
AS FAWSTEN MANGLES YOUR BOY, HE CAN MAKE DESPAIRING ATTEMPTS TO CLIMB TO SAFETY...
HE CAN STAY UP THE TREE FOR A MANDATORY EIGHT COUNT, OR...
..UNTIL FAWSTEN DROPS IT WITH A LEFT!
K77

At sea between Papeete and Uh Uh Island, Albert wrestles with a native canoe...

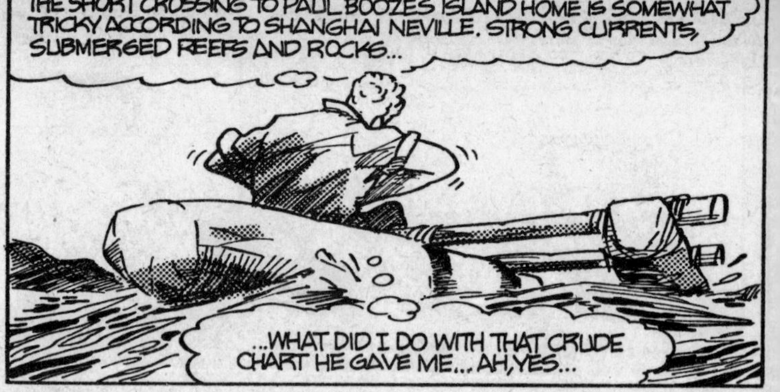
THE SHORT CROSSING TO PAUL BOOZE'S ISLAND HOME IS SOMEWHAT TRICKY ACCORDING TO SHANGHAI NEVILLE. STRONG CURRENTS, SUBMERGED REEFS AND ROCKS...
...WHAT DID I DO WITH THAT CRUDE CHART HE GAVE ME... AH, YES...

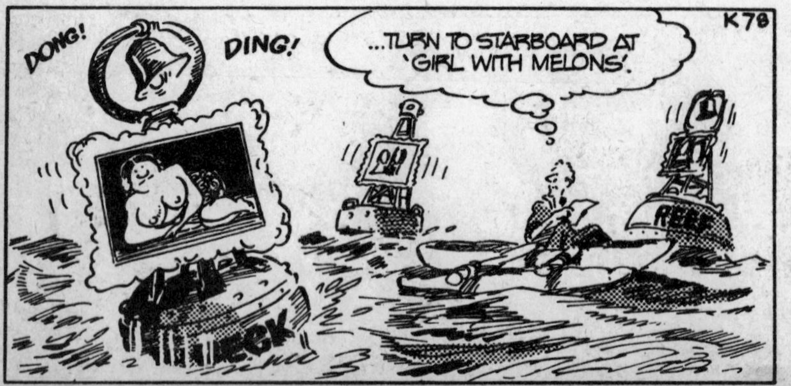
DONG!
DING!
...TURN TO STARBOARD AT 'GIRL WITH MELONS'.
K78
REEF

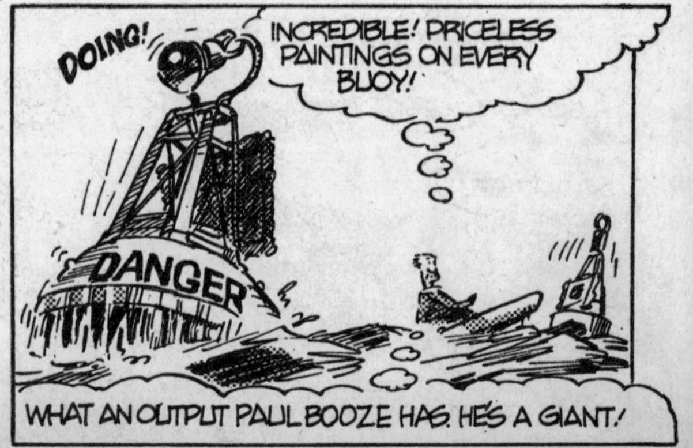
DOING!
INCREDIBLE! PRICELESS PAINTINGS ON EVERY BUOY!
DANGER
WHAT AN OUTPUT PAUL BOOZE HAS. HE'S A GIANT!

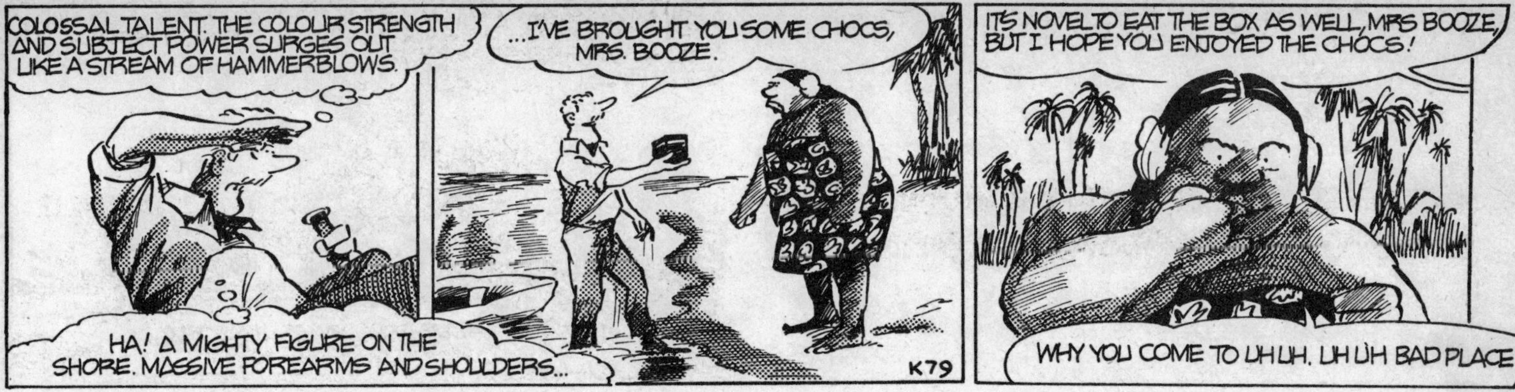
COLOSSAL TALENT. THE COLOUR STRENGTH AND SUBJECT POWER SURGES OUT LIKE A STREAM OF HAMMERBLOWS.
HA! A MIGHTY FIGURE ON THE SHORE. MASSIVE FOREARMS AND SHOULDERS...
...I'VE BROUGHT YOU SOME CHOCS, MRS. BOOZE.
K79
IT'S NOVEL TO EAT THE BOX AS WELL, MRS BOOZE, BUT I HOPE YOU ENJOYED THE CHOCS!
WHY YOU COME TO UH UH. UH UH BAD PLACE!

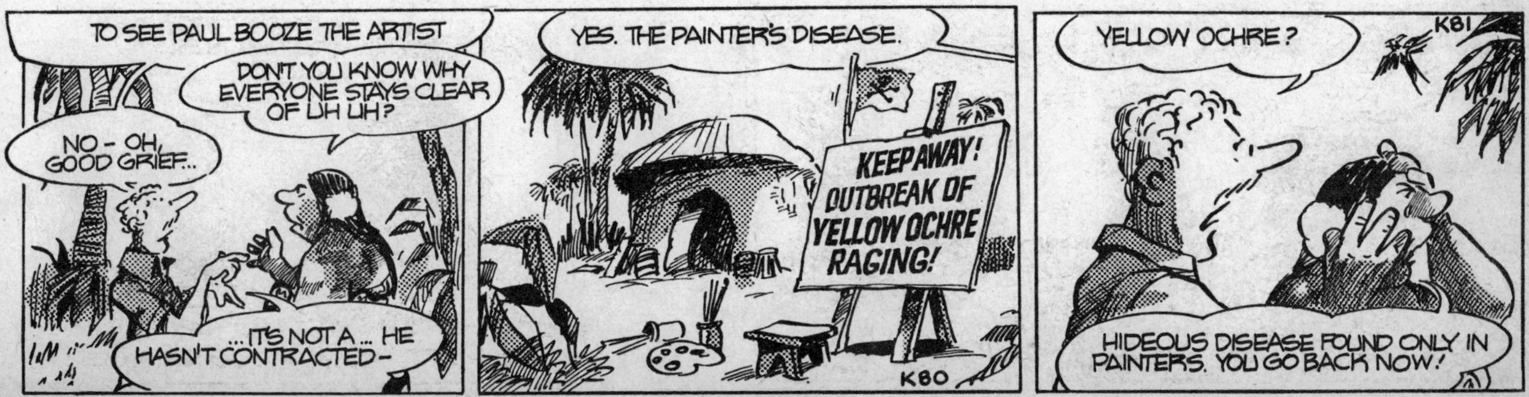
TO SEE PAUL BOOZE THE ARTIST
DON'T YOU KNOW WHY EVERYONE STAYS CLEAR OF UH UH?
NO - OH, GOOD GRIEF...
...IT'S NOT A ... HE HASN'T CONTRACTED-
YES. THE PAINTER'S DISEASE.
KEEP AWAY! OUTBREAK OF YELLOW OCHRE RAGING!
K80
YELLOW OCHRE?
K81
HIDEOUS DISEASE FOUND ONLY IN PAINTERS. YOU GO BACK NOW!

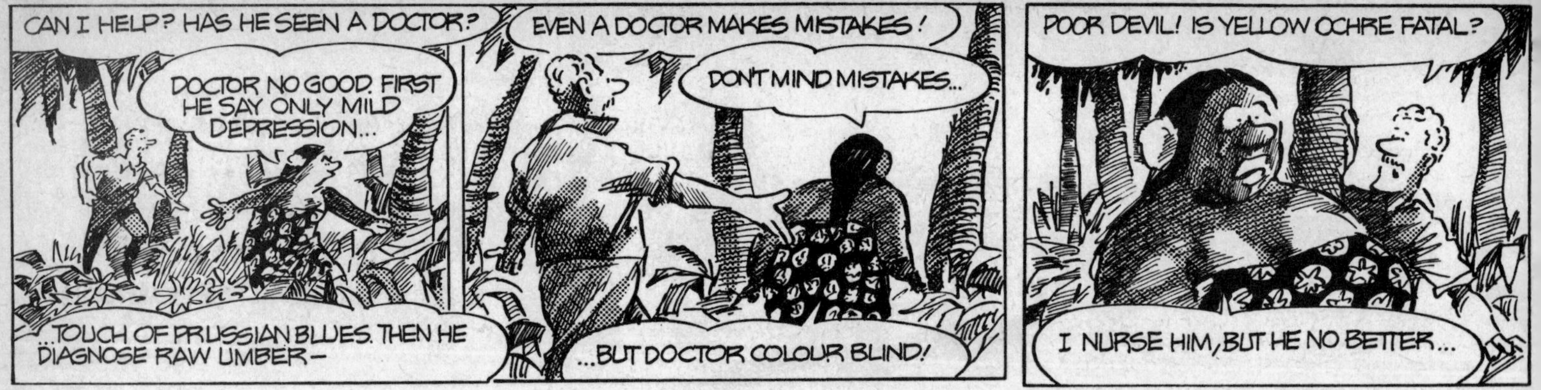
CAN I HELP? HAS HE SEEN A DOCTOR?
DOCTOR NO GOOD. FIRST HE SAY ONLY MILD DEPRESSION...
...TOUCH OF PRUSSIAN BLUES. THEN HE DIAGNOSE RAW UMBER–
EVEN A DOCTOR MAKES MISTAKES!
DON'T MIND MISTAKES...
...BUT DOCTOR COLOUR BLIND!
POOR DEVIL! IS YELLOW OCHRE FATAL?
I NURSE HIM, BUT HE NO BETTER...

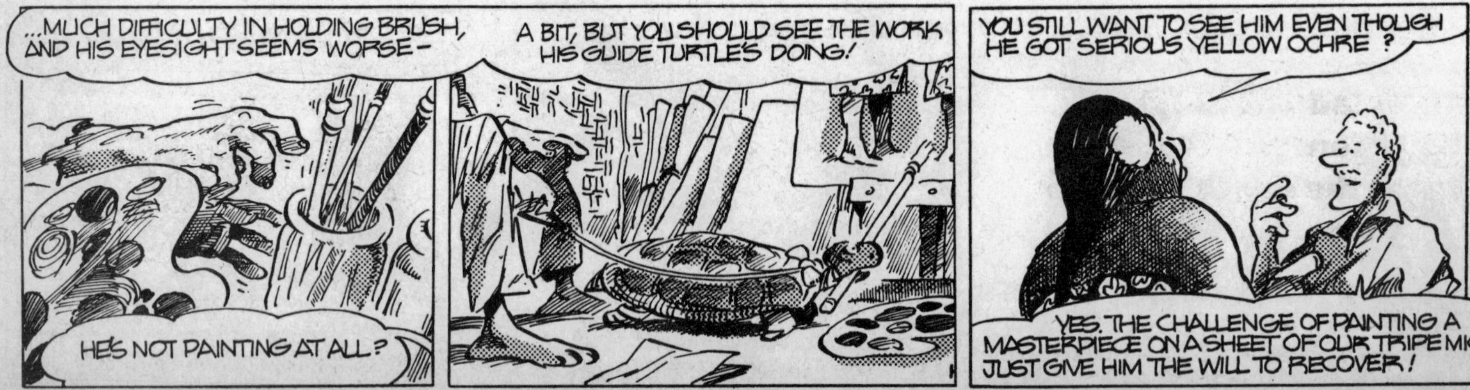
...MUCH DIFFICULTY IN HOLDING BRUSH, AND HIS EYESIGHT SEEMS WORSE–
HE'S NOT PAINTING AT ALL?
A BIT, BUT YOU SHOULD SEE THE WORK HIS GUIDE TURTLE'S DOING!
YOU STILL WANT TO SEE HIM EVEN THOUGH HE GOT SERIOUS YELLOW OCHRE?
YES. THE CHALLENGE OF PAINTING A MASTERPIECE ON A SHEET OF OUR TRIPE MIGHT JUST GIVE HIM THE WILL TO RECOVER!

NO! YOU GO BACK!
WHAT A TRAGEDY TO LET A GREAT TALENT FADE AWAY WITHOUT A FIGHT. I'VE SEEN HIS SUPERB WORK OUT THERE, AND NOT JUST PAINTINGS...
K83
...LOOK AT THAT MAGNIFICENT NOTICE!
KEEP AWAY BLAST YOU! YELLOW OCHRE OUTBREAK!
OK, LET'S GO!

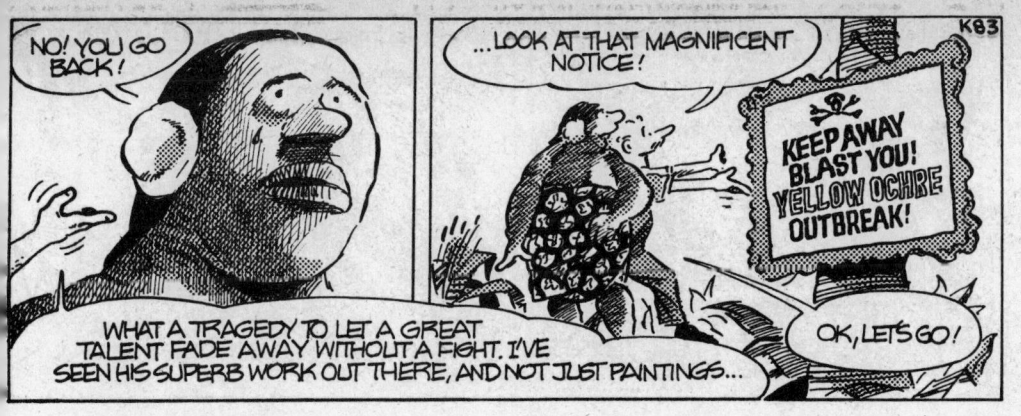

While Albert presses forward on his errand of mercy, ready to fight a fiendish disease for the sake of a piece of painted tripe...

in the Soladorian native village, Tom and Ditchley, rivals to the death, confront each other...

WHAT A ROTTEN, MISERABLE, CHEERLESS, USELESS LIFE I HAVE!
EVERYTHING I DO TURNS TO DUST, EVERY HOPE CRUMBLES...
...I FIND MY ENEMY HELPLESS AT MY FEET, BUT CAN I MAKE HIM COWER ON HIS KNEES? OH NO. THEY BURIED HIM UPRIGHT! HOW UNLUCKY CAN I GET?
I LIKE THAT! IT'S ME WHO'S STUCK HERE UP TO MY NECK!

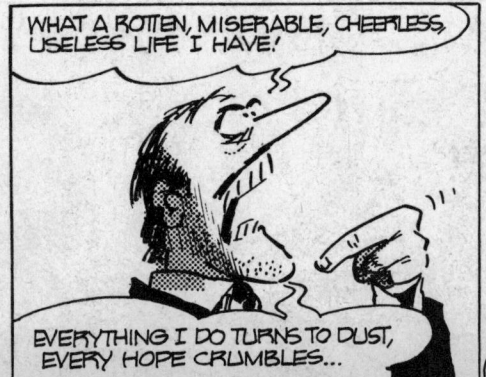

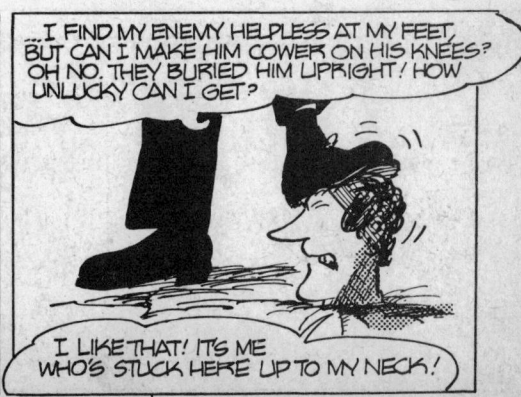

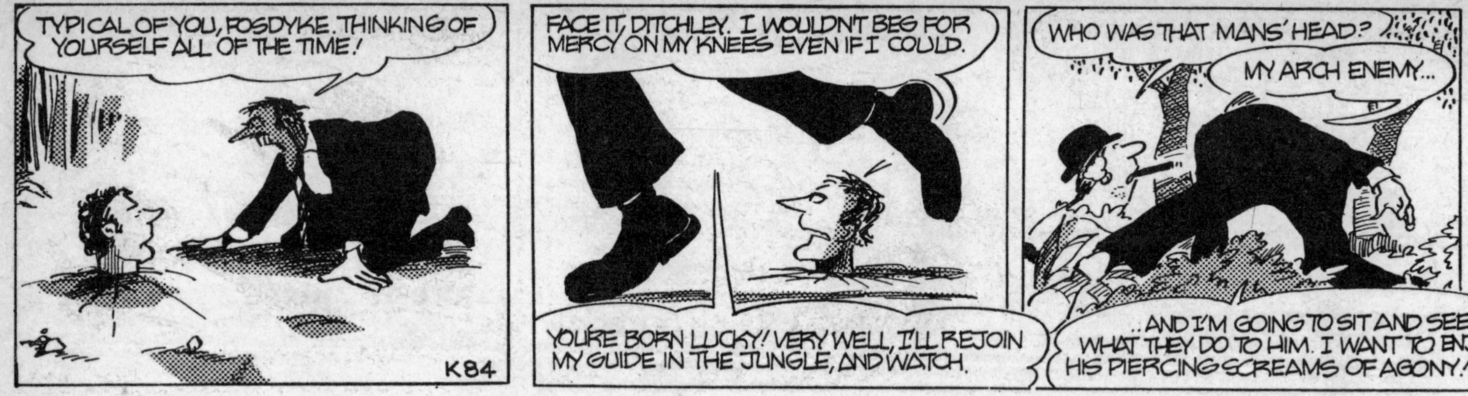
TYPICAL OF YOU, FOSDYKE. THINKING OF YOURSELF ALL OF THE TIME!
K84
FACE IT, DITCHLEY. I WOULDN'T BEG FOR MERCY ON MY KNEES EVEN IF I COULD.
YOU'RE BORN LUCKY! VERY WELL, I'LL REJOIN MY GUIDE IN THE JUNGLE, AND WATCH.
WHO WAS THAT MANS' HEAD?
MY ARCH ENEMY...
..AND I'M GOING TO SIT AND SEE WHAT THEY DO TO HIM. I WANT TO ENJOY HIS PIERCING SCREAMS OF AGONY!

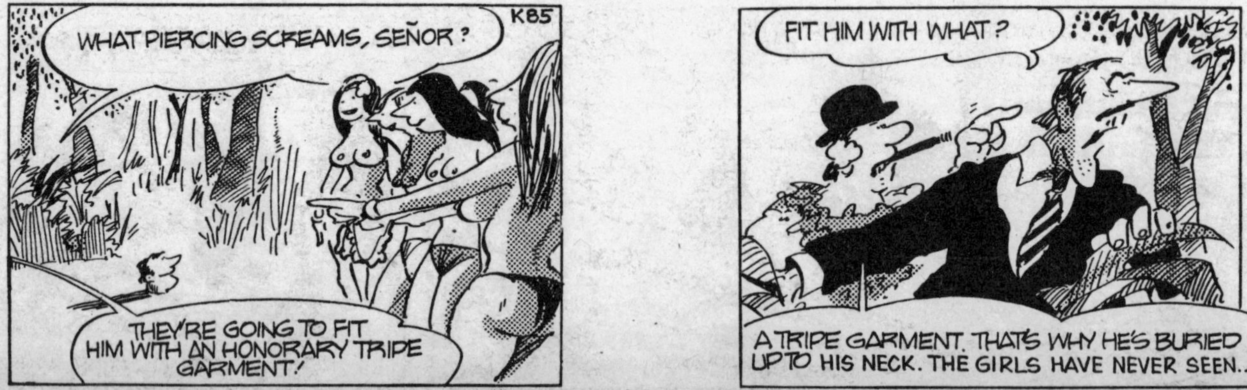
K85
WHAT PIERCING SCREAMS, SEÑOR?
THEY'RE GOING TO FIT HIM WITH AN HONORARY TRIPE GARMENT!
FIT HIM WITH WHAT?
A TRIPE GARMENT. THAT'S WHY HE'S BURIED UP TO HIS NECK. THE GIRLS HAVE NEVER SEEN...

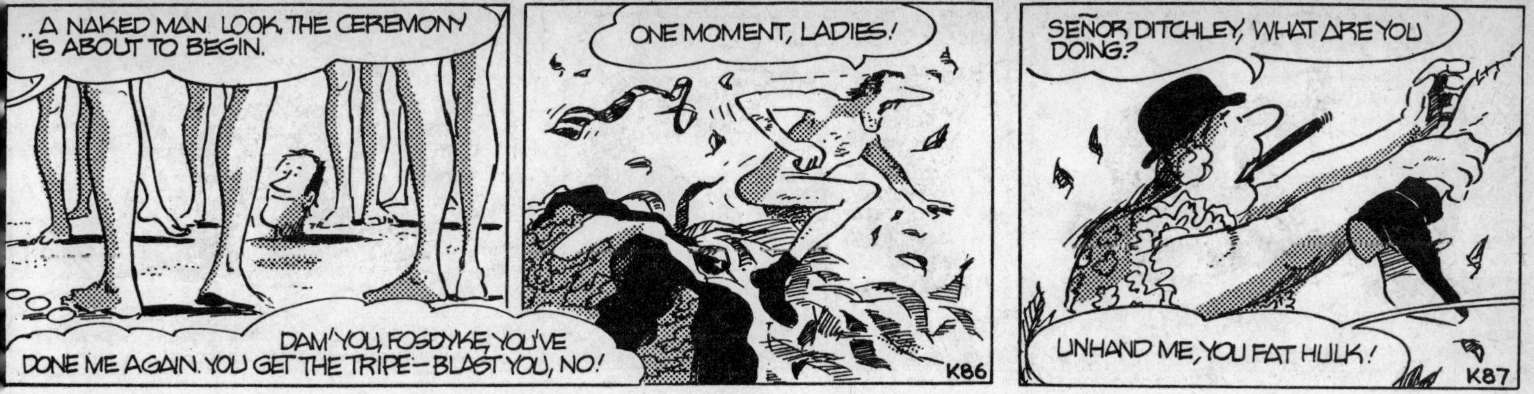
..A NAKED MAN. LOOK, THE CEREMONY IS ABOUT TO BEGIN.
DAM' YOU, FOSDYKE, YOU'VE DONE ME AGAIN. YOU GET THE TRIPE—BLAST YOU, NO!
ONE MOMENT, LADIES!
K86
SEÑOR DITCHLEY, WHAT ARE YOU DOING?
UNHAND ME, YOU FAT HULK!
K87

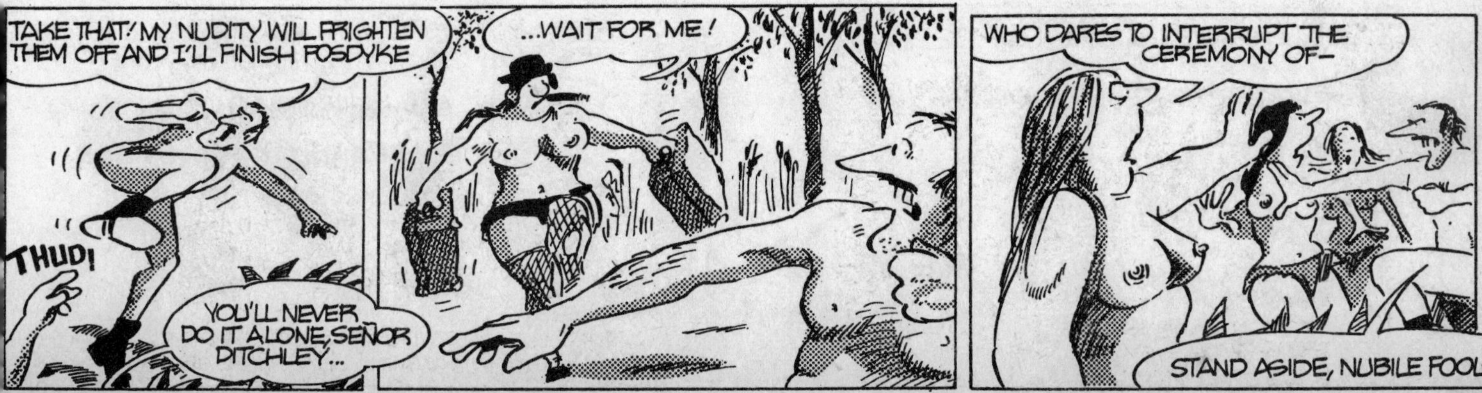
TAKE THAT! MY NUDITY WILL FRIGHTEN THEM OFF AND I'LL FINISH FOSDYKE
THUD!
YOU'LL NEVER DO IT ALONE, SEÑOR DITCHLEY...
...WAIT FOR ME!
WHO DARES TO INTERRUPT THE CEREMONY OF—
STAND ASIDE, NUBILE FOOLS!

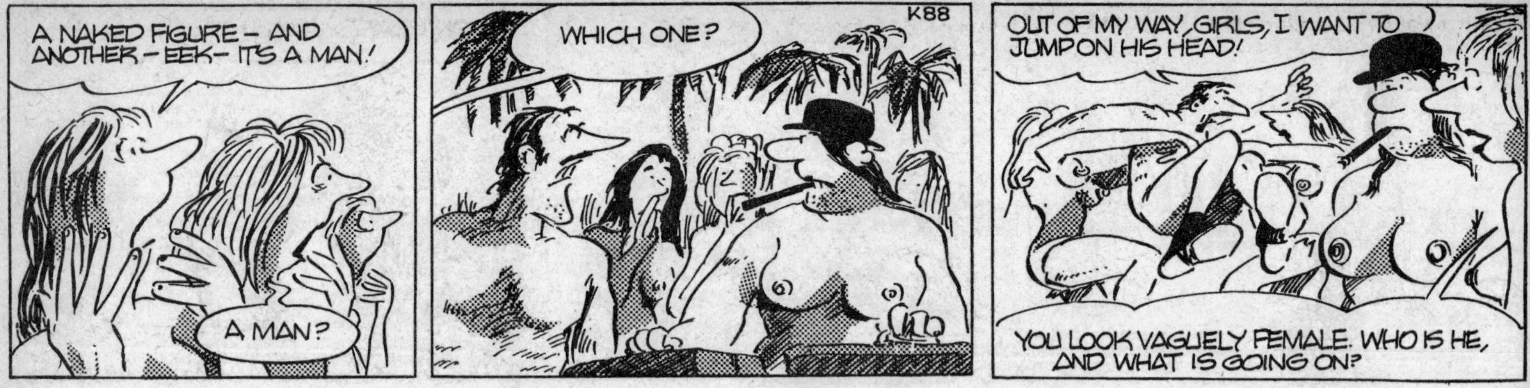
A NAKED FIGURE – AND ANOTHER – EEK – IT'S A MAN!
A MAN?
WHICH ONE?
K88
OUT OF MY WAY, GIRLS, I WANT TO JUMP ON HIS HEAD!
YOU LOOK VAGUELY FEMALE. WHO IS HE, AND WHAT IS GOING ON?

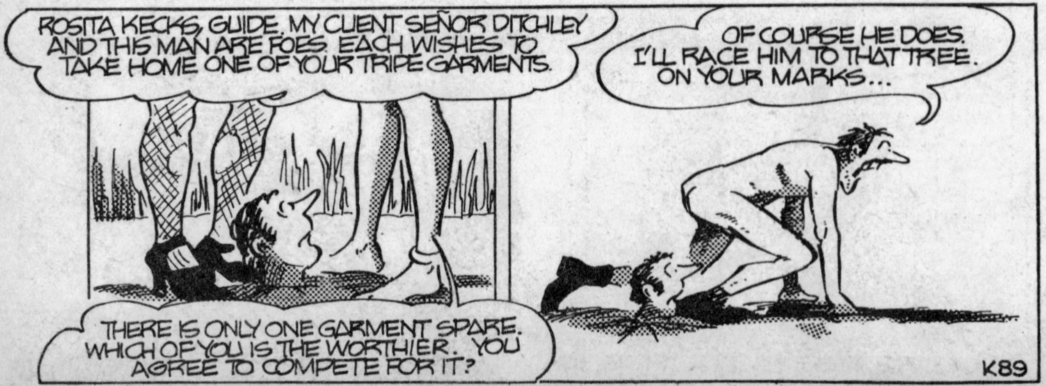
ROSITA KECKS, GUIDE. MY CLIENT SEÑOR DITCHLEY AND THIS MAN ARE FOES. EACH WISHES TO TAKE HOME ONE OF YOUR TRIPE GARMENTS.
THERE IS ONLY ONE GARMENT SPARE. WHICH OF YOU IS THE WORTHIER.. YOU AGREE TO COMPETE FOR IT?
OF COURSE HE DOES. I'LL RACE HIM TO THAT TREE. ON YOUR MARKS...
K89

Meanwhile, in New York Bert's big moment has arrived...

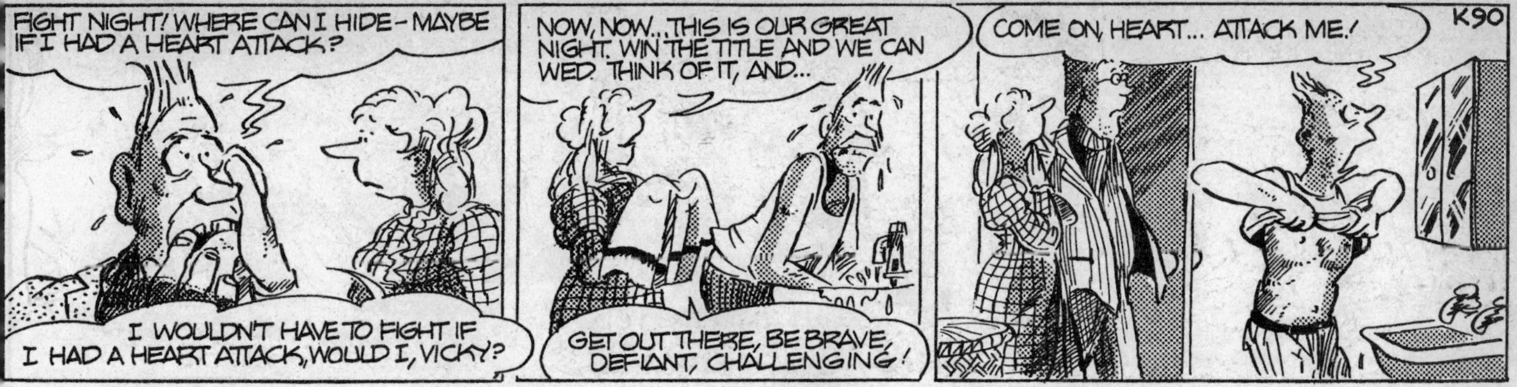
FIGHT NIGHT! WHERE CAN I HIDE – MAYBE IF I HAD A HEART ATTACK?
I WOULDN'T HAVE TO FIGHT IF I HAD A HEART ATTACK, WOULD I, VICKY?
NOW, NOW... THIS IS OUR GREAT NIGHT. WIN THE TITLE AND WE CAN WED. THINK OF IT, AND...
GET OUT THERE, BE BRAVE, DEFIANT, CHALLENGING!
COME ON, HEART... ATTACK ME!
K90

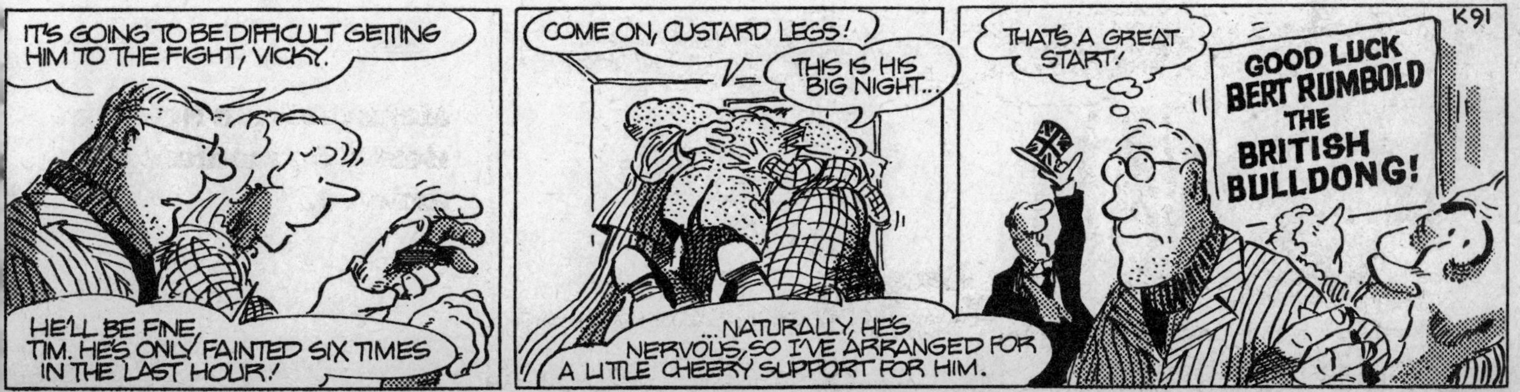
IT'S GOING TO BE DIFFICULT GETTING HIM TO THE FIGHT, VICKY.
HE'LL BE FINE, TIM. HE'S ONLY FAINTED SIX TIMES IN THE LAST HOUR!
COME ON, CUSTARD LEGS!
THIS IS HIS BIG NIGHT...
...NATURALLY, HE'S NERVOUS, SO I'VE ARRANGED FOR A LITTLE CHEERY SUPPORT FOR HIM.
THAT'S A GREAT START!
GOOD LUCK BERT RUMBOLD THE BRITISH BULLDONG!
K91

At the boxing stadium...

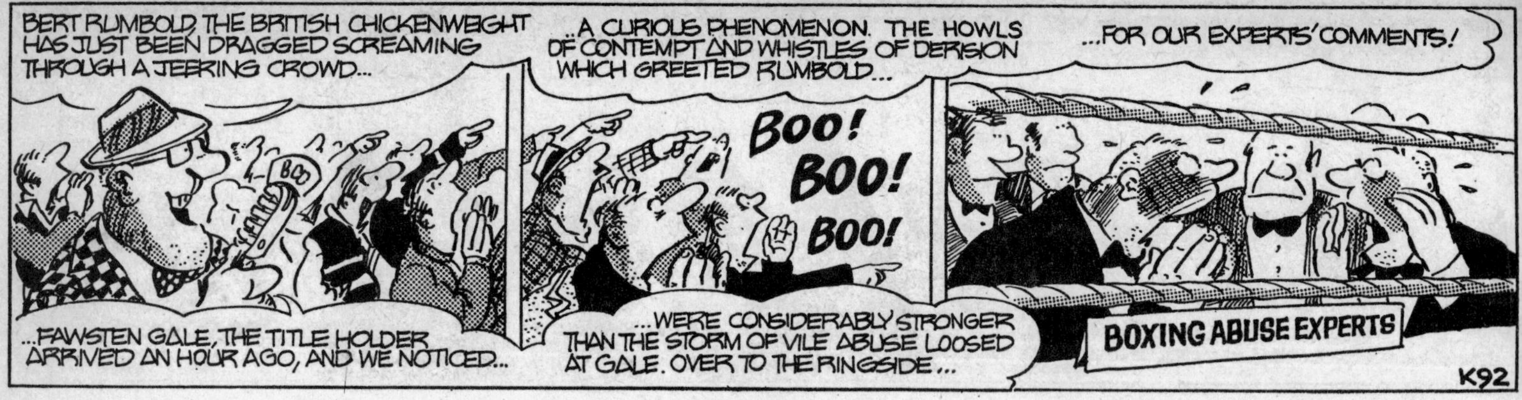
BERT RUMBOLD, THE BRITISH CHICKENWEIGHT HAS JUST BEEN DRAGGED SCREAMING THROUGH A JEERING CROWD...
...FAWSTEN GALE, THE TITLE HOLDER ARRIVED AN HOUR AGO, AND WE NOTICED...
...A CURIOUS PHENOMENON. THE HOWLS OF CONTEMPT AND WHISTLES OF DERISION WHICH GREETED RUMBOLD...
BOO!
BOO!
BOO!
...WERE CONSIDERABLY STRONGER THAN THE STORM OF VILE ABUSE LOOSED AT GALE. OVER TO THE RINGSIDE...
...FOR OUR EXPERTS' COMMENTS!
BOXING ABUSE EXPERTS
K92

And in Bert's dressing room...

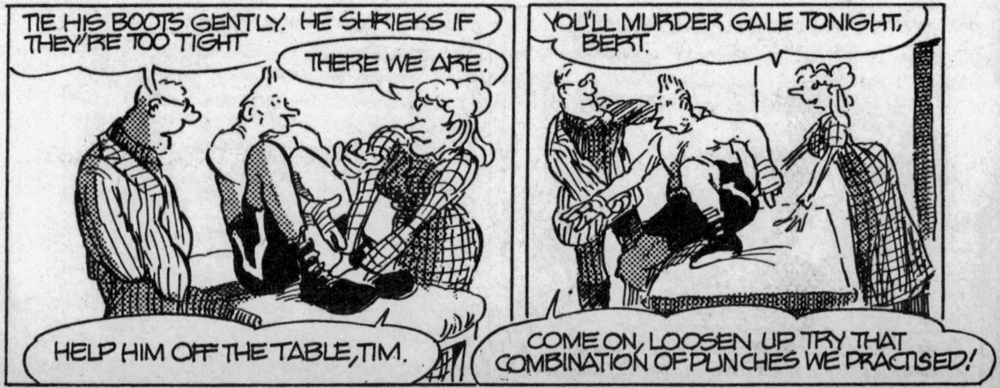
TIE HIS BOOTS GENTLY. HE SHRIEKS IF THEY'RE TOO TIGHT
THERE WE ARE.
HELP HIM OFF THE TABLE, TIM.
YOU'LL MURDER GALE TONIGHT, BERT.
COME ON, LOOSEN UP TRY THAT COMBINATION OF PUNCHES WE PRACTISED!

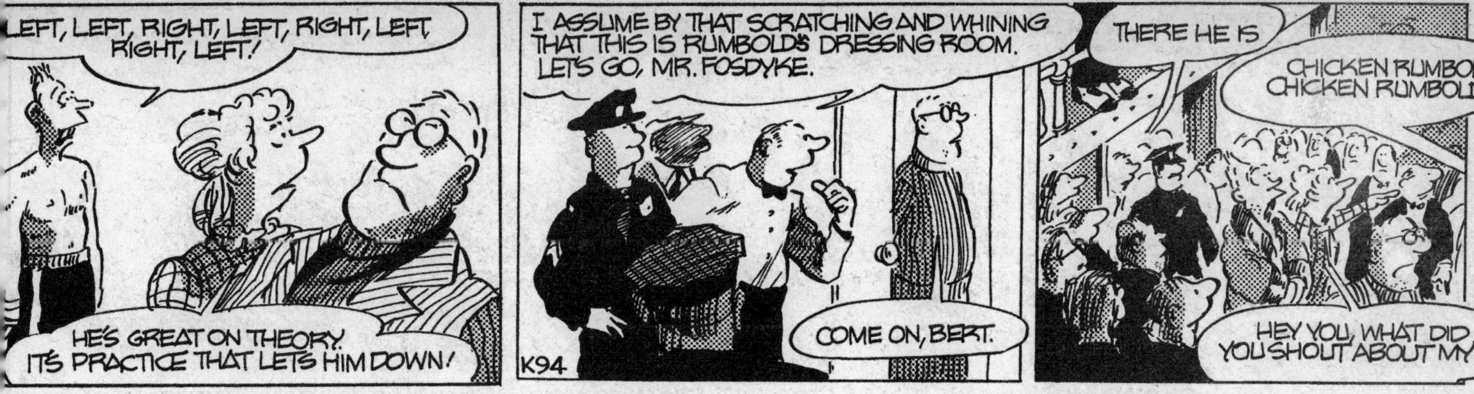
LEFT, LEFT, RIGHT, LEFT, RIGHT, LEFT, RIGHT, LEFT!
HE'S GREAT ON THEORY. IT'S PRACTICE THAT LETS HIM DOWN!
I ASSUME BY THAT SCRATCHING AND WHINING THAT THIS IS RUMBOLD'S DRESSING ROOM. LET'S GO, MR. FOSDYKE.
COME ON, BERT.
K94
THERE HE IS
CHICKEN RUMBOLD, CHICKEN RUMBOLD!
HEY YOU, WHAT DID YOU SHOUT ABOUT MY-

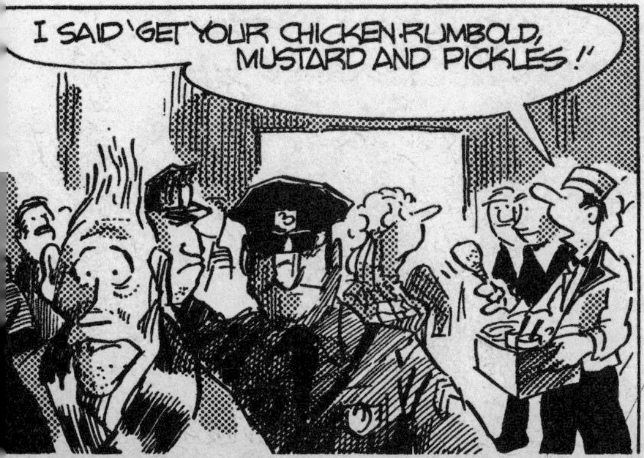
I SAID 'GET YOUR CHICKEN-RUMBOLD, MUSTARD AND PICKLES!'

So, into the ring at last...

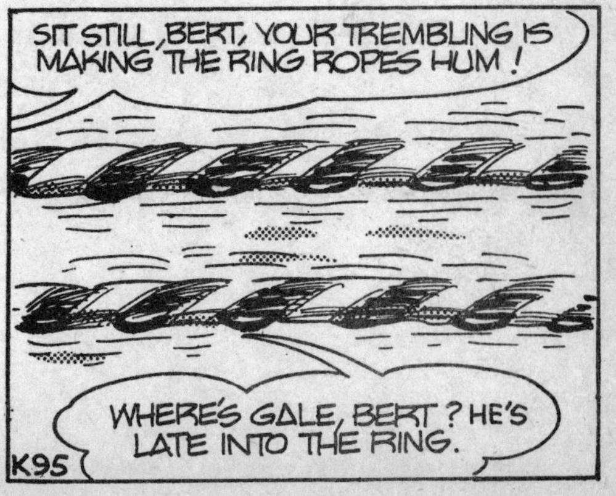
SIT STILL, BERT, YOUR TREMBLING IS MAKING THE RING ROPES HUM!
WHERE'S GALE, BERT? HE'S LATE INTO THE RING.
K95

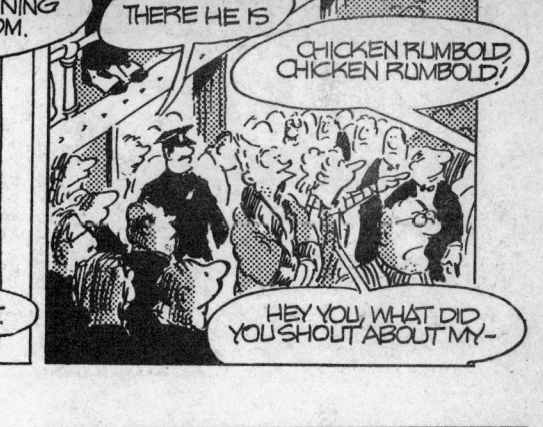

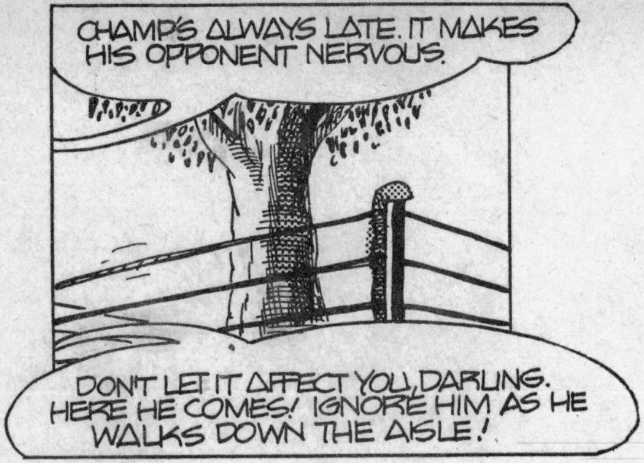
CHAMP'S ALWAYS LATE. IT MAKES HIS OPPONENT NERVOUS.
DON'T LET IT AFFECT YOU, DARLING. HERE HE COMES! IGNORE HIM AS HE WALKS DOWN THE AISLE!

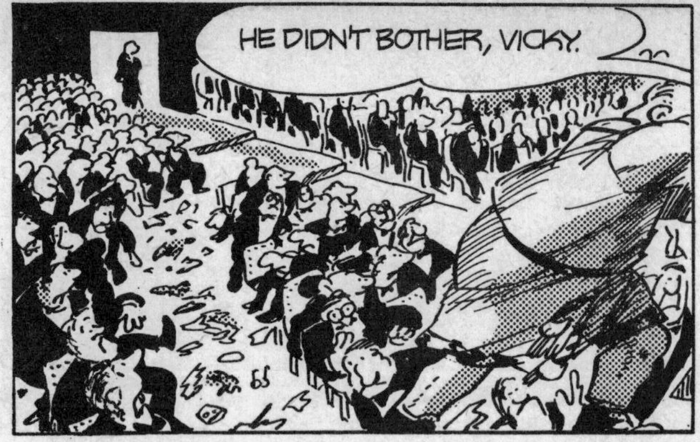
HE DIDN'T BOTHER, VICKY.

Can Bert Rumbold defeat the superhuman Fawsten Gale and wed his Victoria at last? Can Tom spring from his earthy prison to outwit the evil Ditchley and win the prized tripe garment? Will Albert save the genius Paul Booze from his crippling disease?

Wait for Volume Six
or read the strip every day in the DAILY MIRROR